Network Security and Its Impact on Business Strategy

Ionica Oncioiu
Titu Maiorescu University, Romania

A volume in the Advances in Information Security,
Privacy, and Ethics (AISPE) Book Series

Published in the United States of America by
IGI Global
Business Science Reference (an imprint of IGI Global)
701 E. Chocolate Avenue
Hershey PA, USA 17033
Tel: 717-533-8845
Fax: 717-533-8661
E-mail: cust@igi-global.com
Web site: http://www.igi-global.com

Library of Congress Cataloging-in-Publication Data

Names: Oncioiu, Ionica, 1972- editor.
Title: Network security and its impact on business strategy / Ionica Oncioiu,
   editor.
Description: Hershey, PA : Business Science Reference, [2020]
Identifiers: LCCN 2018055607| ISBN 9781522584551 (hardcover) | ISBN
   9781522584568 (ebook) | ISBN 9781522585084 (softcover)
Subjects: LCSH: Business enterprises--Computer networks--Security measures. |
   Data protection. | Computer security.
Classification: LCC HD30.38 .N48 2020 | DDC 658/.0558--dc23 LC record available at https://lccn.loc.gov/2018055607

This book is published in the IGI Global book series Advances in Information Security, Privacy, and Ethics (AISPE) (ISSN:
1948-9730; eISSN: 1948-9749)

British Cataloguing in Publication Data
A Cataloguing in Publication record for this book is available from the British Library.

All work contributed to this book is new, previously-unpublished material. The views expressed in this book are those of the
authors, but not necessarily of the publisher.

For electronic access to this publication, please contact: eresources@igi-global.com.

Advances in Information Security, Privacy, and Ethics (AISPE) Book Series

Manish Gupta
State University of New York, USA

ISSN:1948-9730
EISSN:1948-9749

MISSION

As digital technologies become more pervasive in everyday life and the Internet is utilized in ever increasing ways by both private and public entities, concern over digital threats becomes more prevalent.

The **Advances in Information Security, Privacy, & Ethics (AISPE) Book Series** provides cutting-edge research on the protection and misuse of information and technology across various industries and settings. Comprised of scholarly research on topics such as identity management, cryptography, system security, authentication, and data protection, this book series is ideal for reference by IT professionals, academicians, and upper-level students.

COVERAGE

- Access Control
- Cookies
- Privacy-Enhancing Technologies
- Cyberethics
- Privacy Issues of Social Networking
- IT Risk
- CIA Triad of Information Security
- Network Security Services
- Device Fingerprinting
- Global Privacy Concerns

IGI Global is currently accepting manuscripts for publication within this series. To submit a proposal for a volume in this series, please contact our Acquisition Editors at Acquisitions@igi-global.com or visit: http://www.igi-global.com/publish/.

Titles in this Series

For a list of additional titles in this series, please visit: www.igi-global.com/book-series

Advanced Methodologies and Technologies in System Security, Information Privacy, and Forensics
Mehdi Khosrow-Pour, D.B.A. (Information Resources Management Association, USA)
Information Science Reference • copyright 2019 • 417pp • H/C (ISBN: 9781522574927) • US $285.00 (our price)

Handbook of Research on Information and Cyber Security in the Fourth Industrial Revolution
Ziska Fields (University of KwaZulu-Natal, South Africa)
Information Science Reference • copyright 2018 • 647pp • H/C (ISBN: 9781522547631) • US $345.00 (our price)

Security and Privacy in Smart Sensor Networks
Yassine Maleh (University Hassan I, Morocco) Abdellah Ezzati (University Hassan I, Morocco) and Mustapha Belaissaoui (University Hassan I, Morocco)
Information Science Reference • copyright 2018 • 441pp • H/C (ISBN: 9781522557364) • US $215.00 (our price)

The Changing Scope of Technoethics in Contemporary Society
Rocci Luppicini (University of Ottawa, Canada)
Information Science Reference • copyright 2018 • 403pp • H/C (ISBN: 9781522550945) • US $225.00 (our price)

Handbook of Research on Information Security in Biomedical Signal Processing
Chittaranjan Pradhan (KIIT University, India) Himansu Das (KIIT University, India) Bighnaraj Naik (Veer Surendra Sai University of Technology (VSSUT), India) and Nilanjan Dey (Techno India College of Technology, India)
Information Science Reference • copyright 2018 • 414pp • H/C (ISBN: 9781522551522) • US $325.00 (our price)

Handbook of Research on Network Forensics and Analysis Techniques
Gulshan Shrivastava (National Institute of Technology Patna, India) Prabhat Kumar (National Institute of Technology Patna, India) B. B. Gupta (National Institute of Technology Kurukshetra, India) Suman Bala (Orange Labs, France) and Nilanjan Dey (Techno India College of Technology, India)
Information Science Reference • copyright 2018 • 509pp • H/C (ISBN: 9781522541004) • US $335.00 (our price)

Cyber Harassment and Policy Reform in the Digital Age Emerging Research and Opportunities
Ramona S. McNeal (University of Northern Iowa, USA) Susan M. Kunkle (Kent State University, USA) and Mary Schmeida (Kent State University, USA)
Information Science Reference • copyright 2018 • 170pp • H/C (ISBN: 9781522552857) • US $145.00 (our price)

Security and Privacy Management, Techniques, and Protocols
Yassine Maleh (University Hassan I, Morocco)
Information Science Reference • copyright 2018 • 426pp • H/C (ISBN: 9781522555834) • US $205.00 (our price)

701 East Chocolate Avenue, Hershey, PA 17033, USA
Tel: 717-533-8845 x100 • Fax: 717-533-8661
E-Mail: cust@igi-global.com • www.igi-global.com

Editorial Advisory Board

Table of Contents

Chapter 13

Detailed Table of Contents

This chapter explored communications security through the use of an empirical survey to assess the extent of network and data transfer security management in Ghanaian higher educational institutions. Network security management controls consist of monitoring of networks, posture checking, network segmentation, and defense-in-depth. Data transfer security management includes encryption, media access control, and protection of data from public networks. Data were collected from information technology (IT) personnel. The ISO/IEC 21827 maturity model for assessing IT security posture was used to measure the controls. Overall, the result showed that the institutions were at the planned stage of communications security management. In particular, network monitoring, defense-in-depth, and the protection of data from public networks were the most applied controls. Conversely, posture checking was the least applied control. Higher educational institutions need to review their communications security plans and better manage network and data transfer security controls to mitigate data breaches.

Chapter 2

This chapter highlights aspects of the contribution of an IT program used in cost accounting and its management according to the target costing (TC) and its impact on the business strategy of an economic entity. The authors present the historical evolution of the TC, its implementation steps, and the methodological steps that go into the management accounting. The characteristics of a software program specifically designed for cost accounting and management of TC, its design, implementation stages, execution mode, are presented. The guarantee of a managerial decision is based on the provision of real, accurate, and reliable information that can be obtained and analyzed with this software program. The theoretical and methodological aspects presented are based on the existing literature, university studies, and specialty from all over the world. Through the authors' contribution, a new conceptual-empirical framework is created to discuss issues that impact on the business environment of economic entities.

Chapter 3

Tatiana Dănescu, University of Medicine, Pharmacy, Sciences, and Technology of Targu-Mures, Romania
Alexandra Botoș, 1 December 1918 University, Romania
Ionica Oncioiu, Titu Maiorescu University, Romania

A significant milestone in the evolution of financial reporting systems occurred when the international financial reporting standards (IFRS) were first applied in the year of 1989. The XBRL (extensible business reporting language) phenomenon marked a new stage in the development of global accounting and reporting systems in the year of 2008 when public companies in US began to use this system. Although the two steps have had a significant impact on the process of harmonizing the global financial reporting system, this process is yet not complete. This chapter presents a comparative analysis of some issues emerging from the application of electronic reporting systems in order to identify the risks presented by them and possible solutions to current practices in financial reporting.

Chapter 4

Ionica Oncioiu, Titu Maiorescu University, Romania
Oana Claudia Ionescu, Titu Maiorescu University, Romania

By its nature, the improvement of the individual's health is a service that involves a rigorous sharing of data in real time. Integrating innovative advances in technologies into the healthcare system by organizations from Turkey is a challenge, an approach to the economic and social boundary, and an attempt to balance consumer-oriented actions. This chapter aims to contribute to the decrease of the shortcomings that exist in the healthcare security assessment by focusing on data mining for public institutions and organizations in Turkey.

Chapter 5

Jayapandian N., Christ University, India

The main objective of this chapter is to discuss various security threats and solution in business transactions. The basic working principle and theoretical background of near field communication (NFC) technology is discussed. A component of NFC communication section is to be discussed on various NFC operation modes and RFID tags. NFC technology is used in various fields such as electronic toll collection and e-payment collection for shopping. This device-to-device payment system is facing major security issues. This NFC communication data is transferred from one terminal to another terminal by using short-range radio frequency. Data hackers try to access this radio frequency and attack the business transaction. This hybrid encryption algorithm is used to solve business transaction data security issues. This chapter deals with both key encryption and data encryption processes.

Chapter 6

Dana Maria Constantin, University of Bucharest, Romania
Dan Ioan Topor, 1 Decembrie 1918 University, Romania
Sorinel Căpuşneanu, Dimitrie Cantemir Christian University, Romania
Mirela Cătălina Türkeş, Dimitrie Cantemir Christian University, Romania
Mădălina-Gabriela Anghel, Artifex University, Romania

This chapter illustrates some aspects of the green reporting and its impact on the business strategy of an economic entity. The main objectives of this chapter are to present the green reporting and the green accounting synthesis documents and, also, to present the computer program for the green report of an economic entity. Based on the national and international literature, the authors present the concepts of the green reporting and integrated report and a computer program specifically designed to record green costs and green reporting. They present the types of green costs and the legislation related to the green reporting. The aspects presented by the authors are based on the national and international literature, specialized studies related to the topic of this study. A new theoretical-empirical framework is created by the authors through their contribution, which facilitates the identification of new ideas, themes, and debates of other issues encountered in the world business environment.

Chapter 7

Alexandru Lucian Manole, Artifex University, Romania
Cristian-Marian Barbu, Artifex University, Romania
Ileana-Sorina Rakos, University of Petrosani, Romania
Catalina Motofei, The Bucharest University of Economic Studies, Romania

Information technology instruments are a very important asset in the hands of every manager. The higher education institutions make no exception from these rules. The exposure to the modern technology and communication tools is very quickly assimilated by students, who acquire the skills to address and even master it and have high expectations from the university they study in to provide them with accurate and real-time information on their particular needs. The management of the university should have at its hand data on students, including personal data, data on academic achievements of any kind, housing in hostels, due and paid tuition fees, data on research, emphasizing both resources allocated and the results obtained, even providing links to online platforms and databases that index these results. The authors approach both operational databases and decision-oriented data warehouses and will aim to capitalize their own research interests in the field of IT to synthesize a set of solutions for this type of software.

Tatiana Dănescu, University of Medicine, Pharmacy, Sciences, and Technology of
Targu-Mures, Romania
Ionica Oncioiu, Titu Maiorescu University, Romania
Ioan Ovidiu Spătăcean, University of Medicine, Pharmacy, Sciences, and Technology of
Targu-Mures, Romania

Using accurate and reliable financial information is the primary condition for successful investments on a stock exchange. Nevertheless, some major corporate scandals broke out at the 21st century horizon and concluded with a major capital market crisis in confidence. Recent events have proved that Romanian capital market is no exception. All these unfortunate scandals had in common some ingredients, among which are a poor corporate governance, a lack of accountability, and misrepresentation of financial information. This chapter relates to the need of integrity in financial reporting process, as the basis for adequate, reliable, and comprehensive information used in decision making by investors in general, institutional investors in particular. The main focus is to review the characteristics of financial information in order to identify some patterns and depict an overview for sensitive areas that may be vulnerable to fraudulent behavior, such as fair value measurements, related party transactions, revenue recognition, provisions, or asset impairment (inventories and receivables).

Anca Gabriela Petrescu, Valahia University, Romania
Mirela Anca Postole, Titu Maiorescu University, Romania
Marilena Ciobanasu, Titu Maiorescu University, Romania

The goal of information security is to be able not just to put in place measures to detect and mitigate attacks but also to predict attacks, deter attackers from attacking, and thus defend the systems from attack in the first place. Data protection should be based on the lessons learned over time, both within the organization and in other organizations. Over the time, a large number of methodologies for identifying information security risks were proposed and adopted and simplified approach to different methodologies has led to their classification in quantitative and qualitative, especially in terms of metrics used to quantify risk. This chapter proposes an international overview regarding the quantitative and qualitative analysis methods for information risk analysis. In practice almost always use a combination of these methods, depending on the characteristics of the organization investigated the degree of uncertainty associated with the method of analysis and risk management.

Husam AlFahl, Taibah University, Saudi Arabia

Mobile commerce can be a great potential to generate new streams of revenue for many established and new businesses. The penetration rates for mobile phone subscriptions in many countries show that there are significant opportunities to invest in and introduce mobile commerce services in many of these markets. The aim of this chapter is to explore and identify the various factors that influence the intention to adopt mobile commerce in Saudi banks and telecoms. A number of these factors were included in this research as they are chosen from well-known theories and investigated in the current study within the mobile commerce context using principal component analysis technique. The findings of the research show that seven components can affect the intention to adopt mobile commerce in Saudi banks and telecoms. The three most significant components that can affect the intention to adopt mobile commerce services in Saudi banks and telecoms are performance expectancy, organizational readiness, and mobile commerce features and opportunities.

Chapter 11

Ana Maria Ifrim, Titu Maiorescu University, Romania
Alina Stanciu, 1 Decembrie 1918 University, Romania
Rodica Gherghina, The Bucharest University of Economic Studies, Romania
Ioana Duca, Titu Maiorescu University, Romania

The digital era has brought along the exponential growth of the economic and technological opportunities that entities can access and implement in the development of their own activities, along with a series of threats with strategic impact. Being a global, multinational, sustainable, profitable, and credible concept, it also involves a leadership connected to market threats for the entity. Moreover, this leadership must be adaptable, identifying with the vision of the entity and conveying it to its members through the organizational culture it cultivates, but above all a leader who understands and is aware of the functioning of the entity, both managerially and economically. And in order to achieve this, a permanent assessment and re-evaluation of the entity's performance is imperative. This chapter seeks to understand the economic and managerial mechanisms of operation to base the making of pertinent, real, and especially timely decisions in counteracting the threats of a turbulent environment while increasing the potential of the entity.

Chapter 12

Alok Sharma, Baba Mast Nath University, India
Nidhi Sharma, Baba Mast Nath University, India

This noble algorithm to provide security to online data transfer is an excellent means by which security can be received in transferring data over the network, and it cannot be detected by any technique or tools available in the market with attacker, unwanted parties, and intruder. In this chapter, a noble algorithm to secure data in online transmission is proposed that provides one hundred percent security to online data. This process makes the communication one hundred percent secure.

Chapter 13

Louis Delcart, European Academy of the Regions, Belgium

The literature on the development of SMEs is clear: one of the most important obstacles to developing a private sector that also creates jobs is access to financial resources. This chapter presents the various economic players and their accessibility to finance: the public authorities, national, regional and local, the enterprises, and then in particular the SMEs and the traditional civil society. It also shows the conditions that succeed with the most effective results, incentives for start-ups and further developing companies, and the way targets are to be measured.

Preface

Nowadays' society is becoming more and more dependent on the information infrastructures that represent the backbone of a vital information flow. Thus, the protection of this infrastructure represents a major concern of companies all around the world. The optimal circulation of information ensures the survival and development of the enterprise, as well as its adaptability to the new market challenges and ever-changing conditions of the competitive environment. At the same time, computer security must be seen as a process that is essential in meeting the legitimate needs of partners and customers and not as something that "can be added", while social media have also gained considerable attention in the business world.

On top of that, advances in information and communication technologies have resulted in a vast range of applications leading to innovative business models and processes. There has been an explosion in the use of electronic devices, generating vast amounts of data about consumers and their daily economic and social activities. The resultant 'big data' – or data streams from various sources – can be collected, aggregated and analyzed to provide valuable insights into the minds of consumers. They can lead to efficiencies in a wide range of sectors, leading to innovative new products, as well as services and ways to serve customers. Interestingly, apart from tracking consumers, even business processes and models are changing because of these technologies.

Furthermore, the Network Security requires innovative forms of data collection from various sources and it needs to process it in order to decipher information faster than ever before. Huge data sets are analyzed to aggregate consumer information, preferences and behavior. Data from various sources is streamed, for example from social media sites such as Twitter and Facebook, transaction logs, automated information-sensing devices and geographical information collection. There is also the rise of Deep Learning, Artificial Intelligence, Internet of Things (IoT), and Digital Transformation. Big data analysis promises to usher in a disruptive change in almost every industry.

In other words, the goal of the Network Security is to be able to not just put in place measures to detect and mitigate attacks, but also to preemptively predict attacks, deter attackers from acting and thus defend the systems from attack in the first place. A superficial evaluation of the information security assembly, including security awareness, leads to the lack of feed-back necessary for the decision-making process with regard to the necessity of implementing adequate corrective measures for improving the information security management. This process implies a more profound understanding of the risks associated with each threat, and a better capacity of tailoring the security framework to align with the organization's identified risks, regulatory requirements and perhaps most importantly – the increasing dependencies on information technology. Therefore, in choosing an effective strategy development, the organization should consider the risks and vulnerabilities exposed to treatment solutions adapted to the needs of its risks while also reducing costs, both short- and long-term. In a stage where, as we have pointed out above, information has become a basic resource of any organization, making the best decisions to protect this resource must be based on a coherent analysis.

As suggested by its title, the *Network Security and Its Impact on Business Strategy* volume displays various cross- and multi-disciplinary approaches. The authors of the papers in this volume propose practical solutions which reflect a dynamic and interdependent approach with the added value of the Core of the Business and at the same time the Leadership's ability to rapidly identify existing risk changes in a system in order to introduce them. For this reason, the lessons learnt as a consequence of an incident should contribute to the improvement of the security mechanisms, policies and, overall speaking, of the security management within the organization.

The first chapter, "Network and Data Transfer Security Management in Higher Educational Institutions", shows the extent of network and data transfer security management in Ghanaian higher educational institutions. Winfred Yaokumah and Alex Ansah Dawson emphasize that managing and operating a secure network ensures the protection of information in networks and its supporting information processing facilities. As a result of that, performing these activities can involve network monitoring, posture checking, network segmentation, and putting in place defense-in-depth measures. For this reason, the authors argue that it is expected that the findings of this study would be used by policymakers at the state government's level to review their communications security plans and better manage network and data transfer security controls to mitigate data breaches.

In the next chapter, "Target Costing and Its Impact on Business Strategy: Computer Program for Cost Accounting and Administration", Constantin Anghelache, Sorinel Căpușneanu, Dan Ioan Topor and Andreea Marin-Pantelescu investigate aspects of the contribution of an IT program used in cost accounting and its management according to the Target Costing, along with its impact on the business strategy of an economic entity. The authors also present the historical evolution of the Target Costing, its implementation steps and the methodological steps that go into the management accounting. The results revealed that the Target Costing method can be successfully implemented to increase the organizational performance towards product value creation and increased profitability for both existing products and new ones.

The focus of the chapter "An International Overview of the Electronic Financial System and the Risks Related to It" is on a comparative analysis of the issues emerging from the application of electronic reporting systems in order to identify the risks and possible solutions to current practices in financial reporting. Tatiana Dănescu, Alexandra Botoș and Ionica Oncioiu discuss the impact of the XBRL (Extensible Business Reporting Language) phenomenon on the process of harmonizing the global financial reporting system. They also claim that, compared to the XML system, XBRL has a more efficient semantic explanation but it is more inappropriate for automated logical reasoning. In contrast to these arguments, there are studies that mention the fact that, in the USA, the XBRL adoption transition has been a difficult time for both private and public entities. Currently, XBRL is also considered an opportunity for harmonizing the electronic reporting system in Europe, especially since ESMA (European Securities and Markets Authority) has made it mandatory to use XBRL as of 2020.

The fourth chapter of this book, titled "Healthcare Security Assessment in the Big Data Era: Lessons From Turkey", contributes to the decrease of the shortcomings that exist in the healthcare security assessment by focusing on data mining for public institutions and organizations in Turkey. Ionica Oncioiu and Oana Claudia Ionescu suggest that, in Turkey, the health services are strongly influenced by the changes that take place as a result of the health system reform, which aims to decentralize the health system by increasing the role of local authorities, professional associations, funding institutions and the community. The results of this study show that the data generated by means such as health data are quite large in size, thanks to the developing information technology and cloud computing resources. The processing of this data requires confidential information to be collected over a limited time and it is to be resolved by means of certain large specific database coding techniques.

The purpose of the chapter "Business Transaction Privacy and Security Issues in Near Field Communication" is to highlight aspects related to the Near Field Communication (NFC) transaction and the implications for its use in various fields such as electronic toll collection and e-payment collection for shopping. Jayapandian N explains that the concept of 'hybrid encryption model' has been created to give a reasonable solution to the data attack. Moreover, the main advantage of the homomorphic encryption algorithm is to secure chain transactions without losing their original information. This algorithm is used in different applications, for example in the currency exchange trading and transactions made by shipping companies.

The chapter "Green Reporting and Its Impact on Business Strategy: Computer Program for Evidence and Green Reporting" makes an interesting contribution regarding the green reporting and the green accounting synthesis documents by creating an integrated report and a computer program specifically designed to record green costs and green reporting. Dana Maria Constantin, Dan Ioan Topor, Sorinel Căpușneanu, Mirela Cătălina Türkeş and Mădălina-Gabriela Anghel propose a strategic framework for the accounting and sustainability reporting (Green Accounting and Reporting). The use of sustainability reports in strategic operations gives clear benefits both to long- and short-term companies that develop them, including increased efficiency and cost reduction. The results revealed that the need for transparency and disclosure of sustainability information is a priority for businesses of any small or large company, but also for other stakeholders, including governments, investors or civil society.

Alexandru Lucian Manole, Cristian-Marian Barbu, Ileana-Sorina Rakos and Catalina Motofei in "Information Technology in Higher Education Management: Computer Program for Students' Evidence" investigate the role of the introduction of ICT into higher education management in the context of globalization and the unprecedented development of information technologies. Many decision-makers in the field of higher education strongly support this issue, as this field has suffered over time from the lack of tools specifically created to improve the management of education on all levels. Suitably, as modern technology in the field of communications might allow a better access over wide area networks, the design and implementation of shared data structures should be made while keeping in mind the best practices in optimization of responses to users' requests and also internal data processing. The chapter concludes that the use of educational technologies has increased the curricular learning between faculties and students that promote constructivism.

The chapter "Fraud Risk Management for Listed Companies' Financial Reporting" focuses on the aspects of reviewing the characteristics of financial information in order to identify some patterns and depict an overview for sensitive areas that may be vulnerable to fraudulent behavior, such as fair value measurements, related party transactions, revenue recognition, provisions or asset impairment (inventories and receivables). This approach is due to the fact that the major corporate scandals which broke out at the 21st century horizon had in common some ingredients, among which: a poor corporate governance, a lack of accountability and misrepresentation of financial information. Tatiana Dănescu, Ionica Oncioiu, and Ioan Ovidiu Spătăcean believe that the prevention and deterrence of fraudulent financial reporting are definitely cheaper measures in comparison with the costs related to any fraud magnitude, either financial or, more important, reputational costs. Nevertheless, management, directors, and auditors of companies that meet such profiles should submit the financial reporting practices to a higher level of supervision. As a result, the authors suggest that the fraudulent financial reporting is perceived as a major obstacle in the efficient functioning of capital markets and, despite its relatively few occurrences, it has a tremendous cost reflected upon the investors' credibility.

"The International Experience in Security Risk Analysis Methods" is a chapter which tests a large number of methodologies for identifying information security risks. Anca-Gabriela Petrescu, Mirela Anca Postole and Marilena Ciobanasu outline an international overview regarding the quantitative and qualitative analysis methods for information risk analysis. The impact of each category of security may be associated with the loss of system functionality or other assets of the organization, degradation, reducing response time for legitimate users, loss of public confidence in the organization or unauthorized disclosure of sensitive data. The data reveal that among the advantages of using qualitative methods, in general, there is no need to accurately determine the financial value of assets, but rather their effects in terms of general information security (confidentiality, availability, integrity).

The study "Mobile Commerce Adoption" by Husam AlFahl explores and identifies the various factors that influence the intention to adopt mobile commerce in Saudi banks and telecoms. According to the consolidation methodology, mCommerce is directly linked to eCommerce because both services are carried out by electronic means through computer-based networks and can be accessed using telecommunication networks. The findings of this research show that the three most significant components that can affect the intention to adopt mobile commerce services are performance expectancy, organizational readiness, and mobile commerce features and opportunities.

In Chapter 11, Ana Maria Ifrim, Alina Stanciu, Rodica Gherghina and Ioana Duca focus their attention on using integrated performance indicator systems in the digital economy. They consider that the evolution of a fragmented market, the pragmatic adoption of new technologies represents new opportunities for new market players to innovate and develop business models that generate profit. The study seeks to present the economic and managerial mechanisms of operation which determine the making of pertinent, real and especially timely decisions in counteracting the threats of a turbulent environment while increasing the potential of the entity. The authors argue that the analysis of the organizational evolution is usually associated with other methods of investigation and analysis of organizational performance. Those methods provide the possibility to anticipate the consequences of managerial decisions as a result of the impact of different environmental changes on the organizational performance in order to guide and control the development of the firm.

The chapter "A Noble Algorithm to Secure Online Data Transmission One Hundred Percent at Zero Cost" builds upon an algorithm to secure data in online transmission which provides one hundred percent security to online data. Currently, this algorithm is free of cost, as any internet user with basic knowledge of computer fundamental can use it without any external requirement. Alok Sharma and Nidhi Sharma explain the benefits of the session made using this algorithm, the fact that it can be destined for a life-long use and for other communications like Alpha-numeric communication along with binary communication with zero cost on security software and hardware without any type of network complexity.

The last chapter of the book is written by Louis Delcart and it is titled "Stimulating Local and Regional Economic Projects and Technological Innovation". The author describes the various economic players and their accessibility to finance: the public authorities, national, regional and local, the enterprises and then in particular the SMEs and the traditional civil society. He also suggests that the economy of the future will be made to scale ever higher, will be electronic and will be based on the forms developed by the Internet. The Internet is proving to be successful by creating and improving the shopping and ways of doing business. Soon, this will unfold faster than we can imagine and the specialist Internet economy will be the largest part of the infrastructure of the global economy. Thus, much can be solved by offering guarantees from international development banks, through the organization of serious follow-ups at the banks, by requiring an accounting at the companies, by introducing project-based thinking among the managers of SMEs. In any case, one of the incentives for regional involvement is to stimulate them in taking responsibility on the management of the European Regional Development Funds based upon a regionally developed strategy.

This overview of the content of the volume *Network Security and Its Impact on Business Strategy* outlines that each contributing chapter contains elements that have the potential to open doors for future research. Certainly, the Internet of Things is a new approach that steps outside the classical ICT environment and creates a vast opportunity to young engineers and ICT experts to find new markets. They have to consider various service sectors, such as buildings, energy, consumer and home, healthcare, traditional industries, transportation, retail and public safety, and to find various application groups such as commercial and industrial applications, but also infrastructure, elderly care, entertainment, safety, resource automation, surveillance equipment and tracking, store hospitality and many more. Thereby, Network Security is conceptually positioned with the help of literature in the field, taking into account the time factor in a not too distant future, and the interdependencies with new concepts of the current economic environment. The specialists agree with the idea that the core changes caused by the Network Security consist in creating an environment which encourages and rewards innovation. What nowadays concerns all modern societies is not only how to use more efficiently and continuously the field of information technology, but also to improve the legal framework in which interactions in this field take place.

Finally, it is important to mention that e-business adoption will soon be one of the major factors which determine the competitiveness of a company. The small businesses that redesign their business processes and adapt to e-business before the others will increase their market share and soon will be the leaders of the sector. For that reason, explosion www and communication environments allow us to dream of a future in which most businesses and human activities will take place in a virtual space, communicating "digitally" for transmitting and receiving information, promotional activities, controls, financial transactions. But the realization of this future depends largely on increasing the number of consumers with Internet access.

Ionica Oncioiu
Titu Maiorescu University, Romania

Acknowledgment

I think that in life nothing is accidental, and sometimes when you least expect, there are people coming into one's life who are able to see in one's person more than she can see. Looking back, I realize that I am tremendously indebt to Ms. Elena Druică. I want to thank her for trusting me, for our extremely positive collaboration and for opening thus a door to a new challenge for me: the editorial activity. I wish to thank Ms. Druică for each virtual encouraging smile, for each piece of advice and especially for her on-going generous and kind support.

Last, but by no means least, I wish to thank all the persons who made the publishing of the present volume possible: Jan Travers, Melissa Wagner, Erin Wesser, Christina Henning, Nicole Elliott, Kristina Byrne, Lindsay Johnston, Joshua Witman, Nick Newcomer, Jaimie Watts, Josephine Dadeboe, Sean Eckman, Marianne Caesar, Colby Conway, and many other IGI Global team members, reviewers, collaborators, and all the contributing authors: without your efforts and dedication this editorial project would have never been possible.

Chapter 1
Network and Data Transfer Security Management in Higher Educational Institutions

Winfred Yaokumah
Pentecost University College, Ghana

Alex Ansah Dawson
Kwame Nkrumah University of Science and Technology, Ghana

ABSTRACT

This chapter explored communications security through the use of an empirical survey to assess the extent of network and data transfer security management in Ghanaian higher educational institutions. Network security management controls consist of monitoring of networks, posture checking, network segmentation, and defense-in-depth. Data transfer security management includes encryption, media access control, and protection of data from public networks. Data were collected from information technology (IT) personnel. The ISO/IEC 21827 maturity model for assessing IT security posture was used to measure the controls. Overall, the result showed that the institutions were at the planned stage of communications security management. In particular, network monitoring, defense-in-depth, and the protection of data from public networks were the most applied controls. Conversely, posture checking was the least applied control. Higher educational institutions need to review their communications security plans and better manage network and data transfer security controls to mitigate data breaches.

INTRODUCTION

The increasing number of data breaches in higher educational institutions, coupled with high complexity of emerging network technologies, poses a challenging environment for security professionals and systems administrators to put in place adequate protection on campus networks (Custer, 2010; HEISC, 2014). Computer networks and data transfer technologies have evolved significantly (Choras, 2013). Data transfer technologies encompass the breadth of digital data flows both within an organization and between external entities across network infrastructures. Digital data flow includes transfer of data, voice,

DOI: 10.4018/978-1-5225-8455-1.ch001

video, and the associated signalling protocols. Securing information flow traversing networks requires effective network infrastructure management (HEISC, 2014). Therefore, systems administrators need to learn, understand, and know how to configure networking software, protocols, services, and devices; deal with interoperability issues; install, configure, and create interfaces with telecommunications software and devices; and troubleshoot systems effectively. Information security professionals must understand and analyze security features and fully recognize vulnerabilities that can arise within each of the systems components and then implement appropriate countermeasures (Harris, 2013).

There have been reports on increasing numbers of security incidents in the recent times (Koch et al., 2012). According to the Verizon's annual report, 76% of data breaches were carried out through network intrusion (Verizon, 2013). There have also been a significant number of reported incidents in connection with the widespread adoption of social media (Benjamin & Chen, 2012; Chandramouli, 2011). The rapid pace of data breaches can be attributed to the growing number of network users, human vulnerabilities, the vulnerabilities in applications and operating systems, and the complexity of network infrastructures that connect several devices. As emerging technologies proliferate, organizations have become increasingly vulnerable to cyber-attacks (Pfleeger & Caputo, 2012). In particular, higher educational institutions have been experiencing data breaches in the recent times due mainly to vulnerabilities in the campus network infrastructure. Many security incidents occur over the networks as a result of inadequate management of networks and data transfer services.

Information technologies have changed the way in which higher education is delivered (Martínez-Argüelles, Castán, & Juan, 2010). Higher educational institutions use and store large volumes of data, including personal information of employees and students, sensitive institutional business data, and faculty research data. But the practices to design and institute strong and effective controls to safeguard data are often at odds with higher education's values of collaboration, openness, and sharing (Coleman & Purcell, 2015; Custer, 2010). Notwithstanding, higher educational institutions must protect sensitive and critical data (Gregory & Grama, 2013). A recent study points to the growing number of cyber-attacks on colleges and universities (Garg, 2016); heightening concern among students, parents, alumni, and donors regarding the security of the personal information these institutions store, process and transmit. According to a survey conducted by Symantec, 10% of all the reported data breaches involve the education sector (Symantec, 2014). A rather current statistics show that 35% of all data breaches come from the educational institutions (Garg, 2016). This alarming phenomenon is making information security a growing concern for higher educational institutions (Gregory & Grama, 2013).

While the effect of data breaches usually focuses on the harm to affected individuals, data breaches affect the institution experiencing the breach. Depending on the nature of the breach, potential direct financial costs of a data breach may include legal representation, fines, and the expense of notifying affected individuals (Grama, 2014). In particular, higher educational institutions may face reputational consequences and consumer confidence, which can result in a loss of alumni donations and a reduction in the number of students choosing to apply to or attend the institution (Grama, 2014). Therefore, how to establish sound and effective management of campus network security in colleges and universities has become crucial (Huang & Jiao, 2014). Security professionals and systems administrators in higher educational institutions have to effectively manage security on campus networks and data transfer services to mitigate the risks.

The purpose of this study is to explore communications security (network and data transfer security) through the use of empirical survey to assess the extent of network and data transfer security management of campus networks in Ghanaian higher educational institutions and to provide some strategies for protecting campus information resources. The study assesses the extent to which higher educational institutions manage campus networks and the data traversing the networks. Network and data transfer security management fall under the broad classification of communications security management (ISO/IEC27002, 2013). As classified by ISO 27002 (2013), network security includes monitoring of wired and wireless networks, performing posture checking, segmentation of networks, and implementing defence-in-depth, while data transfer security entails encryption, media access control, control of exchanged data, and protecting data from public networks.

BACKGROUND

Higher Education and Information Security

Higher educational institutions amass astounding collection of information which is available in digital forms and accessible through a campus-wide technology infrastructure. For example, the universities and colleges in Ghana have deployed large information technology infrastructure including networks, operating systems, and data resources to support teaching, learning, and research activities (Yaokumah, Brown, & Adjei, 2015). These institutions have systems such as employee records, students' records, payroll, and enterprise resource planning (ERP) systems normally used by businesses. In addition, Ghanaian universities have from the scholarly information held in library collections to the administrative information stored in structured databases, faculty research, and instructional materials. The situation is more profound by the emerging trends in online and virtual universities, where academic programs are using technologies and methodologies different from the traditional classroom method of course delivery. This results in merging of voice, virtual reality, streaming video, and data traffic into a common digital infrastructure; providing the mesh of connectivity through wired and wireless connectivity on campuses; and the increasing mission-critical reliance on the Internet. Thus, higher educational institutions are regularly uploading study materials and research findings over the Internet for the speedy propagation of information (Kumar & Kumar, 2014). These data are central to learning, outreach, scholarship, and administrative functions of higher education.

Colleges and universities normally provide open academic environment for learning and hence accommodate a wide array of mobile phones, laptops, and other mobile devices that students, faculty, administrative staff, and visitors use on campus or gain access to campus networks remotely (Patton, 2015). This exposes campus networks to various attacks. But good information security practices are essential to reducing risk; safeguarding data, information systems, and networks; and protecting the privacy of the higher education community. However, recent reports mention that in 2015 some leading universities including Pennsylvania State University (PSU), Washington State University, Harvard University, Johns Hopkins University, the University of Virginia (UVA), and the University of Connecticut have suffered cyber-attacks with considerably damage (Garg, 2016).

Accordingly, the higher educational sector including educational institutions in the developing countries present unlimited threats related to data breaches. The reasons and motives behind data breaches are many and varied. There is a very high number of data moving electronically on campus networks owing to increasing students' numbers. There is unlimited exchange of data among academic departments, administration, and academic registries. In addition, high usage of mobile devices for storing contents, ranging from personal information to research data, creates an environment for intentional as well as unintentional data beaches. According to Poll (2015), nearly 86% of college students use smart phones regularly and students, professors and research fellows receive millions of unsolicited requests for sensitive information. Theft of expensive technical know-how and hiring of people within the education system for espionage - are all growing concerns. Thus, without proper security management, the threat can get out of hands, turning an actual incident into a very expensive and stressful aftermath remedial process (Garg, 2016).

Network Security

Network Security is defined as the process of taking physical and software preventative measures to protect the underlying network infrastructure from unauthorized access, misuse, malfunction, modification, destruction, or improper disclosure, thereby creating a secure platform for computers, users, and programs to perform their permitted critical functions within a secure environment (SANS Institute, 2013). Network security involves the use of technologies and the processes to design, build, manage, and operate a secure network (SANS Institute, 2013). Managing and operating a secure network ensures protection of information in networks and its supporting information processing facilities. Performing these activities will involve network monitoring, posture checking, network segmentation, and putting in place defense-in-depth measures.

Network Monitoring

Network monitoring describes a system that constantly monitors a computer network for network usage pattern and performance and hence notifies the network administrator of any abnormality (Downing, 2013). Network exploits take advantage of software flaws in the systems that operate on local area networks (LANs), Bluetooth, and wireless fidelity (WiFi) or cellular networks. Network exploits can often succeed without any user interaction, making them especially dangerous when used to automatically propagate malware. With special tools, attackers can find users on a WiFi network, hijack the users' credentials, and use those credentials to impersonate a user online (US GAO, 2012). Network, server and client misconfiguration offers another avenue for hacking. Network elements, such as routers and gateways, come with a default administrator password, passwords that often never change. Hackers with access to a router can cause all traffic through it to be sent through their own servers, allowing "man in the middle" attacks (US GAO, 2012). Similarly, misconfigured servers can allow hackers to disable or modify websites, inserting code of their own. Such codes are usually intended to steal data from associated databases (Schneider, 2012). But network monitoring can identify internal security threats, virus infection, user activities, network connections, degrading hardware, low drive space, and whether the security settings are meeting compliance requirements (Downing, 2013).

Posture Checking

Posture checking deals with performing penetration testing and network vulnerability assessment. Penetration testing is the process of attempting to gain access to computing resources without having knowledge of authentication credentials to the system (SAINT, 2016; SANS Institute, 2006). Vulnerability testing places emphasis on identifying areas on the network that are vulnerable to a computer attack (SANS Institute, 2006). Penetration tools include packet manipulation tools and password cracking tools. These are also tools that the attacker uses to gain unauthorized access to systems. Packet manipulation tools allow a penetration tester or attacker to create and send all types of specially crafted transmission control protocol/Internet protocol (TCP/IP) packets in order to test and exploit network-based security protections such as firewalls and intrusion detection systems/intrusion prevention systems (IDS/IPS), while the password cracking tools are used to detect and obtain weak passwords (SANS Institute, 2006). Vulnerability scanners have the ability to exploit multiple vulnerabilities on different hardware and software platforms; can detect the vulnerability and further verify whether the vulnerability can be exploited by an attacker (SANS Institute, 2006). As best practice, all network controls should be routinely validated by an authorized external third party through penetration testing and vulnerability assessment.

Network Segmentation

One way to protect confidential and critical systems is to segregate networks along physical or logical lines by grouping information services, users and information systems on networks (ISO/IEC27002:2013). Using virtual LANs (VLANs) to separate systems creates an additional layer of security between regular network and most sensitive systems. This method is often utilized in order to protect data centers, credit card processing systems, and other systems considered to be sensitive or mission critical (HEISC, 2014). Network segmentation improves security; the systems administrators can have a better access control over the network by limiting access to sensitive data (ISO/IEC27002, 2013). An attacker who gains unauthorized access to a network segment would be limited to that segment and might not able to gain further access to the entire network (Reichenberg, 2014).

Defense-in-Depth

A sound network control strategy employs the concept of defense-in-depth to provide optimal security. Defense-in-depth is a security measure that builds layers of defenses to protect digital critical assets (Edge, 2010). Layering is implemented in the physical security plan as well as policy and administration (Edge, 2010). It can be implemented with multiple security controls. For example, firewalls at the network perimeter limit the traffic that is allowed in and out of the network. The IDS/IPS devices detect and prevent traffic that is suspicious or known to be malicious (Schneider, 2012). In addition, internal network isolation limits the visibility of network traffic to devices and users by department or role (HEISC, 2014). To provide additional layer of protection, strong passwords can be enforced for all network computers as computers run host-based firewalls and antivirus software. Certain sensitive network traffic can be encrypted so that it cannot be intercepted. All of these controls are combined together to provide a layered or in-depth defensive strategy (HEISC, 2014).

Data Transfer Security

Data transfer security entails maintaining the security of information being transferred within an organization and with any external entity (ISO/IEC27002, 2013). Providing data transfer security involves encryption of data in transit, controlling access to media, and protection of data from public networks.

Encryption

With the purpose of maintaining the confidentiality of data, encryption can be used to transform data into a form unreadable by persons without a secret decryption key (US-CERT, 2013). Its main purpose is to ensure privacy by keeping the information hidden from anyone for whom it is not intended, even those who can see the encrypted data (US-CERT, 2013).. For example, people may encrypt files on their storage devices to prevent an attacker from reading them. Encryption of certain network traffic is an essential network control. All confidential or sensitive information leaving the network should be encrypted with proven encryption algorithms. Authentication protocols that transmit passwords or encryption keys over the network should also be encrypted (US-CERT, 2013). Secure sockets layer (SSL) is a common encryption protocol used for web traffic (HEISC, 2014).

Media Access Control

Hindering intrusion of unwanted users gaining access to the network is essential to maintaining a secure environment. Impeding such attacks involves creating barriers and blocking unauthorized entry, but establishing boundaries for legitimate users by limiting access to network resources (Edge, 2010). Network security devices consist of security functions that are used to manage networks. These devices include firewall, intrusion prevention/detection systems (IPS/IDS), data loss prevention (DLP) and content security filtering functions such as anti-spam, antivirus or URLfiltering (Schneider, 2012). Moreover, wireless devices contain security features to prevent unauthorized access. However, wireless networks have many security issues. Hackers have found wireless networks relatively easy to break into, and even use wireless technology to crack into wired networks (Kumar & Gambhir, 2014). Therefore, networks should be managed and controlled to protect information in systems and applications. Security mechanisms, service levels and management requirements of all network services should be identified and included in network services agreements, whether these services are provided in-house or outsourced (ISO/IEC27002:2013).

Protect Data From Public Networks

Data interception can occur when an attacker is eavesdropping on communications originating from or being sent to a mobile device (US GAO (2012). Electronic eavesdropping is possible through various techniques, such as man-in-the-middle attacks - when a mobile device connects to an unsecured wireless fidelity (WiFi) network and an attacker intercepts and alters the communication; and WiFi sniffing - occurs when data are sent to or from a device over an unsecured (i.e., not encrypted) network connection, allowing an attacker to record the information (US GAO, 2012). But with communication monitoring technologies, all information within the enterprise can be filtered, recorded, or even blocked in order to reduce the occurrence of data leakages (Mei-Yu & Ming-Hsien, 2013).

METHOD

This study explored communications security through the use of a survey questionnaire to assess the extent of network and data transfer security management of campus networks. The population of the study was the 182 higher educational institutions (public and private universities, colleges of education, polytechnics, and tutorial colleges) accredited by the National Accreditation Board of Ghana (NAB, 2016). Higher educational institutions can be grouped under colleges and universities. Sixty higher educational institutions located within three capital cities of Ghana form the selected samples for the study. One hundred and eighty anonymous survey questionnaires were sent (3 questionnaires to each institution) to the security practitioners, systems administrators, and IT managers working in the selected institutions. The survey instrument (see Appendix), which was based on ISO/IEC 27002 (2013) framework, was adopted from Higher Education Information Security Council for measuring communications security (network and data transfer security) in higher education (HEISC, 2013). The questionnaire consisted of network security management (4 items), data transfer security management (4-items), and 3 items of demographical data (institution type, experience, and job function). Apart from the demographic data, all the items on the questionnaire used a 6-point Likert scale (*not performed = 0, performed informally = 1, planned = 2, well defined = 3, quantitatively controlled = 4, and continuously improving = 5*).

The ISO/IEC 21827 (2008) maturity model was employed to measure the responses because of its particular focus on IT security management. The metrics measure the level of management of information systems security. The description of the scale on the metrics were: *Not performed* - no security controls or plans are in place; *performed informally* - the base security practices of the control areas are generally performed on an ad hoc basis, there is also general agreement within the organization that identified actions that should be performed and are performed when required, but the practices are not formally adopted, tracked, and reported on; *planned* - the base requirements for the control areas are planned, implemented, and repeatable; *well defined* - security processes used are documented, approved, and implemented organization-wide; *quantitatively controlled* - security processes are measured and verified; and *continuously improving* - standard processes are regularly reviewed and updated and improvements reflect an understanding of and response to vulnerability's impact (ISO/IEC 21827, 2008).

The data collected were coded and analyzed using Statistically Package for Social Scientists (SPSS). Firstly, the Cronbach's alpha reliability coefficient which measures the internal consistency of the items on the questionnaire was computed: the network security of 4 items gave a coefficient of .836 and the data transfer security also with 4 items gave an alpha of .869. Thus, the coefficients were within the acceptable range of 0.7 or above, according to Hair et al. (2014). Secondly, descriptive statistics were used to ascertain the network security, data transfer security, and the individual items of the controls.

MAIN FOCUS OF THE CHAPTER

The data analysis ascertained the practitioners' perspectives on network and data transfer security management of their campus networks. The data analysis has been divided into three parts; a) assessing network security management, b) assessing data transfer security management, and c) assessing the overall communications security. Out of the 180 survey questionnaires sent to the security practitioners, systems administrators, and IT managers working in 60 higher educational institutions, 80 responses were returned from 39 of the institutions. This represents 44.4 percent response rate. Table 1 shows the characteristics of the respondents. The vast majority, 57.5% of the respondents had 1 to 5 years experience as IT managers and network administrators in their respective institutions. This may be explained as most of the higher educational institutions are less than ten years old.

Table 1. Characteristics of respondents

Respondents	Frequency	Percentage
Job Functions		
IT Manager/IT Specialist	36	45.0
Systems/Network Administrator	44	55.0
Years of Experience		
1-5 years	46	57.5
6-10 years	28	35.0
11-15 years	6	7.5

$N = 80$

Network Security Management

Firstly, the study assessed the extent to which higher educational institutions protected the campus networks. The network security controls that were measured included monitoring of wired and wireless networks, posture checking, network segmentation, and defence-in-depth. Overall, network security management stood at 48.8 percent. This indicated that the institutions were at the planned stage of network security management (see Table 2).

Figure 2 shows the levels of network security management. With regards to network monitoring, the respondents were asked whether their institutions had controls in place to continuously monitor wired and wireless networks for detecting unauthorized access. The results indicated that on average the institutions were at the level of 59.6% of monitoring their campus networks. Network monitoring ensures the network reliability of the internal network, thereby increases user productivity (Downing, 2013). As such, systems administrators need to monitor traffic on every device (smart phones, cell phones, servers, desktops, routers, switches) connected to the wired and wireless networks on real-time bases and setup automatic discovery on the network to detect devices that are connected, removed or whose configuration settings have changed. Any device that was not registered should be denied access to connect to the campus networks. Moreover, the administrators can use network access control (NAC) to verify whether devices connecting to the network are running antivirus software. NAC can prevent access to the network until antivirus software is installed and any identified vulnerabilities on the equipment are resolved (Hedrick & Grama, 2013).

Moreover, the participants were asked whether they performed vulnerability test to assess the current antivirus software, firewall enabled, open ports, operating system (OS) patch levels of devices and all the devices connected to the network. In Figure 1, the result indicated that the level of posture checking was 41%. The intent of posture checking was to find security weaknesses in computer systems, networks or applications and to ensure that detected vulnerabilities in the system were fixed correctly. For universities to know the resilience of their critical network systems, data residing and traversing their networks to attacks, security activities must include posture checking (performing penetration testing and vulnerability assessment). It is through assessment processes that the administrators can identify security holes and configuration issues, while maintaining system integrity and resilience. Thus, it is often necessary to regularly audit and assess the systems to ensure adherence to university-wide security

Table 2. Network security management

	Network Security Management	NP (%)	PI (%)	PL (%)	WD (%)	QC (%)	CI (%)	Mean	ML (%)	SD
1	Monitoring wired and wireless network	-	15.0	25.0	22.5	22.5	15.0	2.98	59.6	1.302
2	Posture checking	-	40.0	37.5	7.5	7.5	7.5	2.05	41.0	1.211
3	Network segmentation	7.5	7.5	47.5	30.0	7.5	-	2.22	44.4	.968
4	Defence-in-depth	-	22.5	32.5	22.5	15.0	7.5	2.52	50.4	1.211
Levels of Network Security Management		1.88	21.25	32.63	20.63	13.13	7.5	2.44	48.8 (PL)	.965

Not Performed (NP – 0%); Performed Informally (PI – 20%); Planned (PL – 40%); Well Defined (WD – 60%); Quantitatively Controlled (QC – 80%); Continuously Improving (CI – 100%); ML - Management Level, *N*=80

policy. To achieve this, there are several free and commercial vulnerability and exploitation tools that university system administrators can use to assess the health of their networks could include Nmap, Retina, SAINT, Metasploit, CORE IMPACT, and Nessus. At best, higher educational institutions should engage external qualified penetration tester on an annual basis to ensure that security controls are working effectively (HEISC, 2014).

Also, respondents were asked whether they have segmented the network architecture to provide different levels of security based on their information classification. The result revealed that the level of network segmentation stood at only 44.4%. But the universities can benefit from improved security and enhanced performance from network segmentation. For example, in the university, finance and human resources units can have their own subnet because of the sensitive nature of the data they process and store (Reichenberg & Wolfgang, 2014). Similarly, the faculty, students, alumni, and other personnel can have their own different subnets. The WiFi security controls could also be isolated from all other internal networks in order to help maintain the confidentiality and integrity of the wired network (HEISC, 2014). In this case, wireless users could not be able to access resources on wired networks (HEISC, 2014)). Doing this would limit security breaches on campus networks.

Moreover, participants were asked whether they had their servers protected by more than one security layer (firewalls, network IDS, host IDS, application IDS). The result showed that the level of defense-in-depth was a little over 50%. This level of defense-in-depth implementation signified the need for system administrators and security personnel in the universities to put in place stronger defense-in-depth strategies on their computers, servers, and wired and wireless networks which would make it more difficult for attackers to defeat the complex and multi-layered defense system to penetrate university networks. The components of defense-in-depth to be considered should include installation and updates of antivirus software, firewalls, anti-spyware programs, intrusion detection and prevention systems, multiple-factor authentication, and biometric verification systems. Hedrick and Grama (2013) investigated the extent of implementation of firewalls, intrusion detection systems (IDS), access control lists, network access control, and data loss prevention in educational institutions. The study found that firewalls and intrusion prevention systems (IPS) continued to be the most widely used security technology across campuses. In particular, firewalls were used to protect external connections (89% of the institutions studied) and high-security servers and networks (87% of the institutions studied) (Hedrick & Grama, 2013). The in-

Figure 1. Level of network security management

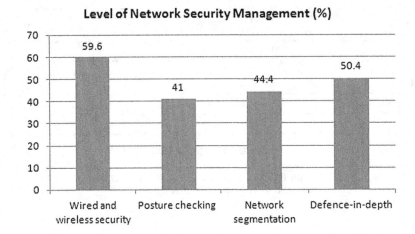

stitutions used IPS to monitor network traffic for malicious activities and to actively prevent attempted intrusions. IPS solutions should be implemented on external Internet connections and in high-security areas to block malicious intrusion (Hedrick & Grama, 2013).

Data Transfer Security Management

Secondly, the study assessed the extent to which higher educational institutions protect the data traversing their campus networks. Overall, data transfer security practices stood at 44.8% (see Table 3), indicating that the institutions were at the planned stage on data transfer security management. Observably, data transfer security management has been lower than network security management (which was 48.8%). This is an indication that the institutions are paying more attention to network security than data transfer security.

In particular, the respondents were asked to indicate their institution's use of appropriate and vetted encryption methods to protect sensitive data in transit. Encryption protects data at rest and in transit. Figure 2 shows the level of encryption at 44.4%, indication the need to encourage the use of encryption software to encrypt sensitive data of their devices and when sent across the network. Data encryption

Table 3. Data transfer security management

	Data Transfer Security Management	NP (%)	PI (%)	PL (%)	WD (%)	QC (%)	CI (%)	Mean	ML (%)	SD
5	Encryption	7.5	22.5	32.5	15.0	22.5	-	2.22	44.4	1.242
6	Media access control	7.5	32.5	15.0	30.0	15.0	-	2.12	42.4	1.236
7	Protect exchanged information	7.5	32.5	7.5	45.0	-	7.5	2.20	44.0	1.316
8	Protect data from public network	7.5	25.0	15.0	22.5	30.5	-	2.42	48.4	1.348
	Levels of Data Transfer Security Management	7.5	28.13	17.5	28.13	17.0	1.88	2.24	44.8 (PL)	1.090

Not Performed (NP – 0%); Performed Informally (PI – 20%); Planned (PL – 40%); Well Defined (WD – 60%); Quantitatively Controlled (QC – 80%); Continuously Improving (CI – 100%); ML - Management Level, *N*=80

Figure 2. Level of data transfer security management

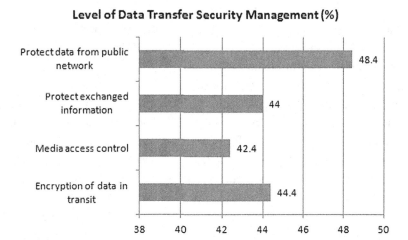

prevents anyone without a decryption key from being able to read the data (Beaudin, 2015). Principally, university community uses smart phones and other mobile devices to store and transmit sensitive data (personal and financial information, intellectual property), mobile data should be encrypted on these devices and when sent across to other devices for protection from potential theft. Even sensitive email messages can be encrypted using public keys. Most email clients have a feature to easily perform this task. The person receiving the message will be able to decrypt it.

Moreover, the respondents were asked whether their institutions have controls in place to protect, track, and report status of media that has been removed from secure organization sites (media access control). The result shows a score of 42.4%. In addition, the level of protection exchanged data stood at 44%, when the respondents were asked whether they had policies and procedures in place to protect exchanged information from interception, copying, modification, misrouting, and destruction. Finally, when asked whether the respondents have a process in place to ensure that data traversing public networks is protected from fraudulent activity, unauthorized disclosure, or modification, the result shows a score of 48.4%.

In order to manage and improve data transfer security, higher educational institutions could adopt some measures. Higher educational institutions could put in place mobile device and acceptable use policies. There is also the need for security education to address basic security literacy (Kaspersky & Furnell, 2014). Training and awareness programs for the university community (faculty, staff, students, alumni, contractors) must focus on how users should protect themselves on the campus and public networks. The faculty should be taught and use Virtual Private Network (VPN) when sending sensitive data among themselves or with other research institutions. VPN creates a private network through public networks and routes data securely to the recipients. Training programs should cover basic security practices such as how to turn off sharing, how to enable firewall to block unauthorized access to their devices. They should be taught how to use Hyper Text Transfer Protocol Secure (HTTPS) and Secure Sockets Layer (SSL). HTTPS is the protocol that ensures data sent between the browser and the website is encrypted and SSL establishes an encrypted link between a web server and a browser. Also, running up-to-date anti-virus software could help protect systems connected to unsecured network.

Communications Security Management

Finally, the study assessed the maturity of the higher educational institutions' overall communication security management. Table 4 and Figure 3 show that the overall level of network and data transfer security practices, among all the institutions, was 46.8% (Level 2), which is the *planned stage* of maturity. This stage indicates that the base requirements for the networks and data transfer security controls are planned, implemented, and repeatable. Specifically, less than 5% of the institutions had no network and data transfer security controls or plans in place; about 25% had the base security practices of network and data transfer control areas generally performed on an ad hoc basis; and about 26% had the base requirements for the network control areas planned, implemented, and repeatable. Moreover, 25% had network and data transfer security processes documented, approved, and implemented campus-wide; about 15% had network and data transfer security processes measured and verified; about 5% have standard processes to regularly reviewed, updated and improve processes to response to vulnerability's impact.

Ideally, for higher educational institutions to attain the highest level of communications security, they should be at Level 5 (continuously improving). At this level, higher educational institutions would have implemented standard processes that would be regularly reviewed and updated. Also, improvements to communications security controls would reflect an understanding of, and response to, a vulnerability's impact through the process of a measured and verified (e.g., auditable) security assessment. In addition, at this level, communications security controls would have been documented, approved, and implemented institution-wide.

SOLUTIONS AND RECOMMENDATIONS

Higher educational institutions have become the target of cyber attacks, which has been evident in several recent reported cases of data breaches (Garg, 2016; Symantec, 2014). This study used a survey to gain deeper understanding of network security (wired and wireless network monitoring, posture checking, network segmentation, and defence-in-depth) and data transfer security (encryption of data in transit, media access control, protection of exchanged information, and protection of data from public networks) management in Ghanaian higher educational institutions.

The results of the study showed that network and data transfer security were not adequately managed in Ghanaian higher educational institutions. The overall level of network and data transfer security

Table 4. Network and data transfer security management

Network and Data Transfer Security Management	NP (%)	PI (%)	PL (%)	WD (%)	QC (%)	CI (%)	Mean	ML (%)	SD
Levels of Network Security Management	1.88	21.25	32.63	20.63	13.13	7.5	2.44	48.8 (PL)	.965
Levels of Data Transfer Security Management	7.5	28.13	17.5	28.13	17.0	1.88	2.24	44.8 (PL)	1.090
Overall communications Security Management	4.69	24.69	25.7	25.07	15.07	4.69	2.34	46.8% (PL)	.986

Not Performed (NP – 0%); Performed Informally (PI – 20%); Planned (PL – 40%); Well Defined (WD – 60%); Quantitatively Controlled (QC – 80%); Continuously Improving (CI – 100%); ML - Management Level, *N*=80

Figure 3. Level of network and data transfer security management

Overall Level of Network and Data Tranfer Security

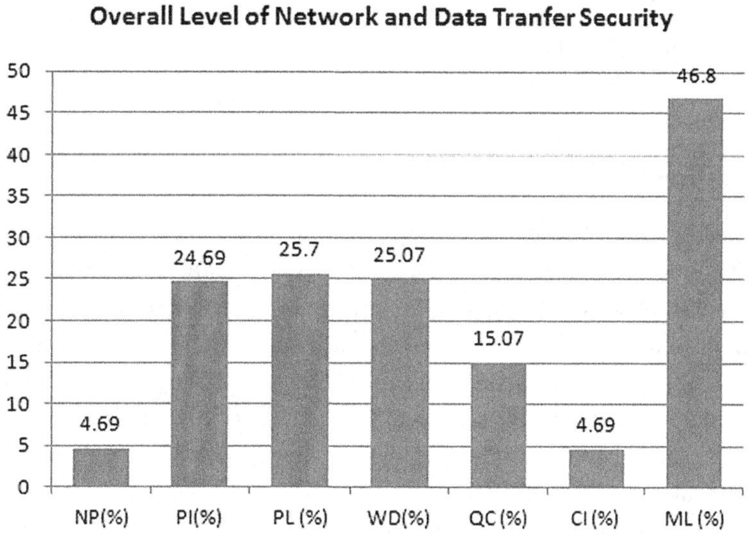

practices among all the institutions stood at 46.8% (Level 2), which is the *planned stage* of maturity. This stage indicated that the base requirements for network and data transfer security controls were planned, implemented, and repeatable. With regards to the eight individual network and data transfer security controls assessed, apart from two controls, the level of management of all the other controls fell below 50%. In particular, monitoring of wired and wireless networks for an unauthorized access was about 60%, whereas protection of critical assets by more than one security layer (defence-in-depth) was about 50%. On the contrary, all the remaining measures fell below 50%. The lowest score recorded was posture checking (41%). Considering the level of data breaches in higher educational institutions, these levels of network and data transfer security management are inadequate. Consequently, higher educational institutions need to review their communications security management plans and implement a more secure network and data transfer security controls.

There are some implications of this study. First, higher educational institutions need to invest in monitoring systems to continually monitor the campus networks for unauthorized access (PWC, 2015). Network monitoring systems monitor an internal network for problems and pre-emptively identify issues such as virus infection, low drive space, and degrading hardware. This can reduce the impact these problems can have on the institutions' productivity (Beaudin, 2015). Second, higher educational institutions can deploy the necessary standards-based authentication, digital signatures (public-key encryption), directory services, and network management systems necessary for inter-institutional collaboration and resource sharing across the network to prevent unauthorized access to sensitive data in transit.

Third, implementing a strategy of defense-in-depth could defeat or discourage all kinds of attacks. Firewalls, intrusion detection systems, well trained users, policies and procedures, strong password, and good physical security are examples of some of the effective security plans that can be put in place. Each of these mechanisms by themselves is of little value but when implemented together will provide an effective security. Fourth, access to wireless and wired networks should be strictly restricted to authenticated faculty members, staff, students, and other authorized persons only. Moreover, all users must be made to change passwords periodically; systems should be deployed to encrypt passwords; and two or three-factor authentication methods can be instituted before access is allowed into campus networks. Fifth, systems administrators and security personnel need to employ standard information security frameworks and best practices to ensure data security.

CONCLUSION

The findings of this study will be useful to IT systems administrators, IT security personnel, and IT auditors by gaining insight into network and data transfer security environment of the campus communications security. The study also showed some disparities in the management of network security between higher educational institutions in developing country, Ghana and that of the developed nations (Hedrick, 2013; PWC Report, 2015). These differences can be useful for benchmarking, which may inform IT strategic planning and management. However, the study had a limitation of low response rate. This is usually the case as evidence suggested that when collecting data of sensitive nature, the researcher should expect very low response (Kotulic & Clark, 2004).

Future research will involve replicating the study in other organizations so as to compare, benchmark, and gain insight of the broader network and data transfer security environment. Moreover, this study focussed on network and data transfer security, which were considered as technical security measures. However, data breaches happened as a result of human behavior (performing risky activities, non-compliance to security policies). As such, multi-disciplinary study including behavioural science theories will be needed to explain user bahavior. Thus, combining behavioural science with communications security (including intrusion prevention, protocol and behavior analysis, application control, vulnerability management, network segmentation, encryption and other defenses) may provide insightful results.

REFERENCES

Beaudin, K. (2015). College and university data breaches: Regulating higher educaiton cybersecurity under state and federal law. *The Journal of College and University Law*, *41*(3), 657–694.

Benjamin, V., & Chen, H. (2012). *Securing cyberspace: Identifying key actors in hacker communities. IEEE International Conference on Intelligence and Security Informatics (ISI)*, Arlington, VA. 10.1109/ISI.2012.6283296

Chandramouli, R. (2011). *Emerging social media threats: Technology and Policy Perspectives. Second Worldwide Cybersecurity Summit*. London, UK: WCS.

Choras, M. (2013). Comprehensive approach to information sharing for increased network security and survivability. *Cybernetics and Systems: An International Journal*, *44*(6-7), 550–568. doi:10.1080/01969722.2013.818433

Coleman, L., & Purcell, B. M. (2015). Data breaches in higher education. *Journal of Business Cases and Applications*, *15*, 1–7.

Custer, W. L. (2010). Information Security Issues in Higher Education and Institutional Research. *New Directions for Institutional Research, 1,* 46. doi:10.1002/ir.341

Downing, M. (2013). *The Importance of Network Monitoring*. Retrieved from http://www.animate.com/the-importance-of-network-monitoring/

Edge, I. E. (2010). Employ five fundamental principles to produce a SOLID, secure network. *Information Security Journal: A Global Perspective, 19*(3), 153-159. doi:10.1080/19393551003649008

Grama, J. (2014). *Just in time research:Data breaches in higher education*. Retrieved from https://net.educause.edu/ir/library/pdf/ECP1402.pdf

Gregory, W. H., & Grama, J. (2013). *Information Security (Research Bulletin)*. Louisville, CO: EDUCAUSE Center for Applied Research. Retrieved from http://www.educause.edu/ecar

Hair, J. F. J., Hult, G. T. M., Ringle, C., & Sarstedt, M. (2014). A primer on partial least squares structural equation modeling (PLS-SEM). *Long Range Planning, 46*, 328. doi:10.1016/j.lrp.2013.01.002

Harris, S. (2013). *All-In-One CISSP Exam Guide* (6th ed.). McGraw Hill.

Hedrick, G. W., & Grama, J. (2013). *Information Security*. Retrieved from https://library.educause.edu/resources/2013/6/information-security

HEISC. (2014). *Information Security Guide - Communications Security*. Retrieved from https://spaces.internet2.edu/display/2014infosecurityguide/Communications+Security

Higher Education Information Security Council (HEISC). (2013). *Information Security Program Assessment Tool*. Retrieved from http://www.educause.edu

Huang, N., & Jiao, Z. (2014). On campus network security system of college and university. *Journal of Emerging Technologies in Web Intelligence, 6*(4).

ISO/IEC 21827. (2008). *Information technology - Security techniques - Systems security engineering - Capability maturity model (SSE-CMM)*. Retrieved from http://www.iso.org/iso/catalogue_detail.htm?csnumber=44716

ISO/IEC 27002. (2013). *Information technology Security techniques - Code of practice for information security controls*. Retrieved from http://www.iso.org/iso/catalogue_detail?csnumber=54533

Kaspersky, E., & Furnell, S. (2014). A security education Q&A. *Information Management & Computer Security, 22*(2), 130–133. doi:10.1108/IMCS-01-2014-0006

Koch, R., Stelte, B., & Golling, M. (2012). *Attack Trends in Present Computer Networks. 4th International Conference on Cyber Conflict (CYCON)*, Tallinn, Estonia.

Kotulic, A. G., & Clark, J. G. (2004). Why there aren't more information security research studies. *Information & Management, 41*(5), 597–607. doi:10.1016/j.im.2003.08.001

Kumar, G., & Kumar, K. (2014). Network security – an updated perspective. *Systems Science & Control Engineering, 2*(1), 325–334. doi:10.1080/21642583.2014.895969

Kumar, U., & Gambhir, S. (2014). A literature review of security threats to wireless networks. *International Journal of Future Generation Communication and Networking, 7*(4), 25–34. doi:10.14257/ijfgcn.2014.7.4.03

Martínez-Argüelles, M. J., Castán, J. M., & Juan, A. A. (2010). Using the critical incident technique to identify factors of service quality in online higher education. *International Journal of Information Systems in the Service Sector, 2*(4), 57–72. doi:10.4018/jisss.2010100104

Mei-Yu, W., & Ming-Hsien, Y. (2013). Enterprise information security management based on context-aware RBAC and communication monitoring technology. *Mathematical Problems in Engineering*, 1–11. doi:10.1155/2013/569562

National Accreditation Board of Ghana (NAB). (2016). *Number of accredited tertiary institutions in Ghana per category as at September 2016*. Retrieved from www.nab.gov.gh

Oblinger, D. G. (2015). *Ten reasons to tackle the top 10 IT issues*. Retrieved from http://er.educause.edu/articles/2015/1/ten-reasons-to-tackle-the-top-10-it-issues

Patton, M. (2015). Battling data breaches: For higher education institutions, Data Breach Prevention is More Complex than for Industry and Business. *Community College Journal, 86*(1), 20–24.

Pfleeger, S. L., & Caputo, D. D. (2012). *Leveraging behavioral science to mitigate cyber-security risk*. MITRE Technical Report 12-0499. Bedford, MA: MITRE Corporation.

Poll, H. (2015). *Pearson student mobile device survey 2015*. Retrieved from http://www.pearsoned.com/wp-content/uploads/2015-Pearson-Student-Mobile-Device-Survey-College.pdf

PWC Report. (2015). *The Global State of Information Security Survey 2015*. Retrieved from http://www.pwc.com/gx/en/issues/cyber-security/ information-security-survey/download.html

Reichenberg, N. (2014). Improving Security via Proper Network Segmentation. *Security Week*. Retrieved from http://www.securityweek.com/improving-security-proper-network-segmentation

Reichenberg, N., & Wolfgang, M. (2014). Segmenting for security: Five steps to protect your network. *Network World*. Retrieved from http://www.networkworld.com

SAINT. (2016). *Vulnerability management, penetration testing, configuration assessment and compliance*. Retrieved from http://www.saintcorporation.com

SANS Institute. (2006). *Penetration testing: Assessing your overall security before attackers do*. Retrieved from https://www.sans.org/reading-room/whitepapers/ analyst/penetration-testing-assessing-security-attackers-34635

SANS Institute. (2013). *Network security resources*. Retrieved from https://www.sans.org/network-security/

Schneider, D. (2012). The state of network security. *Network Security, 2*(2), 14–20. doi:10.1016/S1353-4858(12)70016-8

Symantec. (2014). *Internet Security Threat Report 2014*. Retrieved from http://www.symantec.com

United States Computer Emergency Readiness Team (US-CERT). (2013). *Security tip. Understanding Encryption*. Retrieved from https://www.us-cert.gov/ncas/tips/ST04-019

US GAO. (2012). *Information security: Better implementation of controls for mobile devices should be encouraged.* Retrieved from http://www.gao.gov/products/GAO-12-757

Verizon. (2013). *The 2013 data breach investigations report.* Retrieved from www.verizonenterprise.com

Yaokumah, W., Brown, S., & Adjei, P. O. (2015). Information technology governance barriers, drivers, IT/Business alignment, and maturity in Ghanaian universities. *International Journal of Information Systems in the Service Sector*, *7*(4), 66–83. doi:10.4018/IJISSS.2015100104

APPENDIX

Information Security Management Survey Instrument

The purpose of this study is to assess the level at which network and data transfer security measures have been put in place on campus networks in Ghanaian higher educational institutions and to provide strategies for protecting information resources.

Please, use the scale below to assess the level of network and data transfer security management in institution.

Profile of Respondent

Please indicate your response to the following questions by checking the appropriate boxes.

1. What is your current job title?
    a. Information Security Officer (CISO)
    b. Chief Information Officer (CIO)
    c. IT Manager /IT Specialist
    d. Internal Auditor
    e. Network Adminstrator
2. How many years of experience do you have at your current position?
    a. 1-5 Years
    b. 6-10 Years
    c. 11-15 Years
    d. 16-20 Years
    e. Over 20 Years

Table 5. ISO 21827 International Standards Scale for Measuring Maturity Levels

Code	ISO 21827	Definitions
0	Not Performed	There are no security controls or plans in place. The controls are nonexistent.
1	Performed Informally	Base practices of the control area are generally performed on an ad hoc basis. There is general agreement within the organization that identified actions should be performed, and they are performed when required. The practices are not formally adopted, tracked, and reported on.
2	Planned	The base requirements for the control area are planned, implemented, and repeatable.
3	Well Defined	The primary distinction from Level 2, Planned and Tracked, is that in addition to being repeatable the processes used are more mature: documented, approved, and implemented organization-wide.
4	Quantitatively Controlled	The primary distinction from Level 3, Well Defined, is that the process is measured and verified (e.g., auditable).
5	Continuously Improving	The primary distinction from Level 4, Quantitatively Controlled, is that the defined, standard processes are regularly reviewed and updated. Improvements reflect an understanding of, and response to, vulnerability's impact.

Network Security

Please, indicate your reaction to each of the following statements by marking the checkbox that represents the level at which your institution has put in place the following network security measures.

Data Transfer Security

Please, indicate your reaction to each of the following statements by marking the checkbox that represents the level at which your institution has put in place the following data transfer security measures.

Table 6.

	Description of Items						
NTSEC1	My institution continuously monitors our wired and wireless networks for unauthorized access.	0	1	2	3	4	5
NTSEC2	My institution has a process for posture checking, such as current antivirus software, firewall enabled, OS patch level, etc., of devices as they connect to your network.	0	1	2	3	4	5
NTSEC3	My institution has segmented network architecture to provide different levels of security based on the information's classification.	0	1	2	3	4	5
NTSEC4	Internet-accessible servers are protected by more than one security layer (firewalls, network IDS, host IDS, application IDS, etc).	0	1	2	3	4	5

0. Not Performed 1. Performed Informally 2. Planned 3. Well Defined 4. Quantitatively Controlled 5. Continuously Improving

Table 7.

	Description of Items						
DTSEC1	My institution use appropriate and vetted encryption methods to protect sensitive data in transit.	0	1	2	3	4	5
DTSEC2	Controls are in place to protect, track, and report status of media that has been removed from secure organization sites.	0	1	2	3	4	5
DTSEC3	My institution has policies and procedures in place to protect exchanged information (within my organization and in third-party agreements) from interception, copying, modification, misrouting, and destruction.	0	1	2	3	4	5
DTSEC4	My institution has a process in place to ensure data traversing public networks is protected from fraudulent activity, unauthorized disclosure, or modification.	0	1	2	3	4	5

0. Not Performed 1. Performed Informally 2. Planned 3. Well Defined 4. Quantitatively Controlled 5. Continuously Improving

Chapter 2

Target Costing and Its Impact on Business Strategy:
Computer Program for Cost Accounting and Administration

Constantin Anghelache
The Bucharest University of Economic Studies, Romania

Sorinel Căpușneanu
ⓘ https://orcid.org/0000-0003-3799-3993
Dimitrie Cantemir Christian University, Romania

Dan Ioan Topor
1 Decembrie 1918 University, Romania

Andreea Marin-Pantelescu
The Bucharest University of Economic Studies, Romania

ABSTRACT

This chapter highlights aspects of the contribution of an IT program used in cost accounting and its management according to the target costing (TC) and its impact on the business strategy of an economic entity. The authors present the historical evolution of the TC, its implementation steps, and the methodological steps that go into the management accounting. The characteristics of a software program specifically designed for cost accounting and management of TC, its design, implementation stages, execution mode, are presented. The guarantee of a managerial decision is based on the provision of real, accurate, and reliable information that can be obtained and analyzed with this software program. The theoretical and methodological aspects presented are based on the existing literature, university studies, and specialty from all over the world. Through the authors' contribution, a new conceptual-empirical framework is created to discuss issues that impact on the business environment of economic entities.

DOI: 10.4018/978-1-5225-8455-1.ch002

INTRODUCTION

This century begins with a revolution in the field of computers, especially by using and implementing computerized applications, information systems and information technology (IT) in all business practices of larger or smaller companies. The emergence and adoption of Web-based applications and technologies, information, and telecommunications has multiplied the capabilities and benefits of computers. The importance of computers and software in business can no longer be ignored or overestimated. Large, medium or small businesses use Internet-based communications technologies, networks, or programs that enable employees and professionals to quickly communicate, collaborate, and work across geographic locations across the globe, thereby contributing to streamlining workflows. Starting from the overall cost targeting framework, we focused our attention on creating an IT program able to manage the flow of financial and economic operations that took place in a small company. The program presented is an original one and is based on the technology provided by Microsoft Office through Access. The main objectives of this chapter are: (1) *the presentation of some aspects of the target costing method, the implementation steps and the methodological steps in the management of a small company*, and (2) *the creation of a computerized program necessary for the management of the target costing accounting, adapted to the general accounting plan for managerial accounting from Romania.*

BACKGROUND

Conceptual Approaches of Target Costing

The emergence and application of the concept of determining the target costing of products was found at the beginning of the 19th century at Ford in the United States and Volkswagen Beetle in Germany in 1930 (Feil et al., 2004). During this time, Americans created a concept to maximize the attributes of a product by minimizing its cost, which was later transformed into a technique called VE (Value Engineering). This technique was taken over by Japanese companies to cope with the competitive environment and was an innovative incentive for the Japanese Managerial Accounting System to implement the Target Costing approach.

VE, known as "Genka Kikako", was used for the first time at Toyota in 1963 and was not mentioned in Japanese literature until 1978 (Tani et al., 1995) when it was called "target costing" (Kato, 1993). Its implementation as a cost management technique was carried out by Japanese accounting officers (Kato, 1993; Tani et al., 1994; Tani, 1995) and the development of the TC system was initially made by Toyota Motor Production in 1959 being the oldest and technically advanced (Gopalakrishnan et al., 2007). Target Costing has emerged as a market-oriented system that effectively manages the new costs of a product during the design and development phase and, along with the Kaizen Costing method, helps the Japanese automotive industry to achieve their goals (Monden & Lee, 1993).

As defined by CAM-I (Consortium for Advanced Management International), Target-Costing (TC) is a "a set of management tools and methods aimed to design and plan activities for new products, which provides the basis for controlling subsequent operation phases and which makes sure that the products achieve their goals in terms of profitability throughout their life cycle" (CAM-I, 1994).

Several organizations around the world have adopted and implemented the TC technique to meet the objectives of manufacturing and internal management processes such as management controls or strategic and environmental considerations. Thus, in response to increasing supply chain pressures associated with capital market pressures, many companies in the US and Europe are adopting this technique (Paunica et al., 2009; Juhmani, 2010). Supply Chain Management plays a key role in uniting TC's objectives with customer desires and market requirements through interactive supplier engagement in TC practice, contributing to the success of implementing this technique while providing credible market information (Hamood et al., 2011).

The most popular innovative methods and techniques used in cost accounting and management in the 1980s included: Activity-Based Costing, Target Costing, Theory of Constraints, Value-Added Management, Vertical Integration (Smith, 1999). According to US and European reports, companies have begun to adopt TC in the late 1980s (Ansari et al., 1997a) for several reasons: disciplining the PDP product development process (Cooper & Slamulder, 1997), improving cost management and increased competitiveness (Feil et al., 2004). This is a concern for cost management and not for the mitigation and control of costs, but also for supply chain management to be involved in TC practice as the main source of information to insure the value of products.

There are few studies about the implementation or non-implementation factors of TC and include: industrial affiliation, competition degree, uncertainty in the business environment and the strategy perceived by the managers (Ansari et al., 1997b).

After its implementation, the Target Costing method has become the necessity of a compromise born between the rapidity of changing customer expectations and the execution of products with low costs and high quality and utility. Thus, the Target Costing method turns from a cost-cutting technique into a profit management tool after the 1990s and demonstrates its sustainability in a highly competitive, contemporary environment. Some specialists noted the positive relationship between the implementation of the Target Costing method and the intensification of competition (Dekker & Smidt, 2003), between increasing competition and stimulating and encouraging a dynamic environment (Kocsoy et al., 2008), while other specialists find that the method targeting costs was perceived as tool for cost-cutting, then for customer satisfaction, product quality and opportunity (Rattray et al., 2007). The positive argument for the implementation of the Target-Costing method is based on forecasts of customer requirements and competitor market behavior, and the negative argument for non-adoption of the Target-Costing method is based on the rigid targets identified in the forecasts of customer requirements and perceptions in an uncertain environment that suggests using the method only as a tool to maintain competitiveness.

Since 2000, some cost accounting techniques have been developed that integrate strategic management (Adler et al., 2000) and are indispensable for a company's continued activity much more than a feedback from the control system or market orientation to the detriment of production (Nishimura, 2002). This is also demonstrated by a case study of a Romanian company that indicates that accountants are the main observers of the impact of market competitiveness and the increase/decrease in prices and costs for the Target Costing method and the transmission of these signals to the company's management (Căpuşneanu & Briciu, 2011).

Japanese companies regard the Target Costing method as an integral part of the design and development of the production process and not just as a stand-alone calculation technique. A number of specialists have put forward in their studies: the benefits of integrating the Target Costing Method (TC) along with the ABC-costing method in the target cost allocation process within American companies (Cokins, 2002);

the benefits of TC integration with the BSC by adopting the four perspectives of the BSC to support the frequent processes needed to cover the gap between the Target Cost and the estimated cost, and which leads to a balance between cost, quality and functionality (Souissi & Ito, 2004); the advantages offered by the similarities between TC and BSC in meeting customer needs and the requirements for achieving financial goals and global strategic goals (Yilmaz & Baral, 2010).

Other specialists have argued that the presence of the Target Costing method after the 2000s is rather a product development system rather than a costing technique (Burrows & Chenhall, 2012); the Target Costing method is an integrated system of several economic instruments that allows the three dimensions (cost, quality, time) to be used efficiently, but also to control product cost and increase the profitability of the company (Pakizeh et al., 2013). The specialists focus to identify ways in which the Target Costing method can be successfully implemented to increase organizational performance towards product value creation and increased profitability for both existing products and new products.

Purpose and Stages of Target Costing

The purpose of the Target Costing method is to identify the production cost of the product being tracked so that the sale brings the profit margin that the company desired. The Target Costing method focuses on reducing the cost of a product in the design phase where changes affect the entire life cycle of the product in question. These definitions imply that the Target Costing objective is characterized by (1) *the market price and the desired profit*, and (2) *the start of the product life cycle*. Atkinson et al., (1991) argue that Target-Costing is a cost-planning method that focuses on products in discrete manufacturing processes and short life cycles of products (Atkinson et al., 1991). During the life cycle of the product, such firms would gradually improve their processes using the Kaizen Costing method. Many US companies use standard computing systems to control costs in the manufacturing phase. The focus of the Kaizen Costing method is very different from other systems. In general, standard cost systems focus on cost control, while Kaizen Costing focuses on continuous improvement.

According to the TC method, costs become fixed as soon as the product is in production, i.e. at the beginning of its life cycle. Applying a major redesign process becomes irrelevant when manufacturing a product, especially when its lifecycle is shorter. These two attempts to reduce the costs of the start-up phase of a product production become useless and inefficient. According to the TC principle, its methodology is applied even from the first design phase of the product. We believe that this methodology can be applied throughout the lifecycle of a product, from launch to maturity. This point of view is shared by other specialists like Horvath who wrote: *"Target-Costing is just part of the cost management function of a product throughout its life cycle. The target cost must be met by meeting the customer's requirements, using different methods to identify the potential for cost reduction"* (Horváth et al., 1993). By its restrictive descriptive content, most managers and other specialists have understood that this methodology cannot be applied to existing products, which has led them to continue to use inefficient cost management systems. The Institute of Management Accouting also advises companies to apply the TC methodology to new and existing or modified products. Changes in production techniques occur when the company is ready and motivated to move to another level, but this usually involves different production costs and profitability. If managers are of the opinion that only changes in product design are possible during manufacturing, then the company might lose some significant strategic opportunities.

In the literature, the specialists identified the following general steps underlying the Target Costing (Briciu & Căpușneanu, 2013):

1. **Setting the Target Price:** It is based on an assessment of the market's needs, competitive analyzes or company's preliminary plans based on the manufacture of a new or modified product according to the characteristics or requirements of the customers.

2. **Setting the Target Profit Margin:** This is set according to the company's long-term strategic and financial goals or as a result of the efforts made to plan a profit share. The general equation is as follows:

$$Tm = Tp - Tc, \tag{1}$$

In which: Tm = target margin; Tp = target price; Tc = target cost (assignable).

The assignable cost consists of: costs of raw materials, direct wage costs, depreciation costs, instrumentation costs, development costs, general manufacturing costs, administrative costs, investment costs.

3. **Determining Estimated Cost and Target Cost:** If a company wants to change an existing product, it has the necessary cost-base information and can only determine potential costs for the new product if the specifications and manufacturing method of the new product are identical to the existing product (old). Based on these, the costs of the new product or the current costs are determined. The general equation is as follows:

$$Tp - Tm = Etc \tag{2}$$

In which: Etc = Estimated Target Cost (subject to Kaizen Costing). The estimated cost is reduced using the Kaizen Costing technique to achieve the target cost proposed by the entity.

4. **Calculation of Estimated Cost of Estimated Products and Activities:** It is determined by summing up the direct and indirect costs of the product.

5. **Calculate the Target Cost, the Amount to Reduce Costs:** Applying value engineering is done when the estimated cost > the target cost proposed by the company. Adjustment is done from bottom to top, starting with indirect costs and then with direct expenses, if applicable.

Adapting the General Accounts Plan to Target-Costing: Methodological Steps

Considering the life cycle of the manufactured products, the principles of the Target Costing method were adapted to the specifics of the technological processes and the types of manufacturing. Thus, our option consisted of adapting the principles of the Target Costing method to the General Accounts Plan in Romania by using Class 9 "Management Accounts" in the developed version of double-managerial accounting. This chart of accounts helps simplify the technique of recording and determining product costs by correctly reflecting the economic and financial operations that take place within a company (Briciu & Căpușneanu, 2011).

Being subject to accounting normalization and based on information pluralism, managerial accounting provides accounting information geared to several categories of users such as: state, company management, investors, shareholders, etc. Managerial accounting satisfies the information needs and aims at internal analysis of the result on organizational structures. By using Class 9 "Management Accounts" a concrete capture of the operational flows performed in each phase of the life cycle of the manufactured products (including the target price, the target costs or the target profit margin pursued by the company) is achieved. By adapting all the above-mentioned aspects, the chart of accounts presented the following synthetic structure (Briciu & Căpușneanu, 2011):

Group 90 "Internal Settlements" comprising the following accounts: 901 "Internal Settlement of Expenses"; 902 "Internal Settlements of Output"; 903 "Internal Settlement of Cost Differences"; 904 "Internal Sales Settlements"

Group 92 "Calculation accounts" comprising the following accounts: 921 "Basic activity expenses"; 923 "Indirect costs"; 924 "General Administration Expenses"; 925 "Expenditure on disposal".

Group 93 "Cost of Production" composed of the following accounts: 931 "Cost of Finished Production"; 935 "Cost of production sold".

Group 95 "Analytical results accounts" consisting of a single account, 951 "Analytical result".

The way of functioning of the accounts in class 9 "Administration accounts" is presented as follows (Căpușneanu & Briciu, 2011):

Group 90 *"Internal Settlements"*. The ways of adapting to the Target Costing method required that the name of some of the accounts be changed in order to accommodate the flexibility requirements of the respective expenditures, respectively, of the obtained revenues.

Account 901 *"Internal Reimbursement of Expenses"* is a bifunctional account but acts as a passive account. It helps to keep track of direct costs (basic activity) and indirect costs (production, general administration, sales). It is credited during the month for the settlement of operating expenses by destination (cost or expense locations) through the debit of the accounts: 921 "Basic Expenditures", 923 "Indirect Production Expenses", 924 "General Expenditures administration", 925 "Expenditure on disposal". At the end of the month, the actual cost of production sold through account credit is charged: 935 "Cost of production sold". It has no balance.

Account 902 *"Internal Settlements of Output"* is a bifunctional account. It helps to keep track of the internal cost of production at the end of the month at actual cost. It is credited during the month with the estimated cost of finished production obtained through the debit of account 931 "Cost of production achieved". At the end of the month, the target cost of production is accrued through the credit of the account: 921 "Basic Expenditures". It has no balance. In analytics this account develops on calculation objects (orders, products, executed works, etc.).

Account 903 *"Internal Settlement of Cost Differences"* is an asset account and records the differences in cost calculated at the end of the month between the new actual costs calculated as a result of the customer's compliance with the actual cost of production achieved within the entity. It is charged at the end of the month when the difference in cost (favorable or unfavorable) is determined and recorded by the account credit: 902 "Internal Settlements on Output" and through the debit of account 935 "Cost of Sold Production" with Final Actual Cost. It has no balance. In analytics this account develops on calculation objects (orders, products, executed works, etc.).

Account 904 *"Internal Sales Settlements"* is a passive account. It helps to keep track of: the proceeds from the sale of finished products at the selling price; the settlement of the actual cost and the result obtained from the sale of the finished production. It is credited at the end of the month when settling the target cost of the production obtained and sold, respectively the margin on the target profit obtained from the sale of the production, through the debit of the account 951 "Analytical result". At the end of the month, the amount of revenue generated from the sale of finished products is debited through the same 951 account "Analytical result". It has no balance. In analytics this account develops on calculation objects (orders, products, executed works, etc.).

Group 92 "*Calculation accounts*" is a homogeneous group in terms of the economic content and accounting function of the accounts.

Account 921 "*Expenditures related to the main activity*" is an asset account. It helps to keep track of the expenses related to the core business of the entity. It is debited: (1) during the month, when collecting the direct expenses related to the core business, through the credit of account 901 "Internal Settlement of Expenses"; (2) At the end of the month, when allocating allowances from indirect costs (taking into account specific cost drivers), the credit of the accounts: 923 Indirect Production Expenses, 924 General Expenditures and 925 Retail Expenditure ". It is credited at the end of the month with the target Cost of Finished Production through the debit of account 902 "Internal Settlements of Output". It has no balance. In analytics, this account is developed on calculations (orders, products, executed works, etc.), on calculation items (raw materials and direct materials and salaries and direct payroll accessories).

Account 923 "*Indirect Production Expenses*" is an asset account. It helps to keep track of indirect production costs. It is charged during the month for the collection of costs by production activities through the credit of account 901 "Internal Settlement of Expenses". At the end of the month, at the end of the month, it is credited with the allocation of the share of the expenses related to main activity (indirect production) operations based on the specific cost inductors through the debit of account 921 "Basic activity expenses". It has no balance. Analytically, this account grows over indirect production activities.

Account 924 "*General Administration Expenses*" is an asset account. It serves for the bookkeeping of administrative expenditure. It is charged during the month for the collection of administrative expenditure by the credit of account 901 "Internal Settlement of Expenditure". At the end of the month, it is credited with the allocation of the share of the expenses related to the main (indirect management) operations based on the specific cost inductors through the debit of account 921 "Expenditures related to the main activity". It has no balance. In analytics, this account grows over general government activities.

Account 925 "*Retail Expenditure*" is an asset account. It helps to highlight spending on commercial activities. It is charged during the month for the collection of expenses by commercial activity through the credit of account 901 "Internal Settlement of Expenditure". At the end of the month, at the end of the month, it is credited with the allocation of the share of the expenses of the main (indirect) selling operations based on the specific cost inductors through the debit of account 921 " Expenditures related to the main activity ". It has no balance. In analytics, this account develops through indirect sales activities.

Group 93 "*Cost of production*" is the group that highlights aspects of the cost of production from two points of view, namely: the finished output and the sold production. Both accounts described below show an asset accounting function.

Account 931 "*Cost of Finished Production*" is an asset account. It helps to keep track of the finished production, consisting of finished products, executed works. It is debited during the month with the registration price of the finished target output obtained through the credit of account 902 "Internal payments on the obtained output". It is credited at the end of the month by settling the target cost of the finished output obtained through the debit of account 935 "Cost of production sold". It has no balance. In analytics, this account develops on calculations (orders, products, executed works, etc.).

Account 935 The "*Cost of Sold Production*" is an asset account and records the finished output for sale (orders, products, works executed at the sales price) It is charged at the end of the month with the recording of the finished output obtained at the estimated cost (target) through the credit of account 931 "Cost of Finished Production." It is credited at the end of the month by settling the estimated cost (target) of the production obtained on account 901 "Internal Settlement of Expenditure." It does not have balance. It is similar to the previous account (orders, products, executed works, etc.).

Group 95 *"Analytical results accounts"* is the group containing results accounts obtained as a result of the difference between the income and expenditure of an entity's output.

Account 951 *"Analytical result"* is a bifunctional account. It keeps track of the analytical result obtained from sales of finished products. Credits are credited at the end of the month with the selling price of the target sold product through the 904 "Internal Sales Settlements" account. It also flows at the end of the month with the target cost of the finished output obtained and the margin on the target profit obtained as the difference between the revenue recorded at the target sales price and the target cost of the sold output through the credit of the same account 904. It has no balance. In analytics, this account develops on calculation objects (orders, products, executed works, etc.)" (Căpușneanu & Briciu, 2011).

In our opinion, the methodological steps on management accounting and cost calculation using the Target Costing method are as follows (Căpușneanu & Briciu, 2011):

1. *Accounting the turnover into the target sales price.* It is made through the debit of account 904 "Internal sales settlements" and credit of account 951 "Analytical result".

904"Internal sales settlements" = 951"Analytical result"

2. *Establishing and recording the estimated profit margin (target).* It is made through the debit of account 951 "Analytical result" and the credit of account 904 "Internal sales settlements".

951"Analytical result" = 904"Internal sales settlements"

3. *Calculate and record the estimated cost (assignable, target).* It is made at standard cost by debiting account 931 "Cost of Finished Production" and crediting account 902 "Internal Settlements on Output".

931"Cost of Finished Production" = 902"Internal Settlements on Output"

4. *Establish estimated cost destinations (assignable, target).* At this stage there is the allocation of the total cost of the sums by destinations, i.e. places of expenses (processes, activities) and cost carriers using the cost inductors or precise weights established by the Target Costing Method Implementation Team.

921"Expenditures related to the main activity"

923"Expenditures related to the main activity"

924"General Administration Expenses"

925"Retail Expenditure"

= 901"Internal Reimbursement of Expenses"

Analytical accounts can be opened for the following direct expenses: raw materials, direct salaries and other direct expenses. For Indirect Expenses, analytical accounts are opened for each type of activity evidenced in the appropriate process.

5. *Assignment of indirect costs related to activities on products,* works or services provided using specific cost drivers (a list of cost drivers specific to each type of indirect expense or the scales set by the deployment team).

921"Expenditures related to the main activity"

= 923"Indirect Production Expenses"

924"General Administration Expenses"

925"Retail Expenditure"

6. *Calculation and settlement of actual cost.* It is made by debiting account 902 "Internal Settlements of Output" and Account 921 "Expenditures related to the main activity". There are no changes to traditional costing methods.

902"Internal Settlements of Output" = 921"Expenditures related to the main activity"

7. Calculation and recording of cost differences between the new actual cost as determined by recommendations based on customers' requests and the actual cost determined by component within the entity.

903"Internal Settlement of Cost Differences" = 902"Internal Settlements of Output"

8. *Settlement of current actual cost of production sold.* It is made through the debit of account 935 "Cost of production sold" and credit of account 931 "Cost of production obtained".

935"Cost of Sold Production" = 931"Cost of Finished Production"

9. Distribution of cost differences on sold production.

935"Cost of Sold Production" = 903"Internal Settlement of Cost Differences"

10. *Settlement of current actual cost on target result.* It is made through the debit of account 951 "Analytical result" and the credit of account 904 "Internal sales settlements".

951"Analytical result" = 904"Internal sales settlements"

11. *Closure of expenditure accounts (cost-production interface).* It is made through the debit of account 901 "Internal Reimbursement of Expenses" and credit of accounts 935 "Cost of Sold Production".

901"Internal Reimbursement of Expenses" = 935"Cost of Sold Production"

Computer Program for Cost Accounting and Administration

In this subchapter, the authors also present the model of a software solution for managing Target Costing method, built around a database. This solution is a model which, due to the expansion of modern development environments, can be replicated in any (more or less) similar tool, and integrated into a more comprehensive IT solution for managerial accounting. The solution presented has the following aims:

1. To assist the user(s) throughout the steps of the Target Costing method implementation within a company;
2. To automatically generate inputs regarding the accounting records and the management of the accounts dedicated to managerial accounting (class 9, according to the Romanian accounting plan).

This approach involves the use of an application which includes both procedural programming and support for database management. In this respect, the authors have selected the Microsoft® Access relational database management software to build and develop the application. The procedural component dedicated to the first aim will follow the steps presented in the previous section of the chapter. It shall automatically calculate output indicators and store them in the dedicated section of the database, and they will provide input data for the second stage, that is the generation of accounting records. As both stages involves a database as storage instrument for the data processed within the Target Costing method, the database was designed according to the principles of the relational model, compatible with the DBMS (Data Base Management System) proposed.

The structure of the model involves the main tables presented below:

ACCOUNTS (Account_ID, Account_name)

DEBT (ACC, Op_ID, Calc_ID, Sumd)

CREDIT (ACD, Op_ID, Calc_ID, Sumc)

OPERATIONS (Op_ID, Description)

COST_CALCULATIONS (CID, Date)

CALCULATIONS (CID, Phase_ID, Prod_ID, QP, TUSP, TPM, TUC, NTC, NRC)

INDICATORS (Ind_ID, Ind_name, Type).

COST_COMPONENTS(Calculation,Component,Weight)

PRODUCTS (<u>Prod_ID</u>, Prod_name, Description)

PHASES (<u>Phase_ID</u>, Phase_name)

The model designed is described by the following characteristics:

- The first four tables are used to manage the accounting records with the accounts member of the 9th class. This approach follows the model specified by Roşca et al. (1993) and allows the input of accounting formula with more than one account on each side of the balance. To be noted, the operations are predefined, see the list of values below (Table 1).
- *COST_CALCULATIONS* defines the calculation operations, which is the transaction most comprehensive in our database, covering all other transactions. A complete calculation will follow all the steps described above, and their implementation should be subsequently explained.
- *CALCULATIONS* includes the data necessary to initiate a cost calculation (as defined above): the quantity, the target unit price, target profit margin, target unit cost, new target cost, new effective cost. The data are stored for each phase, and each product.
- The *PRODUCTS* table manages data about the products of the company. Each product is uniquely identified by the value of the primary key (the first column of the table);
- The *INDICATORS* table holds the list of indicators used in the process; they reflect the components of the cost, grouped by type.

The physical model of the database, as represented in Microsoft Access, is presented in Figure 1.

The database functionalities are managed via a set of interfaces (forms), all of which can be accessed in a central panel: For all calculation operations presented above, the authors have defined a special control form, which allows the user to consult and interact with the data, in correlation with the calculation steps specific to the Target Costing method. The interface of the form is presented in the Figure 2.

Table 1. Predefined operations that allow accounting records to be managed within the database

Operations	
OP_ID	**Description**
1	Accounting the turnover into the target sales price
2	Establishing and recording the estimated profit margin (target)
3	Calculate and record the estimated cost (assignable, target)
4	Establish estimated cost destinations (assignable, target)
5	Assignment of indirect costs related to activities on products
6	Calculation and settlement of actual cost
7	Calculation and recording of cost differences between the new actual cost as determined by recommendations based on customers' requests and the actual cost determined by component within the entity
8	Settlement of current actual cost of production sold
9	Distribution of cost differences on sold production
10	Settlement of current actual cost on target result
11	Closure of expenditure accounts (cost-production interface)

Figure 1. Database diagram
Source: Authors' work, as presented by ACCESS

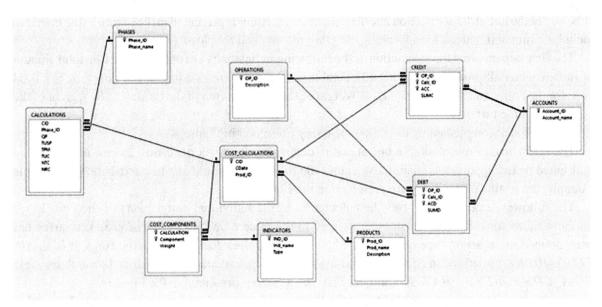

Figure 2. Control form for applying the target costing method
Source: Authors' work, as presented by ACCESS

TARGET COST CALCULATIONS

Step 1. Add calculation data | Calculation data interface

Step 2. Compute calculation indicators | Initial calculation indicators

Step 3. Calculate individual components of the cost | Individual cost components

Step 4. Input real cost data | Input real cost data

Step 5. Deviations calculation | See calculation cost deviations

Step 6. New target and real costs | New target and real costs

Step 7. Generate accounting records | Generate

Enter calculation number | 1
Enter phase number | 1

PREVIEW CALCULATION JOURNAL

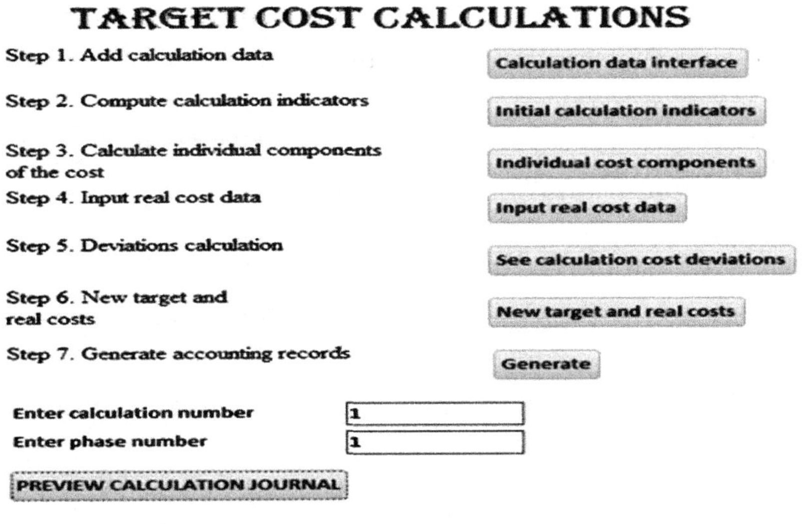

The steps of the calculation, according to the specifications of the Target Costing method, are presented in the following section. Users are to use the *Calculation data interface* form, accessible by using the button with the same name, in order to entry the initial data for the calculation. The structure of the form allows for the input of the following attributes: (1) Calculation identifiers: ID and Date; (2) The product for which the calculation is realized; (3) Forecasted quantities; (4) Target unit sale prices; (5) The target profit margin; (6) The target unit cost.

Apart from the first two items, the other indicators are introduced for each phase defined. At a subsequent step, new indicators are inputted, namely the new target cost and the new effective cost. The structure of the initial data collection interface (the main section) is presented in the Figure 3 (the interface includes command buttons for appending, deleting records and for closing the form).

The first step involves the calculation of the following indicators: (1) Total turnover (the total amount of money when all products are sold); (2) Total target profit, corresponding to the turnover; (3) Total cost, for the entire quantity forecasted; (4) Weight of the profit margin in the turnover; (5) Weight of the target cost in the turnover.

This task is accomplished by the following query presented in Figure 4.

The query makes use of simple operations to determine the result measures, as unit indicators are multiplied by the appropriate quantitative value, and the result is stored in a new attribute. For a simple example, the results of the query are presented in the Figure 5.

The following operation involves the calculation of the individual components of the cost, based on the weights for each component type, defined in the table *COST_COMPONENTS*. The query has been defined as an action-type query, which has associated the *APPEND* operation (thus, it is an *APPEND QUERY*, as defined in ACCESS), and the records obtained are used to fulfill the auxiliary table *COST_COMPONENT_PHASES*). Our query has the structure presented in the Figure 6.

The results of the query are presented in the Figure 7 (a preview before the actual append operation is executed):

The query capitalizes the weights associated with the current calculation, as specified by the *INNER JOIN* relationship between the tables CALCULATIONS and *COST_COMPONENTS*, and computes the unit and total component per phase. The next phase involves the input of real cost data for the current phase and calculation, by updating (manually) the values of the *REAL_COST* field in the *COST_COMPONENTS_PHASES* table. Following this operation, the next step takes into account the calculation of

Figure 3. Data entry interface
Source: Authors' work, as presented by ACCESS

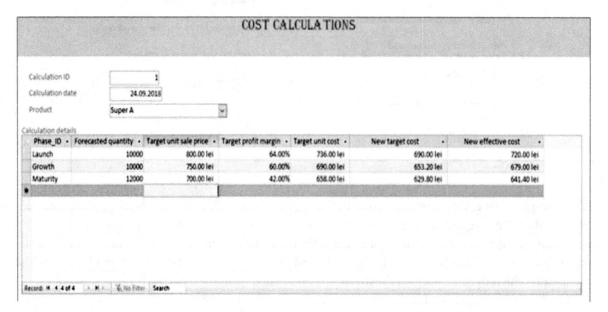

Figure 4. Query for calculation target cost indicators per phase
Source: Authors' work, as presented by ACCESS

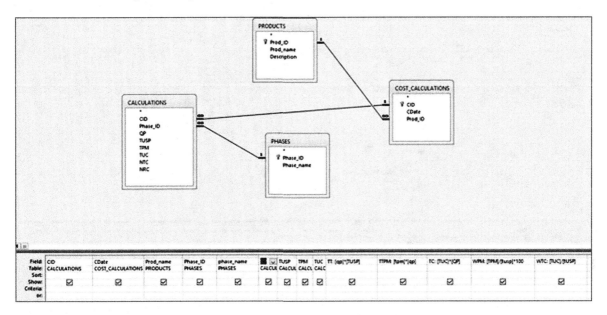

Figure 5. Query results for calculation target cost indicators per phase, only a section is presented
Source: Authors' work, as presented by ACCESS

Calculation	CDate	Product nan	Phase_ID	phase_nam	Forecasted quantity	Target unit sale price	Target profit margin	Target unit cost
	24.09.2018	Super A	1	Launch	10000	800.00 lei	64.00%	736.00 lei
1	24.09.2018	Super A	2	Growth	10000	750.00 lei	60.00%	690.00 lei
1	24.09.2018	Super A	3	Maturity	12000	700.00 lei	42.00%	658.00 lei

the unit and total deviations for the operational calculation. A simple, select-type query, provides the necessary results presented in Figure 8.

Having the cost components per phase together with the deviations allows us to move to the final stage of cost calculation, which assumes the calculation of the new real and target costs, for the current calculation and phase. These results are achieved by using the following query presented in Figure 9.

The final major set of operations in our database is the automatic generation of the managerial accounting records that reflect the movements of cost components within the dedicated accounts, belonging to class 9. This objective is achieved by building and ensuring the controlled running of a set of dedicated append queries, who upload the necessary records into the *DEBT* and *CREDIT* tables. Each append query has been defined starting from the structure of the destination tables. The source fields were designed and populated with values according to the requirements of each operations (there are 11 operations, described in the first section of this chapter, for which the table OPERATIONS has been designed and populated.

Several queries are presented further on, in order to exemplify the application of this instrument for the stated requirement: the automatic generation of the accounting records (formulas). The use of the automated query running mechanisms is governed by the control form presented in Figure 2, and the specification of the calculation and phase for which the users want to manipulate data. The queries for

Figure 6. Query for calculation target cost components per phase
Source: Authors' work, as presented by ACCESS

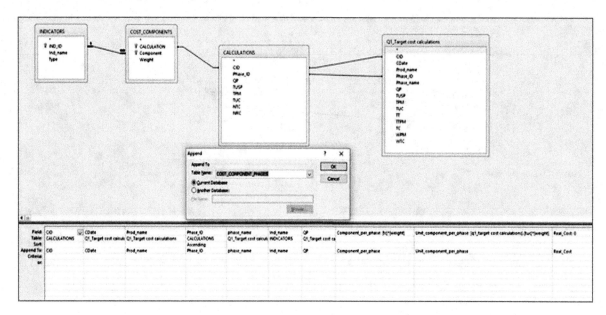

Figure 7. Query for calculation target cost components per phase - results preview, in section
Source: Authors' work, as presented by ACCESS

CID	CDate	Product nam	Phase_ID	phase_nam	Ind_name	Forecasted quantity	Component_per_phase	Unit_component_per_phase
	24.09.2018	Super A	1	Launch	Raw materials	10000	1,472,000.00 lei	147.20 lei
1	24.09.2018	Super A	1	Launch	Maintenance	10000	1,840,000.00 lei	184.00 lei
1	24.09.2018	Super A	1	Launch	Batch management	10000	1,104,000.00 lei	110.40 lei
1	24.09.2018	Super A	1	Launch	Publicity	10000	736,000.00 lei	73.60 lei
1	24.09.2018	Super A	1	Launch	Montage	10000	1,472,000.00 lei	147.20 lei
1	24.09.2018	Super A	1	Launch	Direct wages	10000	736,000.00 lei	73.60 lei

Figure 8. Query for calculation deviations in cost components per phase
Source: Authors' work, as presented by ACCESS

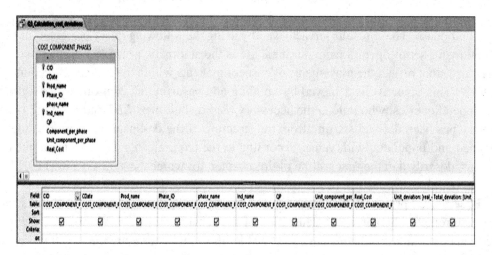

Figure 9. Query for calculation of the new real and target costs
Source: Authors' work, as presented by ACCESS

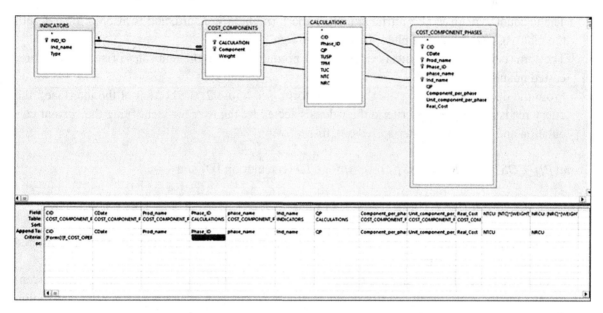

the first operation, namely "*Accounting the turnover into the target sales price*", the queries are presented in the Figure 10.

In compliance with the structure of the record, as presented in the first section of the chapter, correlated with the database structure proposed, the construction of the queries respected the following considerations:

Figure 10. Query that automatically generates the accounting record for the step accounting the turnover into the target sales price. The first half is the query for debt; the second half solves the problem of the credit part of the formula
Source: Authors' work, as presented by ACCESS

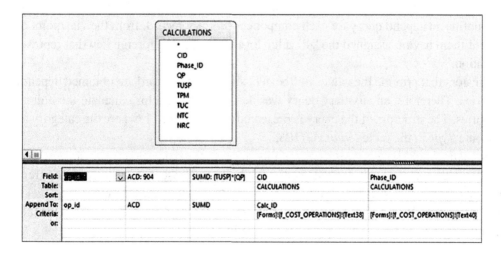

- The operation number is given, as correlated with the corresponding value of the primary key in table *OPERATIONS*;
- The account symbol is also attributed, since the formula is standard, and is also correlated with the table *ACCOUNTS*, as it plays the role of foreign key here;
- The sum (either debt or credit) is calculated as product between the unit sales price, and the forecasted quantity;
- From the dedicated text boxes in the control form (see figure 2, the bottom of the interface), the query reads and applies as criteria the values selected by the user for identifying the current calculation and phase. The criteria used are, respectively:

[Forms]![f_COST_OPERATIONS]![Text38] for *CID* (calculation ID) and

[Forms]![f_COST_OPERATIONS]![Text40] for *Phase_ID*.

Those principles are applied for both queries and, upon running the queries; the record is entered into the *DEBT* and *CREDIT* tables.

Note: the two tables use a composite primary key, which prevents the user from entering two identical records for the same phase defined under the same calculation. Therefore, from this viewpoint, redundancy is excluded. Also, there is no issue in defining the foreign keys in the form proposed by the authors, as the following arguments apply:

- The list of operations is standard (11 operations, 11 methodological steps, as defined in the first section of the chapter);
- Each calculation is a unit of transactions that allows the application of the target cost for as many phases as the users need, respecting the methodological steps;
- The list of phases is pre-defined;
- The control of generating new records is automated by the attribution of values in each step, and the possibility of the users to select which calculation or which phase they want to solve.

Operations 2 and 3 are similar as record structure. A particular configuration was applied for operation 4, which assumes more accounts for the debt part of the accounting formula. Thus, the authors have resorted to define an append query for each component (unitary record, from the viewpoint of the table *DEBT*), all of them having assigned the "4" value for the destination foreign key that represents the ID of the operation.

The indicators that provide the values for the debt sums in this record are obtained depending on the cost categories. Therefore, an auxiliary query was defined, which helps calculate the unit cost for the three categories. The structure of the query is presented in the Figure 11, where the category is indicated by the attribute *Type* in the table *INDICATORS*:

The Calculation and Phase are restricted, at this stage, to the data selected by the user in the control form, in order to ease subsequent query definitions. The query presented is a classical aggregated functions query, where the *NRCU* is the argument for the *SUM* function, and the other three fields are used for grouping the data. Based on this auxiliary instrument, the structure of the query for the first debt account, in the case of operation 4, is presented in the Figure 12.

Figure 11. Auxiliary query that calculates the unit cost per categories
Source: Authors' work, as presented by ACCESS

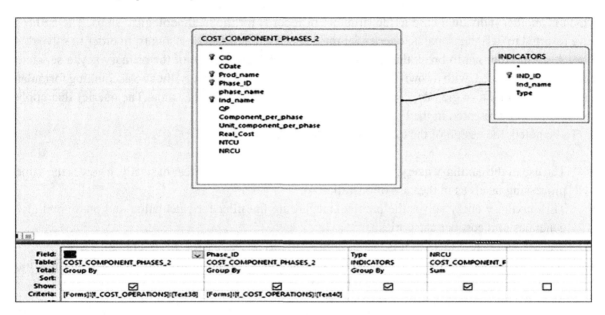

Figure 12. Query that generates first debt formula, operation no. 4
Source: Authors' work, as presented by ACCESS

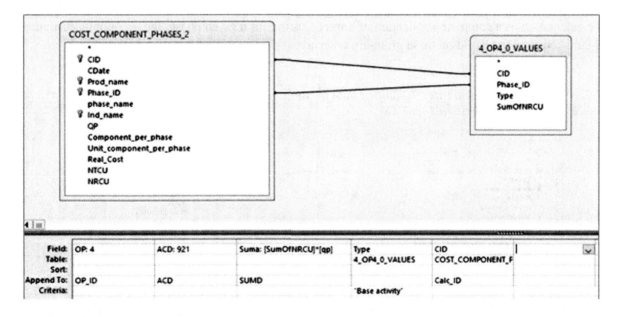

As the criteria for calculation and phase were solved during the design (and will apply during the running) of the auxiliary query, in this step, there is only necessary the criteria that selects the cost category for account *921*, namely "*Base activities*". Furthermore, the debt sum is computed by multiplying the unit cost (result of the auxiliary query) with the forecasted quantity. For the next formula, the structures are the same, excepting the fact that the reference value of the criteria is the one corresponding to the debt account. Operation no. 5 involves two separate records, each having a single account on either side, which is another individual case in the structure of records for the methodological steps. The authors have resorted to defining separate queries for the respective records and accounts, in order to solve this case. Also, in order not to break the rule for unique values in the scope of the primary key, a separate operation was defined, with its own ID, for the second record. Alternatively, the two accounting formulas can be unified into a single one, considering that the debt account is the same. The queries that apply this solution are presented in the Figure 13.

To be noted, the design of the query includes the following elements:

- The use of the auxiliary query, in the right side of the data source area (basically, it solves the same processing needs as in the case of operation 4);
- This auxiliary query solves the problems regarding the filter for calculation and phase and also generates unit cost per categories;
- The account is provided, as it is *921* in both formulas necessary for this operation;
- As the debt sum is computed as general total, regardless of the categories, an aggregate function (*SUM*) was applied, to calculate the total cost;
- Also, the operation number is given, and the calculation ID is taken from the auxiliary query.

The other operations do not pose significant problems; the structure of their formulas is simple, account "against" account. The dataset regarding the accounting records can be presented to the user as a report, an accounting journal for the calculation and phase currently in operation. As we have defined the calculation as a complete application of Target Costing for a given phase, the accounting formulas should be presented based on these grouping criteria: calculation and phase.

Figure 13. Query that generates the unified debt formula, operation no. 5
Source: Authors' work, as presented by ACCESS

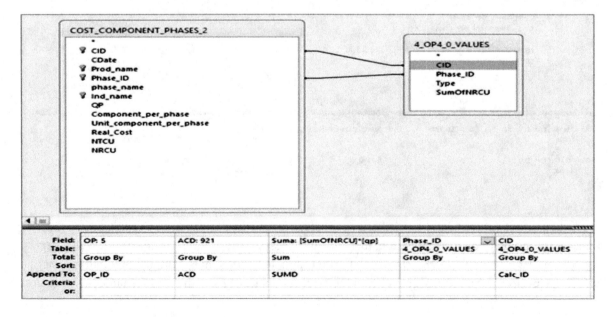

The structure of the report, proposed by the authors, is detailed in the Figure 14.

The journal reveals all account data and formulas on a certain calculation. It can be accessed for viewing from the main interface, as the calculation and phase numbers are read from the same window.

SOLUTIONS AND RECOMMENDATIONS

Starting from the topic discussed in this chapter, we propose to the specialists and to all those interested the following solutions to improve our approach:

- Adoption and implementation of Target Costing accounting alongside other management accounting methods. The results of specialist studies have shown that there are real hybridization possibilities between Target Costing accounting and methods such as Activity-Based Costing, Activity-Based Management etc. (Briciu et al., 2012).
- Expanding the software program or creating other target-based software programs aimed at: highlighting and managing performance (creation of specific environmental indicators including), creating a set of synthesis documents specific to the Target Costing method, highlighting relationships between suppliers and collaborators, etc.

Taking into consideration the conceptual approaches and software presented and based on the literature, we would like to recommend to specialists and those interested in deepening and implementing or adapting the Target Costing method to the specifics of a particular entity or organization, the following:

- Analyzing the principles and factors of the Target Costing method that Influence Company cost management. An analysis and implementation team will be set up. It will study and analyze all of these issues and will guarantee for successful implementation within the selected company.
- Researching the specialty literature on the degree of successful adoption and implementation of the target costing approach or adjusting the chart of accounts, if any. In this regard, different specialized institutions or research institutes can come to the conclusion that they can come up with viable solutions to ensure the successful adoption or implementation of the Target Costing method within the selected company.

Figure 14. Calculation journal report
Source: Authors' work, as presented by ACCESS

CALCULATION JOURNAL

Calculation	Date	Product name	Phase_name	Debt	Debt sum	Credit	Credit sum
1	24.09.2018	Super A	Launch				
OP.ID	Description						
1	Accounting the turnover into the target sales price			904	8,000,000.00 lei	951	8,000,000.00 lei
2	Establishing and recording the estimated profit margin (target)			951	6,400.00 lei	904	6,400.00 lei
3	Calculate and record the estimated cost (assignable, target)			931	6,900,000.00 lei	902	6,900,000.00 lei
4	Establish estimated cost destinations (assignable, target)			924	720,000.00 lei	901	7,200,000.00 lei
4	Establish estimated cost destinations (assignable, target)			923	4,320,000.00 lei	901	7,200,000.00 lei

- Expanding IT programs dedicated to managing a company's costs or performance by using the Target Costing method. This can be done by using more specialized software programs dedicated to the objectives pursued by a particular company that wants to implement them.

FUTURE RESEARCH DIRECTIONS

Through the set goals, the approaches and the presentations made, the authors are of the opinion that the aim of this chapter has been reached, addressing both established professionals from the business environment, as well as specialists or academics. The approaches presented and analyzed from the internal and international literature highlight the synthesis of a large amount of information presented and processed by the authors and covering the topic chosen for the debate, while leaving new possibilities for quantifying future researches. In this respect, the new directions proposed by the authors for the expansion of the theoretical and empirical framework launched aim at:

- Analyzing the possibilities of adapting the principles of the Target Costing method to the specifics of the different companies that like this method of cost management and performance highlighting;
- Analysis of the impact of the managerial decisions resulting from the adaptation of the principles of the Target Costing method to the specifics of the different companies, including the use of a software program dedicated to cost management and performance highlighting;
- Analyzing the possibility of creating new software programs needed to monitor and measure the performance of a company based on the principles of the Target Costing method.

CONCLUSION

This chapter covers a wide range of themes based on the conceptual approaches of the Target Costing method, its stages in a company, and the presentation of the methodological steps in the managerial accounting by adapting the chart of accounts to its specificity. Also, the chapter also presents original authors' contributions to creating a computerized program needed to manage costs by Target Costing within a company. As strong points of this chapter we can mention:

- Helps fill existing gaps in managerial accounting and apply the principles of the Target Costing method within companies precisely through interpretations of conceptual approaches and by presenting the software specifically created for this purpose;
- Presenting the positive impact of implementing and using the IT program on management and employees through: (1) *cost analysis involving staff from all departments, encouraging the responsibility for cost management;* (2) *source of information for other routine management activities (process and product design, cost allocation and control, procurement process, pricing policies, performance appraisal);* (3) *making impact analyzes of new products on the market and the competitive environment* (taking into account the full life cycle of the product, the total costs of both the manufacturer and the customer are significantly reduced).

Through our contribution, we believe we have increased our knowledge of the cost-implementation and cost management capabilities through a company-wide cost targeting approach while opening up new opportunities for future research. The chapter presented remains open to any enlargement needs coming from specialists or other stakeholders. Along with them, we express our desire to extend our research, trying to diversify the problems that have arisen or been reported by specialists. We also remain open to any suggestions from the business or academic environment to continue or expand our research by developing partnerships or collaborations.

REFERENCES

Adler, R., Everett, A. M., & Waldron, M. (2000). Advanced Management Accounting Techniques in Manufacturing: Utilization, Benefits, and Barriers to Implementation. *Accounting Forum*, *24*(2), 131–150. doi:10.1111/1467-6303.00032

Ansari, L. S., Bell, J. E., Cypher, J. H., Dears, P. H., Dutton, J. J., Ferguson, M. D., ... Zampino, P. A. (1997b). *Target Costing: The Next Frontier in Strategic Cost Management*. Chicago: Irwin Professional Publishing.

Ansari, S. L., & Bell, J. E.CAM-I Target Cost Care Group. (1997a). *Target Costing: The Next Frontier in Strategic Cost Management*. Chicago: Iwrin Professional Publishing.

Atkinson, J. H., Hohner, G., Mundt, B., Troxel, R. B., & Winchell, W. (1991). *Current Trends in Cost of Quality - Linking the Cost of Quality and Continuous Improvement*. Montvale, NJ: NAA.

Burrows, G., & Chenhall, R. H. (2012). Target costing: First and second comings. *Accounting History Review*, *22*(2), 127–142. doi:10.1080/21552851.2012.681124

CAM-I (Consortium for Advanced Management–International) et SMAC (Society of Management Accounting of Canada). (1994). *Implementing Target Costing, Management Accounting Guideline, April*. Author.

Căpușneanu, S., & Briciu, S. (2011). Analysis of the Possibility to Organize the Management Accounting through the Target Costing (TC) Method in the Romanian Entities. *Theoretical and Applied Economics*, *9*(562), 71–88.

Cokins, G. (2002). Integrations of Target Costing and ABC. *Journal of Cost Management*, *6*(4), 13–22.

Cooper, R., & Slagmulder, R. (1997). *Target Costing and Value Engineering*. Portland, OR: Productivity Press.

Dekker, H., & Smidt, P. (2003). A survey of the adoption and use of target costing in Dutch firms. *International Journal of Production Economics*, *84*(3), 293–305. doi:10.1016/S0925-5273(02)00450-4

Feil, P., Yook, K.-H., & Kim, I.-W. (2004, Spring). Japanese Target Costing: A Historical Perspective. *International Journal of Strategic Cost Management*, 10-19.

Gopalakrishnan, B., Kokatnur, A., & Gupta, D. P. (2007). Design and development of a target-costing system for turning operation. *Journal of Manufacturing Technology Management, 18*(2), 217–238. doi:10.1108/17410380710722917

Hamood, H. H., Omar, N., & Sulaiman, S. (2011). Target Costing Practices: A Review of Literature. *Asia-Pacific Management Accounting Journal, 6*(1), 1–24.

Horváth, P., Niemand, S., & Wolbold, M. (1993), Target Costing: State of the Art Report. Arlington, TX: Computer Aided Manufacturing-International (CAM-I).

Juhmani, O. I. H. (2010). Adoption and Benefits of Target Costing in Bahraini Manufacturing Companies. *Journal of Academy of Business and Economics, 10*(1), 113–122.

Kato, Y. (1993). Target costing support systems: Lessons from leading Japanese companies. *Management Accounting Research, 4*(1), 33–47. doi:10.1006/mare.1993.1002

Kocsoy, M., Gurdal, K., & Karabayir, M. E. (2008). Target Costing in Turkish Manufacturing Enterprises. *European Journal of Soil Science, 7*(2), 92–105.

Monden, Y., & Lee, J. (1993). How a Japanese auto maker reduces costs. *Management Accounting, 72*(2), 22.

Nishimura, A. (2002). Asia Economic Growth and Management Accounting. *Malaysian Accounting Review, 1*(1), 87–101.

Pakizeh, F., Vali, S., Hanzaei, T., & Moradi, M. (2013). Feasibility Assessment of Target Costing in Yasuj Cement Factory. *International Journal of Advanced Studies in Humanities and Social Science, 1*(4), 290–297.

Paunica, M., Matac, M. L., Motofei, C., & Manole, A. (2009). Some aspects regarding the use of business intelligence in the financial management. *Metalurgia International, 1*(14), 180–181.

Rattray, C. J., Lord, B. R., & Shanahan, Y. P. (2007). Target costing in New Zealand manufacturing firms. *Pacific Accounting Review, 19*(1), 68–83. doi:10.1108/01140580710754656

Roşca, I. (Ed.). (1993). Designing financial and accounting information systems. Didactic and Pedagogical Publishing House.

Smith, M. (1999). *Management Accounting for Competitive Advantage* (1st ed.). Sydney: LBC Information Services.

Souissi, M., & Ito, K. (2004). Integrating target costing and the balanced scorecard. *Journal of Corporate Accounting & Finance, 15*(6), 57–62. doi:10.1002/jcaf.20057

Tani, T. (1995). Interactive control in target cost management. *Management Accounting Research, 6*(4), 399–414. doi:10.1006/mare.1995.1028

Tani, T., Okano, H., Shimizu, N., Iwabuchi, Y., Fukuda, J., & Cooray, S. (1994). Target cost management in Japanese companies: Current state of the art. *Management Accounting Research*, 5(1), 67–81. doi:10.1006/mare.1994.1005

Yilmaz, R., & Baral, G. (2010). Target costing as a strategic cost management tool for success of balanced scorecard system. *China-USA Business Review*, 9(3), 39–53.

ADDITIONAL READING

Briciu, S., & Căpuşneanu, S. (2011). Aspects of the normalization of managerial accounting in Romania on a microeconomic level. *Theoretical and Applied Economics*, 3(556), 95–106.

Briciu, S., & Căpuşneanu, S. (2013). Pros and cons for the implementation of target costing method in Romanian economic entities. In *Proceedings of the 8th International Conference Accounting and Management Information Systems* (AMIS 2013, June 12-13 pp. 1032-1044), Bucharest, ASE Publishing House.

Briciu, S., Căpuşneanu, S. & Topor, D. (2012). Developments on SWOT analysis for costing methods, *International Journal of Academic Research*. 4(4), Part B, 142-150.

KEY TERMS AND DEFINITIONS

Activity-Based Costing (ABC): An accounting method that identifies the costs of (indirect) activities and then allocates these costs to the products. Allocation of product costs to products is done through cost drivers.

Data Base Management System (DBMS): All the programs used to create, query, and maintain a database. Includes two categories of modules: modules that are common to those of computer operating systems and modules with database-specific functions.

General Accounts Plan: A classification system consisting of a list of all accounts used in accounting by an economic entity, ordered by economic content and accounting function.

Kaizen Costing (KC): A cost reduction system defined as the maintenance of present cost levels for products currently being manufactured via systematic efforts to achieve the desired cost level.

Microsoft Access: A program for creating and managing a Microsoft-based relational database that is part of the Microsoft Office suite.

Chapter 3
An International Overview of the Electronic Financial System and the Risks Related to It

Tatiana Dănescu
University of Medicine, Pharmacy, Sciences, and Technology of Targu-Mures, Romania

Alexandra Botoș
1 December 1918 University, Romania

Ionica Oncioiu
Titu Maiorescu University, Romania

ABSTRACT

A significant milestone in the evolution of financial reporting systems occurred when the international financial reporting standards (IFRS) were first applied in the year of 1989. The XBRL (extensible business reporting language) phenomenon marked a new stage in the development of global accounting and reporting systems in the year of 2008 when public companies in US began to use this system. Although the two steps have had a significant impact on the process of harmonizing the global financial reporting system, this process is yet not complete. This chapter presents a comparative analysis of some issues emerging from the application of electronic reporting systems in order to identify the risks presented by them and possible solutions to current practices in financial reporting.

INTRODUCTION

International commercial transactions have become an increasingly common practice among corporations as well as among medium and small entities (Hoffman & Raynier, 2017). At the same time, investors are much more open than previous practices to allocate significant amounts to projects in other countries based on the opportunities they identify. Due to the evolution of the economy and the two above mentioned effects, it is a concern of all investors and of all the commercial entities to harmonize the processes and instruments used in the elaboration of financial reports and to facilitate their correct interpretation

DOI: 10.4018/978-1-5225-8455-1.ch003

by any foreign citizen. The mission of this chapter is to critically and professionally analyze the overall framework of financial reporting in the era of digitization.

In the case of electronic financial reporting, one of the most recognized and used system is the XBRL (Extensible Business Reporting Language). XBRL is founded by a non-profit organization and is used in over 50 countries around the world, including United States of America, England, United Arab Emirates, Brazil, Spain, Germany, Belgium, England, Denmark, Indonesia, Japan and others (European Security and Markets Authority, 2017).

XBRL replaces reporting systems based on PDF or HTML files, still used in many countries of the world (European Security and Markets Authority, 2017). Also, the XBRL system has created techniques to replace the current system used by EIOPA (European Insurance and Occupational Pensions Authority), namely the T4U system, proving itself to be a flexible alternative that can boost to a stronger harmonization development of financial reporting systems, on certain market segments in the European Union.

One of the challenges for foreign investors is to adapt to the different electronic reporting systems, in addition to the differences presented by national standards in the country where they invest their resources, which usually are different in many perspectives from the ones from his native country. This issue is trying to be solved by different ways by each and every country that wants to attract foreign investors. A good example of this practice can be found in China, where the government has created special policies to meet the needs and challenges that the foreign investors face throughout their work. The main objective of this chapter is to observe the application of the electronic financial reporting system in the various national contexts of the world and to identify the similarities and differences in its application.

There are also electronic systems that facilitate the development of financial reporting in cloud, such systems are: Cognos - made by IBM, Dynamics 365 - made by Microsoft, Xero, and others. Moving processes and systems from physical platforms to electronic platforms has meant a rapid step for reporting systems. This process took place without giving the opportunity for a thorough analysis and for the development of risk-taking procedures before the electronic era. Currently, the rapid transformation can now be seen, from the electronic platform to the cloud platform. This is why it is considered appropriate to prepare a detailed analysis of the system before this new transit that the financial reporting system will inevitably follow. A second objective of this chapter is to identify the risks involved in preparing and transmitting financial reporting using the new informational systems.

The use of the XBRL and cloud-based systems is becoming more and more common. Currently, XBRL is considered an opportunity for harmonizing the electronic reporting system in Europe, especially since ESMA (European Securities and Markets Authority) has made it mandatory to use XBRL as of 2020. This announcement gives a more urgent note to the need to analyze electronic financial reporting systems for the benefit of Europe's commercial entities and investors.

BACKGROUND

Nowadays, the definition of an accounting information system has changed, in comparison whit the original definition, due to its development over time, so Fontinelle (2018) considers this system to be a program running on a computerized platform that identifies accounting activity through technological resources, although this it is generally valid to note that there are entities who still keep the written financial information on paper and there are no legislative obligations to motivate them to do otherwise (Hoffman, 2006).

Similar to all the functions within an entity and the accounting system, financial reporting is implicitly influenced by the emergence of innovative technologies. Entity management decides to change a reporting system in favor of another in response to changes in the environment, and in particular due to the emergence of new, more advanced technologies (Derman, 2005). The primary goal of the digitization of financial reports according to Hoffman (2017) is to improve and develop the accounting institution; given the increasing volume, complexity and importance of financial information, the digitization option becomes relevant.

International Financial Reporting Standards are currently of major importance for developers of new technologies for the financial reporting system. These are either mandatory or voluntary in around 120 jurisdictions; they are the only common root of financial reporting systems around the world. On the adoption process, Holger et al. (2008) presents the statistical results of a study conducted on a sample of 3100 entities from 26 countries that have adopted IFRS. Accordingly, the mandatory adoption of IFRS may lead to an increase in financial market liquidity by between 3-6% and therefore to a decrease in the entity's capital cost.

In today's technology, an important element in the financial reporting system is human-computer interaction, which has been in development for over thirty years. The primary purpose of this interaction is to transpose information from the physical plane into the digital one. But this can trigger many risks.

Ilias et al. (2015) suggests that in order to promote an effective financial reporting system, an important factor is the adoption of XBRL. Gunn (2007) points out that the XBRL system resonates with individual concepts in financial reporting, allowing for a universally valid understanding of each financial information. Cohen (2015) also claims that compared to the XML system, XBRL has a more efficient semantic explication but is more inappropriate for automated logical reasoning. In contrast to these arguments, there are studies that mentions that in the USA the XBRL adoption transition has been a difficult time for both private and public entities. In June 2011, IFAC together with ISACA developed a "Leverage XBRL for Value in Organizations" project, which aims to support accountants in capitalizing on XBRL adoption initiatives and compliance requirements. The two entities argue that the benefits and opportunities to incorporate XBRL into internal processes can streamline management communication, thus increasing the value of information used within an organization. The materials provided include numerous examples and case studies.

"As XBRL is being implemented in financial markets around the world, it raises important questions: How will it help to increase the credibility of financial reporting? What does XBRL mean for professional accountants and auditors of financial information and for users of this information? What implications and challenges must be considered before the impact of XBRL on the supply chain of corporate reporting reaches its full potential? "(Gunn, 2007)

INTERNATIONAL FINANCIAL REPORTING SYSTEMS

Due to the fact that a financial reporting system is formed both from the information system and from the legal framework that regulates it, an individual analysis of the national reporting systems is needed to find similarities and differences. Therefore, in Table 1 one can observe the particular situations in 53 states around the world.

By geographically structuring countries according to the situation of global financial reporting systems, a division of the world into four categories is achieved. States that adopt international report-

Table 1. Situation of financial reporting systems in 53 countries

No.	Country	Regulatory Framework for the Financial Reporting System	Use of XBRL
1	Afghanistan	IFRS required for all non-small business entities and for all banks. Micro-enterprises are allowed accounting on the basis of receipts and payments.	Annual reports are submitted by commercial entities in printed form to government authorities.
2	Albania	IFRS required for all listed entities, financial institutions and large private entities.	Many government institutions and agencies, banks and other financial institutions, as well as many private individuals, commercial entities (large and medium-sized) use electronic reporting solutions.
3	Australia	IFRSs are mandatory for listed companies and financial institutions. Alternatively, foreign business entities can use home standards if they are approved by the scholarship. For other SMEs, no specific reporting framework is required.	Transmission of financial reports is done electronically in .tif, .pdf or .rtf format along with the XML format and / or the standard format.
4	Austria	All national companies whose securities are traded on a regulated market are required to use the IFRS standards adopted by the EU in their consolidated financial statements. Except where a foreign entity whose national jurisdictions are considered by the EU to be equivalent to IFRS, they may use their own national standards.	Submission of financial reports to the Company Registry is made in PDF format.
5	Belarus	The application of IFRS is required for all listed entities and financial institutions.	XBRL (Reisinger, 2017)
6	Belgium	IFRS standards are required for national public entities and for entities listed on the stock exchange.	The National Bank of Belgium is responsible for preparing national situations. In order to contribute to this process, Belgian business entities provide the central bank with an annual XBRL template balance sheet.
7	Brazil	Entities quoted on a stock exchange and any banking entity that is legally required to publish financial statements in Brazil must publish consolidated financial statements in accordance with IFRSs. A Portuguese version of the IFRS for SMEs was also adopted as an option for Brazil's SMEs.	Brazilian government entities use XBRL to efficiently collect and improve data quality for the Brazilian National Treasury.
8	Bulgaria	IFRS standards are required for national public entities and for entities listed on the stock exchange.	Non-listed business entity reports may be submitted either in electronic format in PDF or physically in a standard format at the Registration Agency. The listed entities electronically transmit financial reports to the authorities' portal.
9	Cambodia	All Cambodian public interest entities quoted on the stock exchange must comply with IFRS. IFRS for SMEs is an option for all SMEs in Cambodia, except for those of public interest.	There is no legislative provision on the transmission of financial reports to national authorities.
10	Canada	Application of IFRS is mandatory starting in 2011. However, reporting entities in the United States are entitled to apply US GAAP.	Financial reporting issuers are required to submit reports in PDF or XBRL format on the SEDAR (System for Electronic Document Analysis and Retrieval) portal.
11	Chile	All listed entities or other types of commercial entities are accountable for the use of IFRSs in preparing financial statements. SMEs are required to use IFRS for SMEs. Banking institutions are required to apply national accounting standards as published by the Superintendence of Banks and Financial Institutions (SBIF).	The Securities Regulatory Authority of Chile requires listed companies to submit financial statements in XBRL format. Data is republished on its XBRL web site and can be used by global market participants, including data providers, investors and analysts.

continued on following page

Table 1. Continued

No.	Country	Regulatory Framework for the Financial Reporting System	Use of XBRL
12	China	China's national standards are converging with IFRS. Chinese entities representing more than 30% of the total market capitalization of the domestic market produce financial statements consistent with IFRS due to their dual registrations in Hong Kong and other international markets.	The format for submitting financial reports may vary by location. If the reporting entity transmits its online reports, then the financial reports will be sent to the authorities using the format provided by the system.
13	Columbia	Public interest entities and large entities that: a) are subsidiaries of parent companies that report under IFRS; b) are the parent companies of branches reporting under IFRS; and c) are entities that export or import more than 50% of the value of the turnover; adopt IFRS. Large and medium sized companies other than those included in the first category adopt IFRS for SMEs. Micro-enterprises apply standards specifically developed for their needs (Normas de Información Financiera para Microempresas).	Colombian financial institutions complete financial reports in XBRL format and send them to the responsible authority, "Superintendencia Financiera de Colombia". Also, the Columbia Business Registrar asks for the presentation of the balance sheet, profit and loss account and cash flows through its online XBRL Express portal, which feeds information into the SIRFIN Integrated Financial Reporting System.
14	Denmark	IFRS standards are required for national public entities and for entities listed on the stock exchange.	The Danish Business Authority has asked all Danish companies to provide either a XBRL format or the iXBRL format a digitally signed version of their annual financial reporting for market registration and market information.
15	Switzerland	Compliance with national accounting standards is required from all entities. However, compliance with IFRSs ensures compliance, and therefore many large entities have followed IAS / IFRS for many years. Companies whose shares are listed must prepare their financial statements either under IFRS or under US GAAP.	There is a program in development whereby the financial reporting of commercial entities is transmitted in accordance with the Swiss Code of Obligations in XBRL format.
16	UAE	All entities listed on the Dubai Financial Market are required to publish IFRS financial statements. Also, all United Arab Emirates banking entities are required by the United Arab Emirates Central Bank to publish the IFRS financial statements.	The Securities and Goods Issuing Authority shall request quarterly financial statements in XBRL format from listed entities on the Abu Dhabi and Dubai stock exchanges and brokers operating in that country.
17	Finland	IFRS standards are required for national public entities and for entities listed on the stock exchange.	banking institutions are required to use the XBRL format, while quoted entities have the option to use this voluntary format (Enachi & Andone, 2015).
18	France	IFRS standards are required for national public entities and for entities listed on the stock exchange.	All financial institutions are subject to the requirement of the Banking Commission and the French Bank to send financial reports in XBRL format (Enachi & Andone, 2015).
19	Germany	IFRS standards are required for national public entities and for listed entities that prepare consolidated financial reports. Non-listed entities producing consolidated financial reports have the option of choosing between HGB (Handelsgesetzbuch) and IFRS. Entities preparing financial statements in simplified form are required to apply the HGB.	Corporations are required to send digital files in E-Bilanz format (XBRL format) using a wide range of industry-specific taxonomies. In addition to the main taxonomy, based on the German Commercial Code, taxonomies were created for the banking industry, insurers and pension funds. Specific taxa were also produced for hospitals, health care institutions, transport-specific entities, local municipal enterprises and agricultural farms.
20	India	National Accounting Standards (Ind AS) are based on and are substantially converged with IFRS Standards.	The four categories of entities that have the obligation to report in XBRL format are: all business entities, all of the contingent entities and corporations, financial and banking institutions, insurance institutions, and private pensions.

continued on following page

Table 1. Continued

No.	Country	Regulatory Framework for the Financial Reporting System	Use of XBRL
21	Indonesia	Indonesia's prospect of adopting IFRS is to maintain national GAAP (Indonesian Financial Accounting Standards) standards and to gradually converge with IFRS as much as possible. Currently, listed entities do not have the option of fully complying with IFRS.	The Indonesian Bank collects monthly financial statements from 34 Islamic banks, files being validated and sent in XBRL format directly to BI. The data are mainly used for surveillance purposes.
22	Ireland	IFRS standards are required for national public entities and for entities listed on the stock exchange. SMEs can use national standards that are based on the IFRS Standard for SMEs but with significant changes. Alternatively, they can use IFRS adopted by the EU.	The Central Bank of Ireland offers all institutions of creditors the option to submit special reports in XBRL format. The Registration Office of Business Entities also offers this option to all business entities to submit financial reports in this format. (Enachi & Andone, 2015)
23	Israel	All national entities whose securities are traded on a public market only in Israel are required to use IFRS. Banking institutions comply with regulatory accounting standards. Domestic entities whose securities transactions both in Israel and on foreign stock exchanges are allowed to file financial statements in Israel in accordance with IFRS, IFRS, or US GAAP.	Only listed entities have the obligation to submit financial reports electronically in PDF format, accompanied by an XHTL format that is converted to XML or XBRL.
24	Italy	Brokers, issuers of widely distributed financial instruments, banks, brokerage institutions, fund managers, regulated financial institutions and insurance institutions are required to apply IFRSs.	The Italian bank offers the possibility for commercial entities that have intra-community or international activities to send XBRL reports. The Trade Registry requires financial entities to report financial reports in XBRL format. (Enachi & Andone, 2015)
25	Japan	Japanese Accounting Standards ("Japanese GAAP") are developed by the Japan Accounting Standards Board. GAAP are considered to be converging with International Financial Reporting Standards (IFRS) but are not identical, are considered to be equivalent to those adopted in the European Union in 2008.	Tax authorities have requested that XBRL corporations submit their annual financial reports, half-yearly financial reports, quarterly financial reports, and securities registration statements. The new generation EDINET also introduced Inline XBRL.
26	South Korea	National standards are identical to IFRSs, with short-term differences when changing the latter. National standards are required for listed companies and financial institutions. Foreign-listed entities are entitled to use either IFRS or IFRS adopted in Korea or US GAAP. SMEs are entitled to use full IFRS standards.	Transmission of reports is done in XML or XBRL format, electronically on the governmental portal of all types of entities.
27	Latvia	IFRS standards are required for national public entities and for entities listed on the stock exchange.	Records to SRS (State Revenue Service) can be printed, XML files or filled in the online web form. Deposits to the FCMC (Financial and Capital Market Commission) are either printed or in PDF format.
28	Lituania	IFRS standards are required for national public entities and for entities listed on the stock exchange.	The Reclamation Center requires submission by electronic HTML or XML formats and, if necessary, accompanied by PDF files. A printed version it is not necessary.
29	Luxembourg	IFRS standards are required for national public entities and for entities listed on the stock exchange. Luxembourg's accounting principles are required for separate and consolidated financial statements of non-listed entities.	The Financial Sector Supervision Commission requires entities in its area of authority to submit reports in XBRL format. (Enachi & Andone, 2015)
30	Malaysia	Public entities and any entity registered in Malaysia must use the Malaysian Financial Reporting Standards (MFRS) framework that is in line with IFRS.	Financial, banking and insurance institutions as well as corporations transmit financial reports in a standardized format. It is expected that this year (2018) will launch the platform for XBRL electronic transmission of financial reporting of SME Entities.

continued on following page

Table 1. Continued

No.	Country	Regulatory Framework for the Financial Reporting System	Use of XBRL
31	Malta	IFRS standards are required for national public entities and for entities listed on the stock exchange.	Annual reports are submitted by commercial entities in printed form to government authorities.
32	Mexico	All listed entities must comply with IFRS, except for financial institutions and insurance institutions, which must comply with national standards. Foreign business entities can use either IFRS or US GAAP.	Mexican Stock Exchange entities submit financial reports, including the statement of financial position, income statement and cash flows and changes in equity, in XBRL format, which are then posted on the stock exchange's website.
33	Moldova	Compliance with IFRS is required for listed companies and financial institutions.	Annual reports are submitted by commercial entities in printed form to government authorities.
34	Mongolia	The Accounting Act requires that all profit-making and non-profit entities, including small and medium-sized enterprises (SMEs), state-owned enterprises (SOEs) and other entities, prepare financial statements in full compliance with IFRSs.	Financial reports must be submitted electronically via the Ministry of Finance system. Printing in print format is acceptable but cannot replace electronic transmission.
35	Myanmar	Public entities and financial institutions are required to use International Financial Reporting Standards in Myanmar (MFRS), which are substantially in line with the 2010 version of the IFRS. Myanmar has adopted the IFRS for SMEs as the Financial Reporting Standard for SMEs, hate. SMEs are allowed to use MFRS for SMEs or full IFRSs.	Annual reports are submitted by commercial entities in printed form to government authorities.
36	New Zealand	New Zealand has adopted national standards equivalent to IFRS for all public entities. Foreign entities with subsidiaries in New Zealand are required to use NZ-IFRSs if they are not granted specific exemptions by allowing them to use another financial reporting framework, including IFRS.	Financial reports are submitted electronically in PDF format or delivered in printed format to the competent authorities.
37	Holland	Compliance with IFRS is required for listed companies and financial institutions.	The Netherlands Finance Ministry offers the possibility to send financial reports and economic statistics in XBRL format to all commercial entities. The Association of Water Councils also offers this option to all members of the Association. The Dutch bank offers this option to all credit institutions. (Enachi & Andone, 2015)
38	Panama	All listed national private entities are required to use the US IFRS or GAAP. SMEs, as defined by the IASB, need to adopt IFRS for SMEs for annual financial reporting.	Peruvian banks complete financial reports in XBRL format and send them to "Superintendencia de Bancos de Panama". Financial reports are available to the public online.
39	Papua New Guineea	Compliance with IFRS is required for listed companies and financial institutions.	Financial reports are filled in electronically on the Government Authority Portal or can be submitted in printed format.
40	Peru	IFRS standards are required for all national entities whose securities are traded on a public market in Peru other than banks, insurance institutions and pension funds. Banks, insurance institutions and pension funds have to comply with the accounting standards issued by the government regulator. The Peruvian Accounting Standards Board (CNC) also adopted IFRS for SMEs. This Standard may be applied by all Peruvian entities with a total assets and / or net income of less than 3,000 UITs.	Securities supervised entities, with the exception of Intermediate Agents and Entities supervised by the Banking and Insurance Supervisor, use templates in Excel to record, validate, and generate reports in XBRL.

continued on following page

Table 1. Continued

No.	Country	Regulatory Framework for the Financial Reporting System	Use of XBRL
41	Romania	IFRS standards are required for national public entities and for entities listed on the stock exchange. The accounting principles should be applied in the financial reports of all non-listed entities.	Transmission of financial reports is done electronically in pdf format along with the XML format and / or the standard format.
42	Russia	The IFRS standards required for listed companies, financial institutions and some state-owned entities.	XBRL (Reisinger, 2017)
43	Rwanda		Financial reports shall be submitted in printed form to the competent authorities.
44	Saudi Arabia	IFRS standards are mandatory for all listed entities, banks and insurance institutions.	Deposit requirements in XBRL are implemented by all entities registered with MCI. Also, non-listed entities transmit financial reports together with PDF files.
45	Singapore	Entities listed in Singapore are required to use the Singapore Financial Reporting Standards (SFRS), which are substantially convergent to IFRS. However, with the permission of the securities regulator, listed entities may use IFRS. The SINGAPORE Financial Reporting Standard for Small Entities is based on IFRS for SMEs.	All entities (commercial, financial, banking, insurance) have the possibility to submit annual financial reports in XBRL format, except for limited guarantee entities and foreign entities with branches in Singapore.
46	Slovenia	The IFRS standards required for listed companies, financial institutions and some state-owned entities.	Financial reports are sent electronically as a PDF, Word or Excel file. Small and Medium Entities can send annual reports via the web application by directly entering or importing an XML file. Medium and large businesses submit annual reports for statistical purposes through standardized forms and audited and / or consolidated annual reports as PDF files.
47	South Africa	South African entities are permitted to use International Financial Reporting Standards (IFRS), IFRS for SMEs, or South African GAAP standard based on the entity's public interest score.	XBRL (Reisinger, 2017)
48	Spain	IFRS standards are required for national public entities and for entities listed on the stock exchange.	All entities submitting financial reports are required to submit them to the Trade Registry and the control authority in XBRL format, which is then made public online.
49	USA	National public entities must use US GAAP. At present, over 500 ESA foreign applicants with a market capitalization of $ 7 trillion use the IFRS standards to develop US financial reporting.	FFIEC obliges US banks to provide quarterly "call reports" in XBRL format. Entities must provide 3 quarterly (10-Q) and 1 year deposit (10-K) in the EDGAR system of the Regulatory Authority. The data is used by the Safety and Market Commission (ESA) to analyze the entity's compliance with its disclosure obligations, as well as to identify abnormalities and exceptional values that could indicate fraud. Data is republished in XBRL format and is freely available to market participants with special use for a range of groups including data providers, research firms and analysts.
50	Sweden	The IFRS standards required for listed companies, financial institutions and some state-owned entities.	The Registry of Business Entities provides the possibility to send annual financial reports and the auditor's report, by small and medium sized entities and those subject to national GAAP, in XBRL format. (Enachi & Andone, 2015

continued on following page

Table 1. Continued

No.	Country	Regulatory Framework for the Financial Reporting System	Use of XBRL
51	Turkey	National standards that are fully compliant with IFRS are required for listed companies, financial institutions and other public interest entities.	Currently, financial reports of any type of entity are transmitted electronically within the Government Authorities Portal in XML format accompanied by the PDF.
52	UK	IFRS standards are required for national public entities and for entities listed on the stock exchange. SMEs can use a national standard based on the IFRS Standard for SMEs, but with significant changes. Alternatively, they can use IFRS adopted by the EU.	The UK tax authority requires all listed entities to provide tax records in the iXBRL format. Also, the British Companies Registry requires all UK entities to file annual financial statements in iXBRL format.
53	Uganda	The IFRS standards required for listed companies, financial institutions and some state-owned entities.	Financial reports shall be submitted in printed form to the competent authorities.

Source: Realized by processing the information found in bibliographic references

ing standards or have converging standards with them and have implemented the XBRL system; States that have only adopted international reporting standards without implementing XBRL; States that only adopted XBRL without implementing international reporting standards; States that do not apply either of the above mentioned criteria.

On the world map, the spread of IFRS standards at the same time as the use of the XBRL system, and the geographic areas covered by purple color, Blue Areas are the only application of IFRS, and the orange areas only apply XBRL; the remaining white areas are represented by states that do not adopt either. It is noteworthy that the map is based on all the information identified so far including the adoption of XBRL in South Africa's reporting system starting in July 2018, with the indication that the map will continue to change especially since 2020 when all EU countries will be subject to XBRL adoption.

There are sustained efforts to implement IFRS, but the level of convergence is different, in particular due to certain economic, social and administrative elements that can accelerate or slow the convergence process. However, there is a large difference between the adoption of XBRL and IFRS. Considering this observation and the fact that there are already companies who use cloud computing financial reporting systems that are currently not standardized by any institution, the speed of new technology development can be a major drawback for the process of harmonizing the global system financial reporting.

Due to the fact that IFRSs are uniformly applied throughout the European Union and all national banking entities have the obligation to transmit XBRL reports to the European Central Bank, and since 2020, States that do not currently apply XBRL will have to apply this system, it is relevant to analyze the situation as a whole. According to ESMA, financial reports will be made in HTML, with the help of XBRL, which can be opened with any standard web browser. Reports can also be easily converted to SQL or Excel. A special XBRL taxonomy will be performed according to IFRS by the IFRS Foundation, being an extension of the original taxonomy. To help professionals, ESMA has created a user manual to help them with simple problems in generating Inline XBRL files.

Based on the information available so far, some states under review implement national financial reporting standards or accounting law, which in some cases are in line with IFRS but have avoided adopting IFRS for one of the following reasons:

- Particular economic situations and specific to the local economy for which, to date, the coverage of the provisions of the general standards, IFRS (ex. Cuba) has not been met;
- Low national level of regulation of the financial reporting system in order to give freedom to non-listed entities (ex. Paraguay);
- Disadvantaged state political governance for the adoption of international systems.

Considering the states that have adopted only the XBRL system, the ASIA region is the only one with such states: India, Iran, Saudi Arabia and Indonesia.

According to the information found, among the reasons why most states have not yet implemented the XBRL system for financial reporting are:

- Resistance to change, many states currently have a functional reporting platform in place, and changing this platform would involve changing the entire national system, this change affecting all entities in that state;
- Economic disadvantage or warfare. Some states currently lack the favorable internal environment for developing their internal financial reporting system;
- The cost of implementing the XBRL system, in order for the financial reporting system to be changed, needs financing of this process, some states do not have the financial possibility of updating the digital financial reporting system to the new technological trends.

Currently, at international level, the following formats used for the purpose of transmitting financial reports to responsible institutions can be highlighted:

- XBRL;
- HTML;
- PDF or Smart PDF;
- Printed forms

It is noted that if the digital system works efficiently, any of the systems using digital formats is much quicker and easier compared to the written submission of financial reports. Digital transmission is also preferred due to the reduction of paper waste and the reduction of bureaucracy. For the other three digital formats, these have advantages and disadvantages to each other. For example, the size of PDF files can take up more storage space than an HTML file, and the information presented in PDF format is harder to handle than HTML.

There are studies that have attempted to observe users' financial reporting preferences about their format. Rowbottom and Lymer (2003) noted a preference for the PDF report of a UK business entity's financial report while Hodge (2004), which analyzed updated traffic logs, found a slightly higher preference for HTML versus PDF, of financial reporting. Also, Jones (2011) claims that in the case of quarterly reports, researchers have found a user preference for the PDF format.

The main difference between HTML and XBRL is the XML format. HTML format is predefined so that financial reporting information can be presented on World Wide Web platforms, while XML does not replace this format brings added flexibility to other devices such as tablets, phones, and so on, XBRL to Difference from HTML is an XML schema that is specifically designed for financial reporting. XBRL has now begun to replace the HTML system within the financial reporting system. Inline XBRL offering the possibility to translate financial reports into French, German, Japanese, Spanish and English, and can be adapted to both IFRS and GAAP.

DIGITALIZATION AND INNOVATION OF FINANCIAL REPORTING SYSTEMS

Among the reasons entities adopt changes in financial reporting systems are the desire to lower costs or the desire to increase efficiency and performance by increasing the quality of the reporting information system (Deloitte, 2018). Thanks to the new data storage option in the Cloud Computing System, entities have the option of reducing the cost of maintaining the accounting information system and, at the same time, increasing the level of accessibility of information.

In the financial reporting process, the use of the cloud computing facility has become a very attractive option today. In a study by Shkurti and Muça (2014) it is presented that accounting professionals believe that with the implementation of a cloud-based system the biggest advantage is the cost savings with data storage systems and lower purchase costs of software licenses. In addition to this cost-cutting advantage, the increased transparency of information is highlighted, similar to the faster speed of accessing real-time financial information, and increased accessibility under the availability of an internet network.

One of the products that enable this feature and helps with financial reporting is the Oracle E-Business Suite, a set of technologies that provides integrated reporting. According to the information provided by them on their web site, the group was made available to corporations, especially the European region and Australia, when passing to the adoption of IFRS, at present it provides dual financial support in accordance with IFRS, and in accordance with GAPP.

G-Account for Xero is another alternative to using Cloud Computing, being a special application for XERO users in the bookkeeping system. This application allows Google-based automation of financial reporting via Google Cloud platforms. This means using a very simple system based on Excel files, being very accessible to any user.

Another innovation in this area is mobile applications that allow access to financial-accounting analysis software, suites like Oracle E-Business, as well as access to financial statements and reports. Therefore, the financial reporting system presents a continuous development along with the technological development, but can cause the number and complexity of the risks attributed to it. Also, both XERO and G-Account for Xero are available in Desktop and Mobile.

This innovative software integrates with other automated payment and collection systems such as PayPal, Bill.com, Shopify and more. These facilities increase the flexibility of businesses using these accounting programs, but these programs are usable by small and medium business entities and less when considering the large amount of data in large entities and corporations.

IDENTIFIED RISKS

In the decision of implementing a digitized financial reporting system, the risk level can be higher for a State that has not opted for the adoption of IFRS or US GAAP. Developing XBRL in a global international financial reporting platform can also pose risks for every entity on a global level.

In the XBRL system the following risks can be highlighted:

- Information denaturation due to the XBRL tagging system, each country or system that uses the XBRL choses the tags that the system will imply, this system may be in some cases a disadvantage in the interpretation of financial reporting information,
- Incompatibility and loss of information due to national accounting regulations or standards that are different from IFRS or US GAAP,
- Resistance to change by the reporting entities, this may occur especially in national reforms when implementing new systems, some entities will comply less when the reporting process changes,
- Inefficient data mining, due to the large amount of data that will be imported by the government after implementing the XBRL system. In the PDF and XML system there are a lot of information's that do not enter the data base and remain strict as documents, like the management's reports and other annexes, when implementing the XBRL all of this information will be flowing in the data base.

When choosing an accounting information system based on Cloud computing as a whole, the following risks can be attributed to this change:

- Choosing software for the accounting system and in advance of financial reporting that does not present a complete vision of the entity. In the case of small and medium-sized entities, it may lead to the distortion of the image presented in the financial reports, which becomes inconsistent with reality;
- The transition from a desktop software to the accounting information and financial reporting system to a Cloud Computing based application can lead to multiple issues that are closely related to the transfer of information and complementary to their loss;
- Using an innovative system such as Cloud Computing can lead to the emergence of resistance to change by the reporting entity's staff, especially the poorer staff that is more adaptable to the functionality of such a system;
- Cyber-attacks that have become real problems for some states can also pose threats to the entity's financial reporting system, especially when using the Cloud platform that is not alert to unauthorized infiltration. Also, the lack of knowledge of the existence of an authority or institution responsible for combating these risks may become problematic in the case of the Cloud Computing system by commercial entities.

SOLUTIONS AND RECOMMENDATIONS

The XBRL system may indeed present a solution to the needs of management and national authorities, but it must be perceived as a tool of the financial reporting information system, a tool that does not eliminate the vulnerabilities and risks that detract from financial reporting.

Regarding the adoption of XBRL, it is recommended that management should be aware that due to the use of certain labels within the XBRL system, the meta-data can be used inconsistently, requiring factual verification and quality control of financial reporting. Cohen (2004) noted that the development of the taxonomy could lead to the elimination of this risk. However, the XBRL taxonomy is quite efficient, this system using a number of 2845 well-defined labels, and its expansion could lead to a loss of value and relevance of information.

Another possibility to prevent the risk of non-compliance is to develop accounting software so that it facilitates the verification and auditing of financial reports using the XBRL system. They may incorporate certain automatic alarms and if the financial reports are incomplete or inconsistent with the financial statements in the accounts, alert the professional who produces them.

Cybernetic resistance testing of the system can be simulated in order to identify vulnerabilities but also gaps, to test methods of response and information retrieval in the event of a timely attack. This practice can become a very important one in the process of preventing and protecting financial reporting systems, especially for corporations. The disadvantage of such a practice is that it would claim the constant existence of a team that can track and counteract such attacks, which would increase costs. In view of the above-mentioned argument for adopting an innovative technology system, namely cost reduction, an entity is unlikely to want to set up a new office / department to perform this role if management is not aware of the risks and their consequences.

In view of the above, it is relevant that, alongside the XBRL system, there is a system that standardizes the use of Cloud Computing when it is the basis for the financial reporting process. In addition, regardless of the change to the financial reporting system, whether it is updating to XBRL format or updating to a cloud computing software, the adoption of new criteria for assessing the quality of the financial reporting system is also important.

It would be beneficial for both users and software vendors for the accounting information system, including financial reporting, to create a new profession of consultants who have economic and computer skills to provide objective advice at that time when an entity wants to upgrade the above mentioned systems.

FUTURE RESEARCH DIRECTIONS

It is relevant that future research on financial statements and situations be directed to the mobile application area, which is a very new area but is beginning to show great interest in the corporate management view that accessibility to information is most important. Currently, this area cannot be investigated due to the fact that it is not possible to identify the entities that benefit from such a service.

CONCLUSION

Due to the rapid development of technologies and the desire of states to have the most efficient financial reporting system, a favorable environment is created to manifest the risk of non-compliance of financial reporting with the economic reality caused by the adoption of digital accounting systems and processing of reports that are not suited to issuers in all matters requiring public reporting.

At present, technological development exceeds the ability to absorb new products in many situations, which is why the most useful step in making the right decisions about the accounting information system and / or financial reporting is the use of advice from a professional, who is acquainted both in technology, accounting and economics.

REFERENCES

Cohen, E. (2004). Compromise or Customize: XBRL's Paradoxical Power. CAP Forum on E-Business: Compromise or Customize: XBRL's Paradoxical Power. *Canadian Accounting Perspectives*, *2*(3), 187–206. doi:10.1506/YAHN-CAE8-5CWQ-H4TE

Cohen, E. (2015). XBRL: The standardised business language for 21st century reporting and governance. *International Journal of Disclosure and Governance*, *4*(2), 368–394.

Deloitte. (2018). *Effective dates of IFRSs and amendments.* Retrieved from https://www.iasplus.com

Derman, D. T. (2005). Avoiding Accounting Fixation: Determinants of Cognitive Adaptation to Differences in Accounting Method. *Contemporary Accounting Research*, *22*(2), 351–384. doi:10.1506/RQ40-UR50-5CRL-YU8A

Enachi, M., & Andone, I. (2015). The Progress of XBRL in Europe – Projects, Users and Prospects. *Procedia Economics and Finance*, *20*, 185–192. doi:10.1016/S2212-5671(15)00064-7

European Security and Markets Authority. (2017). *ESEF Reporting Manual.* https://www.esma.europa.eu

European Security and Markets Authority. (2017). *European single electronic format.* Retrieved from https://www.esma.europa.eu

Fontinelle, A. (2018). *Introduction to Accounting Information Systems.* Investopedia. Retrieved from https://www.investopedia.com/

Gunn, J. (2007). XBRL: Opportunities and Challenges in Enhancing Financial Reporting and Assurance Processes. *American Accounting Association.*, *1*, A36–A43.

Hodge, F. D., Kennedy, J. J., & Maines, L. A. (2004). Does search-facilitating technology improve the transparency of financial reporting? *The Accounting Review*, *79*(3), 687–703. doi:10.2308/accr.2004.79.3.687

Hoffman, C. (2006). *Financial Reporting Using XBRL.* UBmatrix Inc.

Hoffman, C. (2017). *Digital Financial Reporting Manifesto.* Universal Public Domain Dedication.

Hoffman, C., & Raynier F. (2017). *Intelligent Digital Financial Reporting.* CC0 1.0 Universal Public Domain Dedication.

Holger, D., Luzi, H., Christian, L., & Rodrigo, V. (2008). *Mandatory IFRS Reporting Around the World: Early Evidence on the Economic Consequences. Initiative on Global Markets.* University of Chicago, Graduate School of Business.

Ilias, A., Razak, M. Z. A., & Rahman, R. A. (2015). The expectation of perceived benefit of extensible business reporting language (XBRL): A case in Malaysia. *Journal of Developing Areas*, *49*(5), 263–271. doi:10.1353/jda.2015.0060

Jones, D. (2011). *New ideas and tips for PDF financial reports.* Retrieved from http://irwebreport.com

KPMG. (2018). *Asia Pacific Tax Profiles.* Retrieved from https://home.kpmg.com

Oracle's Financial Management Solutions: Transition to IFRS with Oracle E-Business Suite. (n.d.). Retrieved from www.oracle.com

Reisinger, B. (2017). XBRL in Progress – Financial Reporting Policy Frameworks and their Effects on the Adoption of XBRL. *Financial Communications*, *8*, 1–20.

Rowbottom, N., Allam, A., & Lymer, A. (2005). An exploration of the potential for studying the usage of investor relations information through the analysis of web server logs. *International Journal of Accounting Information Systems*, *6*(1), 31–53. doi:10.1016/j.accinf.2004.08.002

Shkurti, R., & Muça, E. (2014). An Analysis of Cloud Computing and Its Role in Accounting Industry in Albania. *Global Perspectives on Accounting Education*, *8*(2), 219–229.

ADDITIONAL READING

Dong, W., Yujing, C., & Jing, X. (2016). Knowledge Management of Web Financial Reporting in Human-Computer Interactive Perspective. *EURASIA Journal of Mathematics Science and Technology Education*, *13*(7), 3349–3373.

Edel, L. (2018). Inline XBRL New Emerging Technology. *Global Journal of Management and Business Research*, *1*(1), 26–29.

Fourny, G. (2017). *The XBRL Book. Create Space Independent Publishing*. Platform.

Ivana, M., & Ana, O. (2013). Information Technology and Accounting Information Systems' Quality in Croatian Middle and Large Companies. *Journal of Information and Organizational Sciences*, *37*(2), 117–126.

Pfeifer, J. W. (2018). Preparing for Cyber Incidents with Physical Effects. *The Cyber Defense Review*, *3*(1), 27–34.

Tatiana, D., & Alexandra, B. (2016). Research on the International Accounting Harmonization Process. *Annals of the University of Craiova. Economic Sciences Series*, *1*(44), 66–75.

Wu, J., & Vasarhelyi, M. (2004). *XBRL: A New Tool for Electronic Financial Reporting. Business Intelligence Techniques*. Berlin, Heidelberg: Springer.

Xiuping, Z., & Bruce, C. (2018). *Policy of Overseas Investment, Investing in China and Chinese Investment Abroad*. Singapore, China: Springer.

KEY TERMS AND DEFINITIONS

Entity: In the present context, it means any institution, organization, or economic entity in its own right, which presents a form of legal organization and is subject to financial reporting.

Financial Reporting: Individual financial statements prepared in accordance with IFRS, annual, semestrial, or whenever required in accordance with the national regulations of the reporting entity.

Informational Accounting System: The set of elements, processes, and practices involved in the process of collecting, transmitting, processing, and compiling financial reports.

Inline XBRL: Inline xtensible business reporting language provides a mechanism for embedding XBRL tags into HTML documents. This allows XBRL users to associate the labeled data with a legible presentation of a report under the control of the reporter.

Prevention: Contextually, it means to avert a possible risk, to take all necessary measures to avoid triggering and creating a risk.

Risk: Possibility to manifest a phenomenon, act, or fact that may cause damage, loss, or may have a negative impact on the activity of an entity.

Taxonomy: Taxonomy is comprised of a schema file or links and direct link links mentioned in this scheme. The taxonomy scheme together with the link files defines the concepts and relationships that form the basis of the taxonomy. The set of relationships, schemas, and relationship files is taxonomy.

Chapter 4

Healthcare Security Assessment in the Big Data Era:
Lessons From Turkey

Ionica Oncioiu
Titu Maiorescu University, Romania

Oana Claudia Ionescu
Titu Maiorescu University, Romania

ABSTRACT

By its nature, the improvement of the individual's health is a service that involves a rigorous sharing of data in real time. Integrating innovative advances in technologies into the healthcare system by organizations from Turkey is a challenge, an approach to the economic and social boundary, and an attempt to balance consumer-oriented actions. This chapter aims to contribute to the decrease of the shortcomings that exist in the healthcare security assessment by focusing on data mining for public institutions and organizations in Turkey.

INTRODUCTION

The transition from the industrial society to the information society, technologically-oriented developments also contributed to the increase of the importance of knowledge by accelerating the production, storage, processing and sharing of the data (Frese & Fay, 2001). The rapid progress in information technology has brought many changes, from the daily life of people to the work processes of public and private sector organizations, from the provision of public services such as health and education to the emergence of new areas of expertise and professions (Pettigrew, Woodman & Cameron, 2001).

The use of information in administrative processes, adaptation to information and communication technologies is seen as an element that provides comparative advantage of competition among countries as well as between countries (Mikalef & Pateli, 2017). For this reason, investments for organizations and for information and communication technologies for countries have become a strategic priority (Grimson, Grimson & Hasselbring, 2000).

DOI: 10.4018/978-1-5225-8455-1.ch004

Today, traditional hardware and software it is now possible to store, process, share and analyze large volumes of data, which are costly to be stored and analyzed by their solutions, thanks to developing information technologies, hardware and software solutions (Şener & Yiğit, 2017). In the 1990s, states and public organizations changed the procedures and procedures, using public facilities and facilities, as well as traditional means, introduced public goods and services, developed and implemented public policies (Ibbs & Kwak, 2000).

At the same time, data mining is a relatively new phenomenon for governments and the public sector, with an advanced implementation network in sectors such as banking, marketing, information, telecommunications and healthcare (Ericksen & Dyer, 2005).

The process of adaptation of the healthcare security assessment to information technology, starting with the state of affairs, now faces new challenges in Turkey such as social media and Web 2.0, open source software, large data, machine learning and open data (Yiğit, 2017).

Many field data mining applications are often found, such as risk analysis and irregularity detection, customer acquisition, credit card fraud detection, customer loss determination, fraud detection, line density estimates, medical diagnosis and appropriate treatment processes (Low & Chen, 2012). The large amount of data and data mining to government programs in Turkey, are included in development plans and policy documents such as the top national action plans (Bolman & Deal, 1999).

It is understood that this area is very dynamic and evolving. Nevertheless, it seems that public services and policies are limited to specific areas such as health. The first question that needs to be answered is "What should the purpose of health policy be?" It is not enough to define the goal as simply "providing each patient with treatment". Because protecting healthy people from diseases and accidents is as important and necessary as being treated. For this reason, this chapter aims to contribute to the decrease shortcomings that exist in the healthcare security assessment by focusing on data mining for public institutions and organizations in Turkey.

In this context, the objective of government policy in Turkey, development plans and action plans as senior policy papers with the strategic plans of the ministries big analyzed using content analysis method data and data mining on public policies and services. Thus, examples of good practice developed especially in the ministries have been identified.

BACKGROUND

The presentation of public services and the decision to implement public policies have been reshaped since the 1980s with the wave of administrative reform (Ozcan, 2008).

As a result of adopting the private sector in the organizational structure and processes, a similar relation is established between the public organizations and the citizen with the market mechanisms and the innovative service methods are started to be applied. Living change accounted for public administrators and to increase public organizations' productivity.

At the same time, the provision of organizational decentralization has led public administrators to be held responsible for their performance targets and the restructuring of public organizations (Narcı, Ozcan, Sahin, Tarcan & Narcı, 2015).

Professional governance, open performance standards and criteria in the public sector, focus on control of output, recruitment, application of private sector management techniques, productivity and discipline in resource use are the basic principles of the wave of reforms, called new public administration (Crowley, Gold, Bandi & Goel, 2016).

International organizations such as the World Bank and the International Monetary Fund have recommended and encouraged operator reforms, public administration has spread on a global scale (Liu, Zhang, Keil & Chen, 2010). In the 1990s, developments in information and communication technologies became a new wave of reform in the public sector.

In fact, the rapid progress in technology has become a driving force for change in both private and public sector management. Innovations such as the use of information and communication systems such as computer systems, the Internet and new databases have been the prerequisite for inclusion in the public sector, called e-government.

In the US, one of the countries in which YKI emerged, at the beginning of the 2000s, President Bush pursued a policy of making more use of information technologies to reduce costs through productivity growth. In the UK, the use of information and communication technologies, the Labor government, which came to power in 1999 has been one of its main objectives. Discussions within the European Union in this period also focused on efficiency, efficiency and service delivery rather than the democratic potential of new information and communication technologies (Hadad, Hadad & Simon-Tuval, 2013).

With the widespread use of other developed and developing countries, e-government applications have gained an international character and spread all over the world (Bukachi & Pakenham-Walsh, 2007). In this period, public organizations have been adapting applications such as e-mail, web site management, online transaction and now web based services have become an integral part of the state.

The e-government has been the forerunner of the transformation of individual-state relations in the first quarter of the 21st century (Bostan, 016). Services provided under the e-government, shared data and realized transactions significantly increased the amount of data in circulation. In this period, the development of technologies such as smartphones and tablet computers and the widespread use of the internet have changed the expectations from the state.

Technologies such as customized forum pages, chat rooms, and group emailing have increased the opportunities for mass and private communication (Andreassen et al., 2007). In conjunction with Web 2.0 technologies, which are called next-generation Internet applications, in which an average user can share their participation and knowledge, the Internet has become able to contribute to any content and re-publish existing content, transforming from the static internet structure into a dynamic structure involving collaboration between social networks and users.

Social media tools based on Web 2.0 technologies have steadily increased in number since the early 2000s, and private sector and public organizations have remained indifferent to developments in this area (Pelone, F., Kringos, D.S, Romaniello, Archibugi, Salsiri & Ricciardi, 2015). Public organizations have begun to use corporate social media accounts mainly for information sharing, reporting, interaction and partly for participation and cooperation. Thus, the possibility of public services to be offered more effectively and quickly, citizens to take public decisions and to form politics has been improved.

Following a memorandum issued by President Obama in the United States in 2009, open government and open data policies have emerged that are based on transparency, participation and collaboration and advocate the incorporation of digital transformation possibilities into governance processes (Varabyova & Müller, 2016).

While openness in management is not a new concept, the difference from the previous ones is that it is more holistic enough to include transparency, participation and cooperation and is also used more effectively with the integration of tools such as information technology, the internet and social media.

This goal of open administration also differentiates it from classical e-government applications that prioritize online transaction and service provision. With the influence of international organizations such as the Open Government Partnership established in 2011, open management has become a widespread policy among a large number of countries in a short period of time (Mikalef & Pateli, 2017). Innovations that support the development of open administration include open data and open source software

Open data has helped national and local governments to ensure that users have access to a wide range of data in an easy-to-use format. The widespread use of open source software provides the necessary facilities for processing and analyzing large amounts of data, as well as programs that can be used for data access allowing them to be redesigned accordingly.

In recent years, we can say that we are faced with a new challenge with the development of technologies that can collect and process large amounts of data thanks to the widespread use of the internet and networks.

At present, there are applications called Industry 4.0 in the delivery of certain public services, in the management of production processes of factories and in the delivery of some private sector services (Girginer, Kose & Uckun, 2015). Innovations such as the integration of machine sensors, software, cloud computing and storage systems have opened up the opportunity to use the results obtained from interrogating large data sets as a way to perform organizational operational processes as a feedback.

Thus, the machines and the things we use, such as cars, refrigerators, factory robots, analyze what they collect while performing their functions, solve problems quickly, and develops an advanced personalized product and service mentality.

The impact of the learning of machines and the transformation of goods in terms of public utilities and politics, which are expressed in terms of internet, is not yet extensively addressed (Pettigrew, Woodman & Cameron, 2001). The in-depth study of all these developments is beyond the limits of this chapter. However, it is thought that this study will contribute to the related by evaluating the data mining issue, which has a critical role in processing large data, and the effects of data mining on public services.

On the other hand, data generated by means such as health data, shopping data, stock market and financial data, social media data, public transaction data, private sector data and personal use of the internet are quite large in size, and thanks to developing information technology, hardware and software solutions databases and cloud computing resources.

Hidden data cannot be analyzed by human ability using conventional methods have reached their size (Low & Chen, 2012). For this reason, it is necessary to analyze using special software and programs. This includes the Google-developed GFS file system and the MapReduce programming technique, and the Hadoop ecosystem to run applications that can be used to process large amounts of data on simple servers.

It is an open source infrastructure developed in Java that brings together a distributed file system called Hadoop Distributed File System (HDFS) and MapReduce features (Hasselbring, 2000). Hadoop is software that consists of HDFS and MapReduce components. As a result of that it has become possible to process collected data by using appropriate software, algorithms and technologies on large data, to determine the relationship between them, to determine the coexistence and to remove the patterns.

Anyway, today, besides statistics, data analysis and management are also used by those working in science branches such as information systems (Şener & Yiğit, 2017). In addition, experts examine social problems by integrating text mining techniques, a kind of data mining, into their research processes. Unstructured data is collected in databases and transformed into structured data, stored in tabular format in a specific format.

Data mining studies are carried out with the aim of identifying and predicting data through the structured data contained in the institution's databases and data warehouses. Large data, on the other hand, are often indicative of a non-structural dataset that results from the merging of multiple, unrelated datasets. The processing of this data requires confidential information to be collected over a limited time and to be resolved by means of large database specific coding techniques.

CHALLENGES AND DESIGN CONSIDERATIONS OF THE HEALTHCARE SECURITY ASSESSMENT IN TURKEY

During the Seljuk and Ottoman periods, health services were mostly offered through foundations (Briggs, Cruickshank & Paliadelis, 2012). However, it was not possible for the whole community to benefit from these services because the services were progressing with palace and soldiers.

Private medicine was also developed in the direction of the conditions. Until the end of the 19th century, those who were financially competent were treated by private physicians in their homes and received care (Aytekin, 2011).

The first hospital equipped with the help of the government of the Turkish geography in which we live is accepted as Gülhane. There is no well-equipped health facility up to this turnaround.

However, when the Gülhane Military Hospital was compared with the western hospitals of its era, it was far behind both equipment and information level (Briggs, Cruickshank & Paliadelis, 2012). Together with the publicity of the Republic, health has been one of the primary issues and has been one of the first ministries established.

Over time, the world began to blow, the welfare state and social state currents and Turkey also have the understanding that influenza health care is guaranteed by the state is born. Health services that were socialized in 1960 began to weaken in the face of liberal trends that began to develop in the 1980s and had to change (Du, Wang, Chen, Chou & Zhu, 2014).

In particular, the medical education given here by German teachers is of great importance for Turkish medicine. The training given by Rieder was, in theory, a practical training course, but only at that time. A team of medical information has been discovered a long time ago by Westerners, Rieder still not known and it is taught geography in Turkey have been identified and demonstrated by physicians (Gülsevin & Türkan, 2012). With the establishment of the Ministry, the central organization and the provincial organization have been restructured. Ministry of Health, as the first task; determining the priorities of health services, increasing the achievements in the field of health and allocating resources according to the determined criteria.

A government body and a health directorate have been established for the implementation of preventive health services in line with the identified basic mission (Gemmel, Vandaele & Tambeur, 2001). Treatment services are planned to be performed by municipalities and special administrations, and it is envisaged that poor patients will be treated free of charge by government agencies and other organizations.

In 2003, the Health Transformation Program has brought the country's health system to a completely different position, as well as the first phase of changes in health perceptions (Pan, Johnston, Walker, Adler-Milstein, Bates & Middleton, 2005). The changes that have taken place in Social Insurance Institution premiums and the start of dominance of the public private partnership in the market point to bigger changes in our health care system.

As a result, it has been seen that physicians who make a living with their work in the medical examination have been away from providing preventive services. The health centers suffering from the loss of doctors and nurses were reinstated with the Full Day Law issued in 1978, but remained physicians without any remedy (Škrinjar, Bosilj-Vukšić, & Indihar-Štemberger, 2008).

With the adoption of the Law on the Socialization of Health Services No. 224 in 1961, it was aimed to provide health services in a continuous, widespread and integrated manner to meet the needs of the public (Narcı, Ozcan, Sahin, Tarcan & Narcı, 2015). In accordance with this purpose; health centers, health centers, district and provincial hospitals were opened and a structuring integrated into the province was carried out gradually in the presentation of health services.

In addition to these objectives, the General Health Insurance (GSS), Draft Law, which was enacted in October 2008, was prepared at these times but was not presented to the Council of Ministers. Second Five-Year Development Plan coming to the fore again with the GSS in 1969, Turkey has not been adopted by the Grand National Assembly (SB 2007). The State Planning Organization (DPT) established a master plan on health services in 1990. In the process of evaluating health reforms, the first and second National Health Conferences were held (Uçkun, Girginer, Köse & Şahin, 2016).

The 'Green Card' application, which was enacted in 1992 with the Law No. 3861, providing free public health services for low-income groups with no power to meet health care needs. Health reform studies in general; such as the collection of the social security institution under a single umbrella, the establishment of the GSS, the separation of health care service provision and financing functions, the effective restructuring of the Ministry of Health through supervision and planning tasks, prioritization of preventive health services, autonomy of hospitals, contains basic topics (Ozcan, 2008).

The main targets for health in the scope of Everyone's Health under the Urgent Action plan announced on 16 November 2002 (Celik & Esmeray, 2014) are as follows: functional and administrative restructuring of the Ministry of Health; all citizens to be covered by universal health insurance; the gathering of health institutions under one roof; giving importance to mother and child health; the financial and administrative autonomy of the hospitals; the transition to the practice of family medicine; prevalence of preventive medicine; elimination of the lack of health personnel living in priority regions in development; encouragement of private sector to invest in health field; all the public institutions to the lower levels of authority transfer; the e-transformation project in the field of health is the passing of a dream.

Moreover, Health Transformation Program announced by the Ministry of Health in December 2003 will design the future health system by considering project and reform studies from past to present and plan to make the necessary changes for the transition to this system. This program is structured to address the health sector in all its dimensions and consists of components and subcomponents. Each component is associated with one other component and is basically constructed on three main legs. Bağ-Kur, Retirement Fund and Social Insurance Institution (SSI) programs, which cover different working groups with the province GSS program, are collected under the single insurance institution umbrella in 2006 (Beylik, Kayral & Naldöken, 2015).

In the Ministry of Health hospitals, 'Performance Based Payment System' has been passed on to the requests for health services in the scope of access to health services. In all policies implemented under the SDP, health service provision is increase of to keep the increase in health expenditures in balance and to ensure effective use of resources allocated for health services (Yiğit, 2017).

The model of the Family Physician, proposed by the World Bank in its 2003 document, for the Turkish health system, constitutes the second basic pillar of health reform (Beylik, Kayral & Naldöken, 2015). According to family medicine model, family physicians will provide services in the framework of the practice system by contracting with the General Health Insurance. However, due to the failure of the General Health Insurance system to be fully implemented, family medicine is financed by the MoH (Bayraktutan, Arslan & Bal, 2010). It is envisaged that the financing of family physicians will be provided through agreement after the General Health Insurance system is fully implemented. It is not possible for the citizens who do not regularly pay their premiums to benefit from the family medicine system. The most important feature of the planned family medicine system that is planned to be implemented is that it is a mandatory step in the referral chain.

In the family medicine system, physicians are transformed into entrepreneurs who earn money according to market conditions rather than public element. Family physicians are able to choose their own staff and provide the requirements outside the medical service through subcontracting firms (Akyuz, Yıldırım, Balaban, 2015).

When the Health Transformation Program is examined, it is observed that the provision of services to entrepreneurs, that is to leave the private sector, is aimed to be placed on the health insurance side of the public (Bal, 2013).

This area is a major precedent when it is examined specifically in the context of family medicine, in its current form in the UK, Clinical Commissioning Groups (CCGs), formerly known as Primary Care Trusts. CCGs are family physicians contracted with the National Health Service (NHS). The financing of health services in the UK is actually covered not by general taxation but by health-specific taxation. (Lee, Yang & Chen, 2016).

In the third basic footing of the Health Transformation Program, the Law on the Law No. 663 and the Public Hospital Unions (KHB) reform described in the Official Gazette dated 02/11/2011 take place. The reform goal is to reorganize the second and third level treatment institutions affiliated to the Ministry of Health as 'autonomous' under the roof of public hospital associations (Dogan & Gencan, 2014).

According to Article 30 of the Decree Law No. 663, Turkey Kamu Hospitals Institution establishes second and third level health institutions and public hospital associations at provincial level in order to use resources effectively and efficiently (Sebetci & Uysal, 2017).

Although access to health services for individuals is facilitated after the health transformation program, there are differences between regions in terms of the supply of health services and it is observed that injustice is not remedied. A comparison between regions in terms of the number of beds per 10,000 people is located well below the average of the Southeastern Anatolia Region of Turkey and Istanbul (Bal & Bilge, 2013). Therefore, it is seen that physicians and bed numbers are not done in proportion to the population in the supply of health services.

At the same time, the projects of city hospitals, which are being carried out by public private partnership, have begun to take place in our lives. It is certain that these investments, which have come to fruition with very high investments, will also affect the insurance structure. It is unlikely that the Turkish Health System will be kept away from the changes that are taking place in the world for sustainability.

RESULTS

The environment in which health organizations are operating today is constantly changing, requiring a thorough knowledge of changes, factors of influence, and future developments. The shift from product orientation to market orientation towards the consumer has forced health organizations to adopt ways of knowing it.

In Turkey, health services are strongly influenced by the changes that take place as a result of the health system reform, which aims to decentralize the health system by increasing the role of local authorities, professional associations, funding institutions and the community (Bircan, 2011). The measures taken have had various consequences both on the supply and the way of financing as well as on the demand. Thus, at the level of the supply and financing system, the development and consolidation of the privatization process, the development of integrated health services (primary care, ambulatory, hospital and emergency care), the creation of a combined financing model, from public resources and private and the introduction of private health insurance. That is why, at the level of health systems, we are discussing the directions for reforming them, due to the fiscal pressures that have accentuated over the years. Emphasis is placed on finding new sources of funding, on efficient management and on finding alternative ways of organizing services.

SOLUTIONS AND RECOMMENDATIONS

From the perspective of change, the complex problems of the Healthcare security assessment face cannot be analysed objectively and continuously within the current tasks (Alamin & Yassin, 2015). The lack of success of many advertising campaigns and the negative effect they generated were considered failures of marketing in health services. Thus, medical staff and consumers considered the publicity made by hospitals to be useless. The skepticism of marketing merits, especially promotion, has led to organizations in the field experiencing serious financial withdrawals during this period. In addition, hospitals were seeking to reduce their costs, and marketing spending was an easy target to operate. As a result, budgets for such activities were cut off, and marketing staff was fired. For some organizations, marketing activities have not been completely eliminated, and they are often embedded in strategic and development plans. In addition, this has enabled marketers to reevaluate that field and focus on developing basic concepts that can be used when marketing is back in place in these organizations. As a result of the diversification of the offered health services, the researches have also increased marketing on the health service consumer.

Governments undoubtedly want to raise their level of health. It is possible to see this interesting in every government's program and in the statements of every politician and manager. Those with political decision-making authority would prefer not to give priority to health, but to other issues, among the many jobs required to be done. Politicians, like everyone, care about their health or their relatives when they are sick. They do not even think that one day they will get sick and find the service they need. The first thing to do is to find the way to influence governments, not academic debates.

CONCLUSION

In order to explain the behavior of the healthcare consumer, it is not enough just to study the behavior of the healthcare consumer, but also the relationship between medical staff - especially the doctor - and the consumer as the main determinant of his behavior and consumption. The significance of this relationship is extremely important for health services because the creation and delivery of services and their quality depend to a large extent on the relationship between the two. Medical staff can help improve this relationship by constantly informing the consumer through a realistic picture of the illness and the judicious use of the possibilities and resources available to the consumer.

Because the medical sector is a highly conditioned technology, it presents some challenges for health service providers in terms of developing and implementing marketing strategies. First of all, it is necessary to continue monitoring of the environment and developments in the field, because the technological breakthroughs lead to the improvement of the quality of the services rendered and to the diversification of the offer, as well as an advantage over the competitors.

New waves of technological change often allow participants from different levels to enter the market. For example, in hospitals, technology has spread to such an extent that procedures that once were only carried out in large hospitals or university institutes can now be achieved in many smaller hospitals or even at the level of medical offices.

In Turkey, the supply of health services is heavily influenced by the changes that take place as a result of the reform of the health care system, which involves the transition from the integrated, centralized, tax-based, government-controlled and state-controlled system to the social security system - decentralized and pluralistic, based on contractual links between health care homes (service buyers) and providers of these services.

REFERENCES

Akyuz, K. C., Yıldırım, I., & Balaban, Y. (2015). Measuring efficiencies of the firms in paper sector by using data envelopment analysis. *International Journal of Economic and Administrative Studies, 14*, 23–38.

Alamin, T. H. M., & Yassin, A. A. (2015). Measuring hospitals efficiency using data envelopment analysis tool: Study on governmental hospitals services at Ministry of Health–Khartoum State. *International Journal of Science and Research, 4*(2), 1586–1592.

Andreassen, H. K., Bujnowska-Fedak, M. M., Chronaki, C. E., Duritru, R. C., Pudele, I., Santana, S., ... Wynn, R. (2007). European citizens' use of E-health services: A study of seven countries. *BMC Public Health, 7*(53), 1–14. PMID:17425798

Aytekin, S. (2011). The performance measurement of the health hospitals with low bed occupancy rates: An application of data envelopment analysis. *Uludag Journal of Economy and Society, 30*(1), 113–138.

Bal, V. (2013). Data envelopment analysis and medical image archiving and communication systems to investigate the effects of the performance of public hospitals. *Journal of Suleyman Demirel University Institute of Social Sciences, 17*, 31–50.

Bal, V., & Bilge, H. (2013). Efficiency measurement with data envelopment analysis in education and research hospitals. *Manas Journal of Social Studies, 2*(2), 1–14.

Bayraktutan, Y., Arslan, I., & Bal, V. (2010). The evaluation of the effects of health information systems to the performance of hospitals by data enveloping analysis: An application in the thoracic medicine hospitals. *Gaziantep Medical Journal, 16*(3), 13–18.

Beylik, U., Kayral, İ. H., & Naldöken, Ü. (2015). Public hospital unions' performance analysis in terms of health care services efficiency. *Cumhuriyet University the Journal of Social Sciences, 39*(2), 203–224.

Bircan, H. (2011). Measurement of the efficiency of village clinics in the Sivas by data envelopment Analysis. *Cumhuriyet University Journal of Economics and Administrative Sciences, 12*(1), 331–347.

Bolman, L. G., & Deal, T. E. (1999). 4 Steps to keeping change efforts heading in the right direction. *Journal for Quality and Participation, 22*(3), 6–11.

Bostan, I. (2016). Investigating the Effectiveness of Programs on Health Financing Based on Audit Procedures. *Iranian Journal of Public Health, 45*(8), 1074–1079. PMID:27928534

Briggs, D., Cruickshank, M., & Paliadelis, P. (2012). Health managers and health reform. *Journal of Management & Organization, 18*(5), 641–658. doi:10.1017/S1833367200000584

Bukachi, F., & Pakenham-Walsh, N. (2007). Information technology for health in developing countries. *Chest Journal, 132*(5), 1624–1630. doi:10.1378/chest.07-1760 PMID:17998362

Celik, T., & Esmeray, A. (2014). Measurement of cost efficiency in private hospitals in Kayseri using by data envelopment analysis. *International Journal of Alanya Faculty of Business, 6*(2), 45–54.

Dogan, N. O., & Gencan, S. (2014). Performance assessment using DEA/AHP integrated method: An application on public hospitals in Ankara. *Gazi Universitesi Iktisadi ve Idari Bilimler Fakultesi Dergisi, 16*(2), 88–112.

Du, J., Wang, J., Chen, Y., Chou, S. Y., & Zhu, J. (2014). Incorporating health outcomes in Pennsylvania Hospital efficiency: An additive super efficiency DEA approach. *Annals of Operations Research, 221*(1), 161–172. doi:10.100710479-011-0838-y

Ericksen, J., & Dyer, L. (2005). Toward a strategic human resource management model of high reliability organization performance. *International Journal of Human Resource Management, 16*(6), 907–925. doi:10.1080/09585190500120731

Frese, M., & Fay, D. (2001). Personal initiative: An active performance concept for work in the 21st century. *Research in Organizational Behavior, 23*, 133–187. doi:10.1016/S0191-3085(01)23005-6

Gemmel, P., Vandaele, D., & Tambeur, W. (2001). Hospital Process Orientation (HPO): The development of a measurement tool. *Total Quality Management & Business Excellence, 19*(12), 1207–1217. doi:10.1080/14783360802351488

Grimson, J., Grimson, W., & Hasselbring, W. (2000). The system integration challenge in health care. *Communications of the ACM, 43*(6), 49–55. doi:10.1145/336460.336474

Gülsevin, G., & Türkan, A. H. (2012). Evaluation of efficiencies of hospitals in Afyonkarahisar using data envelopment analysis. *Afyon Kocatepe University Journal of Sciences, 20*, 1–8.

Hadad, S., Hadad, Y., & Simon-Tuval, T. (2013). Determinants of healthcare system's efficiency in OECD countries. *The European Journal of Health Economics, 14*(2), 253–265. doi:10.100710198-011-0366-3 PMID:22146798

Hasselbring, W. (2000). Information system integration. *Communications of the ACM, 43*(6), 33–38. doi:10.1145/336460.336472

Ibbs, C. W., & Kwak, Y. H. (2000). Assessing project management maturity. *Project Management Journal, 31*(1), 32–43. doi:10.1177/875697280003100106

Lee, Y. H., Yang, C. C., & Chen, T. T. (2016). Barriers to incident-reporting behavior among nursing staff: A study based on the theory of planned behavior. *Journal of Management & Organization, 22*(1), 1–18. doi:10.1017/jmo.2015.8

Liu, S., Zhang, J., Keil, M., & Chen, T. (2010). Comparing senior executive and project manager perceptions of IT project risk: A Chinese Delphi study. *Information Systems Journal, 20*(4), 319–355. doi:10.1111/j.1365-2575.2009.00333.x

Low, C., & Chen, Y. H. (2012). Criteria for the evaluation of a cloud-based hospital information system outsourcing provider. *Journal of Medical Systems, 36*(6), 3543–3553. doi:10.100710916-012-9829-z PMID:22366976

Ozcan, Y. A. (2008). *Healthcare benchmarking and performance evaluation an assessment using data envelopment analysis (DEA)*. Springer.

Pan, E., Johnston, D., Walker, J., Adler-Milstein, J., Bates, D. W., & Middleton, B. (2005). *The Value of Healthcare Information Exchange and Interoperability*. Chicago: Health Information Management and Systems Society.

Pelone, F., Kringos, D. S., Romaniello, A., Archibugi, M., Salsiri, C., & Ricciardi, W. (2015). Primary care efficiency measurement using data envelopment analysis: A systematic review. *Journal of Medical Systems, 39*(1), 1–14. doi:10.100710916-014-0156-4 PMID:25486892

Pettigrew, A. M., Woodman, R. W., & Cameron, K. S. (2001). Studying organizational change and development: Challenges for future research. *Academy of Management Journal, 44*(4), 697–713.

Sebetci, Ö., & Uysal, İ. (2017). The Efficiency of Clinical Departments in Medical Faculty Hospitals: A Case Study Based on Data Envelopment Analysis. *International Journal on Computer Science and Engineering, 5*(7), 1–8.

Škrinjar, R., Bosilj-Vukšić, V., & Indihar-Štemberger, M. (2008). The impact of business process orientation on financial and non-financial performance. *Business Process Management Journal, 14*(5), 738–754. doi:10.1108/14637150810903084

Uçkun, N., Girginer, N., Köse, T., & Şahin, Ü. (2016). Analysis efficiency of public hospitals of metropolitan municipalities in Turkey. *International Journal of Innovative Research in Education, 3*(2), 102–108.

Varabyova, Y., & Müller, J. M. (2016). The efficiency of health care production in OECD countries: A systematic review and meta-analysis of cross-country comparisons. *Health Policy (Amsterdam), 120*(3), 252–263. doi:10.1016/j.healthpol.2015.12.005 PMID:26819140

Yiğit, V. (2017). Technical Efficiency of Physicians In Performance Based Supplementary Payment System: Application In A University Hospital. *Electronic Journal of Social Sciences, 16*(62), 854–866.

ADDITIONAL READING

Crowley, K., Gold, R., Bandi, S., & Goel, A. (2016). *The Public Health Information Technology Maturity Index: An approach to evaluating the adoption and use of public health information technology.* School of Public Health, University of Maryland.

Girginer, N., Kose, T., & Uckun, N. (2015). Efficiency analysis of surgical services by combined use of data envelopment analysis and gray relational analysis. *Journal of Medical Systems, 39*(5), 1–9. doi:10.100710916-015-0238-y PMID:25764507

Mikalef, P., & Pateli, A. (2017). Information technology-enabled dynamic capabilities and their indirect effect on competitive performance: Findings from PLS-SEM and fsQCA. *Journal of Business Research, 70*, 1–16. doi:10.1016/j.jbusres.2016.09.004

Narcı, H. O., Ozcan, Y. A., Sahin, I., Tarcan, M., & Narcı, M. (2015). An examination of competition and efficiency for hospital industry in Turkey. *Health Care Management Science, 18*(4), 407–418. doi:10.100710729-014-9315-x PMID:25515038

Şener, M., & Yiğit, V. (2017). Technical Efficiency of Health Systems: A Research on the OECD Countries. *Journal of Süleyman Demirel University Institute of Social Sciences, 26*, 266–290.

Chapter 5

Business Transaction Privacy and Security Issues in Near Field Communication

Jayapandian N.
Christ University, India

ABSTRACT

The main objective of this chapter is to discuss various security threats and solution in business transactions. The basic working principle and theoretical background of near field communication (NFC) technology is discussed. A component of NFC communication section is to be discussed on various NFC operation modes and RFID tags. NFC technology is used in various fields such as electronic toll collection and e-payment collection for shopping. This device-to-device payment system is facing major security issues. This NFC communication data is transferred from one terminal to another terminal by using short-range radio frequency. Data hackers try to access this radio frequency and attack the business transaction. This hybrid encryption algorithm is used to solve business transaction data security issues. This chapter deals with both key encryption and data encryption processes.

INTRODUCTION

Near Field Communication is a wireless technology to establish a connection between device to device and device to tag. This is technically named as active communication and passive communication. This wireless communication is to create set of networking protocol between smart devices. The communication distance of NFC device is 4cm for each device, it's in and around 10cm to 20cm is a maximum distance of communication. The working principle of NFC is store the payment information in element chip that is named as SEID. This is short name of Secure Element Identifier. This SEID chip is inserted in smart device and NFC active device (Khan, 2016). The advantage of NFC device is contact less business payment transaction. The modern world all the business transaction is deal with digital currency. This digital currency is more secure and easy to handle with transaction. The currency is transformed in many structures, business transaction many customers using credit card or debit card payment. On

DOI: 10.4018/978-1-5225-8455-1.ch005

the time introducing this credit or debit card banking will provide only common password for all transaction, but now banking service is more modernize, they provide one time password for every single transaction. This is the evaluation of any technology; the modern computer world is now transforms in smart device. The day to day life without this smart device can't do any work. The smart device is many devices, like smart phone, smart home and others. This major technology of this smart device is Internet of Things. The device is working the concept of Internet, without internet no use of this smart device. The major drawback of this NFC technology is only short distance communication, but alternate thinking security perspective this short distance communication is provide higher security compare to other communication protocol. The major part of working principle is Radio Frequency Indemnification (RFID). The NFC technology is developed by NXP semiconductors and Sony; previously it is named as Philips semiconductors. The technology is very old but modern applications are used in this technology. On the time of introducing android operating system it is not popular, but now more than 90% of smart phones used in this android OS. The reason of this usage is open source; it's used to reduce the overall selling cost. The business point of view the end user getting lesser cost compare to other operating system mobile. This short distance communication is developed in the form of NFC; this is a joint organization of Sony, Nokia and Philips. This technology is under research department in more than three year, in the year 2004 NFC forum is introduce public usage and feast this technology in common peoples.

Figure 1. NFC technology application

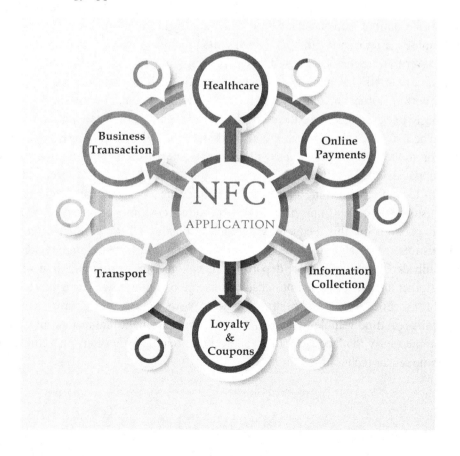

SCOPE OF NFC TECHNOLOGY

The scope of this NFC device is less cost with fast communication. This communication protocol is providing higher security with short distance. The mobile phone transaction is playing a major role. The smart phone is a key concept of this NFC; this NFC is inserted in smart device and use for business transaction. The penetration of smart phone is unavoidable in this modern world (Falaki et al., 2010). The recent survey world population more than 35% of people used this smart phone technology. The growth of this smart phone is in the year 2016 nearly 2.1 billion users used this technology. They expected more than 2.5 billion users in the year 2019. The major usage of this smart phone is China; more than 565 million peoples used this smart phone. The second largest user of this smart phone is United States. The 223 million US peoples used this smart phone technology. This technology is formally accredited at ISO standard in the year of 2003. The purpose of this standard is to maintain some rules during wireless communication. After getting this ISO certificate the communication transfer rate is standardized with the range of 106Kbps, 212kbps and 424kbps. The technology is not a standard version; because any technology is need some latest updates, similar to that in the year 2005 the same accredited company will provide ISO/IEC 21481 standardization certificate. This accreditation is really useful for implement this technology in worldwide in short range of time. This NFC technology is not a used encryption mechanism; they use existing technology of RFID (Finkenzeller, 2010). The main aim of this RFID technology is to get data form tag and retrieve the same data in transceiver device, all this process is made with wireless communication. The purpose of this tag is used to store the information in the form of Non-Line-of-Sight storage. This method is used to easy to identify the object; here object in the form of people, animal, goods and location. The industry is commonly used to tracking their good in barcode technology, after coming this NFC tag method many companies used this technology, even some foreign courier transaction is also used this technology to track their parcel.

The business scope of NFC technology is playing major role. The team leader or manager is easy way to communicate with customer and employee. The major business application is employee communication this part easy to track the employee location. Employee spending time calculation is also done with this technique. The real time data updates are also possible this NFC technology, the immediate boos is give instruction to their employee and pass the customer information. The employee work schedule is dynamically updated and sends their instruction particular time interval. The recent day's most common usage of this technology is online shopping portals use this technology and collects their business payment from customer. This NFC tags placed in their product customer easy way to get all the product details via smart phone using this technology no need to display all the product details. The service department is also used this NFC technology, after providing their service immediately they collect payment and feedback. The major service department is call taxi after providing their service immediately getting customer feedback. Sometimes customer location is monitored using this technology; this is really helpful for secure service. The customer expects more security while travel, using this technic easy to monitor the real time vehicle moments. The public department like restaurant is also used this technology, customers easy to place order in hotel. The Internet of Technology and NFC technology is working with same sensor technology.

E-BUSINESS SECURITY ISSUES

E-Business means electronic business and alternate name of online business. The recent days the growth of this online business is reached billion and millions of dollars. Electronic means sharing the data or information by using internet technology. Commerce means sharing or selling the products through online medium. Main advantage of this business is globalization of products and easy to get buyer and seller. The development of Information and Communication Technology B2B and B2C is evergreen business opportunity (Turner & Dasgupta, 2003). The online business environment is a combination of product delivery, customer feedback and online payment system. The digital environment is to give good opportunity for both buyer and seller. The internet technology is giving a platform of lowest investment and higher profit. The booming of internet technology business environment is totally changed. Major benefit of this E-Business is shop establishment cost is very less and that profit is shared among the customers through some offers. The development of E-business will introduce e-payment method. The e-payment method is secure and convenient method compare to normal payment system. This e-commerce system is handled with variety of application in modern technology (Harshita & Tanwar, 2018). That is named as online fund transfer, Electronic Data Interchange, Supply Chain Management and Inventory Management (Zentner, 2008). The US online sales are reached around 175 billion dollars in the year 2007. The e-commerce security working principle is similar to network security mechanism. This e-business security issues can be categorized into three parts. First one is client side threat; this threat is an active threat. The active threat is a malware and virus. The second one is communication medium threat. This is a major component of information security. This communication channel attack is dealing with three major modules. Those components are confidentiality, availability and integrity. Final threat is server side attack, these is a major attack now a days. The hacker should hack the single server they get many client data. These server side attack is web-server attack, password attack, database attack and interface gateway attack.

Mobile Application Software Issues

Business transaction is used in handheld devices. Most of the handheld devices are working in application software. These mobile applications are another threat, most of the untrusted mobile applications available in internet. Problem of these mobile applications is unknown third party is monitoring the user personal information. Software bug or error is another major problem of business transaction (Zhang & Adipat, 2005). Business industry is slowly moved into physical cashless payment system. These business transactions not implement our own payment platform because of huge investment is need for creating own platform, they automatically tie-up with some payment gateway portal. After coming with this type of payment gateway system small business industry benefited more compare to larger industry.

Network Security Issues

Network security is a one of the hottest topic in business transaction. This NFC technique is purely depending on internet network connection. The network connection is established on basic protocol concept. There are two types of network is generally created. One is private network and another one is public network (El Zarki, Mehrotra, Tsudik & Venkatasubramanian, 2002). This NFC mechanism is working on public network concept. Once the public network many unknown users connected in public domain. Compare to private network higher risk factor is happened in public network. The major problem in this network security is denial of service attack. The e-business concept hacker tries to hack the data from this denial of service attack concept. Business transaction all the systems connected in distributed concept. Distributed denial of service (DDoS) attack is happen in distributed system connection. The customer expect higher security because of these DDoS security issue many customer doesn't trust online e-business.

Hardware and Mobile Device Security Issue

Mobile device is a communication component of NFC business transaction. This mobile device is connected with wireless communication that is internet. This wireless communication most of the time connected with public network. Hardware component is also one of the major security issues. The untrusted mobile hardware devices also used for business transaction. Hacker is easy to get user business transaction data through these untrusted devices. Difference of trusted and untrusted device is simple, licensed manufacturing is called as trusted device. Each device is having unique MAC Id, but this untrusted device is not having this kind of the MAC Id. Another problem is hardware and software compatibility, the higher version of software is not supported in some hardware component (Verdult & Kooman, 2011).

COMPONENTS USED IN NEAR FIELD COMMUNICATION

NFC is commonly used payment system in modern mobile devices. Samsung introduce this NFC based payment system in android phone. The business people always used in these types of handheld mobile devices. After coming these kind of payment method physical currency handling is avoided and it's provide very safe and secure payment gateway. This NFC is deals with many components particularly NFC tag is acted as an identifier and NFC device is a recognizer of that tag. This NFC is a two mode one is active NFC device and another one is passive that is named as NFC tag. The basic working principle of NFC device is named as inductive coupling. The electrons moving to conductor, these electrons produce some magnetic effects (Schamberger, Madlmayr & Grechenig, 2013). These electrons changed in the form of magnetic field this is named as inductive coupling technique. The electrical coil generates this magnetic field by using battery power. Again this magnetic field induces the current in reverse process. This magnetic coil effort is used for NFC communication.

The Figure 2 is to elaborate working method of NFC communication. Smartphone is a sender and opposite receiver is receiving radio frequency signals. The business data is transferred by using this radio

Figure 2. Basic working structure of NFC communication

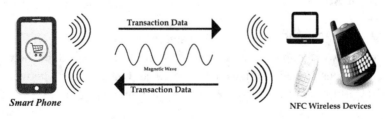

frequency signals. The receiver is also smartphone, computer system and other smart device. The magnetic waves generate the radio signal and send to one terminal to other terminal. There are two types of communication first one is NFC one way communication, it is read the information from NFC tag. The radio frequency read the tag information. Second communication method is NFC two way communication, this is two active device is involved. The main advantage of second method is these devices do the both work that is sender and receiver (Asaduzzaman, Mazumder & Salinas, 2018).

Operation Modes of NFC Device

Near Field Communication device operation mode is categorized in three different methods. The Figure 3 is elaborate basic mode operation of NFC device. First method is read and writes mode operation. This method is used normally used in business billing payment system. The shopkeeper having unique tag, that tag is having all the information like shop name and bank account details. The user read that tag and sends the money through mobile phone. Second mode is peer-to-peer communication mode. In general peer-to-peer means establish the connection between two active devices. This particular mode both sending and receiving operation is deal with mobile device. Final method is smart card emulation mode, this operation active NFC device emulate the smartcard information (Lee et al., 2016).

RFID Tag

The basic working mechanism of Radio Frequency Identification is inductive coupling. This is similar to smartcard, this tag is having some data in inside. RFID reader is used to read the information; smart phone is acted as a RFID reader. The smart phone is generating some magnetic field and read the information from RFID tag. The RFID tag is fixed any one object this smart phone is moving nearby that tag, and then automatically tag information is read from this smart phone. This RFID is generally two types one is active RFID and passive RFID. This passive RFID is having only data there is no power source, but the active RFID is having power source with a data. This RFID is an example of one way communication system (Morak et al., 2012).

Figure 3. Structure of NFC operation modes

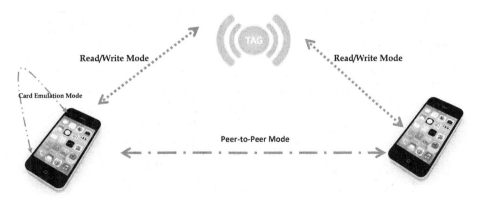

Comparison of NFC and Bluetooth Technology

There are many advantages and disadvantage is there in this NFC communication. The Table 1 is to elaborate some major difference between Bluetooth and NFC technology. This Bluetooth technology is one of the main competitors of this NFC technology. Distance coverage of NFC is very less but it's a higher security protocol. Near Field Communication data transfer distance range is less than 10cm, but its work nearly 20cm (Want, 2011). Bluetooth communication distance range is almost 100 meter. But the main advantage of this NFC secure communication is short distance, because higher distance data leakage problem is possible at both device and network side. This short rage communication security problem is reduced.

APPLICATIONS USED IN NEAR FIELD COMMUNICATION

The Near Field Communication is not only technology; it is one part of our life in future. The NFC stickers or tags places in anywhere and track their moments. This is a simple technique to transfer the data from one device to other. The use of this NFC technology is wallet free transaction. Most of the time forgetting or missing the wallet is a major problem; this NFC technology is providing good solution for this problem. There are many real time applications used for this technology.

Cashless Payment System

The main application of this NFC technique is cashless transaction, no need to carrying the money during shopping or another purpose. The concept of this cashless payment is particular product details and price information is stored in NFC tag, customers just read that tag and get product details. The customer use their smart phone and paying that bill via their mobile. This cashless transaction is slowly moved into digital currency. Most of the government initiates this online payment system, because based on this system government get their tax properly. The corruption and block money problem is avoided due

Table 1. NFC and Bluetooth comparison

S.No	NFC Communication	Bluetooth V2.1 Technology
1	Short range of communication	Wide range communication
2	No Pairing required	Pairing is required
3	Distance range is less than 20 cm	Distance range is nearly 100 m
4	Frequency range is 13.56 MHz	Frequency range is 2.4 to 2.5 GHz
5	Slow Connection	Faster Connection
6	Less power consumption	Higher power consumption
7	Lower Setup time	Setup time is higher compare to NFC
8	Data transfer rate is 424 Kbits	Data transfer rate is 2.1 Mbits
9	Security range is higher than Bluetooth	Less security protocol

to this technology. The online shopping website gives option for cash on delivery. This cash collection is a major task, using this technology product delivery person collect their money using NFC enabled device. The cash collection and monitoring process is very easy compare to other methods (Chen, 2008).

Traffic Violation Monitoring

The modern world billions of individual vehicle transportation is increased day to day. The traffic management is one of the toughest jobs in police. The developing country transportation facility is not good, so automatically traffic violation is happened. Maintenance and traffic violation fine collection is critical task in police, also all this process is to be centralized. The recent days the traffic violation fine collection system is made with online. All the vehicle violation data is collected and maintained in centralized server. The Near Field Communication technology is used for gathering violation vehicle detail and driver details (Xiao & Wang, 2011). This technology is used for scanning driving license and vehicle RC book. This device is used for track the previous vehicle violation details. The traffic violation is automatically captured from CCTV camera and that data is send to this device.

Device Coupling

The device coupling is the process of establishing the short range of connection between two digital devices. This NFC technology is not possible to transfer the file only establishing the communication link. The digital device is already having communication protocol named as Bluetooth or Wifi. The concept of this communication is transfer the file from one device to other device. Before transferring the file connection establishment is needed, this is named as device pairing or coupling. This device pairing is done with this NFC technique (Ortiz, 2006). This NFC is creating and maintains the device connection. This is normally used for frequent communication from one device to other device.

Automobile Industry in Near Field Communication

The growth of automobile industry is endless, reason is automobile industry is always adopt with new technology. Any new technology is incorporated in automobile sector. The combination of electrical and electronic technology is involved in this field. The Internet of Things is also implemented in this auto sector. The latest car there is no manual key is used; the RFID key tag is used for this purpose. If the person is missed the key means easy to trace and locate the key by using RFID signal. Another major application for automobile industry is payment system for vehicle parking and cross the vehicle tolls. This is really need product now a day, because for toll payment heavy traffic is to be happened during payment collection. To avoid this problem RFID tag is pasted in vehicle, NFC enabled device easy to scan the vehicle details and get the payment from that tag. The business purposes all the payment is easy to handle and monitored. This vehicle external data is also collected through this NFC technique (Dias, Matos & Oliveira, 2014). The car agency is used many car, using this NFC tag easy to find the component brand name and details.

Electronic Business Card

The concept of Electronic Businesses Card system is to exchange the buyer and seller information. The business to business transaction contacts is most important one. The business person sharing the visiting card is quit natural. But the maintenance of this contact is really toughest one. This NFC is providing the wonderful solution for maintaining business contacts. The customer information is feted in this small NFC tag, like as name, address and phone number. The dealer just wipes the card in NFC enabled device and makes a call to the customer. Similar to that customer is wipes the card in NFC device they got distributer details (Yang & Papazoglou, 2000).

NFC Based Smart Card

The smart card is the concept of storing the customer information in electronic system. This particular smart card is used to access the any particular system also used to make a payment. This NFC based smart card is used for entry identifications. The banking sector, education sector and many business organization is used this smart ID card. The purpose to this smart card is easy to update the user details, also easy to fix the authentication permission. The education sector library management system is used this method, to track the library book and maintain the library users. The same RFID tag is used to locate the books. The book tracking system is automated due to this NFC technology (Pelletier, Trépanier & Morency, 2011).

SECURITY ISSUES IN NFC TECHNOLOGY

Data security is a heart of modern computer world. Online business is a hot topic of current financial growth. The benefit of this online business is reducing the investment cost of showrooms. This business environment is setup to create connection of user and system. The system means computer, smart phones and other payment devices. This business transaction is purely depending on Information technology with digital information concept. The security is two major attacks one is internal threat and another one is external threat. These digital information process is detection and prevention action is to found while data transaction. The Near Field Communication security is categorized in different levels and types (Haselsteiner & Breitfuß, 2006).

NFC Physical Security

The NFC physical security is the process of secure the physical device from theft, Natural disaster and fire. This security system is to prevent data theft of software, hardware and networking terminals. This physical security mechanism is also deal for user authorization and authentication. This will be helpful for controlling normal user and employee actions. They maintain some security protocol with some limited action to device access. The physical security is to theft data by using some hard disk and pen drive. The NFC device is connected with OTG cable with some biometric identification purpose. Before digitization people get their money by using ATM machine. ATM machine establishment and maintenance cost is very high compare to other digital transaction (Madlmayr, Langer, Kantner & Scharinger, 2008).

Eavesdropping

The concept of eavesdropping is secretly listening others communication without their knowledge. Eavesdropping is a one of the major issue in NFC technology. It is a one type of electronic communication data attack. The basic working method of this NFC communication is to establish a wireless communication in paired device. This wireless communication is made with RF signals. The RF signal used to transfer the data from one device to other device. The attacker is also getting this RF signals by using RF antenna receiver (Kortvedt & Mjolsnes, 2009). Attackers are also having technical skill to hack the RF signals. The digital information sniffing is the part of eavesdropping.

Information Exploitation

Information exploitation is the process of modifying or tries to change the original data. The communication medium data is transferred from source to destination node. The hackers try to modify the original information. This change percentage is very less; this is the major problem of this data corruption. The sender or receiver is very difficult to identify these threats. It is a one type of data error in the process of computer data transmission or storage. The wireless signal transmission data noise is a common problem. This information exploitation and data noise is a similar type, very difficult to identify the difference to both. The only possibility of identification is correct time calculation. The hacker takes little bit time to data exploitation (Azhari, 2014). The modulation and demodulation process is taken some time and difference of this time is taken for data exploitation.

Middle Man Attack in NFC

The Middle Man Attack (MMA) is a common problem in network security. The user tries to access web server and get some information. This Middle Man Attack problem is some unauthorized user try to hack the user information in the middle part of user machine to server machine. The major aim of this attacker is try to hack the user personal information (Conti, Dragoni & Lesyk, 2016). Normally in Near Field communication working principle is also same to send the user information from user terminal to server machine. The target of this middle man attacker is to get user name, date of birth and credit/debit card number. Based on this user personal information hacker is try to access the user personal banking or financial account. The e-commerce business transaction is mostly done with this type of automated machine system.

NFC Data Modification

Near Field Communication device is normally generate the data and transfer from one terminal to other terminal. This communication is done with wired and wireless channel. The data modification is somewhat different from data correction. The NFC wireless RF signals are working in modulation and demodulation process. Hacker or attacker is done with this modulation process in 10% means very difficult to analyze or identify this data change. Business data is normally handling with user financial information. This financial information is include user bank details and account balance. Hacker tries to modify the original data into modified data (Huitsing, Chandia, Papa & Shenoi, 2008). The purpose

Figure 4. Middle man attack in NFC

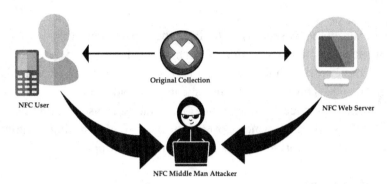

of this modification is future data attack. Example of this data modification is user mobile number, if suppose the hacker is to modify the user original mobile number to attacker mobile number. Recent days all the banking transaction is done with One Time password concept. This OTP process is executed with user mobile number, now hacker is changed that mobile number means he receive OTP and complete that transaction. This is very dangerous problem compare to the data correction.

Data Insertion in NFC

Data insertion is the process of insert the message between the data exchange in two wireless devices. The business transaction sometimes automated device answer mechanism is involved. This type of mechanism is not possible to find the original message or inserted message. The attacker inserts the wrong data between the data exchange process. The network security system this data insertion operation is prevents by using firewall, traffic inspection and load balancer technique. This NFC data insertion is also similar to network security problem.

POSSIBLE SOLUTION FOR NFC SECURITY ISSUES

Near Field Communication is deal with many security and privacy issues. Section six is to elaborate many hardware and software security issues in NFC. The business transaction is slowly moved in wallet gateway system. This wallet payment is facing many security threats; generally wallet system is used in public places. This public places people get free public network connection, these kind of public network is not advisable for payment transaction.

Handling for Physical Security

Physical security system is to prevent the personal information form hackers. There are many protection is involved in this physical security that is hardware system, physical storage and networking component. Physical security is mainly safe from natural disaster and theft. This physical security is mainly three components Figure 5 is to elaborate physical security. The major component is controlling the system access. Then secondary component is surveillance system. Testing is also one of the additional com-

Figure 5. Physical security component

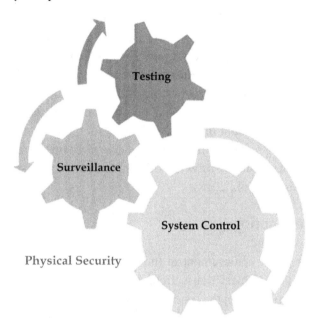

ponents this component is occasionally used. System control is the process of managing the hardware and software system. In general system should be managed and controlled administrator. This system control is similar to administrative rights.

This system is control the unauthorized access. Example of this access control is biometric system; this biometric system is used to control the system access. Surveillance system is one of the major physical security systems. This system is monitoring the system by using CCTV camera. This system is more useful but main drawback is some human monitoring is needed for this system. Testing is last but least physical security system (Fennelly, 2016). This system is frequently test the hardware and software system. Industry safety mechanism is mostly used this testing component.

Avoiding Middle Man Attack

Middle Man Attack is a common network communication problem. The private network connection attacker hack all the data. Then the receiver receive both sender and receiver data. This entire network connection is controlled by this middle man that means attacker. The attacker tries to inject their own message for this private and public network. The NFC business data transaction is used in RF signal, this signal is tracked very easy way. The major aim of Middle Man Attacker is to gather user login credentials; this login information is misused for somewhere. This information is gathered from banking application, financial loan application and some e-commerce website. There are three different spoofing attacks is happened in this NFC business transaction. Internet Protocol spoofing is a common attack. The attacker is changing packet header in normal IP address. That means hacker is to create duplicate website similar to original website. This IP spoofing is transfer the original link into duplicate link, the business transaction these type of attack is quite normal. Another problem is Address Resolution Protocol spoofing; this attack hacker link the user MAC address into IP address, then the entire data packet is diverted into hacker's machine. Final spoofing method is Domain Name System spoofing; this type of attack is change the website address database. There are many technique is there to avoid these kind of attacks. The common solution of this kind of attack is avoiding public network. That means public Wi-Fi network like as hotel rooms, public transportations. This public network connection is used only for other purpose like browsing, media file view. Business transaction is involved and linking with our bank account, so always this kind of transaction our own private internet connection is advisable. Sometime emergency purpose public network usage is unavoidable that kind of situation after using our personal mail account or some other bank account immediately logout for our account. Unknown browser usage is also another problem; avoiding untrusted internet browser is most important one. Sometime hacker is install some unwanted software in public browser, this type of software easily catch our personal data and send to that hacker (Alsmadi et al., 2018).

Secure EMV Card Transaction

The cashless transaction is major achievement in this century. Before coming to the wallet payment this card transaction is heart of cashless transaction. The major goal of EMV card system is replace magnetic strip card into IC chip card. On the time of ATM card invention this magnetic strip technology is used. User information is stored in this magnetic strip, major problem of this technology is hackers easy to scan this credit or debit card details. After introduce this microprocessor chip technology many credit/debit card fraud is reduced. Abbreviation of this system "E" stands for Europay, "M" stands for MasterCard and "V" stands for Visa. This EMV is world standardized technology; it is ISO/IEC 7816 standard technology (Hajji, Ouerdi & Azizi, 2018).

Card Authentication Methods

In business transaction normally used for credit and debit card, this card is authenticating by using verification code. This verification code is normally generating two types. First one is static verification; this method standard verification pin is mapped with user account. Technical name of this static method is Static Data Authentication (SDA). Second one is dynamic verification; this method service provider generate dynamic one time verification pin and send through email or mobile phone. Technical name of this method is Dynamic Data Authentication (DDA). These two methods not use in cryptography technic, but user expect more security in now a day. Third one is combination of above cryptography and dynamic system that is name as Combined DDA with Application Cryptogram (CDA). The concept of static data authentication is working in magnetic strip information authentication. It's very old method also not secure in public key crypto system. The bank issuer singed static certificate and process the authentication (Laur & Nyberg, 2006). The major drawback is hacker easily read magnetic information and create duplicate card. This duplicate card is processed bank issued PIN number; sometime bank employee is also misuse customer account. Dynamic data authentication is needed for microprocessor chip, it is working public cryptography concept. The unique concept of this method is each and every transaction is to create unique cryptogram. The short certificate chain system is verifying this unique PIN in common terminal like as Mastercard or VISA. This type of dynamic PIN generation is to avoid attacks and microprocessor chip system is preventing card data theft. Combined DDA with Application Cryptogram is introduced in the year 2000. This is highly secure and similar to dynamic authentication method. RSA cryptography algorithm is used for data encryption and decryption process. The additional advantage of this method is generating the second dynamic PIN for particular transaction; also they check that particular transaction process (Jayapandian, Rahman, Koushikaa & Radhikadevi, 2016). It provides higher security system compare to other method because of both dynamic PIN generation and encryption algorithm implementation.

ENCRYPTION ALGORITHMS USED IN ONLINE PAYMENT

Online payment system is processed with different modes. Most common method is card payment; this card payment is more reliable and secure. This card is previously used in magnetic strip technology, by using this method card information is stored in credit or debit card. The magnetic card reader is read the information and processes the further steps. That situation single password system is used to access our card information. The hackers easily scan credit or debit card information and make a duplicate card. This is one type of attack; another attack is all this transaction is processed online. This transaction is happened internet technology, again hackers hack the user transaction information. These two attacks is a major problem in business transaction. The latest technology is solving this problem; duplicate card system is avoided by using microprocessor chip technology credit or debit card. All the user information is stored in this Integrated Circuit (IC). It's highly secure compare to older method. Second problem of business transaction is hacking user information while communication. This problem is avoided by using encryption algorithm. This section is discuss about various encryption algorithm is used in this online payment system.

This card transaction system first time they used in RSA algorithm. This algorithm is very powerful on the time of introduce. The public key cryptography method is very powerful method of inverse system (Jayapandian, Rahman, Radhikadevi & Koushikaa, 2016). Main advantage of this RSA algorithm is factoring the larger integer values. The calculation power is high compare to other algorithm. After coming Elliptic Curve Cryptography (ECC) algorithm is RSA algorithm is not used (Huo, Dong & Chen, 2015). This business transaction system computation power is more important. Because based on this computation power payment transaction time is reduced. This ECC algorithm signature generation process time is very less compare to other algorithm. Public key size is another important problem, RSA algorithm public key size is not larger than 1984, due to this problem service provider migrate from RSA to ECC. Elliptic Curve Digital Signature Algorithm (ECDSA) is also altering method of RSA algorithm because business transaction memory requirement is also important. This ECDSA is reducing computation power with memory requirement (Johnson, Menezes & Vanstone, 2001).

Transaction PIN generation is another important role to complete payment transaction. This PIN encryption is also used basic working principle of elliptic curve method that is name as Elliptic Curve Integrated Encryption Scheme (ECIES). This algorithm is generating the key between user and server (Smart, 2001). Based on the card information the send information from user terminal to server, that server generates PIN and sends to the user mobile or mail.

HYBRID ENCRYPTION ALGORITHM USED IN NFC DEVICE

The hybrid encryption system is join public key cryptography method. This is effective method of symmetric encryption scheme. This encryption method is providing higher security system; also data should be transmitted securely from sender terminal to receiver terminal using secret key method. Block diagram of hybrid encryption architecture is elaborate in Figure 6. There are two encryption scheme is commonly used that is key encryption and data encryption. This key encryption technical name is public key cryptography. Data encryption is named as symmetric key cryptography scheme. The combination of symmetric and asymmetric method is providing better security compare to other methods. Near Field Communication system is also deals with transmit the data by using radio frequency signals. This signal is attacked from the nearby attackers. Encryption algorithm is used by avoiding this kind of data attack, but recent day's attackers easy to hack these encrypted data. The concept of hybrid encryption model is to give reasonable solution for these data attack.

There are many NFC standards currently available that is name as NFCIP-1. Some standard NFC protocol is also used; most commonly used protocol is ECDH protocol. ECDH means Elliptic Curves Diffie-Hellman method. This ECDH is used for key encryption process. Data encryption most powerful algorithm is used that is name as Advanced Encryption Standard algorithm. The proposed model for key encryption same Elliptic Curves Diffie-Hellman method is used. The data encryption special hybrid encryption method is used, that is named as probabilistic with homomorphic encryption (Jayapandian & Rahman, 2017). The basic working principle of probabilistic method is random data encryption. The similar data is encrypted in several times, not possible to read the original message. This is a public key encryption method different ciphertext is used. This encryption method original message is working with YES or No method. Suppose attacker try to attack means deterministic encryption method is used to avoid data attack. This encryption message is stored in common table. Second encryption method is homomorphic encryption algorithm. The purpose of encryption is providing higher security at the same time computation time is also more important. Business transaction is to be done with in a second, if suppose hybrid encryption is take more time for execution means it doesn't suitable for payment transaction. That is reason basic working method of homomorphic encryption is computation on data. This encryption technique should take less computation time compare to other method. Main advantage of this homomorphic encryption algorithm is secure chain transaction without losing original information. This algorithm is used in different applications, for example currency exchange trading and transaction is made from shipping companies. The government sector is also using this algorithm for the purpose of secure voting system. The figure shows the working method of hybrid encryption algorithm in NFC communication. In general hybrid method takes more execution time compare to single encryption but

Figure 6. Hybrid encryption in NFC

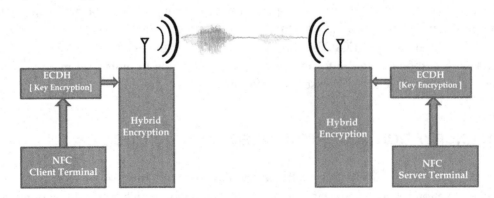

provides higher security. The combination of probabilistic and homomorphic method is take same single execution time because homomorphic encryption is reducing computation time.

SUMMARY

The online business transaction is unavoidable in modern world. The modern technology many online payment gateway method is used. Credit or debit card transaction is very old method. Smart phone usage is gradually increased day to day. Smart phone is not only used for communication purpose, this should be used for social media access, browsing purpose and this kind of payment usage. This chapter is reviewing many online payment method merits and demerits. Moving to latest technology all the user information is handling with digital format. This is a major headache of this digital world, because hacker easy to hack the user personal information and misuse it. This chapter is to solve security problem in business transaction. In business transaction many methods are used for online payment, one of those methods is NFC. The proposed idea is to give reasonable security solution for NFC transaction. NFC transaction is happened with mobile to mobile and mobile to NFC tag. This chapter is reviewing and analyzing various payment security systems. The proposed idea is choosing hybrid encryption technique to provide data security. This method is to give importance for key encryption and data encryption. Hybrid encryption is choosing two best encryption methods; first one is probabilistic encryption. It takes random encryption method for data communication. Second algorithm is homomorphic encryption, it is a computation process.

REFERENCES

Alsmadi, I., Burdwell, R., Aleroud, A., Wahbeh, A., Al-Qudah, M. A., & Al-Omari, A. (2018). *Network Security. In International Conference on Practical Information Security* (pp. 121-138). Springer.

Asaduzzaman, A., Mazumder, S., & Salinas, S. (2018). A promising security protocol for protecting near field communication devices from networking attacks. *International Journal of Security and Networks*, *13*(2), 98–107. doi:10.1504/IJSN.2018.092448

Azhari, F. (2014). Quick detection of NFC vulnerability: Implementation weakness exploitation. *Information Management & Computer Security*, *22*(2), 134–140. doi:10.1108/IMCS-09-2013-0067

Chen, L. D. (2008). A model of consumer acceptance of mobile payment. *International Journal of Mobile Communications*, *6*(1), 32–52. doi:10.1504/IJMC.2008.015997

Conti, M., Dragoni, N., & Lesyk, V. (2016). A survey of man in the middle attacks. *IEEE Communications Surveys and Tutorials*, *18*(3), 2027–2051. doi:10.1109/COMST.2016.2548426

Dias, J., Matos, J. N., & Oliveira, A. S. (2014). The charge collector system: A new NFC and smartphone-based toll collection system. *Procedia Technology*, *17*, 130–137. doi:10.1016/j.protcy.2014.10.220

El Zarki, M., Mehrotra, S., Tsudik, G., & Venkatasubramanian, N. (2002, February). Security issues in a future vehicular network. *International Conference on European Wireless*, 2.

Falaki, H., Mahajan, R., Kandula, S., Lymberopoulos, D., Govindan, R., & Estrin, D. (2010, June). Diversity in smartphone usage. In *Proceedings of the 8th international conference on Mobile systems, applications, and services* (pp. 179-194). ACM.

Fennelly, L. (2016). *Effective physical security*. Butterworth-Heinemann.

Finkenzeller, K. (2010). *RFID handbook: fundamentals and applications in contactless smart cards, radio frequency identification and near-field communication*. John Wiley & Sons. doi:10.1002/9780470665121

Hajji, T., Ouerdi, N., Azizi, A., & Azizi, M. (2018). EMV Cards Vulnerabilities Detection Using Deterministic Finite Automaton. *Procedia Computer Science*, *127*, 531–538. doi:10.1016/j.procs.2018.01.152

Harshita, S. T., & Tanwar, S. (2018). Security Issues and Countermeasures of Online Transaction in E-Commerce. In Mobile Commerce: Concepts, Methodologies, Tools, and Applications (pp. 982-1013). IGI Global.

Haselsteiner, E., & Breitfuß, K. (2006, July). Security in near field communication (NFC). In *Workshop on RFID security* (pp. 12-14). Academic Press.

Huitsing, P., Chandia, R., Papa, M., & Shenoi, S. (2008). Attack taxonomies for the Modbus protocols. *International Journal of Critical Infrastructure Protection*, *1*, 37–44. doi:10.1016/j.ijcip.2008.08.003

Huo, W., Dong, Q., & Chen, Y. (2015). *ECC-based RFID/NFC Mutual Authentication Protocol*. Academic Press.

Jayapandian, N., & Rahman, A. M. Z. (2017). Secure and efficient online data storage and sharing over cloud environment using probabilistic with homomorphic encryption. *Cluster Computing*, *20*(2), 1561–1573. doi:10.100710586-017-0809-4

Jayapandian, N., Rahman, A. M. Z., Koushikaa, M., & Radhikadevi, S. (2016, February). A novel approach to enhance multi level security system using encryption with fingerprint in cloud. In *Futuristic Trends in Research and Innovation for Social Welfare (Startup Conclave), World Conference on* (pp. 1-5). IEEE. 10.1109/STARTUP.2016.7583903

Jayapandian, N., Rahman, A. M. Z., Radhikadevi, S., & Koushikaa, M. (2016, February). Enhanced cloud security framework to confirm data security on asymmetric and symmetric key encryption. In *Futuristic Trends in Research and Innovation for Social Welfare (Startup Conclave), World Conference on* (pp. 1-4). IEEE. 10.1109/STARTUP.2016.7583904

Johnson, D., Menezes, A., & Vanstone, S. (2001). The elliptic curve digital signature algorithm (ECDSA). *International Journal of Information Security*, *1*(1), 36–63. doi:10.1007102070100002

Khan, A. A. (2016). *Spoofing protection for secure-element identifiers*. U.S. Patent Application No. 14/474,737.

Kortvedt, H., & Mjolsnes, S. (2009, November). Eavesdropping near field communication. In *The Norwegian Information Security Conference (NISK)* (*Vol. 27*, p. 5768). Academic Press.

Laur, S., & Nyberg, K. (2006, December). Efficient mutual data authentication using manually authenticated strings. In *International Conference on Cryptology and Network Security* (pp. 90-107). Springer. 10.1007/11935070_6

Lee, J. I., Kim, K. Y., Park, H. W., Park, S. J., & Kim, J. H. (2016). *Image forming apparatus supporting function of near field communication and method of setting NFC operation mode thereof.* U.S. Patent No. 9,256,386. Washington, DC: U.S. Patent and Trademark Office.

Madlmayr, G., Langer, J., Kantner, C., & Scharinger, J. (2008, March). NFC devices: Security and privacy. In *Availability, Reliability and Security, 2008. ARES 08. Third International Conference on* (pp. 642-647). IEEE.

Morak, J., Kumpusch, H., Hayn, D., Modre-Osprian, R., & Schreier, G. (2012). Design and evaluation of a telemonitoring concept based on NFC-enabled mobile phones and sensor devices. *IEEE Transactions on Information Technology in Biomedicine, 16*(1), 17–23. doi:10.1109/TITB.2011.2176498 PMID:22113811

Ortiz, S. (2006). Is near-field communication close to success? *Computer, 39*(3), 18-20.

Pelletier, M. P., Trépanier, M., & Morency, C. (2011). Smart card data use in public transit: A literature review. *Transportation Research Part C, Emerging Technologies, 19*(4), 557–568. doi:10.1016/j.trc.2010.12.003

Schamberger, R., Madlmayr, G., & Grechenig, T. (2013, February). Components for an interoperable NFC mobile payment ecosystem. In *Near Field Communication (NFC), 2013 5th International Workshop on* (pp. 1-5). IEEE. 10.1109/NFC.2013.6482440

Smart, N. P. (2001, December). The exact security of ECIES in the generic group model. In *IMA International Conference on Cryptography and Coding* (pp. 73-84). Springer. 10.1007/3-540-45325-3_8

Turner, E. C., & Dasgupta, S. (2003). *Privacy And Security In E-Business.* Academic Press.

Verdult, R., & Kooman, F. (2011, February). Practical attacks on NFC enabled cell phones. In *Near Field Communication (NFC), 2011 3rd International Workshop on* (pp. 77-82). IEEE. 10.1109/NFC.2011.16

Want, R. (2011). Near field communication. *IEEE Pervasive Computing, 10*(3), 4–7. doi:10.1109/MPRV.2011.55

Xiao, L., & Wang, Z. (2011). Internet of things: A new application for intelligent traffic monitoring system. *Journal of Networks, 6*(6), 887.

Yang, J., & Papazoglou, M. P. (2000). Interoperation support for electronic business. *Communications of the ACM, 43*(6), 39–47. doi:10.1145/336460.336473

Zentner, A. (2008). Online sales, Internet use, file sharing, and the decline of retail music specialty stores. *Information Economics and Policy, 20*(3), 288–300. doi:10.1016/j.infoecopol.2008.06.006

Zhang, D., & Adipat, B. (2005). Challenges, methodologies, and issues in the usability testing of mobile applications. *International Journal of Human-Computer Interaction, 18*(3), 293–308. doi:10.120715327590ijhc1803_3

ADDITIONAL READING

Amine, F. M., & Abdelkader, G. (2017). Hybrid Approach of Modified AES. *International Journal of Organizational and Collective Intelligence*, *7*(4), 83–93. doi:10.4018/IJOCI.2017100105

Ba, S. (2001). Establishing online trust through a community responsibility system. *Decision Support Systems*, *31*(3), 323–326. doi:10.1016/S0167-9236(00)00144-5

Jayapandian, N., & Md Zubair Rahman, A. M. J. (2018). Secure Deduplication for Cloud Storage Using Interactive Message-Locked Encryption with Convergent Encryption, To Reduce Storage Space. *Brazilian Archives of Biology and Technology*, *61*(0), 1–13. doi:10.1590/1678-4324-2017160609

Liu, K., & Shi, J. (2018). A systematic approach for business data analytics with a real case study. In *Operations and Service Management: Concepts, Methodologies, Tools, and Applications. The University of Hong Kong*. Hong Kong: IGI Global. doi:10.4018/978-1-5225-3909-4.ch043

Raina, V. K. (2017). *NFC Payment Systems and the New Era of Transaction Processing*. India: IGI Global. doi:10.4018/978-1-5225-2306-2

Shrivastava, S., & Pateriya, R. K. (2018). Secure Framework for E-Commerce Applications in Cloud Environment. In *Improving E-Commerce Web Applications Through Business Intelligence Techniques* (pp. 82–109). IGI Global. doi:10.4018/978-1-5225-3646-8.ch004

KEY TERMS AND DEFINITIONS

Data Security: Data security provides storage and transmits security by using encryption algorithm.

E-Payment: Electronic payment is online payment system without using physical money transaction.

Hybrid Encryption: Combination of any two encryption algorithms is called as hybrid encryption.

NFC: NFC is near field communication; it's used for sharing short-range data transmissions.

RFID: RFID is radio frequency identification; it's used to transfer the data by using radio frequency signals.

Chapter 6
Green Reporting and Its Impact on Business Strategy:
Computer Program for Evidence and Green Reporting

Dana Maria Constantin
University of Bucharest, Romania

Dan Ioan Topor
1 Decembrie 1918 University, Romania

Sorinel Căpușneanu
Dimitrie Cantemir Christian University, Romania

Mirela Cătălina Türkeş
Dimitrie Cantemir Christian University, Romania

Mădălina-Gabriela Anghel
Artifex University, Romania

ABSTRACT

This chapter illustrates some aspects of the green reporting and its impact on the business strategy of an economic entity. The main objectives of this chapter are to present the green reporting and the green accounting synthesis documents and, also, to present the computer program for the green report of an economic entity. Based on the national and international literature, the authors present the concepts of the green reporting and integrated report and a computer program specifically designed to record green costs and green reporting. They present the types of green costs and the legislation related to the green reporting. The aspects presented by the authors are based on the national and international literature, specialized studies related to the topic of this study. A new theoretical-empirical framework is created by the authors through their contribution, which facilitates the identification of new ideas, themes, and debates of other issues encountered in the world business environment.

DOI: 10.4018/978-1-5225-8455-1.ch006

INTRODUCTION

Many companies around the world have included the environment as part of the global business strategy. Important business issues have become: the waste disposal, the greenhouse gas emissions reduction or various ways of promoting the use of electricity. The Global Resource Initiatives (GRI), the most widely used worldwide report framework, is applied globally by companies offering a standardized approach that demonstrates a strong corporate commitment to the environmental policy. The GRI framework has been developed by a network of people from more than 60 countries and is part of different areas such as: education, government, business etc.

This paper aims to propose a strategic framework for the accounting and sustainability reporting (Green Accounting and Reporting). The Green Accounting realizes how management acts and registers the effects of using the environment. Accounting and its awareness are done through reports which require transparency of the shareholders or other stakeholders. Starting from the specialized studies, a clearer delimitation of the strategic framework between the sustainability reporting and its impact on the business strategy has been attempted by using the information provided by an appropriate IT program. The objectives of this chapter are to: (1) *highlight the implications of accounting* as a *green reporting tool; (2) achieving the integration between the green accounting and the green reporting through the information provided by an appropriate IT program, and (3) highlighting the impact of the accounting/ green reporting information on a company's business strategy.*

BACKGROUND

Conceptual Approaches of Sustainability

In the evolution of the concept of sustainability, the basic idea remained the same, but the specialists have presented several interesting approaches. Thus, some authors have focused on the essence of enhancing and preserving the environment (Shrivastava and Hart, 1992; Santos and Filho, 2005) and the sustainable society (Elkington, 1997), while other authors have reached the economic aspect of the concept of sustainability. According to experts, a sustainable society must meet three conditions: its rates of renewable resources use should not exceed their regeneration rates; its rates of renewable resources use should not exceed the rate at which the alternative sustainable suppliers have developed; and the pollution emission rates must not exceed the capacity of the environment assimilation (Elkington, 1997). Sustainability is a fundamental and complex construction that helps maintain the balance of several factors for the long existence of the planet (Aras & Crowther, 2009). This construction has continued to gain the attention of the specialists, becoming one of the most important problems faced by mankind due to the continuing pressure of the society and investors (Ambec & Lanoie, 2008; Epstein, 2008; Lippman, 2010).

Sustainability represents the development of the society and its evolution towards a rich and more comfortable world, where the natural environment and cultural achievements are reserved for future generations. Nowadays, in addition to the benefits of the future generations, the viability offers gains of value and finance (Dyllick & Hockerts, 2002). Other conceptual approaches to the notion of sustainability refer to the expectations of improving the social and environmental performance of the present generation without including the ability of the future generations to meet their social and environmental needs

(Brundtland et al., 2003). The sustainability framework is a flexible one in the specialized literature, and the opinions of the specialists provide a wider range of concepts:

- Related to the environment such as: innovation in the sustainable marketing (Iles, 2008), Sustainable Reporting (Blengini & Shields, 2010), sustainability and consumer perception (Mc Donald and Oates, 2006); production construction and sustainability (Yan et al., 2008);
- Related to the social environment and the environment such as: promoting sustainability (Frame & Newton, 2007), sustainable society (Dewangga et al., 2008);
- Related to the social and economic environment such as: sustainability and marketing (Kirchgeorg & Winn, 2006);
- Related to the social, economic and environmental environment such as: sustainable corporate performance (Collins et al., 2007).

A Contribution to Sustainability: Sustainability Reporting

Nowadays, the companies have to take responsibility for revealing their operations on the business environment, society and the environment. The Sustainability reporting has become a common practice in the companies in order to respond to the expectations and critics of the stakeholders who want to be better informed about the social and environmental issues and about the impact on the business activities (Boiral, 2013).

The Global Reporting Initiative defines the concept of the Sustainability reporting as "the organizational performance practice of measurement, disclosure and being responsible towards the internal and external stakeholders in order to achieve the Sustainable Development" (Global Reporting Initiative, 2011).

This concept is considered to be synonymous with other concepts such as: corporate social responsibility reporting (CSR), non-financial report, triple bottom line reporting etc. In other words, a Sustainability reporting is that report that is published by a company about the economic, social and environmental impact caused by its day-to-day activities. This reporting presents the values of the company and the governance model and demonstrates the link between its strategy's adoption and its commitment to a global sustainable economy. This reporting helps companies measure, understand and communicate their performance (economic, social, environmentally), set goals and manage actions in a much more efficient way. It is an intrinsic element of the Integrated Ratio Report, combining the analysis of the financial performance with the non-financial performance.

The main providers of guidance in reporting Sustainability are: GRI (GRI Sustainability Report Standards), Organization for Economic Cooperation and Development (OECD Guidelines for Multinational Enterprises), United Nations Global Compact (Communication on Progress), International Organization for Standardization (ISO 26000, International Standard for Social Responsibility).

The General Frame of Green Accounting and Green Reporting

The green management accounting includes the identification, collection, selection, calculation, analysis and the internal report of the environmental cost information and its use in the decision-making process with impact on the economic and the natural environment. Furthermore, the green management accounting can also reflect the impact of the human activities on nature and natural resources, and the assessment of their effectiveness can lead to solve the current environmental problems. The national environmental legislation and the environmental policy regulatory authorities establish measures, in which the companies must regulate their pollution emissions, manage the waste disposal and develop their product packing (Esty & Winston, 2006). The degree of adoption and implementation of the green accounting and green reporting has been influenced by: the regulatory pressures and adoption requests (Bell, 1997; Kurasaka, 1997), ethics of awareness (Lehmann, 1999), the available economic and financial initiatives (Richardson & Welker, 2001; Al-Tuwaijri et al., 2004), the sense of responsibility and transparency of information (Cox et al., 2004; Cormier et al., 2004), the management and efficient operation (Montabon et al., 2000; Husseini, 2001; Anton et al., 2004).

The general framework of green accounting and green reporting enables a company's decision makers, the management and strategic team to use a conceptual model in order to ensure and guarantee the success of its implementation within a corporate strategy. From our point of view, this framework of green accounting and green reporting is particularly important because: (1) *its conceptual-strategic development is reflected in the development of a model focused on the multi-level potential strategies of a company;* (2) *these strategies can be implemented and generally integrated in the corporate strategies;* (3) *they outline the role of accounting function in supporting the green corporate strategy and in the business strategists.*

Integrating the Green Accounting and Green Reporting in the Corporate Strategy

The strategy aims to understand and approach the issues that have an impact on the ability of the company to fulfill its mission that its products/services can be produced to meet the needs of the markets which the efficient configuration of resources serves, in order to build and sustain the competitive advantage (Galbreath, 2009). However, firstly, a company needs to revise its commitment to the environmental or green governance before it can decide the strategy to be adopted at firm, industry, country and the level of society.

According to Valentine and Savage (2010) the deep commitment is demonstrated by the availability of a quantitative environment, by the environmental performance, disclosures which reflect the company's high value commitment to setting up systems and structures to monitor the engagement. The company must make a real attempt to integrate the environmental concerns within the existing ones and the decision-making process in all the aspects of a corporate management. On the other hand, the extreme superficial employment companies offer vague, qualitative vocations, with lack in the environmental initiatives and with no substance in its disclosure.

The companies might take into account a number of factors, before deciding on improving their commitment to the green accounting integration: the shareholders' interests, the accounting management, the implementation limits and options, the potential costs (Rubenstein, 1994). Once decided, the companies must integrate the green policies in the corporate and business strategy and the success depends on the study and understanding of certain forces: macro elements, the secondary elements of the stakeholders, the industry-specific elements; the elements specific to the company and the functional elements (Valentine, 2009).

The introduction of the green policy means reflecting a superior commitment of a company's management and includes: planning, measuring, monitoring and reviewing. *Planning* is the process of identifying all the environmental aspects of the operations carried out, outlining the effective environmental management procedures. It includes: (1) improving the environmental objectives; (2) training; (3) improvement; (4) awareness of campaigning promotion; (5) appropriate documentation for implementation; (6) Emergency preparation. *Measurement* is the process that means procedures involved in collecting, integrating, and directing the relevant environmental data to the specialized departments, according to their needs. *Monitoring* is the measurement and reporting of the environmental performance as well as the necessary preventive and corrective actions specific to the risk assessment procedures. *The review* includes the responsibility of the management to continuously assess and review the effectiveness of the policy, being conducted with the possibility of extending to the audit of the environmental data and environmental performance.

Through their studies, a number of specialists have identified some issues in adopting the green policy and in implementing the green accounting such as: (1) *integrating the environmental policy into the company's strategic and business policy;* (2) *preparing the accounting and reporting system at the level of the company's accounting department;* (3) *adaptation of the green accounting information to the existing standards and regulations and their suitability to the system reflected in the annual financial statements of the company* (Grinnell and Hunt, 2000).

Green Business Strategy and the Corporate Strategy

A unified business strategy refers to how a company is concerned about the competition from a particular market or industry, and at this level, the company must focus on improving the corporate reputation, either by reducing production costs or by resorting to quality products and services. The efforts to integrate the environmental policy into the business strategies continue, and despite the regulatory efforts in the environmental field, many companies have not adapted yet, to these requirements. The only way to adapt along the way is to keep the interest and information about its evolution and to maintain the adaptability to the regulated changes when it is possible (Valentine, 2009). The adaptation to the new environmental regulations as quickly as possible is more advantageous than the late adaptation that will be mandatory and will have some repercussions on the company by sanctioning it. The reflection of this proactive attitude on environment of a company is given by: the analysis of the life cycle of processes and products, the environmental policies implemented within the supply chains; the monitoring and auditing environmental performance; the accounting for environmental costs and savings; the product recycling, restoration and redesign, eco-labeling (Yakhou and Dorweiler, 2004). Profitability can also be achieved by saving electricity and minimizing the waste, which are ultimately only possible after reaching the levels of environmental policy integration.

The degree of integration of the environmental policies should be tested on a daily basis and then, the decision taken at the organizational level. The integration may be conventional or unconventional (Fryxell and Vryza, 1999) and it is the ideal solution to solve conflicts that might arise such as: specialization differences, training, technical terms or jargon used. For this purpose, the use of EMS along with the ISO 14001 Standards would help to integrate the system functions via the interface provided with the input and output functions. EMS provides the life cycle accounting and the environmental cost accounting which are so useful to a company's accounting department.

The corporate strategy focuses on the area of activity where a company is competitive on a particular market or industry (Galbreath, 2006) and must focus on the capital management (Valentine, 2009). Galbreath (2006) presents four strategists that the companies can use for the corporate social responsibility:

1. *The shareholders' strategy* which states that the only responsibility towards the society is an economic one;
2. *The altruistic strategy of the* community (groups or causes) in the form of monetary donations;
3. *The mutual strategy* which considers that by taking on social responsibilities, a company offers improved benefits to the society, but also receives tangible and financial rewards;
4. *Citizenship strategy* which is the strategy that provides a direct link between citizens and companies, so that, by disclosing the environmental reports by the companies which ensure transparency and availability, the citizens can inform and may help protect the environment and warn of emerging environmental issues.

The specialists suggest five great strategies that the companies can use to improve environmental management (Valentine, 2009):

1. *The green positioning strategies*, meaning those strategies incorporating eco-friendly features into a product or service;
2. *The financial strategies*, meaning those strategies that allow the companies to access the green investment funds;
3. *The brand protection strategies*, meaning those strategies designed to strengthen the reputation of a company or reduce the consumer perceptions;
4. *The quality strategies*, meaning those strategies that eliminate the inefficiencies in inputs, outputs or processes;
5. *The cost control strategies*, meaning those cost savings strategies by improving the environmental management techniques and preventing the future events that may cause them: fines, penalties or lawsuits because of not respecting the environmental legislation.

The Role of the Environmental Indicators for the Green Reporting

In the current context of the variability and climate change, sustainability is a problem of attitude, not a technological one (Dobrescu, 2010), where each economic player must assume the environmental management because the environmental protection has become a problem of general interest. The environmental or ecological management requires a systematic and integrated approach (Figure 1), in which the green reporting is the control tool.

Within this management, there are a number of principles that need to be fulfilled such as: the environmental conservation, the environmental quality improvement, the pollution prevention, the environmental damage prevention and the precaution against an unknown risk. In order these principles to be fulfilled, the permanent assessment and monitoring of the environmental components (air, water, soil, biodiversity and human health) and (Constantin et al., 2016) and also emission levels are required (Duțu, 2010). These are done with the help of the environmental indicators, which are used in the green reporting, which is a control and planning tool of the companies which have implemented an environmental management system.

The green reporting is an intermediate step in quantifying the status of the environment and the company's responses to diminish and/or eliminate the environmental impact and preserve the natural resources for sustainability (Figure 2).

The environmental indicator consists of a piece of information that quantifies the status of the environmental quality at a moment. It can be characterized by a minimum, average and a maximum value in relation to the reference values or the maximum admissible concentration (Ionac and Ciulache, 2005; Ivan et al., 2017).

The environmental indicators provide information about:

- The integration of the environmental concerns into the company's overall management;
- The assessing of the environmental performance;
- The report on the status of the environment;
- The company's response to improving the status of the environment.

With the help of these environmental indicators, the green reporting is carried out and it consists in a process of permanent transmission of the monitoring and evaluation information of the environmental factors, on the basis of which the environmental status of the environment is established, meaning if it is polluted and how much is polluted. After Țuțuianu, in 2006, the environmental indicators are based on data or information which can be:

- Direct values obtained by measurements, being considered primary data;
- Values calculated on the basis of formulas, being considered data analized;

Figure 1. The components of the environmental management and green reporting
Source: Adapted after Dumitriu, 2003

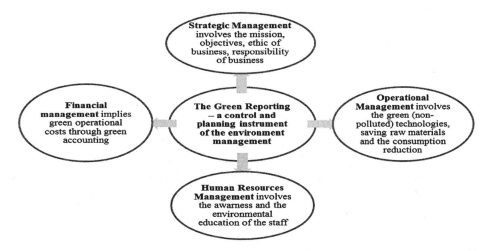

Figure 2. The place of green reporting in the sustainability reporting
Source: Adapted after Țuțuianu, 2006

- Relative values are in the category of the first two, but reported to reference values or values calculated as percentages of the total;
- Indexed values are the data converted into units that are compare over time against a reference point;
- Weighted values are the data modified by applying a factor according to its importance, being used mainly in the calculation of indices;
- Aggregate values are the data obtained from different sources, collected and expressed as a total amount.

In order these environmental indicators may ensure the quality of the green reporting, some requirements must be accomplished:

- They must be comparable and highlight changes in impacts on the environmental quality;
- They must objectively reflect the environmental performance;
- They must continually improve the environmental performance;
- They must be measured in comparable units;
- They must be determined on a daily, weekly, monthly, quarterly, semi-annual and yearly basis, ensuring regimes and concentrations;
- They must be clear to users;
- They must meet the information requirements of the users.

The environmental indicators can be classified according to a wide range of criteria. In this chapter, we refer to the criterion of the global appreciation of the status of the environment, in which the environmental indicators are:

- Air quality;
- Water quality;
- Soil quality;
- The lack of registered plants and animals, and the health of the population (Rojanschi et al., 2004).

The quality assurance of the green reporting by the environmental indicators depends on the cycle of surveillance or the environmental quality monitoring as summarized in Figure 3.

In order the monitoring of the environmental indicators may be objective, there must be reduced and eliminated a series of problems which can appear in the structure and monitoring methodology of the environment quality which can lead to a poor reporting such as:

- The spatial distribution and poor density of the sampling points;
- The too short sampling time;
- The inadequate selection of the environmental indicators in relation to the research environments;
- The absence of the sampling procedures;
- The lack of quality assurance procedures;
- The reference and standard materials are inadequate;
- The lack of standard procedures for sampling, analysis and data integration.

The set of the environmental indicators constitute the most important tools for monitoring, reporting and controlling of the environmental performance of a company, providing the feedback to motivate the human resources, supporting the implementation of the environmental management and identifying the market opportunities and possibilities of decreasing costs.

The green reporting, on the basis of the environmental indicators, contributes to solving some major responsibilities of the companies in the environmental protection activity, in order to achieve sustainability. By the temporal analysis of the environmental indicators, the weaknesses and optimization of potentials can be established, as shown in the below-mentioned IT proposal for a green accounting and green reporting.

Computer Program for Evidence and Green Reporting

In this chapter, the authors propose a software application to solve the environmental modeling of the selected/desired indicators, centered around a database, with the potential to store necessary data and provide access to information drawn from this data. The model of the database can be incorporated in a more complex application for managing the environmental policy, and the fact that is built on the relational model means that it can be implemented in any RDBMS.

As specified, the application will pursue the following objectives:

- To provide a data storage solution for environmental values (organized on indicators);
- To offer the necessary data processing and information presentation platform.

The authors have selected the Microsoft® Access relational database management software to build and develop the application. The database has a simple structure, which is presented, as a physical model, in the figure 4.

The tables presented have the following means:

- **Time**: Provides the time periods (months and years) for which data are collected. There is no need to manually input data directly into the table, because data can be collected on an external data

Figure 3. The stages of the environmental quality monitoring for the green reporting
Source: Adapted after Rojanschi at al., 2008

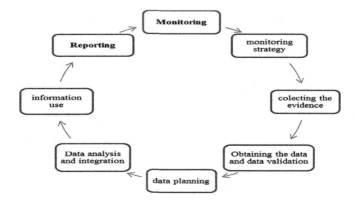

Figure 4. Database diagram (physical model)
Source: Authors' work, as presented by ACCESS

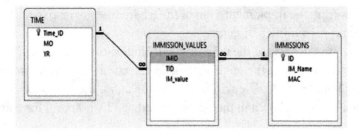

source, such as a worksheet, and imported into the database, from which the data for this table can be easily uploaded, by using an append query;

- **Imissions**: Provides the list of imissions for which the data are collected. The table includes the maximum acceptable concentration, for comparison purposes;
- **Imission_Values**: The table in which data resulted from measurements are stored, grouped by imissions and time.

Once the data have been uploaded, they can be analyzed, under various forms.

The first data analysis we propose is the centralized situation of the values measured, grouped both on the time dimension and the imission type. In this scope, the authors have used a cross-tab query, structured as follows:

- On the row heading section, the time attributes;
- On the column heading, the imission type;
- The value section holds the actual measures.

The structure of the query is presented in the Figure 5.

Figure 5. Crosstab query structure, used for centralized presentation of imission values
Source: Authors' work, as presented by ACCESS

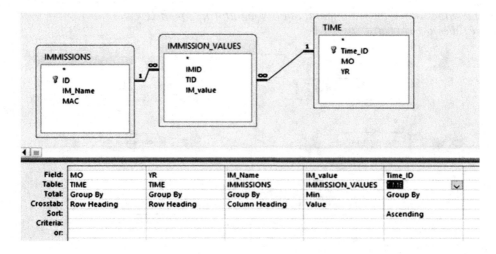

The results of the query are presented in the Figure 6. *Note:* the authors have uploaded a sample of data only for presentation purposes.

For beneficiaries of information provided by such application, there is an important need to observe the correlation between the actual values of the imissions and the threshold represented by the accepted concentration. Thus, the gap between the values is also to be included in the results of data processing. The authors have designed the following query, which measures the gap and presents it in a centralized manner (Figure 7).

The *IGAP* field is calculated as a difference between the maximum admissible concentration (*MAC*) and the actual values. The usage of the *TID* field ensures the calendar-based sorting solution, as the name of the month might be written as is, regardless the language of the user.

Figure 6. Crosstab query results, used for centralized presentation of imission values
Source: Authors' work, as presented by ACCESS

Month	YEAR	HF	PM	SO2
	2014	0.0053	0.16	0.005
February	2014	0.0054	0.1	0.006
March	2014	0.0053	0.11	0.006
April	2014	0.0055	0.13	0.0255
May	2014	0.0053	0.1	0.02
June	2014	0.0053	0.1	0.013
July	2014	0.0053	0.1	0.023
August	2014	0.0052	0.11	0.026
September	2014	0.0051	0.13	0.022
October	2014	0.0053	0.11	0.019
November	2014	0.0053	0.1	0.012
December	2014	0.0054	0.1	0.014
January	2015	0.0054	0.1	0.015
February	2015	0.0054	0.13	0.012
March	2015	0.0055	0.1	0.014
April	2015	0.0054	0.08	0.007
May	2015	0.0051	0.09	0.006
June	2015	0.0054	0.09	0.013
July	2015	0.005	0.11	0.008
August	2015	0.0052	0.08	0.011
September	2015	0.0051	0.09	0.008
October	2015	0.0053	0.1	0.007
November	2015	0.0054	0.11	0.017
December	2015	0.0054	0.086	0.005

Figure 7. Crosstab query structure, used for centralized presentation of imission gap values
Source: Authors' work, as presented by ACCESS

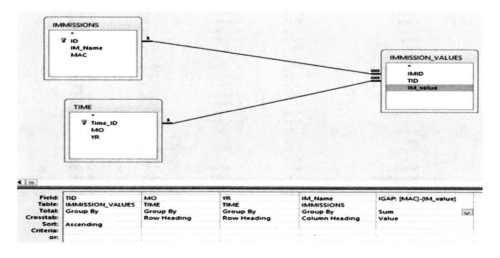

A positive value of the gap means that the imission has not reached the critical level, while a negative value reveals an unfavorable situation. The authors have chosen this formula considering the sensible correlation between the possible sign of the gap and its meaning for the protection of environment.

As the month and year were represented under the form of separate attributes, they occupy the *ROW HEADING* section of the crosstab. The aggregate function used, as there is a requirement for this type of field, in combination with the *VALUE* property, poses no problem, as the argument is represented, at this stage, by a singular value. The results of the query are presented in the Figure 8.

The interpretation of the query results displays a single negative value, that is for *PM* imissions in January, 2014. Considering that the application will be able to store high amounts of data, measured for extended periods of time, the authors have pursued in the next stage the calculation and representation of aggregate values, based on various statistical functions. The aggregation criteria used were the year and the type of imission. The structure of the query for annual average values is presented in the Figure 9 and the results of the query are presented in the Figure 10. The next step in the analysis of environmental data is the comparison between the average values and the maximum admissible concentrations. This result is achieved by applying the following query from the Figure 11.

All calculation formulas are visible in the figure above. The query allows the simultaneous calculation of average imission value per year, and of the average gap, as the grouping levels are the same and do not pose any kind of conflict. The results of the query are displayed in the Figure 12.

As the result formula was constructed on the same logic as the comparison between individual values, a positive difference means a favorable result.

SOLUTIONS AND RECOMMENDATIONS

Taking into consideration the aspects discussed in this chapter, we propose the following:

Figure 8. Crosstab query results, used for centralized presentation of imission gap values
Source: Authors' work, as presented by ACCESS

Month	YEAR	HF	PM	SO2
	2014	0.0097	-0.01	0.345
February	2014	0.0096	0.05	0.344
March	2014	0.0097	0.04	0.344
April	2014	0.0095	0.02	0.3245
May	2014	0.0097	0.05	0.33
June	2014	0.0097	0.05	0.337
July	2014	0.0097	0.05	0.327
August	2014	0.0098	0.04	0.324
September	2014	0.0099	0.02	0.328
October	2014	0.0097	0.04	0.331
November	2014	0.0097	0.05	0.338
December	2014	0.0096	0.05	0.336
January	2015	0.0096	0.05	0.335
February	2015	0.0096	0.02	0.338
March	2015	0.0095	0.05	0.336
April	2015	0.0096	0.07	0.343
May	2015	0.0099	0.06	0.344
June	2015	0.0096	0.06	0.337
July	2015	0.01	0.04	0.342
August	2015	0.0098	0.07	0.339
September	2015	0.0099	0.06	0.342
October	2015	0.0097	0.05	0.343
November	2015	0.0096	0.04	0.333
December	2015	0.0096	0.064	0.345

Figure 9. Crosstab query design, used for calculation the average imission values
Source: Authors' work, as presented by ACCESS

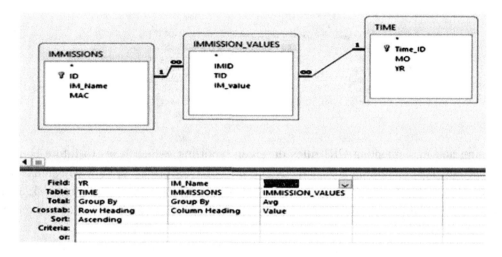

Figure 10. Crosstab query results, average imission values
Source: Authors' work, as presented by ACCESS

YEAR	HF	PM	SO2
2014	0.005308	0.112500	0.015958
2015	0.005300	0.097167	0.010250

Figure 11. Crosstab query design, gap between average imission values and the maximum admissible concentration
Source: Authors' work, as presented by ACCESS

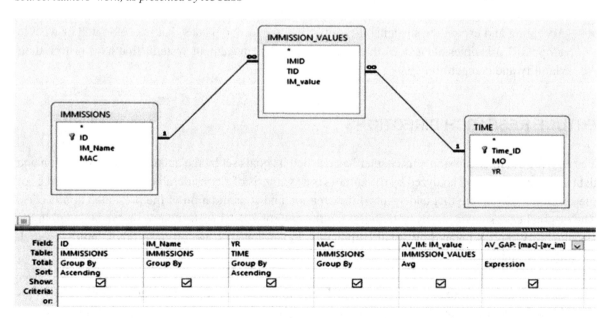

Figure 12. Crosstab query results, gap between average imission values and the maximum admissible concentration
Source: Authors' work, as presented by ACCESS

ID	IM_Name	YEAR	Maximum adm	AV_IM	AV_GAP
	HF	2014	0.015	0.0053	0.0097
1	HF	2015	0.015	0.0053	0.0097
2	SO2	2014	0.35	0.0160	0.3340
2	SO2	2015	0.35	0.0103	0.3398
3	PM	2014	0.15	0.1125	0.0375
3	PM	2015	0.15	0.0972	0.0528

- Adopting and implementing GRI rules on green reporting, which leads to future benefits for a company such as: increasing transparency and financial performance, increasing stakeholder access to capital, increasing innovation and efficiency, reducing waste, managing risk, increasing consumer confidence in manufactured products, increased employee confidence and recruitment, increased reputation and other social benefits;
- The need for sustainability helps companies manage their social and environmental impacts as well as improving operational efficiency and natural resource management, remaining a vital component of shareholders, employees and other stakeholders;
- Sustainability is a differentiation factor in a competitive industry, favoring investor confidence, confidentiality and loyalty of employees.

By presenting environmental performance, the information presented in the sustainability reports becomes valuable to all parties involved in environmental, economic and social activities. In view of the above, we would like to recommend the following:

- Research of empirical literature to identify those opportunities to adopt and implement GRI principles and adapt them to other management accounting methods that allow and highlight environmental reporting;
- Accepting and expanding sustainability reporting across companies that have adopted or wish to adopt GRI principles alongside other accounting and management systems that have proven their viability and compatibility.

FUTURE RESEARCH DIRECTIONS

Through the assumed mission, this chapter has reached its goals set by the authors. The information and data used, processed and analyzed by the authors is a synthesis of a considerable amount of resources of the specialized literature that underpinned the creation and consolidation of the presented approaches. The original case study is a way of highlighting the environmental performance that is included in the sustainability reports created by small companies. Regarding this, we propose other future research directions such as:

- Analyzing the possibility of adapting GRI principles to other managerial accounting or environmental accounting methods or systems;

- Analyzing the impact of managerial decisions resulting from the adaptation of GRI principles to other managerial accounting/environmental accounting methods or systems, including environmental reporting;
- The analysis of the possibility of creating new instruments for monitoring and measuring the environmental performance based on the principles of GRI and the principles of other managerial/environmental accounting methods or systems.

CONCLUSION

It is obvious that the need for transparency and disclosure of sustainability information is a priority for businesses of any small or large company, but also for other stakeholders, including governments, investors or civil society. From the understanding and the actual implementation of the GRI principles in terms of sustainability reporting, a considerable period of accommodation, harmonization and harmonization should take place. Increasing demand for sustainability reports is attributed to the needs of business communities and political leadership. The information contained in the environmental reports must be credible, reliable and robust, relevant and strategic to the appropriate user categories.

Business leadership has to support the sustainability strategy, introduce it into their businesses, and thus see the value it can offer to them, but also to society in general. Also, political leadership should support sustainability reporting, especially due to increased reporting and information requirements, but also to the fact that they are of particular importance in the sustainability landscape. Credibility and understanding of the impact of sustainability reports make the difference in a competitive market. The use of sustainability reports in strategic operations gives clear benefits both to long-term and short-term companies that develop them, including increased efficiency and cost reduction.

REFERENCES

Al-Tuwaijri, S. A., Christensen, T. E., & Hughes, K. II. (2004). The Relations among Environmental Disclosure, Environmental Performance and Economic Performance: A Simultaneous Equations. *Approach. Accounting, Organizations and Society, 29*(5-6), 447–471. doi:10.1016/S0361-3682(03)00032-1

Ambec, S., & Lanoie, P. (2008). Does it pay to be green? A systematic overview. *The Academy of Management Perspectives, 22*(4), 45–62. doi:10.5465/amp.2008.35590353

Anton, W. R. Q., Deltas, G., & Khanna, M. (2004). Incentives for Environmental Self-regulation and Implications for Environmental Performance. *Journal of Environmental Economics and Management, 48*(1), 632–654. doi:10.1016/j.jeem.2003.06.003

Aras, G., & Crowther, D. (2009). The durable organization in a time of financial and economic crisis. *Economics and Management, 14,* 210–216.

Bell, C. L. (1997). The ISO 14001 Environmental Management Systems Standard: One American's View. In C. Sheldon (Ed.), *ISO 14000 and Beyond: Environmental Management Systems in the Real World* (pp. 61–92). Sheffield, UK: Greenleaf Publishing. doi:10.9774/GLEAF.978-1-909493-05-6_5

Blengini, G. A., & Shields, D. J. (2010). Green labels and sustainability reporting: Overview of the building supply chain in Italy. *Management of Environmental Quality*, *21*(4), 477–493. doi:10.1108/14777831011049115

Boiral, O. (2013). Sustainability reports as simulacra? A counter-account of A and A+ GRI reports. *Accounting, Auditing & Accountability Journal*, *26*(7), 1036–1071. doi:10.1108/AAAJ-04-2012-00998

Bruntland, G. H., Julio, F., & Cristopher, J. L. M. (2003). Who Assessment of Health Systems Performance. *Lancet*, *361*(9375), 2155. doi:10.1016/S0140-6736(03)13702-6 PMID:12826452

Collins, C., Steg, L., & Koning, M. (2007). Customers' values, beliefs on sustainable corporate performance, and buying behavior. *Psychology and Marketing*, *24*(6), 555–577. doi:10.1002/mar.20173

Constantin, D.M., Topor, D.I., & Căpuşneanu, S., Barbu & C.M., Bogan, E. (2016). The monitoring of carbon monoxide air pollutant, as part of the air quality management. Case study: Olt County, Romania. *Annales Universitatis Apulensis Series Oeconomica*, *2*(18), 27–34.

Cormier, D., Gordon, I., & Magnan, M. (2004). Corporate environmental disclosure: Contrasting management's perceptions with reality. *Journal of Business Ethics*, *49*(2), 143–165. doi:10.1023/B:BUSI.0000015844.86206.b9

Cox, P., Brammer, S., & Millington, A. (2004). An Empirical Examination of Institutional Investor Preferences for Corporate Social Performance. *Journal of Business Ethics*, *52*(1), 27–43. doi:10.1023/B:BUSI.0000033105.77051.9d

Dewangga, A., Goldsmith, S., & Pegram, N. (2008). *Social responsibility guideline and sustainable development: Integrating a common goal of a sustainable society* (Master's thesis). Retrieved from WorldCat Dissertations. (OCLC: 747412684)

Dobrescu, P. (2010). *Viclenia globalizării. Asaltul asupra puterii americane*. Bucureşti, România: Institul European.

Dumitriu, C. (2003). *Management şi marketing ecologic. O abordare strategică*. Iaşi, România: Editura Tehnopress.

Duţu, M. (2010). *Dreptul mediului*. Bucureşti, România: Editura C.H. Beck.

Dyllick, T., & Hockerts, K. (2002). Beyond the business case for corporate sustainability. *Business Strategy and the Environment*, *11*(2), 130–141. doi:10.1002/bse.323

Elkington, J. (1997). *Cannibals with forks – Triple bottom line of 21st century business*. Stoney Creek, CT: New Society Publishers.

Epstein, M. (2008). *Making sustainability work: Best practices in managing and measuring corporate social, environmental, and economic impacts*. San Francisco: Greenleaf.

Esty, D. C., & Winston, A. S. (2006). *Green to Gold*. Yale University Press.

Frame, B., & Newton, B. (2007). Promoting sustainability through social marketing: Examples from New Zealand. *International Journal of Consumer Studies, 31*(6), 571–581. doi:10.1111/j.1470-6431.2007.00600.x

Fryxell, G. E., & Vryza, M. (1999). Managing environmental issues across multiple functions: An empirical study of corporate environmental departments and functional co-ordination. *Journal of Environmental Management, 55*(1), 39–56. doi:10.1006/jema.1998.0241

Galbreath, J. (2006). Corporate social responsibility strategy: Strategic options, global considerations. *Corporate Governance, 6*(2), 175–187. doi:10.1108/14720700610655178

Galbreath, J. (2009). Building corporate social responsibility into strategy. *European Business Review, 21*(2), 109–127. doi:10.1108/09555340910940123

GRI. (2011). *Sustainability Reporting Guidelines*. Amsterdam: Global Reporting Initiativ.

Grinnel, D. J., & Hunt, H. G. (2000). Development of an integrated course in accounting: Focus on environmental issues. *Issues in Accounting Education, 15*(1), 19–42. doi:10.2308/iace.2000.15.1.19

Husseini, A. (2001). *Industrial Environmental Standards and Their Implementation in the World*. National Environmental Management Seminar (EM 2001), Kuala Lumpur, Malaysia.

Iles, A. (2008). Shifting to green chemistry: The need for innovations in sustainability marketing. *Business Strategy and the Environment, 17*(8), 524–535. doi:10.1002/bse.547

Ionac, N., & Ciulache, S. (2005). *Ghid de cercetare environmentală*. Bucureşti, România: Editura Ars Docendi.

Ivan, O. R., Căpuşneanu, S., Topor, D. I., & Oprea, D. M. (2017). Environmental changes and their influences on performance of a company by using eco-dashboard. *Journal of Environmental Protection and Ecology, 18*(1), 399–409.

Kirchgeorg, M., & Winn, M. (2006). Sustainability marketing for the poorest of the poor. *Business Strategy and the Environment, 15*(3), 171–184. doi:10.1002/bse.523

Kurasaka, H. (1997). *Status and Progress of Environmental Assessment in Japan*. Paper presented at the Recent Developments with National and International Environmental Impact Assessment Processes, New Orleans, LA.

Lehmann, J. (1999). *Befunde empirischer Forschung zu Umweltbildung und Umweltbewusstsein (Findigs from empirical research on environmental education and environmental awareness)*. OpladenŞ Leske and Budrich.

Lippman, E. (2010). *Case study on sustainability: Accountants' role in developing a new business model*. Retrieved from http://papers.ssrn.com/sol3/papers.cfm?abstract_id=1662648

McDonald, S., & Oates, C. J. (2006). Sustainability: Consumer Perceptions and Marketing Strategies. *Special Issue: Sustainability Marketing, 15*(3), 157–170.

Montabon, F., Melnyk, S. A., Sroufe, R., & Calantone, R. J. (2000). ISO 14000: Assessing its perceived impact on corporate performance. *The Journal of Supply Chain Management, 36*(2), 4–16. doi:10.1111/j.1745-493X.2000.tb00073.x

Richardson, A. J., & Welker, M. (2001). Social disclosure, financial disclosure and the cost capital of equity capital. *Accounting, Organizations and Society, 26*(7), 597–616. doi:10.1016/S0361-3682(01)00025-3

Rojanschi, V., Grigore, F., & Ciomoș, V. (2008). *Ghidul evaluatorului și auditoriului de mediu*. București, România: Editura Economică.

Rubenstein, D.B. (1994). *Environmental Accounting for the sustainable corporation – Strategies and Techniques*. Quorum Books.

Santos, M., & Filho, W. (2005). An analysis of the relationship between sustainable development and the anthropsystem construct. *International Journal of Environment and Sustainable Development, 4*(1), 78–87. doi:10.1504/IJESD.2005.006775

Shrivastava, P., & Hart, S. (1992). Greening organizations. *Academy of Management Best Paper Proceedings, 52*(1), 185–189. doi:10.5465/ambpp.1992.17515480

Țuțuianu, O. (2006). *Evaluarea și raportarea performanței de mediu. Indicatori de mediu*. București, România: Editura AGIR.

Valentine, S. V. (2009). The Green Onion: A Corporate Environmental Strategy Framework. *Corporate Social Responsibility and Environmental Management*. doi:10.1002/csr.217

Valentine, S. V., & Savage, V. R. (2010) A Strategic Environmental Management Framework: Evaluating The Profitability of Being Green. In *Sustainability matters- Environmental Management in Asia*. Academic Press. Retrieved from http://www.worldscientific.com/worldscibooks/10.1142/7901#t=doi

Yakhou, M., & Dorweiler, V. P. (2004). Environmental accounting: An essential component of business strategy. *Business Strategy and the Environment, 13*(2), 65–77. doi:10.1002/bse.395

Yan, W., Chen, C., & Chang, W. (2009). An investigation into sustainable product constructualization using a design knowledge hierarchy and Hopfield network. *Computers & Industrial Engineering, 56*(4), 617–626. doi:10.1016/j.cie.2008.10.015

KEY TERMS AND DEFINITIONS

Environment: The environment in which a company operates, including air, water, soil, flora, fauna, man, and relationships between them.

Environmental Indicator: Information that quantifies the state of quality at a time.

Environmental Monitoring: Monitoring, forecasting, warning and intervention for the systematic assessment of environmental components in order to know the state of its quality in order to decide in accordance with reality.

Environmental Performance: Results that can be measured by a company's environmental management.

Green Reporting: (GR): Report on the financial situation of a company based on information on costs and environmental indicators.

Software Program: Algorithm in a source code, written in a certain programming language, used to accomplish a purpose.

Sustainability: The current economic and social development without damaging the natural environment.

Chapter 7
Information Technology in Higher Education Management:
Computer Program for Students' Evidence

Alexandru Lucian Manole
Artifex University, Romania

Cristian-Marian Barbu
Artifex University, Romania

Ileana-Sorina Rakos
University of Petrosani, Romania

Catalina Motofei
The Bucharest University of Economic Studies, Romania

ABSTRACT

Information technology instruments are a very important asset in the hands of every manager. The higher education institutions make no exception from these rules. The exposure to the modern technology and communication tools is very quickly assimilated by students, who acquire the skills to address and even master it and have high expectations from the university they study in to provide them with accurate and real-time information on their particular needs. The management of the university should have at its hand data on students, including personal data, data on academic achievements of any kind, housing in hostels, due and paid tuition fees, data on research, emphasizing both resources allocated and the results obtained, even providing links to online platforms and databases that index these results. The authors approach both operational databases and decision-oriented data warehouses and will aim to capitalize their own research interests in the field of IT to synthesize a set of solutions for this type of software.

DOI: 10.4018/978-1-5225-8455-1.ch007

INTRODUCTION

At the beginning of the millennium, education crosses a process of development to meet the current demands of society, a process marked by the phenomenon of globalization and the unprecedented development of information technologies. We are witnessing a series of economic, technological and cultural changes that come both in good parts and in more difficult parts, which imply the need for adaptation in everyday life.

The introduction of ICT into higher education management has quickly received an air of inevitability, with most decision-makers in the field of higher education strongly supporting this issue, as the field of education has over time suffered from the lack of tools specifically created to improve the management of education at all levels. Thus, the last decades have transformed information technology from a product intended for a small number of people, due to high acquisition costs and relatively large dimensions, into a ubiquitous instrument in the professional and personal lives of the citizens of the country.

The advantages of using ICT are not negligible, which has attracted the rapid spread of formal and non-formal educational activities. One of the most visible benefits that ICT brings is accessibility of information. Education has used the opportunity offered by ICT to rethink how to deliver educational content in a manner that improves managerial performance. The management of the beneficiaries of educational services can be improved by creating tools to track the progress achieved - both by each student and by the academic community.

BACKGROUND

Information technology in education, according to foreign specialists - is defined as a combination of processes and tools involved in addressing educational needs, using computers and other electronic resources and technologies (Ball & Levy, 2008; Roblyer, 2006), and information technology applications in education are called "educational technologies" (Bernard & Abrami, 2004; Kingsley, 2007). In education, an example of IT is the type of wireless connection used for online learning, management systems, Internet technologies, high-speed communication infrastructure, emerging technologies for visual presentation, access to course materials through Internet resources and artificial intelligence (Ball and Levy, 2008). A classification of educational technologies is made by them in three categories, as follows: (1) training, (2) productivity, (3) administration.

Nowadays, most academics use ICT Information Applications - for teaching purposes, such as tutorials, research, simulations, and other forms of instruction. The use of online learning systems by faculties is more and more frequent, Bernard and Abrami (2004) suggesting that the use of educational technologies has increased curricular learning between faculties and students that promote constructivism. In addition to the many benefits, the use of information technology also has some challenges (Schmidt, 2002), such as: "the effective replacement of traditional classrooms is one of the greatest challenges in placing the course on the internet."

The idea of the information-based society was launched in the US and became of great interest in Europe after writing a famous report of the European Union, named after its coordinator, famous today, today's controversial Martin Bangemann. UNESCO's Objective by UN Charter is the UNESCO's key objective of contributing to peace and security in the world by promoting collaboration among nations through education, science, culture and communication, promoting universal respect for justice and respecting the law, and the fundamental rights and freedoms of man, indifferent to the country, regardless of nation, sex, language or religion. The UNESCO Principles on ICT in Education can be summarized as follows:

- Old and new technologies must be used in a balanced way - equally important is on-line and interactive education;
- The achievement of international educational goals requires considerable investment in teachers/teachers training institutions;
- The demand for higher education cannot be satisfied in the less developed and developed countries, rather than in the presence of the virtual teaching-learning mode;
- Training needs cannot be met without virtual classes, virtual labs, etc.;
- Educational objectives cannot be met without gender equality. Whenever possible, the proposed indicators will address the need to measure the gap between women and men.

Information technology in the management of higher education is undoubtedly one of the most important requirements of any result of the actions taken. Any activity aimed at detecting problems, assessing their influence and finding solutions to solve them is for any higher education institution - the key to progress. The higher education institution can present an integrated picture of its missions when it is conceived as a „learning organization".

METHODOLOGY OF RESEARCH

We chose this direction for the study because we considered it useful to bring such research into consideration as there is a wide range of issues that can be debated, not just information technology discussions in the management of higher education institutions. Therefore, in order to pertinently draw a line of knowledge around them, we consider it appropriate to relate to the studies conducted to date with implications from the perspective of the chosen research theme. The approach of the study is thus one of the baseline analysis of the literature, focusing on determining the direction of research approached and the findings of the studies.

At the same time, this chapter also aims at conducting an empirical study on the particularities of the different types of evidence regarding the students, the disciplines in the program, the teachers and the marks obtained after the evaluation.

The *proposed methodology* for carrying out the study, as well as for achieving the objectives, is based on the *preliminary documentation* for understanding the theoretical aspects of information systems and information technology, as well as the understanding of the management of higher education institutions. The theoretical research describes and analyses the current state of knowledge, making contributions in completing it and clarifying certain aspects necessary for subsequent application. The starting point of the research is the theoretical documentation by going through the literature specific to the field, which allows the formulation of opinions at the end of the chapter.

The theoretical approach is complemented by a series of informational applications on the application of information technology in the management of higher education institutions.

THE INFORMATION MANAGEMENT SYSTEM OF THE UNIVERSITY

The information system of the university management represents all the information, information flows, procedures and means of information processing meant to contribute to the achievement of the university objectives. Therefore, it is made up of a multitude of related elements, such as: data and information, information flows, procedures and means of handling information. The university information system can contribute to the achievement of the objectives of higher education only in the conditions in which the specific functions of the university are fulfilled. The information system as a direct result of IT progress is the most dynamic and flexible component of the management system. The educational process is constantly under the influence of changes in society, which must be elastic and receptive to technical and technological novelties and integrate on a large scale of modern information technologies.

University managers often claim that manual data processing invokes costs, major delays and the failure to meet deadlines. In this case, a well-developed information system would intervene, able to collect very large volumes of information in short time and to highlight the anomalies discovered in the course of time. Thus, the role of university management is not to cumulate and process whole volumes of data, but to see exactly what consequences and what impact certain decisions are taking in the process. "It may be said that the role of the information system of the university management can be expressed through the advantages it assures in the dynamics of the managerial activity", as Professor Petrescu I. points out in his work „University management treaty" (Petrescu, 2003).

Universities have the obligation, according to the law of education, to keep records of students and to keep track of what happens to them after graduation, and those who do not produce what the market demands will be withdrawn from their funding. The classification of universities and the hierarchy of the study programs will allow for funding to be made on a performance-by-job basis, and the capacity of a university to produce graduates for the labor market will lead to resource concentration where the quality is. This is done in the major universities of the world, with the direct result of a very clear set of development strategies that the university pursues. A student will not choose a university; he will not go to a specialization that will not later bring him the opportunity to find a job.

Entry Document: Students' Records

Documents for the record of the students' professional activity are:

1. The Registration Form
2. The Admissions List
3. The Admissions Book
4. The Matriculation Register
5. The Student Gradebook
6. The Examination Gradebook
   a. The Examination Gradebook
   b. The Equivalent discipline Gradebook
7. The Grades Centralizer
8. The Final Examination Gradebook (Licence/Bachelor's degree, Dissertation)
9. The Graduation Certificate

The Registration Form

It is the standardized document, proposed by the faculties, approved by the Board of Directors, which contains the candidate's personal data and is filled in by the candidates enrolling in the admission contest or by the students transferred from other faculties/university centers, re-enrolled and foreign students. The application form is used to enter the personal data of students enrolled in the school management program database. The admissions lists are verified and signed by the Central Admissions Commission Responsible at the University.

The admission lists can be:

- Lists of candidates enrolled in the study programs/specializations;
- Lists of admitted/rejected candidates;
- Lists of candidates in descending order of the grades;
- Lists of registered candidates, on faculty/specializations. These documents form the basis of the registration decision of the candidates admitted to the admission exam and registered in the I year and have a permanent retention term.

The Admission Books

These are documents drawn up by the secretariats of the faculties containing the first and last name of the candidates in alphabetical order and the grades they have obtained in the competition tests. The gradebooks are signed by members of the candidates' examination committee. The gradebooks used, stamps and serial numbers are kept in the archive.

The Matriculation Register

The document contains, for each matriculation number, all the disciplines in the educational curriculum of the promotion with the number of credits and hours related to each discipline. The document is filled in by the secretary of the faculty, immediately after the student's enrolment, with their identity information. The surname(s), the initial of the father (the mother, if the father is unknown) and the first name of the holder enrolling in the matriculation register and the study papers are those on the birth certificate and are capitalized, unique, and valid for the entire study period. If, at the time of enrolment or during the period of study, a student submits a request for completion of the name, accompanied by certified copies of the official documents giving the new name - in relation to the name on the birth certificate, based on the head of the institution's approval for the request, shall proceed to the completion required by writing in parentheses after the last first name in the Register of Matriculation.

At the end of the academic year, for the student, the faculty secretary completes the columns with the marks. In the case of repetition, interruption of studies, etc., the unsustainable years are mentioned in the observations. After completing the final examination, the secretary enrols in the matriculation register the result obtained on the exam. The matriculation register is filled in with no blanking. Incorrect or filled empty tabs are cancelled. Entries on each tab of the Register must be signed by the faculty secretary, dean and stamped. The matriculation register is kept permanently in the archive, under full security.

The Student Gradebook

The document is filled in with the student's identity data by the secretary of the faculty and signed by the dean. At the beginning of each academic year the student gradebook is signed by the secretariat. Teachers will fill in the student gradebook, immediately after examination, with the exam grade.

The student gradebook is the only student's legitimate document and will be permanently carried by the student. Issuing a duplicate for the student gradebook implies the public announcement (newspaper) of the cancellation of the first gradebook. Upon expelling, retreat or transfer, the student gradebook is retained at the secretariat. The gradebooks are documents that include students' grades during the school year. These gradebooks can be:

The Examination Gradebook

The document is automatically generated by the school management program under the management of faculty secretariats, by years of study, study programs/specializations, educational subjects and forms of verification. The examination gradebook is sent in the exams to the teaching staff responsible for examining the students. The examiner enters the grade in the examination gradebook and in the student gradebook, confirmed by his signature. Upon completion of the exam, the examination gradebook is handed over to the secretariat within 24 hours to transcribe the grades into the centralized results of the students in the examination sessions (where applicable) and electronically, in the school management program.

The Equivalent Discipline Gradebook

The document is drawn up by the secretariat of the faculty for any student in one of the following situations: repeat, re-enrolled, transferred, admitted to further education, second faculty and includes the equivalent disciplines established by the Faculty Council for alignment with the curriculum of the series in which it is enrolled. The discipline holder enters the grade in the gradebook, confirmed by his signature. Upon completion of the exam, the gradebook is handed over to the secretariat within 24 hours to transcribe the grades into the centralized results of the students in the examination sessions (where applicable) and electronically in the school management program.

All these types of gradebooks are archived on study/specialization programs, years of study and educational forms, with a permanent retention term, in full security.

The Gradebook Centralizer

The gradebook centralizer is the document centralizing the results obtained by each student, following exams in a university year. The centralizer is based on study programs/specializations, years of study, comprising students in the alphabetical order. It is a working document, optional, for the secretariat, which is kept permanently alongside the Matriculation Register.

The Final Examination Gradebook

These documents are drawn up on study programs/specializations, filled in by the secretary of the faculty with the data on the identity of the graduates enrolled in the examination and sent to the commission for the final examination. The grades given by the committee shall be entered in these gradebooks, which shall be signed by the members of the examination board. The gradebooks are handed over to the college secretary and the results obtained are transcribed in the matriculation register, electronically in the school management program and the diploma awarded to the graduate. These documents are archived with a permanent term.

The Graduation Certificate

It is the document drawn up by the secretariat of the faculty, which is issued to the graduates who have passed or not the examination of completing the studies. The graduation certificate for graduates who passed the final examination exam includes the graduate's personal data, data on the study program/specialization completed and the results of the study completion exam. For graduates who have not passed the final examination, the certificate will include the graduate's personal data, details of the study/specialization program completed and specified: "without a study completion exam". This document is valid for 12 months. The student and master students' information system is composed of client server applications, applications that allow the centralized management of personal, but also financial, schooling data. The modules of the system include secretarial, administrator, caseries, accounting, web.

The Department of IT Services and Support (DSSIT) of a university manages the entire hardware and software IT infrastructure and provides specialized IT support to legitimate users of this infrastructure. The existing hardware and software IT infrastructure at faculty and department level enables high level and effective teaching, research and administrative work, in line with the tasks and objectives set by the management of the higher education institution. The IT platform integrated with universities offers sets of IT services that address well-defined user categories: students, teachers, researchers, collaborators, administrative and public staff.

The computer network architecture is designed to provide users with quality IT services regardless of the access point. DSSIT's tasks and responsibilities are defined according to the specificity of the activity, by harmonizing with the regulations and norms that stipulate the operating framework and the strategic plan of the respective institution. IT services are provided in a transparent way to end-users, so their management and coordination is based on analyzing and integrating the workflows of all departments.

IT services are provided to all departments, coordination of DSSIT activities takes into account the IT infrastructure dimension, flow management/task management, requirements management, real time IT resource planning and allocation in accordance with existing requirements. The IT Service and Support Department (DSSIT) is headed by a hierarchically and functional subordinate of the rector. The strategic decisions of DSSIT are analyzed by the DSSIT director together with the rector and communicated to DSSIT members.

The DSSIT Director supervises and supervises the DSSIT activities, and has meetings with the Rector at least every three months. The responsibilities and tasks of the DSSIT, as well as the procedures for the activity carried out within the DSSIT, are communicated to the DSSIT members.

The responsibilities and tasks of the DSSIT are as follows:

- Designing, managing and monitoring network infrastructure;
- Monitoring and maintenance of hardware equipment (desktop systems, server systems, active and passive network equipment);
- Monitoring and maintaining software applications that are approved and validated by dssit, overseeing the legality of using software applications;
- Defining, designing, deploying, managing and monitoring it services (saas, paas, iaas) provided by the it infrastructure to its users, including it service availability management, it resource management, it service continuity management, it service security management (it services set is reassessed annually);
- Debugging and removing hardware and software malfunctions of it services to the extent that tools and resources are available to manage these actions;
- Defining the levels of importance of IT services in the context of ensuring their continuity and competitive allocation of existing and functional IT resources;
- Saving and managing critical data in digital format in accordance with their established leadership (database backup) levels;
- Providing specialist support to legitimate it infrastructure users (employees, students, collaborators);
- Ensuring the quality and availability of it services in line with existing and functional hardware and software resources;
- Continuous auditing and monitoring of it security and compliance with all compliance standards as set out in all security-specific regulations;
- Compilation of individual sheets for each computerized system identified by the inventory number, specifying the software applications installed;
- Defining, validating and enforcing digital identity management of legitimate it users;
- Defining user types, roles associated with user types and credentials of access to hardware and software it resources;
- Allocating to each user, individually depending on the type and role, the set of credentials on authentication, authorization and access to hardware and software IT resources;
- Tracking compliance with the Software Use Regulations (Licensing Laws and User Rights for Users to Access IT Software Resources), the Rules of Use and Access to Computing Systems and the Computer Network (rights set by users for accessing hardware IT resources and computer network), the Guidelines for Ethical Standards on the Use of IT Technologies, the IT Security Policy (including the Digital Personal Data Processing Policy) by all legitimate users;
- Validation and tracking of hardware and software IT purchases;
- Formulating and validating the proposals and specifications sets passed to management on the improvement of the entire hardware and software IT infrastructure;
- Formulating, validating and submitting the responsibilities/tasks of DSSIT to the management;
- Formulating, validating and submitting the operational procedures for the DSSIT (the DSSIT operational procedures are reassessed annually), to the operational management;
- Formulating, validating and submitting all Regulations defining the hardware and software IT infrastructure management, the Guidelines for the use of IT Technologies and the IT Security Policy, to the management;
- Formulating, validating and submitting the DSSIT payrolls and the corresponding job descriptions, to the management;

- Formulating, validating and submitting the requirements and measures to enable the DSSIT members to work in good working order, to the management;
- Formulating and reporting to the management of all non-compliances arising in the operation of hardware and software IT infrastructure, non-compliance by legitimate users of the Software Usage Regulations (Licensing Law and User Rights for Access to IT Software Resources), access to computer systems and the computer network (user rights for access to IT hardware and computer network resources), the Guidelines for the Use of IT Technologies, the IT Security Policy;
- Formulating and reporting to the management of all issues that impede and/or restrict the proper functioning of the DSSIT;
- Implementation and monitoring of sanctions and constraints and limitations on the use of hardware and software resources imposed by management on users who do not comply with the Hardware and Software IT Infrastructure Use Regulations, the Guidelines on Ethics for the Use of IT Technologies and the IT Security Policy;
- Creating specific training sessions for IT infrastructure users, as needed.

In order to launch the program, the desktop application icon that includes the components used for student and master management is accessed. Because access to the program is secure, the user must enter a user account and password in the window, these data being provided by the IT service to each user. In the application, for any operation, navigation is done with mouse help by clicking on the tab displayed in the interface. For the registration of students and master students, the "Entries" tab is selected and operations can be performed here: entry to the admission exam for students and master students, operations related to the enrollment of students and master students in the higher year, enrollment of students in a supplementary year, enrollment of repeat students, enrollment of newly transferred students, or re-enrolled students.

Also, the students are enrolled in a single register, a database with all the information related to their academic activity and the diplomas obtained, whether they have been enrolled in state or private faculties, which prevents forgery. Besides, part of the information in this database, i.e. those related to the graduation diploma, will be accessible to the general public and, implicitly, to the employers. In this way, all students from Romania, from the time of enrollment to graduation to graduation, are kept.

The matriculation in the first year, undergraduate/master's degree studies is done by the rector, only by decision, following the admission exam. Based on the Matriculation Decision, each student/master student is enrolled in the register, under the unique number, valid for the entire period of the faculty. The enrollment of the student to the budget/fee, bachelor's/master's degree studies, is only made after signing of the schooling contract with the rector of the university, as the state empowered person. The tuition agreement specifies the reciprocal rights and obligations, according to the rules in force. The student can enter into a contract with an economic agent - individual, legal person, etc. to receive material support during the studies. The student's registration in the matriculation register is based on the documents from the personal file which must include:

- The application form for the first year of study;
- The baccalaureate diploma or equivalent, in original or legalized copy. If a student submits a baccalaureate diploma in a legalized copy, he/she will automatically enroll in toll-paid education;
- The birth certificate in legalized copy;

- The bachelor's/master's degree or equivalent, graduation supplementary sheet, analytical curriculum, for those who follow a second specialization, etc.;
- A medical certificate indicating that he/she can frequent collectivities;
- A copy of the i.c.;
- The schooling contract.

As a rule, papers in the original are not issued during the studies. Exceptionally, with the Dean's approval, for a maximum of 48 hours, they can be released to solve personal problems. Otherwise, students receive certified college copies after their original studies. After joining the faculty, the Dean releases each student the following nominee documents:

- The student gradebook;
- The student card;
- The student tickets card.

The student gradebook includes all grades obtained during the evaluation, including those not promoted. Presenting the student card, and the IC, as appropriate, to the examiner is mandatory. The student card - annually stamped - serves to obtain the facilities granted under the law. The tickets card is personal, non-transferable and serves only for the purpose for which it was issued. No corrections are allowed in the student's/master student's documents. In case the student loses the nominal documents, it is issued duplicate after the announcement in the press of the loss and payment of the fees set by the Senate. In case of retirement from the college, transfer etc., the student is obliged to return the nominal documents.

The student's enrollment to the undergraduate (bachelor)/master's degree in all forms of education in Year II and the following is done by the Dean in the first decade of October, but not later than October 15, based on the results obtained by the student and the number of the faculty credits and known by the student by contract.

The budgeted/scholarship student/CPNV declared repeat student, will be enrolled, upon request, under the fee scheme, at the amount of the year of study in which he/she is to be enrolled. Additional school duties are set by the Faculty Council. Starting from Romania's accession to the European Union, the citizens of the EU Member States, the European Economic Area and the Swiss Confederation have access to all forms and levels of education under the same conditions as those provided for by law for Romanian citizens, for the tuition fees. The enrollment file of foreign citizens to undergraduate/master's degree studies will necessarily include the following documents:

- The baccalaureate diploma or equivalent, in original and certified translation in Romanian or in an international language;
- For enrolling in master's degree studies: the graduation diploma of a long-term higher education institution and the matricol or diploma supplement, in original and certified translation in Romanian or in an international language;
- The graduation certificate of the preparatory year, certificate of linguistic competence or, as the case may be, educational documents certifying the completion of at least 4 years of study at a school with teaching in Romanian (if the undergraduate/master's degree studies are conducted in Romanian language);
- The birth certificate in legalized translation in Romanian;

- The passport in legalized copy;
- The written approval of the Ministry of Education, Research and Innovation - Directorate for International Relations.

During the schooling period the student file is filled in with:

- The documents required for scholarships;
- Personal requests for professional activity: interruptions, delays, motivations, etc.;
- Documents attesting studies in other universities in the country and abroad, etc.;
- Other personal documents.

In this section, the authors propose a model for a software solution dedicated to the management of students' results at examinations and verifications, at the end of each session. The application's data structure, presented below, can be integrated into a wider database, dedicated to the management of the entire activity of the university.

Also, the contents of each data segment presented (students, disciplines, study programs, teachers etc.) can be expanded to provide support for additional informational needs. The database is loaded with a set of test data (no personal data are used in the application), used only to demonstrate the functionalities and to argument its usability with similar, real data. Not in the last row, the data structure can be uploaded in another compatible RDBMS, to be integrated in a client-server or n-tier application.

The activity is managed on the basis of academic years. Each academic year must be explicitly defined as a record in the corresponding table.

The process of enrollment collects the data solicited by regulations, and makes them compatible with the requirements of the National Students' Register. A sample form used for data collection is presented in the Figure 1.

Figure 1. Form interface, enrollment of students
Source: Authors' work, as presented by ACCESS

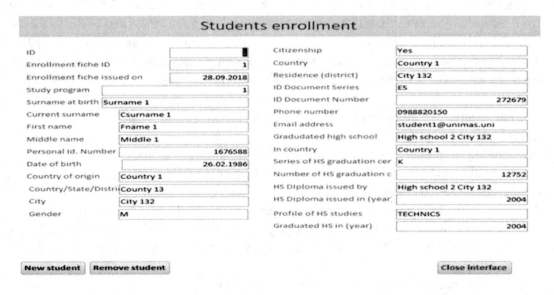

This form can also be used to manage, in the future, following enrollment, the data from students' personal files, as is necessary. Following enrollment, students must be assigned to groups and series (studies formation). This can be done automatically, by enforcing an algorithm which ensures strict alphabetical order and includes batches of students in each group, provided the maximum number of students allowed by the current educational quality standards. The interface that allows the distribution of students for the first year has the structure presented in Figure 2.

The interface reads the number of students per group/series and automatically generates the records in the tables that hold the evidence of students' repartition on groups and series. A part of the code used for this purpose is presented in Figure 3.

The management of teachers involves a form gathering the data about teachers. It allows the run of create, read, update and delete data, this is presented in Figure 4.

The data structure behind the form involves three separate tables:

- *Teachers*, which provides the data for the main form;
- *Degrees*, which acts as a nomenclator for teaching degrees, as specified by the national law;
- *Teach_degrees*, which holds the evidence of career track for each teacher, specifying each degree awarded and the date of award.

Figure 2. Form design, distribution of students per student formation
Source: Authors' work, as presented by ACCESS

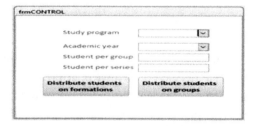

Figure 3. Sample of code, distribution of students per student formation
Source: Authors' work, as presented by ACCESS

```
Option Compare Database
Dim ng As Integer 'number of groups

Private Sub Command15_Click()
Dim j As Integer 'counter variable
Dim a As Integer 'counter variable
Dim b As Integer 'counter variable
Dim strsql As String 'sql string to be used to add the groups
a = 1
b = 30
For i = 1 To ng
For j = a To b
strsql = "insert into student_groups values(" & j & "," & 100 + i & ")"
DoCmd.RunSQL strsql
Next
a = a + 30
b = b + 30
Next
End Sub

Private Sub Command3_Click()
Dim i As Integer      'counter variable
Dim n As Integer      'number of students
Dim spg As Integer    'maximum number of students per group
Dim ns As Integer     'number of series
Dim sps As Integer    'maximum number of students per series
Dim strsql As String 'sql string to be used to add the series
Dim intsp As Integer    'study program ID
Dim stryear As String   'academic year
Dim strec As String
Dim sno As Integer
Dim id As Integer
Dim rext As Recordset
Dim db As Database
Set db = CurrentDb()
stryear = Combo7.Value
strec = "students_years"
Set rext = db.OpenRecordset(strec)
n = rext.RecordCount
```

Figure 4. Form for managing teacher data
Source: Authors' work, as presented by ACCESS

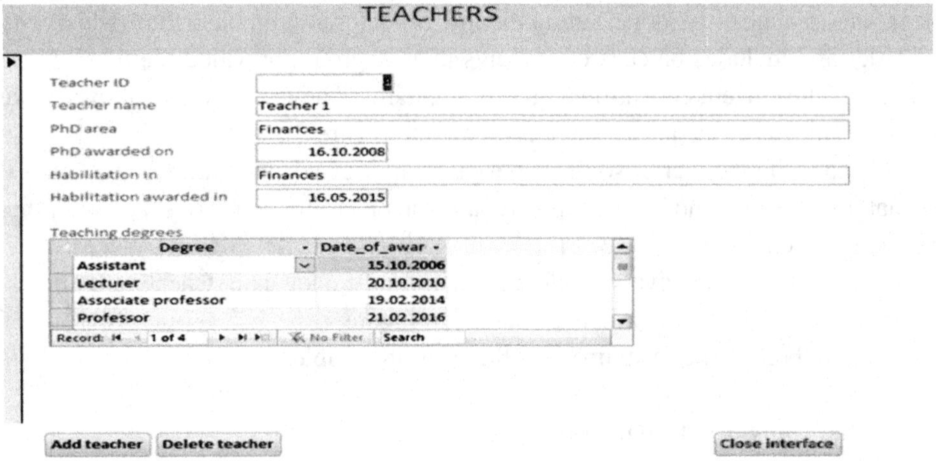

To present the evolution of the teacher's career, a subform is used, based on the third table specified in the above list.

As the evidence of students, the dataset on teacher and the segments regarding the organization of the academic year, by series and groups were solved, the following function of the application will solve the assignment of teachers by disciplines.

The teaching load of each person is configured in compliance with its degree and depending on the existence of habilitation. The director of the department assigns the disciplines, for each teacher, upon consultation with each member of the department and within the legal rules and quality standards.

For this purpose, the authors have defined a form, which presents itself as a continuous form (a presentation closer to the spreadsheet view than the traditional columnar interface, which has default value set for the present academic year and fields designed to accommodate all necessary values for the source table.

The layout of the form is presented, as form view, in Figure 5.

The form includes a functionality that allows for the analysis of unassigned activities (considering that all series shall have the all disciplines in the learning plan assigned to them). This functionality is achieved by using two queries, in cascade. The structure of the first query is presented in the Figure 6.

Figure 5. Form for assigning courses
Source: Authors' work, as presented by ACCESS

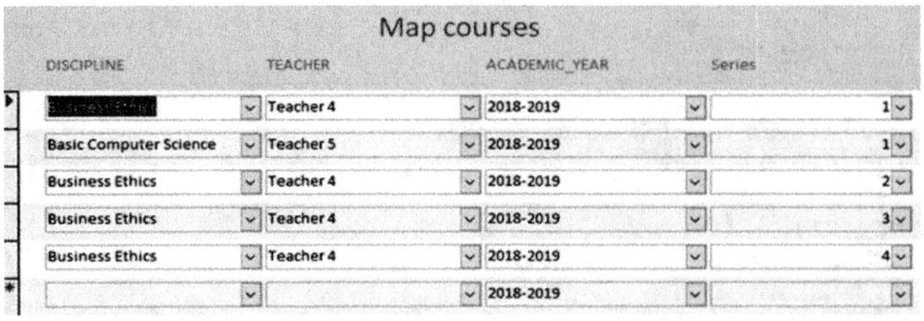

Figure 6. Query design for retrieving the courses in the educational offer
Source: Authors' work, as presented by ACCESS

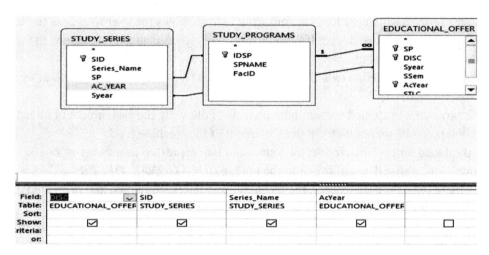

The results of the query are presented, in section, in the Figure 7.

The second query, which actually provides the data necessary to the user, has the structure presented in the Figure 8.

As it can be seen from the structure of the two queries, the attempt to merge them in a single one should lead to an error message about ambiguous outer joins (these outer joins are needed to identify the

Figure 7. Query results for retrieving the courses in the educational offer
Source: Authors' work, as presented by ACCESS

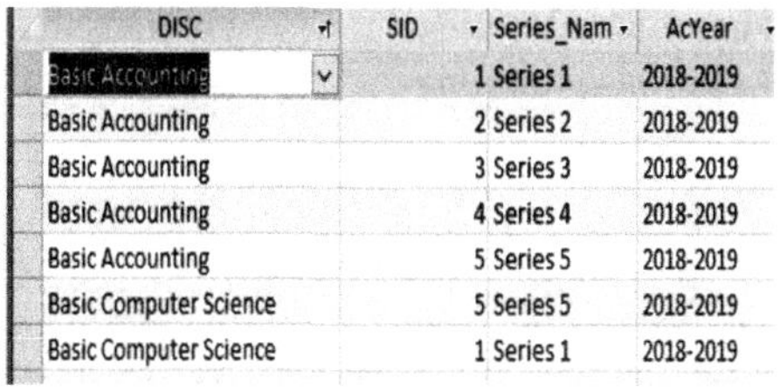

DISC	SID	Series_Nam	AcYear
Basic Accounting	1	Series 1	2018-2019
Basic Accounting	2	Series 2	2018-2019
Basic Accounting	3	Series 3	2018-2019
Basic Accounting	4	Series 4	2018-2019
Basic Accounting	5	Series 5	2018-2019
Basic Computer Science	5	Series 5	2018-2019
Basic Computer Science	1	Series 1	2018-2019

Figure 8. Query structure for retrieving the unassigned courses in the mapping process
Source: Authors' work, as presented by ACCESS

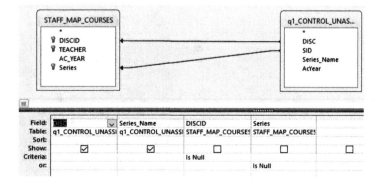

data missing from the mapping table, on the left side of the figure above, with the arrowheads pointing towards it.

In the footer of the assignment form, a command button allows the user to access the list of unassigned activities. The query updates itself following each new record added or changed in the form and, subsequently, in the source table.

This instrument is supposed to ease the work of users, and its results are presented, in section, in the Figure 9.

The same procedure is applied for seminars and labs. Following the assignment of all activities, the teaching activities can be measured from the viewpoint of the teaching load.

The standard load for each discipline, by course and lab, expressed as number of hours, is specified in the learning plan, whose data are stored in the table *EDUCATIONAL_OFFER*.

Based on those data, for each teacher, the teaching load can be computed and presented in a centralized report. The query in the Figure 10 extracts the teaching load per courses.

Query produces the following results (in section), for teacher 4. The three links between the source objects prevent creation of unrelated records, based on the Cartesian product operation. To ensure proper saving of data, the data are appended to a temporary table, as the query in the figure above is an append

Figure 9. Query results for retrieving the unassigned courses in the mapping process
Source: Authors' work, as presented by ACCESS

DISC	Series_Name
Mathematics	Series 1
Mathematics	Series 2
Mathematics	Series 3
Mathematics	Series 4
Mathematics	Series 5
Financial accounting	Series 1
Financial accounting	Series 2

Figure 10. Query design for teaching loads per courses
Source: Authors' work, as presented by ACCESS

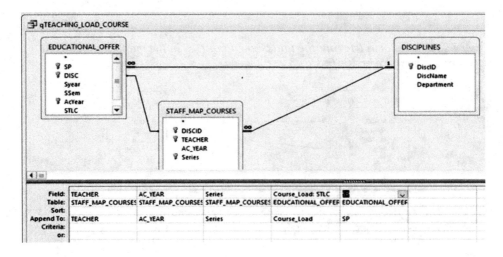

query. All teaching loads will be stored in the temporary table for the academic year, allowing for the storage of data for more academic years, as in Figure 11.

The teaching load for seminars is determined in the same manner. All data are also uploaded in the auxiliary table, on the basis of reports on the teacher's load are designed for that academic year. The structure of the query designed to solve this issue is presented in the Figure 12.

A composite primary key prevents duplicate records from being entered into this table.

The centralized situation per teacher can be presented in a report, which allows best graphical presentation of data and summarizing teaching load per course and seminar, shown in Figure 13.

Figure 11. Query results for teaching loads per courses
Source: Authors' work, as presented by ACCESS

TEACHER	AC_YEAR	Series	Standard te	SP
Teacher 4	2018-2019	1	2 Financial management
Teacher 4	2018-2019	2	2 Financial management
Teacher 4	2018-2019	3	2 Financial management
Teacher 4	2018-2019	4	2 Financial management
Teacher 4	2018-2019	5	2 Financial management

Figure 12. Query design for teaching loads per seminars/laboratories
Source: Authors' work, as presented by ACCESS

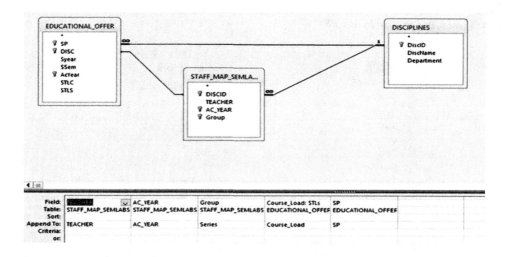

Figure 13. Report for teaching loads per academic year
Source: Authors' work, as presented by ACCESS

ACTIVITY ASSIGNMENT			
ACADEMIC YEAR	TEACHER	Study formation Load	STUDY PROGRAM
2018-2019			
	Teacher 4		
		107	1 Financial management
		101	1 Financial management
		5	2 Financial management
		4	2 Financial management
		3	2 Financial management
		2	2 Financial management
		1	2 Financial management
		Total load	12

The next function developed for the application is the management of students' results, which is actually the purpose of this section. Based on the existing tables, an auxiliary table is used, the catalogue table, which is designed initially and then populated with actual catalogues, loaded with students' grades. Regardless the organization of the exams, the catalogues are designed for each group of students. Scheduling the exams is a prerequisite task for catalogue operation. In this respect, the authors have designed an auxiliary table, whose structure is presented in the Figure 14.

The composite primary key prevents duplicate records from being inputted into the table, with a complex combination of values that fits the needs of faculty staff. Also, the table is correlated with the other tables from which the external keys that form its primary key come from. These considerations provide a reliable approach towards ensuring data integrity for this segment of the database.

The table can be loaded with the help of an append query, under the control of a dedicated from. On the form, the users specify the session for which exams are to be programmed, as seen in the figure below. A scheduling algorithm will consider the three situations:

- Winter session, for the exams due to be taken for the 1st semester;
- Summer session, for the disciplines belonging to the second semester;
- Re-exams or special session for exams failed by some students, all disciplines will be scheduled for examination within these two sessions. These aspects are shown in Figure 15.

Figure 14. Table design for scheduling the exams, for each semester
Source: Authors' work, as presented by ACCESS

	Field Name	Data Type
	EX_ID	AutoNumber
♀	SPNAME	Text
♀	AcYear	Text
♀	Syear	Number
♀	SSem	Text
♀	disc	Number
♀	Group	Number
♀	Session	Text
	Exam_date	Date/Time
	Room	Text

Figure 15. Control scheduling the exams, for each session
Source: Authors' work, as presented by ACCESS

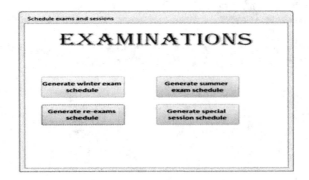

Once the table was loaded with data, the dedicated form can be accessed in order for the calendar assignment and room allocation to be inputted as in the example in Figure 16.

After all the data have been entered, the schedule can be displayed for the information of students and all people interested. The name of the teacher for each discipline can be added to the data taken from the scheduling per-se, and included in the official information on the session schedule.

Following the generation of the exam schedule, the catalogue can be predefined for each group, this requires an auxiliary table in which the teacher has the opportunity to input the grade for each student as shown in the Figure 17.

Figure 16. Form for entering data for exams, for one session
Source: Authors' work, as presented by ACCESS

EXAMINATION SCHEDULE

EXAM_ID	Study year	Semester	Discipline	Group	Date	Room
	Academic year:	2018-2019	STUDY PROGRAM			
	Session		Financial management			
	1	1st Semester	Business Ethics	114		
707	1	1st Semester	Business Ethics	115		
708	1	1st Semester	Business Ethics	116		
709	1	1st Semester	Business Ethics	117		
710	1	1st Semester	Business Ethics	118		
711	1	1st Semester	Business Ethics	119		

Figure 17. Query design for generating catalogue data
Source: Authors' work, as presented by ACCESS

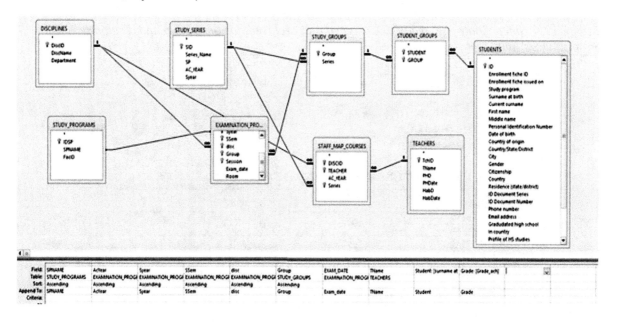

The next step involves the input of data regarding the grades, by the teachers. The teacher will be granted access only to the exams he/she supervises, and the grades can be inputted between 1 and 10, or 0 for absent students, as shown in the Figure 18.

The completed catalogue can be presented as a report, and can be printed for each group and discipline through a control form that includes parameters for the two fields. Also, the printed catalogue can be signed and archived. The structure of the catalogue report is presented in the Figure 19.

Based on the grades, the students' average grads can be computed. Also, the failed exams, either due to low score or absence can be emphasized. The students can be granted access to their own results, via a fiche that displays their scholar achievements, in terms of grades. Securing the application means to assign user accounts, passwords and rights proper to each segment of data. Also, an excellent method of

Figure 18. Form for entering data for electronic catalogue, for one session
Source: Authors' work, as presented by ACCESS

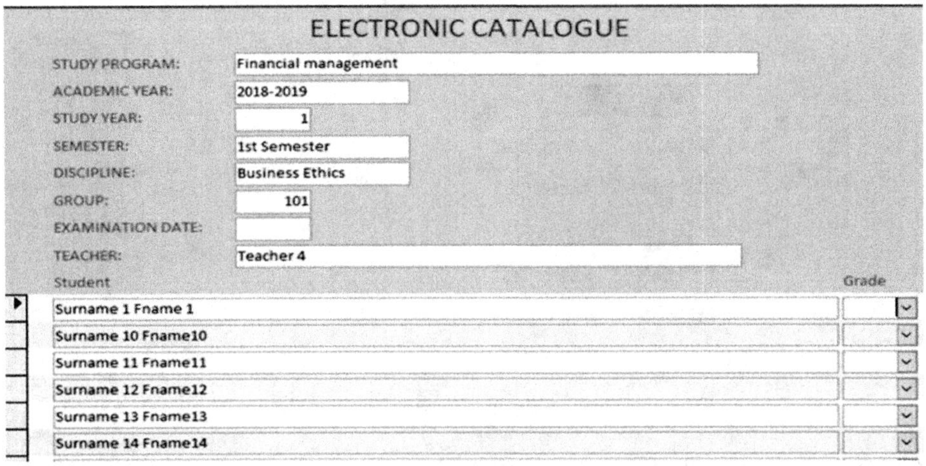

ELECTRONIC CATALOGUE

STUDY PROGRAM:	Financial management
ACADEMIC YEAR:	2018-2019
STUDY YEAR:	1
SEMESTER:	1st Semester
DISCIPLINE:	Business Ethics
GROUP:	101
EXAMINATION DATE:	
TEACHER:	Teacher 4

Student	Grade
Surname 1 Fname 1	
Surname 10 Fname10	
Surname 11 Fname11	
Surname 12 Fname12	
Surname 13 Fname13	
Surname 14 Fname14	

Figure 19. Printed catalogue, ready to be signed and archived, for one group and discipline
Source: Authors' work, as presented by ACCESS

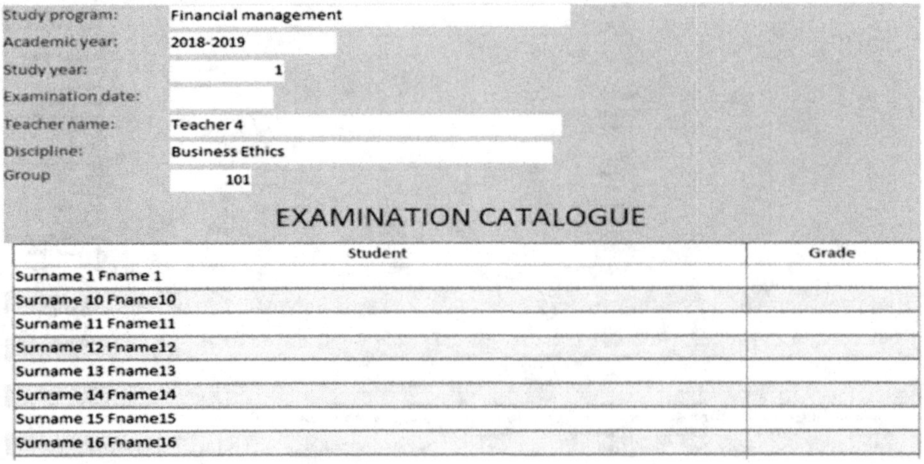

Study program:	Financial management
Academic year:	2018-2019
Study year:	1
Examination date:	
Teacher name:	Teacher 4
Discipline:	Business Ethics
Group	101

EXAMINATION CATALOGUE

Student	Grade
Surname 1 Fname 1	
Surname 10 Fname10	
Surname 11 Fname11	
Surname 12 Fname12	
Surname 13 Fname13	
Surname 14 Fname14	
Surname 15 Fname15	
Surname 16 Fname16	

ensuring the confidentiality of data involves the distribution and further configuration of the interfaces according to users' rights. So, if users do not have access to the instruments that manipulate data, they cannot access the respective data (through the application).

The Evidence of the Disciplines: The Curriculum

The curriculum includes *four defining components*:

1. The *temporal* component, which represents the way of planning the training process in time (week, semester, year, cycle);
2. The *formative* component, which represents the way of distribution for content units (course unit, course packages, modules);
3. The *accumulation* component, which reflects the modalities of allocating study credits;
4. The *evaluation* component, which represents the modalities of the current and final assessment of the learning outcomes and competences obtained by the student at the course unit/module.

The curricula for the *first cycle - undergraduate*, are developed by specialties, according to the *Nomenclature of Vocational Training and Specialties*. The procedure for the elaboration, updating and approval of the curricula is applied within the framework of the management of each faculty. The procedure aims at describing the process of elaborating, approving and updating the curricula of bachelor/undergraduate and master study programs in all forms of education. Selection of the disciplines to be included in each study cycle, their character (compulsory, optional, facultative, fundamental, specialty and complementary), the number of hours allocated for courses, seminars, practical papers, number of credits foreseen for each discipline, as well as the form of verification of the knowledge and skills acquired by students/master students/trainees is achieved through the curricula, in accordance with the legal provisions in force and ARACIS standards.

The curricula are developed in accordance with the following requirements:

1. Clear definition and precise delineation of the professional and transversal competences in the fields of the Bachelor's degree studies in correlation with the corresponding competences of the master studies;
2. Ensuring compatibility with study plans and programs organized by other universities at national and European level, according to ARACIS standards in terms of:
    a. Study disciplines, by consulting the discipline nomenclature;
    b. The duration of study semesters;
    c. Weekly average of classes: 20-28 hours/week
    d. The structure of the didactic activity classes, according to the content of the study disciplines (fundamental disciplines, specialized disciplines, complementary disciplines) specific to each fundamental field of study;
    e. The structure of the didactic activity classes, according to the discipline required by the provision of training (compulsory subjects, optional subjects, facultative subjects) specific to each scientific field;
3. Ensuring a logical succession of disciplines in the curriculum. A discipline scans one semester and ends with the assessment of knowledge.

4.   The number of credits allocated to compulsory courses and optional courses for each semester is 30, plus, as the case may be, the additional credits allocated to facultative subjects.

The curricula are elaborated on a bachelor's and master's degree program by the Dean of the faculty after consultation with the program department. The plan is proposed by the Dean to the faculty council for its approval. Upon endorsement by the Faculty Council, the curriculum is subject to Senate approval. Upon approval by the Senate of the University, the curricula of each study cycle (license/master) cannot be modified throughout their duration. The curricula for bachelor/master study programs evaluated by ARACIS during a university year cannot be changed from the next academic year.

The elaborated curricula will be signed by the Dean of the Faculty and the Rector and approved by the President of the Senate and the Chairman of the Board of Directors. The heads of departments and faculties are responsible for the completion and updating of the curricula within the time limit set by the Senate of the University, according to the provisions of the present procedure. All the related information, study programs, teachers, etc. are found in the Application for the Education Plan.

The Teachers' Records: The Payrolls/the List of the Department Members

The procedure for the establishment of the teaching staff positions in the university departments is applied by the management of each department. The payroll is the legal document on the basis of which the monthly salary of each member of the teaching and research staff is made.

The Description of the Payroll

The payrolls are drawn up within each department by its director, on the basis of the classes orders received from the deans of the faculties and approved by the Rector, as well as the qualifications obtained as a result of the annual multicriterial evaluation of the teaching staff. According to art. 286 paragraph 1 of the National Education Law no. 1/2011, amended and supplemented, the payrolls are drawn up annually, at least 15 days before the beginning of the academic year and cannot be changed during the academic year.

In the departmental functions of the departments, the didactic activities corresponding to the curricula of the bachelor's and master's degree programs, the full frequency and reduced frequency education form, as well as the activities provided by article 287 paragraph 2 of the National Education Law no.1/2011, amended and completed. For DL/RF programs, the payrolls are developed by the ID/IFR Director based on classes orders received from the faculties Deans and endorsed by the Rector, as well as the qualifications obtained as a result of the multi-criteria annual evaluation of teachers.

The elaboration of the department payrolls is based on:

1.   Curricula for undergraduate/bachelor and master study programs managed by the department;
2.   The teaching and associate staff of the department;
3.   Study groups;
4.   Classes orders: between the dean of the faculty and the heads of the departments of the faculties; the completed classes orders are drawn up in duplicate. After completing it by the specialty department, it is submitted to the rector for approval;

5. The university standard norm comprising: the didactic norm; the research norm. The didactic norm comprises the weekly didactic norm established by this procedure and other activities according to the law;

6. The ARACIS mandatory rules on the coverage of teaching positions in the payrolls are as follows: for undergraduate study programs: 70% of the posts must be covered by basic or reserved posts for titulars with higher education qualifications. Of these teachers, at least 25% are professors or associate professors, but no more than 50%; for Master's degree programs, all teaching positions must be covered by teaching staff titled in higher education with the teaching degree of university professor, associate professor or lecturer of which at least 80% are employed on the basis of the basic norm; or reserved post.

The formation of teaching positions and academic norms:

The teaching position represents a position in the payroll of a teaching staff or by one or more teachers by hourly payment. *The didactic norm,* according to the legal provisions may include:

1. Teaching activities;
2. Seminar activities, practical and laboratory work, year project guidance;
3. Guiding the elaboration of the graduation paper;
4. Guiding the development of master dissertations;
5. Other teaching, practical and scientific research activities included in the education plans;
6. Conducting didactic-artistic or sports activities;
7. Evaluation activities;
8. Tutorials, consultations, guidance of students' academic circles, students under the transferable credit system;
9. Participation in councils and committees in the interest of education.

The weekly didactic norm is quantified in conventional hours. For academic teachers and lecturers, the weekly teaching norm can consist of 14 conventional hours of teaching and seminars (88% of the norm), and the rest up to 16 conventional hours is covered by activities (12% of the norm), as the case.

For the lecturer and assistant teaching staff, the weekly teaching norm can be 15 hours of conventional teaching and seminars (94% of the norm), and the rest for up to 16 hours is covered by activities (6% of the norm), as the case. The activities are assumed by each teacher by signing the job description at the beginning of the academic year. The performance of these activities is monitored by faculty deans every month. The vacancies to be put out to completion will consist of the number of conventional/weekly hours stipulated by the legal regulations in force. The total working hours in a teaching or research norm, achieved through the accumulation of activities, is 40 hours per week.

The equivalence of didactic activities included in the weekly teaching norm is as follows:

1. In undergraduate education - teaching hours = 2 conventional hours; hour of seminar, laboratory and year projects = 1 conventional hour;
2. In master university education - teaching hours = 2.5 conventional hours; hour of seminar, laboratory and year projects = 1.5 conventional hours;

3. In the case of full-time teaching in an international language, undergraduate, master and doctoral cycles, the teaching, seminar or other activities can be normalized with a multiplier of 1.25, with the approval of the Board of Directors. Exclusion from this provision is the teaching hours of that language. Teaching positions for professors, associate professors and lecturers should include the titles of each teacher, and, if necessary, disciplines in the same field of specialization. For this, the respective teacher must prove the development of relevant scientific research work in that field.

By way of exception, in the case where the didactic norm cannot be made according to paragraph (10) and (11), article 287 of the National Education Law no. 1/2011, amended and completed, the differences up to the minimum didactic norm are supplemented with scientific research activities, upon proposal of the department director, with the approval of the faculty council, submitted by the Rector for approval to the Administrative Board. The reduction in the didactic norm is at most 1/2 of the norm, and the research time is equivalent to 0.5 conventional hours. The teaching staff maintains their qualification as a holder of the didactic function obtained through the competition. Activities exceeding a weekly teaching timetable set by the Senate may be remunerated on a pay-per-hour basis.

Teachers who are elected or appointed in the public institutions of the state or who carry out activities specific to the public service in ministries or other specialized bodies of the state may carry out didactic activities related to a didactic norm. Retired teachers or retired research staff may carry out teaching activities beyond the age limit of upper secondary education (65 years old) under a pay-time scheme equivalent to a teaching assignment. The appointment to posts is subject to the Senate's approval upon proposal of the Faculty Council and with the approval of the Board of Directors.

The structure of the payroll must meet the following requirements:

1. Didactic position in the payroll;
2. In the payroll, the teaching positions (basic, reserved or vacant) are entered in the hierarchical order of the teaching positions and in the alphabetical order of the titular teachers;
3. The normalization of the disciplines in the optional packages is based on the lists of students' signatures on the subjects chosen from the optional packages until september 10 of each year. If until this date the student has not opted, he/she will automatically be assigned to one of the proposed subjects in the optional package. For each discipline in the package there will be a minimum of a course and a seminar group;
4. Should be signed by the department manager, Dean, Rector, President of the Senate.

The vacancy for the vacant positions is proposed by the director of the department in whose structure the vacant post is located, through a report endorsed by the department council. The proposal will contain a description of the post in the competition which will be made in comprehensive terms according to the University's real needs, with the aim of not artificially limiting the number of potential candidates. The list of positions proposed for the competition is approved by the Dean of the faculty and submitted by the Rector to the Administration Board of the University for approval according to article 213 paragraph 13 of the National Education Law no. 1/2011, amended and completed (according to the Methodology regarding the competition for occupation of vacancies and research positions in each University). The payrolls are drawn up in duplicate by faculty departments, endorsed by faculty councils and approved by the Board of Directors and the Senate.

The Record of Grades: The Gradebooks

It would be useful for the student to be able to verify their school situation and their personal data in an integrated student registration program. In order to be able to access the online gradebook, students need the PIN (in Romanian CNP) and date of birth. For example, the PIN would be a username, and the date of birth would be the password. For example, a database can be created to store the grades given by teachers, students, to each discipline in the exam session. We can design a database of five tables on students' general data and provide information on the subjects studied by them, the teachers teaching the subjects, and the grades obtained by the students during the academic year.

This provides an analysis of the practical ways to use computer tools to develop student's status management systems for a particular university. The advantages of the application are its simple management because it has an intuitive and attractive interface. Users and administrators should not know the Microsoft Access database. The application can be easily modified, so it could be adapted to any type of specialization for tracking the students' school situation.

CONCLUSION

The reform of education to include ICT is considered to be the only and most important factor that will create benefits for the profession. As career preferences are made at an early age, an early focus on computer science, computational logic, and computer science in parallel with digital competencies can provide a solid foundation for the next generation of specialists. Teacher training program needs to focus more and more on IT. While the education systems of the Member States vary significantly, successes with some previous systems point to the use of ICT in pedagogy as a fundamental requirement for all teacher training programs. Since the curriculum is generally a long-term activity, the rapid development of skills for non-field teachers offers a short-term solution during the transition period.

The informational-managerial system can be defined as the set of information, information, flows and information circuits, procedures and means of information processing designed to contribute to the establishment and realization of the organization's objectives. The current trend, which is manifested with a progressive intensity, is to increase the use of automated means of information processing, while restraining manual and mechanized ones. The technical, functional and economical features of the automated means that are amplified at a particularly rapid pace make their proliferation very fast. As a result, there is an increase in both the weight and the role of the informational system in the information system at the level of the university education institutions.

Quality and efficiency in the university environment implies, first of all, quality decisions. In recent years, the decision support systems have become increasingly sophisticated, incorporating multiple functionalities and components to meet the diverse and complex needs of the educational act. Increasing the amount of data stored in operational databases, legal constraints and technological progress are only a few of the challenges facing this type of system to assist in decision-making at all stages.

Thus, any higher education institution is autonomously responsible for the development of a culture of quality that is, consistently applied, well-documented policies, techniques and practices to achieve those results/performances that are consistent with the intended objectives.

SOLUTIONS AND RECOMMENDATIONS

In order to meet modern development trends, higher education needs should address several major challenges:

- To reach a qualitative level to be competitive at national and international level;
- To "improve" their leadership and, in the context of self-management, to increase their funding;
- To permanently diversify its educational and scientific services. These major goals imply changes in higher education that have to be topped up on the political agenda and national strategy of the country.

In order to improve teaching at university level, we propose:

- Enhancing and improving actions and tools to promote the educational offer in order to increase the number of candidates for the admission exam and implicitly the number of students;
- Enhancing the role of departments in evaluating and monitoring the study programs;
- Creating a database of disciplines records from each undergraduate/bachelor and master study program;
- Enhancing the tutoring program at the level of study programs and improving communication with students in order to reduce the dropout rate;
- Further development of relations with the pre-university environment, for increasing the quality of the training of young people at the entrance to the university and their correct guidance towards the appropriate academic fields according to their preferences and level of training;
- Promoting the University at an international level in order to attract students from abroad to the study programs.

The data that are of special interest from the students' viewpoint should be carefully analysed, structured and made available, either in an Internet or Intranet environment. As modern technology in the field of communications might allow a better access over wide area networks, the design and implementation of shared data structures should be made keeping in mind the best practices in optimization of responses to users' requests and also internal data processing.

The database by itself helps in the day-to-day running of the academic institution. However, over time, as the datasets collect more data, these can be used to capitalize their own informational potential in order to positively influence the decisions taken by the university management. The proper setting of instruments dedicated to the decisional processes, which is a business intelligence application, should focus both on the correct and functional structure of the data warehouse that provides raw data, and for the reporting tools used to present the information (results) to the end users. Also, the proper data analysis methodologies should not be put aside, as they help achieve better quality information.

REFERENCES

Abdulghader, A. A., Dalbir, S., & Ibrahim, M. (2012). Potential E-Commerce Adoption Strategies for Libyan Organization. *IJICT, 1*(7), 321–328.

Bonn, S. (2008). Transitioning from Traditional to Hybrid and Online Teaching. In Information and Communication Technology in Education. ICFAI University Press.

Chalikias, M., Kyriakopoulos, G., Skordoulis, M., & Koniordos, M. (2014). *Core ICT indicators: Partnership on ICT measurement for development*. Retrieved from http://www.itu.int/ITU-D/ict/partnership

Creswell, J. W. (2013). *Research Design: Qualitative, Quantitative, and Mixed Methods Approaches* (4th ed.). London: SAGE Publications, Inc.

Croteau, A., & Li, P. (2003). Critical success factors of CRM technological initiatives. *Canadian Journal of Administrative Sciences*, *20*(1), 21–34. doi:10.1111/j.1936-4490.2003.tb00303.x

Farahani, A. J. (2008). E-learning: A New Paradigm in Education. In Tehnologia informaţiei şi comunicării în educaţie. ICFAI University Press.

Gupta, N. (2013). *Customer perception towards online shopping*. Retrieved from retailing.jrps.in/uploads/july 2013/customer _perfection_by_nidhi_gupta.pdf

Smyth, G. (2008). Wireless Technologies: Bridging the Digital Divide in Education. In A. Varma (Ed.), Information and Communication Technology in Education. ICFAI University Press.

van der Wende, M. C. (2001a). The International Dimension in National Higher Education Policies: What Has Changed in Europe over the Last Five Years? *European Journal of Education*, *36*(4), 431–441. doi:10.1111/1467-3435.00080

Varma, A. (2008). ICT in the Field of Education. In A. Varma (Ed.), Information and Communication Technology in Education. ICFAI University Press.

Yusuf, M. O., & Onasanya, S. A. (2004). Information and communication technology (ICT) and technology in tertiary institution. In E.A. Ogunsakin (Ed.), Teaching in Tertiary Institutions (pp. 67-76). Ilorin: Faculty of Education.

KEY TERMS AND DEFINITIONS

Administration: Registering and monitoring users, enforcing data security, monitoring performance, maintaining data integrity, dealing with concurrency control, and recovering information that has been corrupted by some event such as an unexpected system failure.

Data Definition: Creation, modification, and removal of definitions that define the organization of the data.

Database: An organized collection of data, stored and accessed electronically. Database designers typically organize the data to model aspects of reality in a way that supports processes requiring information.

Information and Communications Technology: (ICT): Extensional term for information technology (IT) that stresses the role of unified communications and the integration of telecommunications (telephone lines and wireless signals), computers as well as necessary enterprise software, middleware, storage, and audio-visual systems, which enable users to access, store, transmit, and manipulate information.

Information System: A collection of software, hardware, procedures, data, and computer networks used by people in organizations. An information system is used to collect, store, manage, and distribute data to support specific activities. As organizations and their activities have grown more complex, specialized information systems have emerged.

Personal Identification Number: Introducing redundancy is a numeric or alpha-numeric password used in the process of authenticating a user accessing a system.

Retrieval: Providing information in a form directly usable or for further processing by other applications. The retrieved data may be made available in a form basically the same as it is stored in the database or in a new form obtained by altering or combining existing data from the database.

Update: Insertion, modification, and deletion of the actual data.

Chapter 8
Fraud Risk Management for Listed Companies' Financial Reporting

Tatiana Dănescu
University of Medicine, Pharmacy, Sciences, and Technology of Targu-Mures, Romania

Ionica Oncioiu
Titu Maiorescu University, Romania

Ioan Ovidiu Spătăcean
University of Medicine, Pharmacy, Sciences, and Technology of Targu-Mures, Romania

ABSTRACT

Using accurate and reliable financial information is the primary condition for successful investments on a stock exchange. Nevertheless, some major corporate scandals broke out at the 21st century horizon and concluded with a major capital market crisis in confidence. Recent events have proved that Romanian capital market is no exception. All these unfortunate scandals had in common some ingredients, among which are a poor corporate governance, a lack of accountability, and misrepresentation of financial information. This chapter relates to the need of integrity in financial reporting process, as the basis for adequate, reliable, and comprehensive information used in decision making by investors in general, institutional investors in particular. The main focus is to review the characteristics of financial information in order to identify some patterns and depict an overview for sensitive areas that may be vulnerable to fraudulent behavior, such as fair value measurements, related party transactions, revenue recognition, provisions, or asset impairment (inventories and receivables).

INTRODUCTION

Effective capital markets require that accurate and reliable financial information is provided for stakeholders who have invested in the financial perspectives of a listed entity (Kizil & Burhan, 2018). Some resounding corporate accounting scandals that occurred at the beginning of 21st century raised awareness upon the negative effects of fraudulent financial reporting and determined organizations to act more proactive

DOI: 10.4018/978-1-5225-8455-1.ch008

in fighting fraud (Nelson, Elliot & Tarpley, 2002). Soltani (2007) considered that notwithstanding the measures undertaken by market regulatory forces in the aftermath of such scandals, the audit profession is still under pressure to respond to criticism generated by corporate scandals. Enron, HealthSouth, Kmart, Parmalat, Tyco, WorldCom, Waste Management, Sunbeam, Adelphia Communications or Xerox represent just a few examples of companies that were subject to manipulation of financial information, with undesirable effects upon the investors' community, at the beginning of 21st century. Apart from other corporate failures, Enron, WorldCom, and Tyco highly-publicized scandals provoked over $500 billion in market value declines (Lord & Benoit Report, 2008).

As a result of the major accounting frauds unrevealed within these corporations, investor confidence has been seriously shaken, which has led to the collapse of trading prices despite all management efforts to delay the dissemination of bad news to investors (Kothari, Shu & Wysocki, 2009). According to Louwers, Ramsay, Sinason and Strawser (2007), financial experts have estimated investors' losses to $7 trillion, over a period of three years from peak prices recorded in September 2000. Other authors, such Beasley, Buckless, Glover and Prawitt (2009) described the devastating impact caused by Enron's announcement in 2001 related to an overestimation of the earnings declared over the last four years by $586 million, as well as debt understatement due to past unreported liabilities for estimated dollar amount of $3 billion. The massive and understandable public outcry over Enron's implosion during the fall of 2001 spawned a mad frenzy to determine how the nation's seventh-largest public company, a company that had posted impressive and steadily rising profits over the previous few years, could crumple into insolvency in a matter of months. From the early days of this public drama, skeptics in the financial community charged that Enron's earnings restatement demonstrated that the company's exceptional financial performance during the late 1990s and 2000 had been a charade, a hoax orchestrated by the company's management with the help of a squad of creative accountants (Knapp, 2006).

Another relevant case is related to WorldCom which, in June 2002, announced a restatement of its financial results caused by the capitalization over the most recent two reporting periods of $3.8 billion in expenses. In fact, at the time, the WorldCom scandal was perceived as "the largest accounting fraud in history, with an overstatement of revenue estimated at $11 billion, an overvalued balance sheet of over $75 billion, and shareholders' losses estimated at $200 billion", according to Securities Exchange Commission pronouncements (Ricchiute, 2006).

From examples previously described, one may conclude that fraudulent financial reporting may seriously deteriorate an organization's reputation and financial strength. The companies' market capitalization might drop instantly, causing billions of dollars losses for investors, as a result of financial statement fraud. Even if the balance sheet and income statement do not change substantially, a restatement is likely to damage investors' confidence, and the stock price will deteriorate as a consequence. Also, the auditors may face litigation as a response to investors' losses, which could mean billions of dollars for large public companies (ACFE, 2014).

According to Soltani (2007), the increasing number of public companies and the high valuations of equity securities have put tremendous pressure on management to achieve earnings or other performance targets. Missing those targets, particularly increasing earnings per share and dividend per share each year, can result in significant declines in a company's market capitalization and, consequently, reduced pay for those managers whose income largely depend on achieving earnings or stock-price targets.

Even though the auditor profession has a strong position in fighting against fraudulent financial reporting, unfortunate corporate scandals did not avoid Romanian stock exchange, weakening the investors' confidence. The Romanian case has also a negative connotation among the investor community, due to a total amount of Eur 3.5 million prejudice associated with securities fraud. Furthermore, previous research conducted by the authors proved that investors show little or no interest for audit reports that signal red flags of material misstatements caused by potential fraudulent reporting. On the contrary, evidences of irrational investment behavior were brought to light: increase in stock prices whilst audit opinion was modified. Based on these findings, we consider that red flags suggesting a potential fraudulent financial reporting should receive adequate importance whenever investors formulate their investment decisions.

CORPORATE GOVERNANCE AND FRAUDULENT REPORTING RISK

Solid corporate governance is grounded on the protection of stakeholders' rights to benefit from *information transparency*. The concept of information transparency refers essentially to the process projected, implemented and monitored by a reporting entity, in terms of both *qualitative and quantitative disclosures*, on a timely basis, in order to disseminate relevant and accurate information for the public interest. At this point, the financial auditors play a significant role in forming and reporting an opinion that accompanies an entity's annual financial statements, with the designated purpose of assuring the public interest about the *integrity of the reporting process*. Besides the financial auditor, a solid corporate governance structure involves different other relevant functions, such as: internal auditor, audit committee, risk management and compliance officer, with distinctive responsibilities in assuring the integrity and accuracy of financial information. Such characteristics of financial information primarily require the *absence of fraud* as a source for misrepresentation of financial statements. Therefore, we adhere to the general assertion that the degree of *corporate governance efficiency* significantly influences the occurrence of fraud risk. According to this approach, the weaker the entity's corporate governance system is, the higher probability of fraud risk manifestation one may encounter.

FRAUDULENT FINANCIAL REPORTING DEFINED

Since annual financial statements are the backbone of the financial reporting process, we consider the terms "fraudulent financial reporting" and "financial statement fraud" as being equivalent. The ACFE 2014 International Edition of Fraud Examiners Manual delivers a comprehensive definition for financial statement fraud. Basically, financial reporting is the intentional manipulation of reported financial results to portray a misstated economic picture of the firm, without involving the theft of assets or even the misuse of assets for personal benefits (Rittenberg & Schwieger, 2005). The perpetrators of such a fraud seek gain through the rise in stock price and the commensurate increase in personal wealth. Therefore, there is a tendency to view financial reporting fraud as taking place only in the large companies where the executives are concerned about stock options and their stock prices. In other cases, frauds are committed by senior managers, including managers, to prevent forcing the organization into administration or special measures (Taylor, 2011).

Furthermore, Taylor (2011) described fraudulent financial reporting as a financial statement fraudulent scheme, which involves deliberate manipulation in order to depict a financial position which is in most cases better than the 'true and fair view' required by generally accepted accounting principles. Manipulation of financial statements is, almost by definition, a basic requirement for those frauds known as 'Ponzi schemes' whereby the aim is to attract new recruits to the scheme with fresh capital so earlier investors can keep receiving dividends, thus perpetrating the scheme. In the author's view, lies about financial health of the organization are essential to such schemes.

CHARACTERISTICS OF FRAUDULENT FINANCIAL REPORTING

Fraudulent financial reporting is a primary component of financial statement fraud, besides misappropriation of assets. Much like all types of fraud, financial statement fraud is an *intentional act*, involving either overstating assets, revenues or profits or understating liabilities, expenses or losses, for the purpose of depicting an *artificially inflated financial position* of a reporting entity. In case of listed companies, such a controversial accounting practice could easily fall under market abuse regulations associated with market manipulation, since management acknowledges the release of misstated financial statements on which investors base their decisions. From this perspective, fraudulent financial reporting constitutes *a means* for management to achieve higher performance bonuses or more valuable stock options, *rather than an end* in itself. Therefore, a primary characteristic of fraudulent financial reporting refers to a key person with managerial responsibilities, who has *both the ability* to override controls through force of authority and alter records supporting financial statements *and the incentive* to perform in such manner. Unlike misappropriation of assets, fraudulent financial reporting is more difficult to be uncovered since it usually *involves secrete and complex arrangements* planned by key management personnel.

EARNINGS MANAGEMENT: ESSENTIAL FOR FRAUDULENT REPORTING

Earnings management is a controversial accounting technique used by management to manipulate a company's earnings so that the figures or ratios respond to a pre-determined projection. This fraudulent reporting practice is related to the cases where companies artificially inflate or deflate revenues or profits, in order to manipulate earnings per share figures. Income smoothing is a form of earnings management that involves a shift of revenues and expenses between periods for the purpose of tempering earnings volatility. In that way, instead of having years with outstanding or disappointing earnings, companies will maintain the profitability figures relatively stable. For instance, a company may cut inventory or other assets belonging to an acquired company at the time of acquisition, in order to achieve higher earnings from a later sale. "Companies may also deliberately overstate inventory obsolescence reserves and allowances for doubtful accounts to counter higher earnings" (Arens, Elder & Beasley, 2008).

The incentive to manage earnings is usually encouraged by the management's accountability to guide the company in a manner that provides the achievement of projected performance targets. This motivation may also appear as a result of pressures exerted on management both from outside and inside the company. External pressures are usually associated with stock markets' expectations, since members of senior management are constantly under pressure to attain increase of shareholder value as a result of their leadership. The board of directors is also under external pressures to enhance the company value, and they in turn maintain internal pressures on management to achieve targets that ensure growth and prosperity. When managers or those charged with governance are strongly motivated to meet market expectation, they usually override commonsense business practices and ethical principles in financial reporting. Cases of abusive earnings management must be carefully investigated by external auditors as it is deemed by market regulators to be a material and intentional misrepresentation of results. Moreover, earnings management usually involves intentionally recognizing transactions and other events in an improper accounting period or entering fictious transactions, both of which meet the conditions of a fraud (Soltani, 2007).

FRAUDULENT CORPORATE FEATURES

Rittenberg and Schwieger (2005) referred to a study conducted by the COSO on the incidence of fraud within the companies cited by the Securities Exchange Commission (SEC) during the 1990s. According to this research, the most frequent techniques adopted by management to misstate financial statement information involve improper revenue recognition (e.g. revenues prematurely recorded or fictitious revenue transactions) and overstatement of assets (e.g. overvaluing different type of assets, recording fictitious assets or assets not under ownership, or capitalizing expenses instead of allocating to profit or loss). The study also identified the major characteristics of fraudulent companies. Those characteristics relate to:

- A smaller size than most SEC registrants (under $ 200 million in revenues);
- Management dominance upon the board;
- Absence of audit committees or lack of consistency on behalf of such committees in examining the integrity of financial reporting process;
- Overstatement of revenues and corresponding assets, by premature or fictitious recognition of revenue (e.g. Sales with conditions, long-term contracts, channel stuffing);
- Lack of internal audit departments;
- Relatively long periods over which frauds had been perpetrated (average fraud approached 24 months);
- Imminent financial difficulties (majority in loss situations or nearing break-even) before frauds were committed;
- Dishonest management (the CEO and CFO were involved with the fraud in 83% of the cases);
- High financial interest in company's equity (on average, company officers and members of the board owned 32 percent of the capital stock).

The financial reporting frauds over the past decade have been carried out at times with different levels of sophistication. Rittenberg and Schwieger (2005) portraited an overview of some major financial reporting fraud cases that shook both the American and European corporate history, as described in Table 1.

Boynton and Johnson (2006) referred to a 2003 KPMG Forensic study which addressed 459 executives of publicly held companies that reported revenues over $ 250 million, as well as persons from state and federal government agencies. According to this study, 75 percent of these organizations had encountered fraud in the previous year. Over the same period, one in 14 of the surveyed companies indicated fraudulent financial reporting as the type of fraud with the highest cost. Table 2 describes key elements related to the frequency and magnitude of different types of investigated fraud.

The research also revealed some relevant conditions that favored fraud occurrence within the organization. A four-year period comparison is summarized in Table 3. A significant loop may be seen in case of collusion involving employees and management or external parties while inadequate internal controls registered a major drop. On the other hand, ineffective or nonexistent ethics program seems to be an emerging factor.

Table 1. Summary of major financial reporting frauds

Company	Nature of the Fraud
Enron	Covered up financial problems by: • shifting liabilities to off-balance sheet SPE's; • recognizing revenue from impaired assets by selling them to controlled SPE's; • engaging in round-tripping trades; • numerous other related-party transactions.
WorldCom	Decreased expenses and increased revenues through the following: • bartered transactions recognized as sales, e.g., trading the right to use telecommunication lines in one part of the world to similar rights to another part of the world; • restructuring acquisitions reserves to decrease expenses of future periods; • capitalizing line costs, i.e. rentals expenses paid to phone companies.
Lucent	Enhanced quarterly revenues by "channel stuffing"; i.e., increasing sales at the end of the quarter at amounts greater than customers could actually take.
Parmalat	Company siphoned cash off of subsidiaries through a complex scheme that: • included recording of fictitious cash deposits held at major banks; • understated debt by engaging in complex transactions with off-shore subsidiaries;
HealthSouth	Recorded fictitious revenue across its 250 clinics and hospitals. A wide variety of schemes were used including: • improperly billing group psychiatric sessions, i.e., with ten people in a group the company billed for ten individual sessions instead of one group session; • using adjusting journal entries to both reduce expenses and enhance revenues.
Addeco	Overstated revenue by holding the books open for 20-35 days after the end of the year to record sales from the subsequent period as current period sales.

Source: Rittenberg & Schwieger (2005), p. 313.

Table 2. KMPG forensic 2003 fraud survey: Frequency and magnitude

Type of Fraud	Percentage Experiencing Fraud in the Last 12 mo.	Average Annual Cost of Fraud ($000)
Fraudulent financial reporting	7%	$ 257,932
Medical/Insurance fraud	12%	$ 33,709
Consumer fraud	32%	$ 2,705
Vendor related, third party fraud	25%	$ 759
Misconduct	15%	$ 732
Employee fraud	60%	$ 464
Computer crime	18%	$ 67

Source: Boynton and Johnson (2006), p.350

Identifying and analyzing different type of management fraud detectors was another point of focus for the conducted research. By far, the leading positions are held by internal controls, internal audit and notification by employees. An interesting finding is related to the high frequency of purely accidental detection of management fraud, which may suggest a significant vulnerability in the planning and implementing proper strategy for fighting corporate fraud. Table 4 summarizes nine type of methods involved in unearthing fraud.

Table 3. KMPG forensic 2003 fraud survey: Major fraud factors

Factors Contributing to Fraud	2003	1998	1994
Collusion between personnel and third parties	48%	31%	33%
Inadequate internal controls	39%	58%	59%
Management override of internal controls	31%	36%	36%
Collusion between personnel and management	15%	19%	23%
Lack of directors' supervision	12%	11%	6%
Non-compliance with ethics program	10%	8%	7%

Source: Boynton and Johnson (2006), p.351

Table 4. KMPG Forensic 2003 Fraud survey: Uncovering fraud

Methods of Uncovering Fraud	2003	1998	1994
Internal controls	77%	51%	52%
Internal audit	65%	43%	47%
Notification by employee	63%	58%	51%
Accident	54%	37%	28%
Anonymous tip	41%	35%	26%
Notification by customer	34%	41%	34%
Notification by regulator/law enforcement	19%	16%	8%
Notification by vendor	16%	11%	15%
External audit	12%	4%	5%

Source: Boynton and Johnson (2006), p.361

Table 5 describes some major corporate policies that may be effective in mitigating or preventing management fraud occurrence. These policies were indicated as set in force for a 12 months period prior to the 2003 KPMG Fraud Survey.

The 2004 ACFE Report to the Nation, as cited by Boynton and Johnson (2006), referred to 508 fraud cases that generated a total amount of $761 million in losses, with a distribution that reached every major segment of economy: 42 percent in privately owned companies, 30 percent in listed corporations, 16 percent in government sector, and 12 percent in not-for-profit organizations. The most recent ACFE Report to the Nations (2018) shows that financial statement fraud occurred only in 10 percent of cases as occupational fraud committed (compared with 89 percent in case of asset misappropriation) but provoked the highest financial magnitude (a median loss value of $800,000 compared to only $114.000 in case of asset misappropriation).

A research conducted by Sherman, Young, and Collingwood (2003) supported some conclusions regarding the characteristics associated potentially fraudulent corporate behavior of the New Economy companies. They are summarized into: high-growth firms with declining rates; high-profile glamor companies with extensive business and popular press; new businesses that engage in controversial transactions; companies operating in weak regulatory environments, where low levels of efficiency and honesty may cover high-level corruption; companies that are subject to insignificant scrutiny from reporters, analysts,

Table 5. KMPG forensic 2003 fraud survey: Anti fraud policies

Fraud Mitigation Policies	%
Strengthened internal controls	75%
Instituted periodic compliance audits	44%
Created an employee hotline	42%
Appointed compliance personnel	41%
Established a code of conduct for all employees	40%
Conducted background checks for hires with budgetary responsibility	38%
Instituted fraud awareness training	28%
Tied employee evaluation to ethics or compliance objectives	24%
Other policies	19%

Source: Boynton and Johnson (2006), p.361

and sophisticated investors; companies with complex ownership and financial structures that make key transactions less transparent and give rise to related-party transactions and conflicts of interest; companies whose survival requires them to attract the next round of financing; and companies that strongly link executive compensation to short-term business goals, such as sales, net income or stock price.

The presence of such characteristics is not automatically a sign that a company is tempted to engage in fraudulent accounting practices. Nevertheless, management, directors, and auditors of companies that meet such profiles should submit the financial reporting practices to a higher level of supervision.

CORPORATE RESPONSIBILITES FOR MITIGATING FRAUD RISK

As Tickner (2010) remarked, the only way to estimate with any degree of potential accuracy is to know where all the weaknesses lie within the business controls of the organization and where things have gone wrong before and frauds have come to light. Even then, the cleverest fraudsters may well be committing frauds that are unlikely to see the light of the day.

According to ISA 240 (par.4), the main responsibility for fraud prevention and detection is shared between directors, as individuals charged with governance and the senior management. It is the directors' responsibility to ensure, through supervision of management, that the company establishes and maintains effective controls to provide reasonable assurance of the reliability of financial reporting. Proactive and consistent oversight should restore management's commitment to project and put it place a culture of honesty and ethics. In performing such responsibility, directors should carefully consider the possibility for management to override controls or to exert inappropriate interference within the corporate reporting process, such as management earnings to influence the perception of analysts regarding the company's performance and profitability (Soltani, 2007).

A company's management exercises both the responsibility and the authority to implement measures to mitigate fraud risk. This major responsibility requires a strong emphasis on the reputational benefits associated with an *antifraud corporate philosophy*, which is expected to reduce opportunities to plan and perform fraudulent operations. This approach involves unconditional commitment for creating, enforcing and supervising a culture of honesty and ethical behavior based on relevant corporate governance principles. It is therefore quite usual for listed companies to embrace sharp *code of ethics* and *recruiting procedures* in order to set in place such values and principles. Besides the prevention component, another dimension is concerned with *fraud deterrence*, which could withhold employees to engage in fraud since they are aware of a high probability of detection and punishment. The measures undertaken for prevention and deterrence of fraud can also sustain a competitive and positive workplace environment, which favors the enhancement of the ability to recruit and retain valuable employees (Soltani, 2007).

Fraud prevention and deterrence are primarily preoccupied with fraud committed by employees, such as misappropriation of assets (IAASB, 2015). Nevertheless, fraudulent financial reporting performed or acknowledged by management is far more sensitive and usually involves a greater magnitude in value. From this perspective, a strong corporate governance culture requires an *effectively oversight* conducted by the company's Board of directors towards management's ability to *override internal controls* or to *inappropriate influence the financial reporting process*, for instance artificially inflating earnings or deliberately omitting provisions in order to enhance investors' perception as to the reporting entity's performance and profitability. A sound mechanism *of "whistle blowing"* is also an efficient response to mitigate fraud risk.

Most fraud researchers agree that one of the most effective strategy to fight fraud is to adopt antifraud controls based on corporate core values. These values help create a culture of honesty and ethics upon which is built the foundation for employee's major responsibilities (Arens, Elder & Beasley, 2008). Table 6 summarizes some detailed antifraud programs and control measures, as developed by Whittington and Pany (2008) in accordance with SAS 99 (AU 316) requirements.

Richards, Melancon and Ratley (2008) affirmed that only through ongoing effort can an entity protect itself against acts of fraud. According to their views, the key principles for establishing an environment able to proactively and effectively manage fraud risk are:

Principle 1: A fraud risk management program should be enforced, within corporate strategies, including a policy to describe the directors' and senior management expectations of how fraud risk is managed;

Principle 2: Possibility of fraud occurrence should be measured with a proper frequency to identify schemes and conditions that require prompt actions;

Principle 3: Prevention techniques should be put in place, to mitigate possible impacts of fraud risk upon the organization;

Principle 4: Detection techniques should be enforced to discover fraud when preventive measures fail to prevent fraud or insufficiently mitigated risks are realized;

Principle 5: A reporting mechanism should be put in place to require signals on potential fraud, while thorough investigations and corrective actions should be performed to ensure fraud is addressed in an appropriate and timely manner.

AUDITORS' RESPONSIBILITES AND PROCEDURES RELATED TO FRAUDULENT REPORTING RISK

From a fraud risk approach, the auditor has a major responsibility to develop, project and perform audit procedures that allow obtaining reasonable assurance about whether financial statements do not contain material misstatement resulting from fraudulent reporting (Taylor, 2011). To obtain such assurance, the auditor must permanently maintain professional skepticism (Soltani, 2007).

Table 6. Analysis of antifraud programs and control measures

Measure	Examples
Objective 1: Create and Maintain a Culture of Honesty, Integrity and Ethics	
Set tone at the top	establish, communicate, and enforce a corporate code of conduct with employee involvement; management's activities should show employees that unethical behavior is not permitted; examples of elements that detract from a positive tone: • statement by management of an urging need to achieve financial targets; • establishment of unachievable goals.
Positive workplace environment	encourage and empower employees to help create a positive workplace; motivate employees to attain positive feelings about their employer, by discouraging acts that may induce senses of abuse, threat or ignoration; allow employees to participate in developing and updating the code of conduct; encourage employees to communicate noncompliance with the code of conduct.
Hire and promote appropriate employees	conduct background investigations on employees aiming a position of trust; thoroughly check the candidate's education profile, employment history, and references; train new employees about corporate values and code of conduct; review how employees have contributed to an appropriate workplace environment; periodically objectively evaluate compliance with the entity's corporate values.
Properly train employees	training should include information on the company's values and its code of conduct; training should include information on the need to communicate certain matters and the manner in which it should be done; conduct refresher training; require employees' confirmation regarding their responsibilities to comply with the code of conduct.
Discipline	expectations regarding the consequences of perpetrating fraud should be clearly communicated; appropriate anti-fraud actions should be adopted, including: • a thorough investigation; • appropriate and consistent actions against violators; • assessment and improvement of relevant controls; • communications and training should reinforce the entity's values and code of conduct.
Objective 2: Evaluate the Fraud Risks and Implement Processes, Procedures, and Controls to Mitigate Those Risks	
Identify and measure fraud risks	consider the company vulnerability to financial statements fraud, misappropriation of assets, and corruption (bribery and other such illegal acts); consider organizational and industry-specific characteristics that may induce fraud risks;
Mitigate fraud risks	change certain activities (e.g., cease business in some jurisdictions); change certain processes (e.g., implement lockbox system at a bank instead of receiving payments at the company's various locations).
Implement and monitor controls and other measures	evaluate whether controls have been implemented in areas of high risk of fraud; implement appropriate oversight measure to control the risk of management override of controls.
Objective 3: Develop an Appropriate Oversight Process	
Management	oversee activities of employees;
Audit committee Board of directors	assess management's identification of fraud risks and implementation of antifraud measures; consider likelihood of management override; consider communicating with middle management; have an open dialogue with independent auditors concerning internal controls.
Internal auditors	determine whether fraud has been committed, evaluate fraud risks and deter fraud.
Independent auditors	assist management and audit committee in assessment of company's activities for identifying and assessing fraud risks.

Source: Adapted from Whittington & Pany (2008), p. 294-295

During an audit engagement, the independent auditors must be constantly alert to the possibility that fraud may exist. That vigilance should be more amplified when suspicions appear in relation with management fraud, far more difficult to reveal. In view of the possibilities of fraud committed by management as well as the recent increase in the number of lawsuits against independent auditors, it is strongly recommended for audit firms to conduct any *background investigation* for key management personnel of a potential client, before accepting and audit engagement (Hermanson, Loeb, Saada & Strawser, 1976), especially for listed companies. Such investigation should provide the auditor with an adequate understanding for management motivations to commit fraud and the manner in which fraud may be perpetrated. Furthermore, even if such investigations are performed and no alarming results emerge, independent auditors must stay alert to any *red flags* that may occur during the performance of an audit engagement, suggesting any potentially fraudulent operation. Such a conduct is required under professional skepticism as a basis for fraud risk assessment in the planning phase. Due to professional skepticism, auditors should not be satisfied with an honesty-based perception towards management. It is assumed that in order to estimate the risk of fraudulent reporting, in addition to the factors that determine its occurrence, it is necessary to take into consideration certain indicators whose analysis and evaluation have the purpose of identifying the likelihood of the occurrence and manifestation of financial statement fraud.

Pointers of fraud risk can be unearthed as a result of *discussions* among engagement team, discussions with key members of the Board and management, internal auditors and other key personnel involved in financial reporting process, such as risk officers, law councilors and compliance officers. Effective and transparent discussions allow more experienced auditors to share insights about how the financial statements might be susceptible to fraudulent reporting (Whittington & Pany, 2008). Audit team brainstorming is a form of professional skepticism and should consider each relevant factor that might affect management motivation to misrepresent the financial condition of an entity. This analysis is followed up with a consideration of weaknesses in internal controls that may allow fraudulent reporting to occur and not be discovered by other employees, or could be covered up by other employees (Rittenberg & Schwieger, 2005).

SAS 99 and other literature sources (Messier, Glover & Prawitt, 2008) identify the following specific *brainstorming recommendations*:

- Consider the possibility of a fraud to be perpetrated and covered up;
- Presume fraud in revenue recognition and overstatement of certain assets that are susceptible to manipulation;
- Consider incentives, opportunities and rationalization for fraud, including the nature of executive compensation and pressure to meet earning targets;
- Consider industry conditions and its business environment. Changing technology is important, as is declining customer demand for the company's products;
- Consider operating characteristics and financial stability, especially significant and complex transactions, as well as significant changes in financial condition;
- Consider any unusual or unexpected relationships identified after performance of analytical procedures;
- Understand and investigate unexpected period-end adjustments.

Inquires of management and directors, including audit committee as to their knowledge of confirmed, alleged or suspected fraud, their understanding of fraud risks and programs, systems or controls implemented to mitigate those risks, prove to be effective tools used by auditors in identifying fraud risks. The auditors should also obtain management's perspective regarding the effectiveness of internal control in detecting fraud and whether such perspective has been communicated to the audit committee. Inquiries are also directed to internal auditors to understand their perception about fraud risks and establish whether they have any knowledge of fraud or suspected fraud, including whether management has satisfactory responded to findings over a reporting period. To obtain a complete perspective and collaborate management's responses, auditors should also inquiry other employees, such as operating personnel with no responsibilities in financial reporting, employees responsible for initiating, recording or processing complex or unusual transactions, and legal counsels (Whittington & Pany, 2008). Messier, Glover, and Prawitt (2008) suggested that auditor may consider making inquiries of third parties, such as vendors, customers, or regulators. It can be uncomfortable to inquire about potentially fraudulent activities; it is much more uncomfortable to fail to detect a material fraud.

Analytical procedures projected and performed as risk assessment procedures, within the planning phase of an audit engagement, such as comparisons of reported financial statement numbers with estimates developed by the audit team for reasonableness, may be very useful in identifying unusual relationships among accounts, unexpected transactions or events, ratios and trends that merit additional investigation. According to Taylor (2011), using analytical review procedures as an investigatory tool has the goal of determining whether or not the financial statements tell a coherent story and whether or not some of the numbers may have been manipulated to 'window dress' the figures. Whenever analytical procedures uncover an unusual or unexpected relationship, a signal is fired that the financial statements may be misstated due to fraud. As an example, an unexpected relationship between sales volume from the accounting system and sales volume observed from production statistics listed by operations personnel may indicate fraudulent misstatement of sales (Whittington & Pany, 2008). Moreover, "*a trend analysis of revenues and sales returns during and shortly after the reporting period may signal undisclosed side agreements with customers, which would preclude revenue recognition*" (Soltani, 2007). Other authors promote data mining techniques, such as predictive modeling and deviation analysis, as highly efficient methods to unearth fraudulent operations, due to automatically capabilities of exploring large volumes of data for new, hidden or unexpected information or patterns, without any prior knowledge of fraud (Wadhwa & Virender, 2012).

As a result of audit team discussions, planning and performing the inquiries and analytical procedures, the auditors should obtain a sufficient base to identify fraud risks that require an audit response. In identifying such risks, the auditors consider some relevant factors, among which: the type and significance of the risk, the likelihood that the risk will cause a material misstatement, and its pervasiveness. Since material misstatements associated with financial statement fraud often involve management override of internal controls, auditors ordinarily presume a fraud risk in revenue recognition. For all identified fraud risks, auditors should gain a sufficient understanding of the programs and controls enforced to mitigate those risks (Whittington & Pany, 2008). Table 7 presents some relevant conditions that may strongly suggest presence of fraudulent financial reporting.

Based on identifying and assessing financial reporting fraud risk, the auditors elaborate an appropriate *response* to the results of fraud risk assessment. According to Whittington and Pany (2008) and Rittenberg and Schwieger (2005), most common responses refer to:

Table 7. Conditions of fraudulent financial reporting

Discrepancies in Accounting Records	Conflicting or Missing Evidential Matter	Problematic or Unusual Relationships With Auditors
Transactions not recorded or improperly recorded.	Missing documents Unavailable of other than photocopied or electronic documents.	Access denial to records, employees, and third parties.
Unauthorized balances or transactions.		Undue time pressure imposed by management.
Last-minute adjustments.	Inconsistent, vague, or implausible management or employee responses.	Management complaints about how the audit is performed.
Inadequate employees' access to systems and records.	Unavailable electronic evidence.	Tips or complaints to the auditors about fraud.
	Inability to demonstrate key systems development.	Denial of access to key information technology, staff and facilities.

Source: Adapted from Whittington & Pany (2008), p. 207

1. A modification in the overall audit approach, by:
   a. Designing procedures to gather more reliable evidence;
   b. Obtaining additional corroboration of management's representations involving sensible and material matters, such as third-party confirmation (e.g. Customer confirmation related to specific terms of the transactions), or the use of a specialist;
   c. Assigning additional more experienced audit personnel with specialized professional skills and knowledge;
   d. Reviewing management's selection and application of accounting principles;
   e. Adding an element of unpredictability in designing and performance of audit procedures, such as "surprise" inventory observations.
2. An alteration of audit procedures planned to be performed, by shifting tests from the interim period to near year-end, or increasing the sample size for a particular substantive procedure.
3. Performance of further procedures to address the management override of controls, by:
   a. examining sensible journal entries, such as entries made to unrelated or unusual accounts, with little or no explanation or description;
   b. reviewing the significant accounting estimates to determine whether management judgements and assumptions indicate possible biases;
   c. assessing the business rationale for significant unordinary transactions, especially with related parties;
   d. performing analytical procedures using disaggregated to discover more unusual fluctuations;
   e. inspecting details of major sales contracts and financial viability of customers;
   f. examining all reciprocal or similar transactions, to determine the economic viability and the correspondence with similar transactions in the industry.

Furthermore, Rittenberg and Schwieger (2005) explained how auditors should link audit procedures to some relevant fraud risk indicators, as presented in Table 8.

The auditors' concern about fraudulent financial reporting does not stop at the planning phase of the audit. When *collecting and evaluating evidence* to support management assertions related to financial statements, by performing audit procedures planned as a response to previous fraud risk assessments,

Table 8. Linking audit procedures to fraud risk indicators

Fraud Risk Indicator	Audit Procedures to Address Risk
Pressure to meet earnings objective: Unusual year-end spike in sales	• use audit software (computer analysis) to identify unusual sales or fluctuations; • review all large sales contracts to determine actual shipment of the goods, the existence of unusual terms, and payment date. • verify whether customer is a real business; confirm the terms of major contracts with the customer; examine cash receipts after year-end to determine if receipts were collected.
Potential violation of debt covenants	• perform analytical review of revenue recognition and cost of goods sold; • perform a detailed test of inventory, including observation of inventory and valuation; • review debt covenants to determine potential motivation; • review all changes in classification of liabilities and investigate any unusual entries.
Company is under pressure to show growth	• analytical review for unusual sales spikes near the end of the year; • select sales and note whether actual shipment took place or service was performed; • obtain a list of all related parties and search files for any sales made to related parties.
Pressure to meet projected earnings targets	• review financial statements for unusual ratios, particularly comparison with industry averages; • test capitalization of assets to determine if expenses are being capitalized, examine underlying supporting documents and physically examine the asset; • review all unusual journal entries, including those that involve decreases in previously established "reserves" accounts; • carefully evaluate the reasonableness of estimates.

Source: Rittenberg & Schwieger (2005), p. 315

auditors are required to remain vigilant and professionally skeptic. Any significant discrepancy in the accounting system and supporting documents, any conflicting evidence or missing documentation, any signs of strained relationship with management may result in signals for potential fraudulent financial reporting and should heighten auditor's skepticism. Furthermore, management's response is a key source of evidence, meaning that a vague, implausible or inconsistent response to inquiry, as well as a conflictual or problematic relationship with auditors, can suggest the pervasiveness of fraud (Louwers, Ramsay, Sinason & Strawser, 2007).

Auditors often use Computer Assisted Audit Techniques (CAAT) to screen for fictitious revenues. These tools provide efficient investigations for gaps in document sequences, which may indicate misstatement related to the completeness of liabilities and expense accounts. Audit software may also be used efficiently to sort transactions over a certain amount or containing unusual characteristics (Arens, Elder & Beasley, 2008).

Auditors must prove due care in instrumenting potential fraudulent operations because fraud allegations are always treated with maximum consideration (Boyton & Johnson, 2006). After discovering conditions that indicate fraud, auditors should evaluate the implications. Their fraud suspicions should be *communicated* to an appropriate level of management (generally one level above the personnel involved) as soon as it is practicable and management assistance in further investigations should be required, provided that senior managers seem not to be involved. Nevertheless, unlike some minor frauds involving misappropriation of assets by employees at low organizational levels, fraud suspicions involving senior management are never inconsequential and are required to be communicated directly to the audit committee (Louwers, Ramsay, Sinason & Strawser, 2007). The determination of which party is appropriate to communicate with, requires professional judgement. In case of listed companies, the auditor is required to report valid suspicions of fraud to outside parties, such as a securities regulatory authority. In other cases, the auditor should recognize a duty to disclose fraudulent operations to a funding agency, to a successor auditor; or to court as a response to a subpoena. In very serious situations, when the results of audit procedures indicate beyond any reasonable doubt that a fraud associated with financial reporting has occurred, the auditor should consider withdrawing and communicate the reasons to the audit committee (Messier, Glover & Prawitt, 2008). Such communications, among descriptions related to fraud risk assessment procedures, specific fraud risk factors identified and any additional audit procedures required, need to be properly *documented*.

Rittenberg and Schwieger (2005) pointed out some *important lessons* learned from equity funding practices, lessons that auditors should constantly bear in mind:

- Auditors take a great risk whenever they are not responsible for auditing the whole company;
- Auditors need to analyze the economic assumptions underlying a company's figures and growth rates. For example, a mutual fund in a declining market will not generate the gains needed to pay the investor's insurance premiums linked to that mutual fund investment;
- Whenever the risk of fraud is high, auditors must demand stronger audit evidence, without assuming that all people are honest;
- Computer errors should not be viewed as an excuse, but rather an indication of a problem that should require higher skepticism;
- Dominant clients are a real issue. An audit firm cannot afford to have a client from which it believes it cannot walk away;
- Auditors need to understand the reasons which motivate management to engage in fraudulent reporting, for instance that is the case when all or significant part of management's wealth is tied to stock options.

SOLUTIONS AND RECOMMENDATIONS

Often, fraudulent financial reporting involves more than a conscious act of committing such illegal acts. First of all, management or other relevant employees have an *incentive* or are under *pressure*, each of such condition providing a sufficient reason to engage in fraud. Secondly, there are circumstances that provide an *opportunity* for fraud. Thirdly, the perpetrators are able to *rationalize* committing a fraud, because "*they possess an attitude, character or set of ethical values that support them to intentionally commit a dishonest act*" (Soltani, 2007).

As Ragatz (2015) summarized, a better understanding of the causal factors of fraud can alert leaders to those circumstances that create potentially fraudulent activity. As a response, appropriate measures need to be implemented to reduce the opportunity of committing and concealing fraud. Although the impossibility of completely preventing unethical behavior is generally accepted, the awareness of fraud triangle can provide efficient tools in fighting fraud.

The pressure to commit fraudulent activities occurs when a company's executives are constrained by investors and other stakeholders (e.g. credit institutions or analysts) to reach or even exceed some expected financial results (e.g. analysts' forecast) or certain levels of key performance indicators, to meet debt covenant restrictions, or to artificially inflate stock prices (Bartsiotas & Achamkulangare, 2016). According to Messier, Glover, and Prawitt (2008), even honest individuals can engage in fraud provided that the environment exert sufficient pressure upon them. Fraud risk factors associated with such pressures may include: management compensation schemes; financial pressures for improved earnings or balance sheet; personal need for assets; debt covenant requirements; personal wealth conditioned by either financial results or company's survival.

The opportunity to commit acts of fraudulent financial reporting occurs when a company's internal control system encounters severe vulnerabilities or is not performing effectively, or when a key management personnel finds methods to evade internal controls. Thus, the weaknesses in the internal control system may create *certain opportunities* in which the persons involved are convinced that they can commit those fraudulent acts without being uncovered (Louwers, Ramsay, Sinason & Strawser, 2007). Moreover, the complexity associated with certain transactions may result in the perpetrator's risk assessment of being caught as low. Opportunity is the only triangle factor that can be controlled by the directors and the management, through performance of periodic checks and implementation of effective risk management policies. Some relevant opportunities that should always be considered during fraud risk assessment performance may include:

- The presence of significant related party transactions (e.g. Spe's used by enron);
- Industry dominance, especially the possibility to impose terms or conditions to business partners;
- Subjective judgements made by management regarding assets, revenues or accounting estimates (e.g. inventory valuation is exposed to a high risk of misstatement for those companies which own extremely diversified items of inventory, positioned in many locations, or potentially obsolete);
- Simple transactions are accounted in a highly complex manner through a disjointed recording process;
- Difficult to understand transactions, such as trading futures, options, etf's and other financial derivatives or structured products;
- Inadequate monitoring of management, either because the directors lack independence or is ineffective, or there is an extremely dominant or authoritarian manager;
- A complex or unstable organizational structure, characterized by weak or lacking internal controls, or a significant turnover in accounting personnel.

A rationale behavior occurs when the fraudster is aware of the act of fraud, in terms of nature and consequences (Bishop & Hydoski, 2009). Thus, this condition arises as a result of the attitude and characteristic features of that person which urge him or her to committing such illicit deeds. Alternatively, there may appear circumstances when persons who otherwise would not be capable of committing frauds, still end up acting fraudulent as a result of the environment's pressure.

Many in the accounting profession felt they were generating value by delivering methods to "dress up the financial statements", despite that financial statements did not accurately portray real economic events or conditions. On the other hand, management found they could borrow from the future to recognize current earnings as basis for incentive contracts. As Soltani (2007) stated, fraudulent financial reporting is not necessarily the consequence of a grand plan or conspiracy. It simply occurs when management rationalizes the appropriateness of material misstatement, for instance through an aggressive interpretation of accounting principles, or a temporary misstatement, expecting to adjust when operational results improve. Management has a dominant position in the company's structure and possesses a privileged ability to perpetrate fraud by directly or indirectly altering documents or accounting records.

According to Arens, Elder, and Beasley (2008), the attitude of senior management towards financial reporting is a critical risk factor. If the CEO or other top managers pose a significant disregard for the financial reporting, financial statements fraud has a higher probability.

FUTURE RESEARCH DIRECTIONS

The public expects a proactive approach to fraud detection. The issue of identifying key fraud risk factors (often referred to as "*red flags*"), as indicators of an increased potential for fraud occurring, should be a major preoccupation both for auditors as "watchdogs" for financial reporting integrity and the external users of financial statements. Nevertheless, external users are limited in possibilities to further investigate any fraud suspicion, beyond any alert that they could signal in attention of those charge with governance, regulatory authorities or independent auditors. From the auditor's perspective such an approach must be designed starting with the planning phase of an engagement, based on a proper consideration of the likelihood that fraud may exist within the reporting entity. Efficient planning alerts auditors of potential fraud indicators that must be addressed in an adequately professional manner.

A brief literature review (Louwers, Ramsay, Sinason & Strawser, 2007) indicates relevant *pointers* for potential fraudulent financial reporting, such as: the predominant features of management and their negative influence upon the internal control environment; developments or changes in the business sector, including any regulatory incidence; high competition and reduced demand, as well as the features specific to the company's operational activity and its financial condition.

SAS 99 (AU 316) describes a more detailed picture related to risk factors arising from fraudulent financial reporting in conjunction with the basic coordinates of fraud triangle. Some relevant factors as described by Soltani (2007) refer to:

- Unfavorable economic conditions within the industry;
- Extremely rapid expansion through new business segments or product lines;
- Reduced ability to access funding or restrictive loan agreements;
- High debt and insufficient working capital;
- Frequent cash flow shortages, declining sales and/or profits, and loss of market share;
- Sizable inventory increases without comparable sales increases;
- Difficulty in collecting receivables, amplified by a deterioration in quality of earnings;
- Urgent need for earnings to support high stock prices or to meet earnings forecast;
- Significant litigation, especially between stockholders, directors and management;
- Managers regularly assuming subordinates' duties.

Taylor (2011) added the following key indicators that forensic accountants can use to flag up possible case of manipulation of accounts:

- Better or worse than expected results by a subsidiary or division which is sited away from centralized financial control;
- Subsidiaries or divisions with highly autonomous local management where interventions from the main (i.e. holding company) boar directors or internal audit reviews are resisted or unreasonably delayed.

Once risk factors for fraudulent financial reporting have been identified, the next step is taken forward for the assessment of what possible type of fraud might occur, the likelihood of that fraud to emerge and the pervasiveness (magnitude) of the suspected fraud (Thibodeau & Freie, 2007). Part of this assessment involves taking into consideration controls in place to prevent fraud from occurring or detecting fraud once it has occurred. This approach is highly effective in financial audit engagements, but it also is expected to produce notable results if used by internal auditors and those charged with governance (e.g. the audit committee).

CONCLUSION

Fraudulent financial reporting is perceived as a major obstacle in efficiently functioning of capital markets and, despite its relatively few cases occurrence, has a tremendous cost reflected upon investors' credibility. Corporate responsibilities involved in fighting potentially fraudulent financial reporting are primary carried by those in charge with governance and senior management. Their greatest concern should be focused on designing and implementing a fraud management framework that supports anti-fraud programs and controls. At least same equal as importance, should be viewed the responsibilities of independent auditors in measuring and addressing financial reporting fraud. Professional skepticism is a "must have" character whenever the psychological conditions of fraud occurrence are assessed. Any red flags should therefore be investigated with great concern and vigilance. Most common management frauds involve improper revenue recognition (either premature or fictitious), biased accounting estimates, misstated assets or liabilities values (inventory, accounts receivable, fixed assets, accounts payable, and payroll expenses), and inadequate disclosures or omission of such disclosures. Prevention and deterrence of fraudulent financial reporting are definitely cheaper measures in comparison with the costs related to any fraud magnitude, either financial or, more important, reputational costs. As ACFE recommended, three type of measures could be taken therefore: reduce the pressures, reduce the opportunity and reduce the rationalization of committing management fraud.

REFERENCES

Arens, A. A., Elder, R. J., & Beasley, M. S. (2008). *Auditing and Assurance Services. An Integrated Approach* (12th ed.). Pearson Prentice Hall.

Association of Certified Fraud Examiners (ACFE). (2014). *Fraud Examiners Manual* (International Edition).

Association of Certified Fraud Examiners (ACFE). (2018). *Report to the Nations. Global Study on Occupational Fraud and Abuse*. Retrieved from https://www.acfe.com/fraud-resources.aspx

Bartsiotas, G. A., & Achamkulangare, G. (2016). *Fraud Prevention, Detection and Response in United Nations System Organizations*. Geneva: United Nations. Retrieved from https://www.acfe.com/fraud-resources.aspx

Beasley, M. S., Buckless, F. A., Glover, S. M., & Prawitt, D. F. (2009). *Auditing Cases. An Interactive Learning Approach* (4th ed.). Prentice Hall.

Bishop, T. J. F., & Hydoski, F. E. (2009). *Corporate Resiliency. Managing the Growing Risk of Fraud and Corruption*. John Wiley & Sons, Inc.

Boyton, W. C., & Johnson, R. N. (2006). *Modern Auditing. Assurance Services and the Integrity of Financial Reporting* (8th ed.). John Wiley & Sons.

Hermanson, R. H., Loeb, S. E., Saada, J. M., & Strawser, R. H. (1976). *Auditing Theory and Practice*. Homewood, IL: Richard D. Irwin, Inc.

IAASB. (2015). *Handbook of International Quality Control, Auditing, Review, Other Assurance, and Related Services Pronouncements* (Vol. 1). New York: International Federation of Accountants.

Kizil, C., & Burhan, K. (2018). Accounting Scandals and Eye-Catching Frauds: USA-Japan Comparison by Considering the Role of Auditing. *Journal of Asian Research, 2*(3), 1–14. doi:10.22158/jar.v2n3p123

Knapp, M. C. (2006). *Contemporary Auditing* (6th ed.). Thomson South-Western.

Kothari, S.P., Shu, S. & Wysocki, P.D. (2009). Do Managers Withhold Bad News? *Journal of Accounting Research, 47*(1).

Lord & Benoit Report. (2006). *Do the Benefits of Section 404 Exceed the Cost?* Retrieved from https://www.businesswire.com

Louwers, T. J., Ramsay, R. J., Sinason, D. H., & Strawser, J. R. (2007). *Auditing and Assurance Services* (2nd ed.). New York: McGraw-Hill Irwin.

Messier, W. F., Glover, S. M., & Prawitt, D. F. (2008). *Auditing and Assurance Services. A Systematic Approach* (5th ed.). New York: McGraw-Hill Irwin.

Nelson, M., Elliot, J., & Tarpley, R. (2002). How Are Earnings Managed? Examples from Auditors. *The Accounting Review, 77*, 175–202. doi:10.2308/accr.2002.77.s-1.175

Ragatz, J.A. (2015). *The Fraud Triangle can be an Ethics Crystal Ball*. The American College of Financial Services, TAC Digital Commons, Faculty Publications, Paper 261.

Ricchiute, D. N. (2006). Auditing (8th ed.). Thomson South-Western.

Richards, D. A., Melancon, B. C., & Ratley, J. D. (2008). *Managing the Business Risk of Fraud: A Practical Guide*. Retrieved from https://www.acfe.com/fraud-resources.aspx

Rittenberg, L. E., & Schwieger, B. J. (2005). *Auditing. Concepts for a Changing Environment* (5th ed.). Thomson South-Western.

Sherman, H. D., Young, D. S., & Collingwood, H. (2003). *Profits you can Trust. Spotting & Surviving Accounting Landmines*. Financial Times Prentice Hall.

Soltani, B. (2007). *Auditing. An International Approach*. Harlow, UK: Pearson Education.

Taylor, J. (2011). *Forensic Accounting*. Edinburgh Gate, UK: Pearson Education Ltd.

Thibodeau, J. C., & Freie, D. (2007). *Auditing after Sarbanes-Oxley. Illustrative Cases*. New York: McGraw-Hill Irwin.

Tickner, P. (2010). *How to be a successful auditor. A practical guide to investigating fraud in the workplace for internal auditors and managers*. West Sussex, UK: John Wiley and Sons Ltd Publication.

Wadhwa, L., & Virender, P. (2012). Forensic Accounting and Fraud Examination in India. *International Journal of Applied Engineering Research*, *7*(11), 1–29.

Whittington, O. R., & Pany, K. (2008). *Principles of Auditing & Other Assurance Services* (16th ed.). New York: McGraw-Hill Irwin.

ADDITIONAL READING

Alzola, M. A. (2017). Beware of the watchdog: Rethinking the normative justification of gatekeeper liability. *Journal of Business Ethics*, *140*(4), 705–721. doi:10.100710551-017-3460-3

Dechow, P., Hutton, A., Kim, J. H., & Sloan, R. G. (2012). Detecting earnings management: A new approach. *Journal of Accounting Research*, *50*(2), 275–334. doi:10.1111/j.1475-679X.2012.00449.x

Vladu, A. B., Amat, O., & Cuzdriorean, D. D. (2016). Truthfulness in accounting: How to discriminate accounting manipulators from non-manipulators. *Journal of Business Ethics*, *140*(4), 633–648. doi:10.100710551-016-3048-3

KEY TERMS AND DEFINITIONS

Accounting Estimates: Often made under uncertainty in terms of determining their value as it involves the use of judgment. As a result, the risk of material misstatement is greater when these estimates are involved and in some cases the auditor may determine that the risk of material misstatement is greater, and it requires special attention in the audit.

Creative Accounting: A tool to create a distortion of the quality of financial information, creating uncertainty about the consistency and comparability of information for users, in which case we are dealing with an accounting of intent.

Fair Value: The amount at which an asset is bought or sold in an arm's-length transaction, in which neither party is forced to act.

Financial Reporting: Individual financial statements prepared in accordance with IFRS, annual, semestrial, or whenever required in accordance with the national regulations of the reporting entity.

Risk: Possibility to manifest a phenomenon, act, or fact that may cause damage, loss, or may have a negative impact on the activity of an entity.

Chapter 9
The International Experience in Security Risk Analysis Methods

Anca Gabriela Petrescu
Valahia University, Romania

Mirela Anca Postole
Titu Maiorescu University, Romania

Marilena Ciobanasu
Titu Maiorescu University, Romania

ABSTRACT

The goal of information security is to be able not just to put in place measures to detect and mitigate attacks but also to predict attacks, deter attackers from attacking, and thus defend the systems from attack in the first place. Data protection should be based on the lessons learned over time, both within the organization and in other organizations. Over the time, a large number of methodologies for identifying information security risks were proposed and adopted and simplified approach to different methodologies has led to their classification in quantitative and qualitative, especially in terms of metrics used to quantify risk. This chapter proposes an international overview regarding the quantitative and qualitative analysis methods for information risk analysis. In practice almost always use a combination of these methods, depending on the characteristics of the organization investigated the degree of uncertainty associated with the method of analysis and risk management.

INTRODUCTION

Risk management process within the organization allows managers to handle uncertainty and associated risks and opportunities in an efficient manner, leading to increased ability to create added value (He, Chen, Chan & Bu, 2012; Kurosawa, Ohta & Kakuta, 2017).

Implementation of information security measures, however, is not always a smooth process and not slippery (Tropina & Callanan, 2015). In addition to the issues raised by the high cost of implementing security measures, the authorities control law implementation (enforcement) face a number of problems socially (Peltier, 2010).

DOI: 10.4018/978-1-5225-8455-1.ch009

There are cases where data protection measures may affect the privacy of individuals. In these circumstances arises open conflict between human rights defenders and enforcement authorities, which in some cases lead to legislative and procedural ambiguities, as happens for example if the widespread use of cryptographic mechanisms (Chen, Ge & Xie, 2015).

Information society in which we live requires us to identify new safeguards, on the one hand, the information, which otherwise we are indispensable and, on the other hand, the right to privacy (Agrawal & Tapaswi, 2017).

The essential factor needed to ensure the effectiveness of the risk management process within the organization, however, is the firm commitment of the management (Hiller & Russel, 2013). The commitment must be continuous and must involve the top management. Without this element, the initiative to conduct risk management cannot be successful. Keeping risk management policy up-to-date demonstrates that risk management is a dynamic activity, which benefits from the full support of the management board (Krombholz, Hobel, Huber & Weippl, 2015).

This is why, security mechanisms have to be properly designed and commensurate with the specific threats for the specific types of information (Landoll, 2010). Organizations have to expand and deepen their current information security risk frameworks to address these key threats (Wang & Hu, 2014). This process implies a more profound understanding of the risks associated with each threat, and a better capacity of tailoring the security framework to align with the organization's identified risks, regulatory requirements and perhaps most important – the increasing dependencies on information technology.

BACKGROUND

The risk analysis must be approached methodically to ensure that all activities of the organization were evaluated and all risks associated with these activities have been defined (Stepchenko & Voronova, 2015). The results of the risk analysis can be used to outline a risk profile of the organization that provides a rating of the significance of each risk and to prioritize risk management efforts. This process allows the mapping of risks by fields that affect the description of existing control mechanisms and indicates situations where the investment in controlled measures should be raised, lowered or redistributed (Enagi & Ochoche, 2013).

Risk analysis activity contributes to the efficiency and effectiveness of the organization's operations by identifying those risks that require management attention (Karim, 2007). It facilitates prioritization of risk control actions, depending on the impact on the organization and the potential benefit that they bring control measures organization. In this context, when we talk about treatment risks, the range of responses to risk includes tolerance, treatment, transfer and disposal (Coltman, Tallon, Sharma & Queiroz, 2015). However, organizations may decide that it is necessary to improve the control environment.

Some other external entities of the organization, such as customers, suppliers, business partners, external auditors, regulators and financial analysts often provide useful information for an efficient risk management process, but they are not responsible for the effectiveness of this process and also they are not part of the organizational risk management (Table 1).

Like any factor in a complex system, the benefits of information security are weighed against their total cost (including the additional costs incurred if the system is compromised). If the data or resources cost less, or are of less value, than their protection, adding security mechanisms and procedures is not

Table 1. Roles and responsibilities in the management of organizational risk

Roles	Responsibilities
General manager	• Determining the strategic approach to risk and determining the risk appetite of the organization • Establishing the structure responsible for risk management • Understand the most significant risks • Crisis Management Organization
Compartment managers	• Building risk awareness culture within departments of responsibility • Approval of the performance targets for risk management • Ensure implementation of recommendations to improve the risk posture of the organization to • Identifying and reporting changes in circumstances / risks
Executives	• Understanding, acceptance and implementation of the risk management process • Reporting of inefficient, unnecessary or unworkable • Reporting of loss events and incidents • Cooperate with management in cases of investigation of incidents
Risk manager	• Develop risk management policy and keeping it up to date • Documenting internal risk policies and structures • Coordination of risk management and internal control • Compiling information on risks and reporting to Top Management
Risk management specialists	• Providing support for setting specific risk management policies • Develop action plans for emergency and resumption of • Knowledge-date information in the field of specialty risks • Support investigation of incidents
Internal auditors	• Develop an internal audit program from specific risks • Provide assurance regarding risk management • Reporting on the efficiency and effectiveness of internal control

cost-effective because the data or resources can be reconstructed more cheaply than the protections themselves (Gandino, Celozzi & Rebaudengo, 2017). Unfortunately, this is rarely the case.

Overlapping benefits are also a consideration (Andress, 2003). Suppose the integrity protection mechanism can be augmented very quickly and cheaply to provide confidentiality (Smith, 2005). Then the cost of providing confidentiality is much lower. This shows that evaluating the cost of a particular security service depends on the mechanism chosen to implement it and on the mechanisms chosen to implement other security services. The cost-benefit analysis should take into account as many mechanisms as possible (Fischbacher-Smith, 2016). Adding security mechanisms to an existing system is often more expensive (and, incidentally, less effective) than designing them into the system in the first place.

Changes expected in the future from a society based purely on material resources in a society of intelligent resource already looming today, leading to widespread integration of processing and the management of knowledge and information (Lin, Lin & Pei, 2017). This is a structural change in the conditions of globalization, Internet access, and so on (Choi, Lee, Kim, Jung, Nam & Won, 2014).

THE INTERNATIONAL EXPERIENCE IN SECURITY RISK ANALYSIS METHODS

According with Friedberg et al. (2016) there are two main types of risk analysis, namely the analysis of quantitative and qualitative analysis.

A qualitative method using words or descriptive scales and the form a hierarchical structure that alternates between "rarely" and "almost certainly" (Collins & McCombie, 2012). Such a method is intended to prioritize the likelihood and the consequences of which can range from insignificant to moderate to severe.

For qualitative analysis, management and line staff responsible for risk management at various levels need to work together to develop a risk ranking matrix (Norris, 2001). Each of the criteria for determining the probability and consequences must be considered to place events in proper categories.

On the other hand, quantitative analysis is based criteria to establish the possibility of producing an event and its consequences (Winkler, 2010). The possibility of the occurrence probability is expressed as, not in the form of frequency, thereby ensuring that the risks were compared to a similar base. When we speak of the possibility of occurrence of similar events small possibility of this happening can be treated as a single event.

Method OCTAVE (Operationally Critical Threat, Asset and Vulnerability Evaluation - Evaluation Threats, Assets and Organizational Vulnerability Critical) based on the definition of complex, systematic and contextual essential components of an information system, using a three-stage organization to determine the risks associated with privacy, integrity and availability of information assets critical to the proper performance of the organization considered (Eriksson & Kovalainen, 2015). The method addresses both the organizational, technological and from a modern perspective, which provides an ongoing evaluation process.

The first stage "*Building profiles of assets based on their threats*" involves the evaluation of the entire organization, key areas were identified and analyzed in order to extract relevant information on those assets, the associated threats controls (current and potential necessary) that minimize the threats posed, as well as weaknesses in the approach to policy and practice information security within the organization.

In turn, this stage is divided into four steps:

Step 1: Determining competence in information security for the senior management of the organization;
Step 2: Determining competence in information security for the operational level of the organization;
Step 3: Determination of employee competence in the field of information security.

The first three steps are dedicated meetings with employees from all organizational levels to identify assets with information systems and how they may be affected. Thus, in these meetings participants are asked to identify priority/importance of these assets and the level of safety that are/should be made to protect them.

Step 4: Create profile threats. In this step the participants are exclusively members of the team risk management information that based on the documentation and information obtained in the first three steps selected critical assets in the proper performance of organizational, group and classify these assets, with associated security measures in according to the organizational level that we serve, creating an overview of organizational assets and identify threats to these asset classes and the individual assets.

The second stage "Identification of structural vulnerabilities" involves the systematic evaluation of the informational structure of the organization to determine the effectiveness of current information security solutions, identify weaknesses and vulnerabilities (vulnerabilities classified as conceptual, implementation and configuration). In general, technological aspects are identified by comparison with standards established profile either producers or independent bodies. Generally, at this stage weaknesses of the system are determined based on a variety of automated tools, including tools for testing the integrity of files, antivirus, and system efficiency by limiting access passwords, security communications, and many other instruments.

Once the assets, threats and vulnerabilities were identified, proceed to identify risks to the subject information system (Hong, Kim & Cho, 2010). The purpose of third stage is to determine how the risks associated with certain organizational assets. From the perspective of OCTAVE risk is considered a result of losses caused by the absence of inadequacy of ways to prevent or minimize them (Yang, Wu & Wang, 2014). Measuring losses or impact severity level of risk can be both qualitative and quantitative, depending on available resources and risk management information security system. Determination of information security risks is generally difficult because information about threats and asset values are generally more difficult to obtain and quantify and risk factors are constantly changing. OCTAVE risk analysis based on the methodology involves the use of risk scenarios associated with each critical asset of the organization.

Another mixed method (qualitative and quantitative risk assessment, known as VAR (Value Risk) based on the identification of the most severe effects of the production risks could have on the objectives of the organization, in a horizon type and a given confidence interval and aims to achieve optimal balance between the risks assumed and necessary expenses of minimizing them (Singer & Friedman, 2014). The four steps proposed by the VAR methodology includes identifying threats, estimating the probability of these threats, the calculation VAR (value risk) and determining controls to prevent or minimize the effects of identified risks.

In the first stage are identified risks (current or potential) that may face information system analysis. VAR method recommended classification as fraud, malicious activities, jokes, and attempts to access confidential information, natural disasters, sabotage, and user errors. Concrete ways of experiencing these threats can include DoS attacks, theft, deletion or amendment or affecting the normal operation of networks. These methods are designed to exploit vulnerabilities in information systems and include viruses, Trojan horse programs, and worms, "burst" passwords, intercept electronic mail and packages traded by different applications in computer communication networks, as the assumption of false identities within these networks (spoofing).

Activities in the second stage aimed to determine the probability of threats identified in the previous step. This activity can be performed on the basis of qualitative or quantitative methods described above. In addition, the VAR method recommended secondary sources of information (education provided by government agencies or by market research institutes) to obtain information about the frequency of occurrence of various types of threat. A study published by Khan, Gani, Wahab, Shiraz and Ahmad (2016) conducted in the United States on a representative sample of employees of information technology departments private and governmental organizations found that 80% of the systems that they use or faced with viruses in the last year, the misuse of the organization's information resources was reported by 58% of these, 42% experienced attempted or unauthorized access outside the organization, and 24% of them have had to repair the destructive effects of malicious or accidental activities of their colleagues. Additional sources for this information can be public reports/government journals associated with different systems or applications used historical data or in-depth interviews with relevant personnel information security departments.

Based on the risks identified in the previous stage and the frequency with which they generate threats occur, the method involves calculating VAR variable with the same name, based on market value (PV) of the organization investigated desired type horizon and confidence interval (statistics) to the result obtained by the formula:

$$VAR = \pm a * \sigma * T$$

where a is the confidence interval of the result (for the 99% value is 2.64, 95% 1.96), σ is the estimated market value of the organization, and T is the number of days for which the calculation is made.

The last stage of this method involves selecting different methods of minimizing risk (based on existing standards in the industry and based on secondary sources of information). VAR value is used to determine the level of investment, a company for which this value is less need to invest more modest in information security than companies with a similar higher.

Risk assessment method called Ukrainian (University of California Risk Assessment) developed by scholars at the University of California is an essential quantitative method that closely follows the recommendations of BS7799 standard which sets out a code of practice for information security, tracking its performance assuming a number of new steps (Gaidelys & Valodkiene, 2011).

Stage 1: Establishing the risk assessment team. This team will be responsible for collecting, analyzing and reporting the organization's management. It is essential that all elements of the production cycle of the organization to be represented on this team, including the minimum manpower, administrative and physical security systems.

Stage 2: Define the project goals. Risk assessment team should clarify at the outset the project objective risk assessment, specifying the department, area or function of the organization will be assessed, responsibilities of team members, personnel to be interviewed, standards used, the documentation required in the evaluation, as well as operations or functions to be observed in this process.

Stage 3: Identify the assets involved in the evaluation process. Organizational assets can include (but not limited to) personal, real hardware and software, data and information (including classification of sensitive data and critical for the smooth running of the organization), where operating facilities, as implemented controls to protect their. Identify all assets associated with the project objectives defined in the previous step is essential for project risk management.

Stage 4: Classification of potential losses. This step involves identifying and describing how production risk situations identified will affect the organization and losses (financial or otherwise) that it would incur in this case. Thus, this loss could be the result of physical damage to the equipment, preventing legitimate users from accessing organizational assets, modification, unauthorized access or disclosure of confidential information. And in some cases, losses can be quantifiable, such as the loss of credibility of the organization.

Stage 5: Identify threats and vulnerabilities. A threat is defined as an event, process or action that exploits vulnerability to affect an organization's information assets. Uses and can be no natural threats, human accidental or malicious. More in detail, the threats can result in events such as sags biological contamination or leakage of toxic chemicals, natural disasters, hardware malfunction or software, loss or damage to data integrity, sabotage, theft or vandalism. In turn, vulnerabilities relate to weaknesses in logical or physical security of organizational assets that a threat can exploit to affect them. Vulnerabilities are generally classified as physical security vulnerabilities, menu systems security; communication security processes associated personnel, plans, policies, procedures, management, support, and other types.

Stage 6: Identify existing controls. Different ways of minimizing the risks of adverse events with the organization's information security are generally known as controls. Uses and controls are defined as safety tools designed to reduce the likelihood that a particular threat successfully exploiting a vulnerability information system to successfully attack a particular asset of the organization. This step is concerned with the identification of those controls that are already in place, as well as determining the usefulness and efficiency of the context of the current.

Stage 7: Data Analysis. At this stage all data collected will be used to determine the actual risks faced by assets under the current project risk management. Ukrainian analysis technique involves preparing a list of assets and their associated threats, the types of losses caused by the materialization of such threats and vulnerabilities that facilitated the attacks. Also be estimated frequency with which these threats may occur.

Stage 8: Determination of effective ways to minimize the risks referring to costs implementation. The assessment should provide an estimate of costs associated with implementing the proposed controls, costs and annual maintenance and updating of their life cycle.

Stage 9: Final Report. Project risk management in accordance with Ukrainian methodology involves presenting a formal final report in a form intelligible and useful to the audience being addressed. In general it is a simple and easy to read report and assimilate that conclusions with detailed analyzes that led to their formulation. The report should also include information identified in the organization and list of assets, threats and vulnerabilities associated, as well as determining risks, recommended controls and cost-benefit analysis.

Although there are many methods and approaches to risk management process steps, the most widely accepted view is that the process consists of two stages: risk analysis and risk treatment (Liaudanskienel, Ustinovicius & Bogdanovicius, 2009).

Therefore, risk management covers a wide range of activities rigorously defined and organized, based on the conditions of existence and objectives of the organization, the analysis of risk factors in an optimal and efficient operating concept.

SOLUTIONS AND RECOMMENDATIONS

Many organizations adopt the practice of updating the risk management policy annually (Yami, Castaldo, Dagnino & Le Roy, 2010). This practice ensures that the overall approach to risk management is in line with the latest practices. At the same time, it offers the organization the opportunity to focus on future goals, on the identification of priorities in terms of risk management and to identify emerging risks.

Consequently, the implementation of a continuous and correct process of risk management in all activities of the organization leads to crisis prevention and avoidance of resources waste, by inappropriate reactions to, crisis and poor allocation and use of internal resources (Hadžiosmanović, Bolzoni & Hartel, 2012). It also leads to the minimization of risk and of the probability for negative events to occur in the organization, to protection against negative effects of these events and to real-time control of the organization's activities. At the same time, this process requires a division of responsibilities clearly delineated within the organization, creating a culture of risk prevention at all levels of the organization.

In Romania, according to the Code of internal control standards including management/internal control public entities' risk management methodology is aimed at providing a comprehensive risk control, allowing you to maintain an acceptable level of risk exposure for the public entity with minimal costs.

In addition, as we pointed out previously, management vision must change radically, from a passive or reactive management style to a proactive style, ready at any moment to face the challenges of achieving the objectives of the organization.

FUTURE RESEARCH DIRECTIONS

To be successful, the risk management process must be proportioned according to the risk level of the organization (depending on the size, nature and complexity of the organization), in conjunction with other activities of the organization, to be comprehensive in scope, embedded in routine activities and dynamic to adapt to changing contexts easily (Arukonda & Sinha, 2015).

This approach allows the risk management process to provide positive results, including compliance with the regulatory framework, increasing the confidence of partners and optimize decision making (Hjortdal, 2011). Impact or benefits associated with these results include more efficient conduct of the operations of the organizations more efficient and effective strategy tactics. It is essential that these benefits be measured and sustained.

The first step in understanding risk is to understand the risks in relation to the mission of an organization and its key assets. An appropriate level of understanding can be achieved based on a thorough analysis which risks are identified organization. Once these risks are identified, management organization must decide how to address them.

When an organization is launching a risk analysis team running the process seeks to identify possible sources of problems, formulating questions such as: Under what conditions our activities can fail? What we can identify weaknesses in the security system? We can meet the objectives within the time and on the terms set?

Determining the magnitude or severity of the impact of a particular threat involves identifying potential losses in each category of security (confidentiality, integrity and availability), while the probability associated with its production (Malatras, Geneiatakis & Vakalis, 2016). The impact may be associated with loss of system functionality or other assets of the organization, degradation, reducing response time for legitimate users, loss of public confidence in the organization or unauthorized disclosure of sensitive data.

Finally, determining the level of risk is generally made based on the probability that a given threat exploiting vulnerability in the system and the gravity that having this threat has on the organization's information assets (Tiago, Manoj & Espadanal, 2014). Mathematically, the risk is determined as the product of probability and severity of threats manifestation of their impact on the confidentiality, availability and integrity of the information system of the organization.

Future research is important because certain events with a negative impact on the objectives to be transformed into opportunities if they are identified early.

CONCLUSION

In the context of vehicle information through computer systems and communications, risk is defined as the probability that a threat to exploit the vulnerabilities of property belonging to the organization and thereby cause injury organization (Broadbent & Schaffner, 2016). Risk is measured in terms of probability of delivering a threat and the consequences of this event (impact). The risk may be associated with damage to one or more of the security: confidentiality, integrity, availability and, where appropriate, authenticity and non-repudiation of information, namely information and communication systems.

Over the time, a large number of methodologies for identifying information security risks were proposed and adopted and simplified approach to different methodologies has led to their classification in quantitative and qualitative, especially in terms of metrics used to quantify risk (Singh & Fhom, 2017).

In practice almost always use a combination of these methods, depending on the characteristics of the organization investigated the degree of uncertainty associated with the method of analysis and risk management. Thus, if all the elements of this analysis (the value of assets, impact severity, frequency threats, effectiveness of controls, uncertainty and probability threat materializes) are expressed in quantitative terms, the process can be characterized as a fully quantitative one. Otherwise, depending on the wording of these measurements, risk management is partly or wholly qualitative one.

Risk assessment information based on the six distinct elements considered in risk management: the value of information assets, threat frequency, and severity vulnerabilities exploitation in the production of threats organizational effectiveness of risk minimization procedures (controls), their cost, as the level of uncertainty associated with the process information risk management (Kesan & Hayes, 2012).

Using quantitative methodologies for assessing information security risks involve a number of advantages such as obtaining objective and statistically significant, the quantitative information is expressed more easily understandable by people with marginal training in related areas of information technology, the results are a reliable basis the cost / benefit analysis and the performance of risk management activities is easily evaluated and expressed in a way familiar to the organization's management.

Among the advantages of using qualitative methods is included that in general, there is no need to accurately determine the financial value of assets, but rather their effects in terms of general information security (confidentiality, availability, integrity).

Qualitative assessment of the risks associated with information security also requires a number of disadvantages, including the fact that risk assessment and the results of this process are essentially subjective, influenced by qualified and experienced analysts (Campbell, Kay & Avison, 2005). Also, the lack of numerical values associated costs of identified risks tends to lead to inaccurate perception of them. In addition, this type of evaluation does not provide useful cost / benefit analysis and does not allow objective tracking performance of risk management activities, where all metrics are subjective.

REFERENCES

Agrawal, N., & Tapaswi, S. (2017). Defense schemes for variants of distributed denial-of-service (DDoS) attacks in cloud computing: A survey. *Information Security Journal: A Global Perspective, 26*(1), 1-13.

Andress, A. (2003). *Surviving Security: How to Integrate People, Process, and Technology*. Boca Raton, FL: Auerbach Publications. doi:10.1201/9780203501405

Arukonda, S., & Sinha, S. (2015). The innocent perpetrators: Reflectors and reflection attacks. *Advanced Computer Science, 4*, 94–98.

Broadbent, A., & Schaffner, C. (2016). Quantum cryptography beyond quantum key distribution. *Designs, Codes and Cryptography, 78*(1), 351–382. doi:10.100710623-015-0157-4

Campbell, B., Kay, R., & Avison, D. (2005). Strategic Alignment: A Practitioner's Perspective. *Journal of Enterprise Information Management, 18*(6), 653–664. doi:10.1108/17410390510628364

Chen, H., Ge, L., & Xie, L. A. (2015). User Authentication Scheme Based on Elliptic Curves Cryptography for Wireless Ad Hoc Networks. *Sensors (Basel), 15*(7), 17057–17075. doi:10.3390150717057 PMID:26184224

Choi, Y., Lee, D., Kim, J., Jung, J., Nam, J., & Won, D. (2014). Security Enhanced User Authentication Protocol for Wireless Sensor Networks Using Elliptic Curves Cryptography. *Sensors (Basel), 14*(6), 10081–10106. doi:10.3390140610081 PMID:24919012

Collins, S., & McCombie, S. (2012). Stuxnet: The emergence of a new cyber weapon and its implications. *Journal of Policing. Intelligence and Counter Terrorism, 7*(1), 80–91. doi:10.1080/18335330.2012.653198

Coltman, T., Tallon, P., Sharma, R., & Queiroz, M. (2015). Strategic IT alignment: Twenty-five years on. *Journal of Information Technology, 30*(2), 91–100. doi:10.1057/jit.2014.35

Enagi, M. A., & Ochoche, A. (2013). The Role of Enterprise Architecture in Aligning Business and Information Technology in Organisations: Nigerian Government Investment on Information Technology. *IACSIT International Journal of Engineering and Technology, 3*(1), 59–65.

Eriksson, P., & Kovalainen, A. (2015). Qualitative Methods in Business Research: A Practical Guide to Social Research. *Sage (Atlanta, Ga.)*.

Fischbacher-Smith, D. (2016). Breaking bad? In search of a (softer) systems view of security ergonomics. *Security Journal, 29*(1), 5–22. doi:10.1057j.2015.41

Friedberg, I., McLaughlin, K., Smith, P., Laverty, D., & Sezer, S. (2016). STPA-SafeSec: Safety and security analysis for cyber-physical systems. *Journal of Information Security and Applications, 29*, 1–12.

Gaidelys, V., & Valodkiene, G. (2011). The Methods of Selecting and Assessing Potential Consumers Used of by Competitive Intelligence. *Inzinerine Ekonomika-Engineering Economics, 22*(2), 196–202.

Gandino, F., Celozzi, C., & Rebaudengo, M. (2017). A Key Management Scheme for Mobile Wireless Sensor Networks. *Applied Sciences, 7*(5), 490. doi:10.3390/app7050490

Hadžiosmanović, D., Bolzoni, D., & Hartel, P. H. (2012). A log mining approach for process monitoring in SCADA. *International Journal of Information Security, 11*(4), 231–251. doi:10.100710207-012-0163-8

He, D., Chen, C., Chan, S., & Bu, J. (2012). Secure and efficient handover authentication based on bilinear pairing functions. *IEEE Transactions on Wireless Communications, 11*(1), 48–53. doi:10.1109/TWC.2011.110811.111240

Hiller, J., & Russel, R. (2013). The challenge and imperative of private sector cybersecurity: An international comparison. *Computer Law & Security Review, 29*(3), 236–245. doi:10.1016/j.clsr.2013.03.003

Hjortdal, M. (2011). China's use of cyber warfare: Espionage meets strategic deterrence. *The Journal of Strategic Studies, 4*(2), 1–24.

Hong, J., Kim, J., & Cho, J. (2010). The trend of the security research for the insider cyber threat. *International Journal of Future Generation Communication and Networking, 3*(2), 31–40.

Karim, H. V. (2007). *Strategic security management: a risk assessment guide for decision makers.* Elsevier Inc.

Kesan, P. J., & Hayes, M. C. (2012). Mitigative counterstriking: Self-defense and deterrence in cyberspace. *Harvard Journal of Law & Technology, 25*(2), 474–529.

Khan, S., Gani, A., Wahab, A. W. A., Shiraz, M., & Ahmad, I. (2016). Network forensics: Review, taxonomy, and open challenges. *Journal of Network and Computer Applications, 66,* 214–235. doi:10.1016/j.jnca.2016.03.005

Krombholz, K., Hobel, H., Huber, M., & Weippl, E. (2015). Advanced social engineering attacks. *Journal of Information Security and Applications, 22,* 113–122. doi:10.1016/j.jisa.2014.09.005

Kurosawa, K., Ohta, H., & Kakuta, K. (2017). How to make a linear network code (strongly) secure. *Designs, Codes and Cryptography, 82*(3), 559–582. doi:10.100710623-016-0180-0

Landoll, D. J. (2010). The security risk assessment handbook: a complete guide for performing security risk assessment (2nd ed.). CRC Press, Taylor & Francis Group.

Liaudanskienel, R., Ustinovicius, L., & Bogdanovicius, A. (2009). Evaluation of Construction Process Safety Solutions Using the TOPSIS Method. *Inzinerine Ekonomika-Engineering Economics, 64*(4), 32–40.

Lin, Z., Lin, D., & Pei, D. (2017). Practical construction of ring LFSRs and ring FCSRs with low diffusion delay for hardware cryptographic applications. *Cryptography and Communications, 9*(4), 431–440. doi:10.100712095-016-0183-8

Malatras, A., Geneiatakis, D., & Vakalis, I. (2016). On the efficiency of user identification: A system-based approach. *International Journal of Information Security, 15*(1), 1–19.

Norris, P. (2001). *Digital Divide: Civic Engagement, Information Poverty and the Internet Worldwide.* New York: Cambridge University Press. doi:10.1017/CBO9781139164887

Peltier, T. R. (2010). Information security risk analysis (3rd ed.). CRC Press, Taylor & Francis Group, Auerbach Publications.

Singer, W. P., & Friedman, A. (2014). *Cyber Security and Cyber War: What Everyone Needs to Know.* New York: Oxford University Press.

Singh, A., & Fhom, H. C. S. (2017). Restricted usage of anonymous credentials in vehicular ad hoc networks for misbehavior detection. *International Journal of Information Security, 16*(2), 195–201. doi:10.100710207-016-0328-y

Smith, D. (2005). Dancing with the mysterious forces of chaos: Issues around complexity, knowledge and the management of uncertainty. *Clinician in Management, (3/4)*, 115–123.

Stepchenko, D., & Voronova, I. (2015). Assessment of Risk Function Using Analytical Network Process. *Inzinerine Ekonomika-Engineering Economics, 26*(3), 264–271.

Tiago, O., Manoj, T., & Espadanal, M. (2014). Assessing the determinants of cloud computing adoption: An analysis of the manufacturing and services sectors. *Information & Management, 51*(5), 497–510. doi:10.1016/j.im.2014.03.006

Tropina, T., & Callanan, C. (2015). *Self- and Co-regulation in Cybercrime, Cybersecurity and National Security*. New York: Springer International Publishing. doi:10.1007/978-3-319-16447-2

Wang, W., & Hu, L. (2014). A secure and efficient handover authentication protocol for wireless networks. *Journal of Sensors, 14*(7), 11379–11394. doi:10.3390140711379 PMID:24971471

Winkler, I. (2010). *Justifying IT Security – Managing Risk & Keeping your network Secure*. Qualys Inc.

Yami, S., Castaldo, S., Dagnino, B., & Le Roy, F. (Eds.). (2010). *Coopetition: winning strategies for the 21st century*. Edward Elgar Publishing. doi:10.4337/9781849807241

Yang, C. N., Wu, C. C., & Wang, D. S. (2014). A discussion on the relationship between probabilistic visual cryptography and random grid. *Information Sciences, 278*, 141–173. doi:10.1016/j.ins.2014.03.033

ADDITIONAL READING

Barton, K. A., Tejay, G., Lane, M., & Terrell, S. (2016). Information system security commitment: A study of external influences on senior management. *Computers & Security, 59*, 9–25. doi:10.1016/j.cose.2016.02.007

Hong, W., & Thong, J. Y. (2013). Internet privacy concerns: An integrated conceptualization and four empirical studies. *Management Information Systems Quarterly, 37*(1), 275–298. doi:10.25300/MISQ/2013/37.1.12

Karanja, E. (2017). The role of the chief information security officer in the management of IT security. *Information & Computer Security, 25*(3), 300–329. doi:10.1108/ICS-02-2016-0013

Sarabi, A., Naghizadeh, P., Liu, Y., & Liu, M. (2016). Risky business: Fine-grained data breach prediction using business profiles. *Journal of Cybersecurity, 2*(1), 15–28. doi:10.1093/cybsec/tyw004

KEY TERMS AND DEFINITIONS

Credibility: A concept directly related to risk management. How the organization addresses its credibility influences behavior, and internal and external relations of trust.

Financial Risks: These types of risk may reflect inadequate or unclear definition of strategies and objectives of the organization.

Residual Risk: The risk that remains after security measures are implemented in a computer system and communications, as a consequence of the fact that not all threats can be countered and not all vulnerabilities can be eliminated or reduced to zero.

Risk Analysis: A process of calculating risk. Algorithms for calculating the risk calculated risk as a function of the organization's assets, threats, and vulnerabilities.

Risk Management: A process conducted by the board of directors, the managers and others within an organization, in order to identify potential events that may affect the organization to manage the risks to the organization and to provide reasonable assurance regarding the achievement of organizational objectives.

Strategic Risks: Risks that should be considered by top management of the organization. These risks may affect the strategic objectives set by the organization in the long term.

Threat: A potential cause unwanted incidents that may result in damage to the mission of a system or an entire organization. Security threats can be accidental or deliberate (malicious) and are characterized by elements of threat, attack method, and the goods subject to the threat.

Chapter 10
Mobile Commerce Adoption

Husam AlFahl
Taibah University, Saudi Arabia

ABSTRACT

Mobile commerce can be a great potential to generate new streams of revenue for many established and new businesses. The penetration rates for mobile phone subscriptions in many countries show that there are significant opportunities to invest in and introduce mobile commerce services in many of these markets. The aim of this chapter is to explore and identify the various factors that influence the intention to adopt mobile commerce in Saudi banks and telecoms. A number of these factors were included in this research as they are chosen from well-known theories and investigated in the current study within the mobile commerce context using principal component analysis technique. The findings of the research show that seven components can affect the intention to adopt mobile commerce in Saudi banks and telecoms. The three most significant components that can affect the intention to adopt mobile commerce services in Saudi banks and telecoms are performance expectancy, organizational readiness, and mobile commerce features and opportunities.

INTRODUCTION

Since the introduction of smart phones, there has been a noticeable shift in the use of wireless technologies. We have now reached the stage where almost every new application has an equivalent mobile version. At the same time, telecommunication networks, including wireless, have become sufficiently reliable, fast, and widespread to provide the required connectivity for users around the world. Innovative wireless devices, such as smart phones, allow users to, amongst other things, conduct electronic transactions and access vital information anywhere and anytime (Benou & Vassilakis, 2010). Smart phones and other wireless devices have become ubiquitous tools that enable mobile electronic commerce, known as Mobile Commerce (mCommerce). According to Siau, Lim, and Shen (2001), the interaction between technologies such as the Internet, mobile computing devices, and wireless networks such as mobile networks facilitates the existence of mCommerce.

mCommerce can be considered as the latest version, or next generation, of electronic commerce (eCommerce). mCommerce can be defined as "the use of mobile, wireless (handheld) devices to com-

DOI: 10.4018/978-1-5225-8455-1.ch010

municate and conduct transactions through public and private networks" (Balasubramanian, Peterson, & Jarvenpaa, 2002, p. 349). mCommerce has many applications, such as, using location services to deliver location-based information and for tracking and logistics (Stoica, Miller, & Stotlar, 2005), as well as purchasing from vending machines or paying for fuel using a cell phone's credit. According to Tiwari, Buse, and Herstatt (2006), mCommerce is directly linked to eCommerce because all services in both are carried out by electronic means through computer-based networks and can be accessed using tele-communication networks. The only difference between the two is that eCommerce provides "anytime" access to online services whereas mCommerce potentially allows users to perform online transactions "anytime and anywhere" (Saidi, 2009). This capacity for "anytime and anywhere" access is one of the most significant advantages of mCommerce from a business perspective (Varshney, Mallow, Ahluwalia, & Jain, 2004). According to Siau et al. (2001), mCommerce "is about delivering the right information to the right place at the right time".

Based on the lack of studies about organizational adoption of mCommerce in the Kingdom of Saudi Arabia (KSA) and the significant investment opportunity that the Saudi market is offering for busi-nesses, this research is focused mainly on mCommerce organizational adoption practices in the KSA. This paper presents a model of the factors that influence the intention to adopt mCommerce by Saudi organizations. According to the Gulfnews (2013), the smartphone penetration rate in the KSA is forecast to reach 50 per cent within the next four years and by 2015, the volume of mCommerce in the Middle East and Africa could reach $4.9 billion. By the end of 2013, there were approximately 51 million mo-bile phone subscriptions in the KSA representing an overall penetration of around 169.7 per cent of the Saudi population (CITC, 2014). Based on the large number of mobile subscriptions in the KSA and the rapid development in the Saudi mobile telecommunication market, it can be seen that there is a huge opportunity for organizations to adopt mCommerce services in the KSA.

BACKGROUND

Many gaps can be identified in the current mCommerce literature. For example, Okazaki (2005) sug-gested some insights for future research in the field of mCommerce; these include research comparing eCommerce and mCommerce, research about mobile-based social networks, and the development of research methodologies to study mCommerce. The literature presents a large number of studies in the field of technology adoption. Although mCommerce is still a relatively new technology in carrying out business processes, there are a significant number of articles about its adoption at the individual level. In addition, the number of these articles has noticeably grown in the past few years. On the other hand, there are a limited number of research-based studies about the adoption of mCommerce at the organi-zational level, with few conducted in the KSA.

The following are some of the identified gaps. Stoica et al. (2005) believed that "the patterns of mCom-merce adoption and its impact on the business strategy in an environment which is highly influenced by government participation has yet to be explored in business research" (p. 215). Furthermore, Okazaki (2005) revealed that research in the field of managerial issues in mobile Internet adoption is sparse. Additionally, there is a very limited amount of research in the area of wireless enterprise (Varshney et al., 2004; Varshney & Vetter, 2000; Vrechopoulos, Constantiou, Sideris, Doukidis, & Mylonopoulos, 2003; Yuan & Zhang, 2003).

Apart from the overt focus on adoption studies there are no clear models used to determine exactly what factors influence, drive, and ultimately facilitate successful mCommerce adoption. Studies such as (Bhatti, 2007; O'Donnell, Jackson, Shelly, & Ligertwood, 2007; Sgriccia et al., 2007; Tiwari et al., 2006; Zheng & Ni, 2006) are exploratory in nature, defining conceptual categories and extracting themes from case studies. This has led to a specific set of unrelated exploratory studies with emphasis on adoption, success factors (Zeeshan, Cheung, & Scheepers, 2007) and the impact of payment services (Hassinen, Hyppönen, & Trichina, 2008; Henten, Olesen, Saugstrup, & Tan, 2004; López Catalán & Díaz Luque, 2008; Mallat & Tuunainen, 2008).

Research so far has also not considered organizational factors in much depth and has instead concentrated on broad geographical areas such as Japan for example, or the adoption of specific organizational technologies (Henten et al., 2004; Varshney et al., 2004). A recent review of the literature (Alfahl, Sanzogni, & Houghton, 2012) found that across a broad range of these studies no single research model, unified or otherwise, has been appropriated in the study of mCommerce adoption in organizations. Drawing on the work of others, a series of factors studied in isolation emerges. Alfahl et al. (2012) proposed 15 adoption factors that may affect such adoption. This paper took the challenge by furthering the authors' research questions stated earlier. To achieve this, this research adopt a quantitative research method test the mCommerce organizational adoption model from (Alfahl et al., 2012) for validity. Hence, the main goal for conducting this research is to test mCommerce organizational adoption model from (Alfahl et al., 2012). Such model may help in understanding the different factors that may affect the intention to adopt mCommerce services in organizations. Producing a conceptual model to support organizations when adopting and implementing mCommerce services can be considered a significant contribution to the literature (Narduzzi, 2001; Stoica & Roach, 2006).

FACTORS AFFECTING INTERNET ADVERTISING ADOPTION IN AD AGENCIES

According to Alfahl et al. (2012), mCommerce Organizational Adoption Model contains adoption factors that were identified from the literature by combining many theories and models including diffusion of innovation (Rogers, 2003), unified theory of acceptance and use of technology (Venkatesh, Morris, Davis, & Davis, 2003), technology acceptance model (Davis, 1989; Davis, Bagozzi, & Warshaw, 1989), theory of reasoned action (Fishbein & Ajzen, 1975), and other theories. Alfahl et al. (2012), defines each adoption factor separately with a proposition as well as the supporting literature. These propositions are investigated in the present study to confirm their validity and to see if the factors have an effect on the mCommerce organizational adoption within the Saudi context.

A quantitative research method is applied to this research in order to consolidate the findings from previous research. In this research, a survey questionnaire is designed to test, modify, and refine the conceptual model and the hypotheses adopted from previous research. At this research, a well-known quantitative technique called Principal Components Analysis (PCA) is applied to refine and reduce the number of variables that influence the adoption of mCommerce in organizations and modify the proposed conceptual model. The purposes of conducting this analysis are to reduce the number of independent variables by keeping the ones deemed to be significant and eliminating the less- important ones, to understand the structure and the relationship of the variables included in the study, and to construct a questionnaire that can be used in future research to measure the variables. Field (2013) stated that these three reasons are the main use for PCA. Because it "transforms a large number of correlated variables into a few uncorrelated principal components, PCA is a dimension reduction method" (Saporta & Niang, 2009). In addition, Armeanu and Lache (2008) stated that "PCA is a multivariate data analysis technique whose main purpose is to reduce the dimension of the observations and thus simplify the analysis and interpretation of data, as well as facilitate the construction of predictive models".

The survey questionnaire was designed by identifying the items that can measure the various mCommerce adoption variables identified from the literature. Most of these items or questions were adapted from the existing literature and theories as well as other studies in the field of new technology adoption. Furthermore, a scale to measure different items was designed after identifying the items. As this research is focused on the Saudi market, the information sheet and the questionnaire were translated to Arabic. The information sheet and the questionnaire were translated into Arabic using the back translation technique (Chapman & Carter, 1979). Besides the paper-based version, the questionnaires also had online versions that were designed using Google docs.

The seven components which emerged from the PCA are further contextualized and classified based on the items that cluster around each one. These seven components were grouped into two groups—organizational / environmental and technological—as illustrated in the following section. The resulted seven components are labelled as follows: Performance expectancy (PE); Organizational readiness (OR); mCommerce features and opportunities (MFO); Compatibility of mCommerce services (CMS); Policy and legal environment (PLE); Social influence (SI); Top management support (TMS).

The target population of the survey was employees from both telecommunication and banking sectors within the KSA. From the online survey questionnaire, only 64 responses were received. The response rate was difficult to count since the number of people who came across the online survey is unknown due to the fact that the survey was posted many times to social media sites for two months. The paper-based survey was distributed physically to banks and telecommunication companies. In this research, 80 questionnaires were distributed to both banks and telecommunication companies in a random way, and only 38 valid responses were received. The response rate for the paper-based survey questionnaire was 47.5 per cent. Overall, 102 responses were received, 64 online and 38 paper-based.

When conducting PCA, three main steps should be considered: assessment of the suitability of the data, components extraction, and components rotation and interpretation (Pallant, 2011). In order to assess the suitability of the collected data and know if the sample is adequate to run PCA, the Kaiser-Meyer-Olkin measure of sampling adequacy (KMO) should be applied (Field, 2013; Kaiser, 1970). Many researchers suggest that KMO can be acceptable if its value is above .5 (Field, 2013; Kaiser, 1974). However, Kaiser (1970) stated that "it appears that we don't have good factor-analytic data until measure of sampling adequacy gets to be at least in the .80s, and really excellent data does not occur until we reach the .90s".

In this study, PCA technique was used to extract the components that account for most of the variation in the data. This technique is the right choice since the aim of this study is to explore the data in order to generate future hypotheses (Field, 2013). After applying the previous method to extract the underlying components, the researcher has three techniques that can be used to decide about the number of components to retain. These techniques are Kaiser's criterion, scree test, and parallel analysis (Pallant, 2011). Kaiser's criterion, or the eigenvalue value of 1.0 or more rule, is one of the most commonly used techniques (Field, 2013; Hutcheson & Sofroniou, 1999; Pallant, 2011).

In order to simplify the interpretation of components to be retained, factor rotation can be applied (Hutcheson & Sofroniou, 1999; Pallant, 2011). Researchers can make a simple interpretation for components if a group of points have fallen on or close to the axes; this can be achieved graphically by rotating the axes of the graph, which presents the data points in a way that the variables are loaded maximally to a particular component (Field, 2013; Hutcheson & Sofroniou, 1999). The two types of rotation are orthogonal and oblique (Field, 2013). The most common orthogonal rotation method is the Varimax, as it attempts to minimize the number of variables which have high loadings on each component. On the other hand, the most common oblique rotation technique is Direct Oblimin (Pallant, 2011).

The number of the valid responses obtained from the quantitative survey consists of 102 cases of employees who work in the two target sectors. The 102 collected cases can be divided based on the method of collection, namely online and paper-based questionnaires. An independent samples test which compares paper-based and online surveys was conducted and it shows that there is no difference detected between the results of the two questionnaires. The following are the results of the SPSS analysis that provide a description of the study's sample. Of the participants, 91.2 per cent are between 21 and 40 years of age, and almost 63 per cent are between 31 and 40 years of age.

Moreover, approximately 54 per cent of participants have a high monthly income of more than 11,000 Saudi Riyals. Overall, almost 81 per cent of respondents earn more than 7,000 Saudi Riyals per month.

Almost all participants (99 per cent) use smartphones. In addition, 93.1 per cent of participants are Saudis (see Table 1). Around 58 per cent of the participants are employees in the Saudi banking sector.

PCA was conducted using SPSS on the 47 items included in the questionnaire, by applying varimax rotation. The results showed that twelve components can be extracted, and these components in total explain 74.94 per cent of the total variance. The scree plot was unclear and the determination of the twelve components was based on the Kaiser's criterion (eigenvalue > 1) as suggested by Field (2013), Hutcheson and Sofroniou (1999), and Pallant (2011). Based on the sample size of 102 cases, items that have loading of less than .512 have been ignored as suggested by (Field, 2013). The Kaiser-Meyer-Olkin (KMO), which measures the sampling adequacy for the analysis, is .817. The resulted KMO is acceptable since it is above .5 (Field, 2013; Kaiser, 1974). All KMO values for individual items were above .5 except the two items that measure complexity with values of .404 and .348 as shown in the anti-image matrix from the SPSS output. The communalities table which represent the proportion of common variance within a variable shows that all items have a communality value of more than .605, and the average communality value is almost .75. Based on Rotated Component Matrix, a matrix of the factor loading for each item onto each component, the analysis will be repeated without the eight items that did not load in the first set of the analysis at .512 namely: OC3, TMS3, SF3, ICTI1, SEC2, SN1, SN2, and Compatibility1. In addition, the two items Complexity1 and Complexity2, which have KMO values lower than .5, will be dropped as suggested by (Field, 2013). Therefore, the analysis will be repeated without the inclusion of these ten items.

PCA was again run by loading 37 items and applying varimax rotation as well. The results showed that nine components can be extracted, and the sum of these components explained 72.55 per cent of the total variance. The determination of the nine components to be extracted from the PCA was also based on the Kaiser's criterion (eigenvalue > 1). According to Field (2013), each item must have a loading

Table 1. Participants' nationality

		Frequency	Percent	Valid Percent	Cumulative Percent
Valid	Resident	7	6.9	6.9	6.9
	Saudi	95	93.1	93.1	100.0
	Total	102	100.0	100.0	

of at least .512 to determine if it contributes to the definition of components. The KMO for this set of analysis is equal to .840, which is acceptable since it is above .5 (Field, 2013; Kaiser, 1974). All KMO values for individual items were above .5. Based on Rotated Component Matrix, two items, namely TRU1 and TRU2, did not load at .512 or more onto any of the nine components. Therefore, the analysis will be repeated without the items that did not load as suggested by Field (2013).

PCA was again conducted on the 35 items by applying varimax rotation. The results revealed that only eight components can be pulled out explaining 71.47 per cent of the total variance. The extraction of eight components was based on Kaiser's criterion (eigenvalue > 1). Based on the sample size, an item loading of at least .512 was also used to determine the items that cluster in the same components (Field, 2013). The KMO for this analysis is equal to .837, which is acceptable since it is above .5 (Field, 2013; Kaiser, 1974). Based on the Rotated Component Matrix, two items, namely SEC1 and Compatibility2, did not load to any of the eight components at .512 or more. Hence, the analysis will be repeated without the items that did not load as suggested by Field (2013).

PCA was conducted again on 33 items with varimax rotation. The KMO for this analysis is equal to .838 as presented in Table 3. The KMO is acceptable since it is above .5 (Field, 2013; Kaiser, 1974). In this study the sample size of 102 cases can be described as "meritorious" (Field, 2013; Hutcheson & Sofroniou, 1999; Kaiser, 1974). All KMO values for individual items were above .5. After PCA was run, eight components had eigenvalues over Kaiser's criterion of 1, and in combination they explained 72.90 per cent of the total variance (see Table 2).

An item loading of at least .512 was also used to determine the items that cluster in the same components (Field, 2013) and all the 33 items have loading of more than .512. Table 3 shows the Rotated Component Matrix which presents the item loading after the rotation.

SOLUTIONS AND RECOMMENDATIONS

The aim of PCA as used in this study is mainly to reduce the number of variables that affect the intention to adopt mCommerce in Saudi banks and telecoms and group them under a small number of components. Hence, correlated items are grouped together under one component. The initial approach to the analysis consisted of loading the original 47 items used to measure the fifteen adoption factors in this research project. During the preliminary analysis, and to determine if the resulting components are related, a simple correlation was run on the saved components scores and this test shows there is no relationship between the twelve components that resulted from the preliminary analysis. As a result, an orthogonal rotation strategy should be used as suggested by Starkweather and Herrington (2014). Using an orthogonal rotation is more applicable as this type of rotation allows for component independency.

FUTURE RESEARCH DIRECTIONS

As mentioned before, the main objective for conducting this research project is to identify the factors that influence the intention to adopt mCommerce in Saudi in Saudi telecoms and banks. Attaining such an objective and constructing a conceptual model for mCommerce organizational adoption is the main contribution for this research project.

Table 2. Total variance explained (SPSS output)

	Initial Eigenvalues			Extraction Sums of Squared Loadings			Rotation Sums of Squared Loadings		
	Total	% of Variance	Cumulative %	Total	% of Variance	Cumulative %	Total	% of Variance	Cumulative %
1	10.780	32.667	32.667	10.780	32.667	32.667	7.355	22.289	22.289
2	4.335	13.137	45.805	4.335	13.137	45.805	3.851	11.670	33.960
3	2.031	6.156	51.960	2.031	6.156	51.960	2.503	7.586	41.546
4	1.814	5.498	57.458	1.814	5.498	57.458	2.242	6.795	48.341
5	1.441	4.367	61.825	1.441	4.367	61.825	2.145	6.501	54.841
6	1.338	4.054	65.879	1.338	4.054	65.879	2.111	6.398	61.239
7	1.180	3.576	69.456	1.180	3.576	69.456	1.979	5.998	67.237
8	1.137	3.444	72.900	1.137	3.444	72.900	1.869	5.662	72.900
9	.906	2.746	75.646						
10	.865	2.620	78.266						
11	.739	2.240	80.506						
12	.692	2.096	82.603						
13	.600	1.819	84.421						
14	.585	1.771	86.193						
15	.521	1.578	87.771						
16	.479	1.450	89.221						
17	.451	1.367	90.588						
18	.352	1.066	91.654						
19	.349	1.057	92.711						
20	.317	.960	93.672						
21	.275	.835	94.506						
22	.265	.803	95.310						
23	.229	.695	96.004						
24	.203	.614	96.618						
25	.198	.600	97.219						
26	.186	.563	97.782						
27	.150	.453	98.235						
28	.137	.416	98.651						
29	.125	.379	99.030						
30	.097	.294	99.324						
31	.087	.265	99.589						
32	.076	.230	99.819						
33	.060	.181	100.000						

Table 3. Total variance explained (SPSS output)

	Component							
	1	**2**	**3**	**4**	**5**	**6**	**7**	**8**
PU2	.881							
PU3	.875							
PU4	.854							
PU1	.849							
RA5	.823							
Job-Fit3	.823							
RA4	.815							
Job-Fit2	.718							
RA1	.558							
RA2	.554							
OC1		.804						
ICTI2		.772						
ICTI4		.766						
ICTI3		.728						
OP2		.678						
OP1		.622						
SEC3			.721					
PEU1			.617					
RA3	.548		.607					
PEU2			.556					
Compatibility3				.815				
Compatibility4				.704				
Job-Fit1				.688				
PLE2					.779			
PLE3					.753			
PLE1					.712			
SF1						.796		
SF2						.734		
SN3						.623		
TMS2							.826	
TMS1							.685	
OC2								.755
ICTI5								.652

As this research is only concentrating in Saudi banks and telecoms, there are seven components that may affect the intention to adopt mCommerce in Saudi banks and telecoms. Future work should duplicate the study in other sectors as well as other countries, including both developing and developed nations.

CONCLUSION

This research project successfully identified a number of factors that affect the intention to adopt of mCommerce in Saudi banks and telecoms. Furthermore, producing a conceptual framework for mCommerce organizational adoption can be considered as the main contribution for this research. This research project is one of the first steps needed to develop a framework that can help to explain the organizational intention to adopt mCommerce services. The study delivered an early stage mCommerce organizational adoption model applicable to the KSA. The findings established that the components included in this model explain approximately 72.13 per cent of the total variance in such adoption.

Based on the above findings, performance expectancy (PE) presents the expected gains that can raise both employees and organizational performance when adopting mCommerce services. The above analysis revealed that nine items from three factors (perceived usefulness (PU), relative advantage (RA), and job-fit) load on PE component. The above results revealed that PE has a positive effect on the intention to adopt mCommerce in Saudi banks and telecoms. To support such finding, Venkatesh et al. (2003) found that PE is one of the most significant determinants for the adoption of information technology in organizations. Bhatti (2007), Snowden, Spafford, Michaelides, and Hopkins (2006), and (Yaseen & Zayed, 2010) believed that PU affects the adoption of mCommerce. The literature also revealed that PU significantly affects the adoption of new technologies (Davis, 1986; Davis et al., 1989; Grandon & Pearson, 2004; Subramanian, 1998). Additionally, RA can be a significant factor that affects the adoption of new technologies (Moore & Benbasat, 1991; Rogers, 2003; Sait, Al-Tawil, & Hussain, 2004). Furthermore, job-fit can be considered a direct determinant of user acceptance of new technologies (Thompson, Higgins, & Howell, 1991).

The above analysis suggested that organizational readiness (OR) is based on the organization's readiness to adopt mCommerce services in three areas: culture, policies, and infrastructure. The above findings showed that six items from three factors: information and communication technologies infrastructure (ICTI), organizational culture (OC), and organizational policy (OP) loaded on the OR component. The previous analysis revealed that OR can have a positive effect on the intention to adopt mCommerce in Saudi banks and telecoms. Molla and Licker (2005) found that eCommerce adoption by businesses in developing countries is significantly influenced by some dimensions of organizational e-readiness. On the other hand OR, including financial and technological resources, was not found to be a significant factor in the decision to adopt eCommerce by small and medium US businesses (Grandon & Pearson, 2004). The reason behind such insignificance may occur as they investigated a different technology in different country and settings than the current study. ICTI, OC, and OP affect the adoption of new technology which is supported by the work of Léger, Cassivi, and Fosso Wamba (2004); Yang (2005); Elahi and Hassanzadeh (2009); Premkumar and Ramamurthy (1995). OECD (2007) revealed that business self-regulation is a requirement to produce mCommerce regulations in any country and protect customers.

The above results showed that mCommerce features and opportunities (MFO) as a component represent the expected features that are embedded in mCommerce services and the potential opportunities of providing such service. The five items which are associated with the three factors (perceived ease of use (PEU), RA, and security) loaded on this component. The analysis of the data revealed that mCommerce features and opportunities can have a positive effect on the intention to adopt mCommerce in Saudi banks and telecoms. This is also supported by Bhatti (2007), Snowden et al. (2006), and Yaseen and Zayed (2010). The literature also suggests that PEU can be considered an important adoption factor affecting the adoption of new technologies (Davis, 1986, 1989; Davis et al., 1989; Grandon & Pearson,

2004; Subramanian, 1998; Venkatesh et al., 2003). Furthermore, two studies considered security a significant factor that affects the adoption of mCommerce services (O'Donnell et al., 2007; Yang, 2005).

The above analysis revealed that compatibility of mCommerce services (CMS) to the employee's work as well as to the current organizational systems can be represented by this component. As shown in the analysis above, three items from two factors (compatibility and job-fit) loaded to CMS. The above findings revealed that CMS can have a positive effect on the intention to adopt mCommerce in Saudi banks and telecoms. Compatibility of eCommerce to the firm's culture, value, and preferred work practices were found to be influential factors in the decision to adopt eCommerce by small and medium US businesses (Grandon & Pearson, 2004). The literature also showed that compatibility can be a significant factor that affects the organizational adoption of new technologies (Elahi & Hassanzadeh, 2009; Moore & Benbasat, 1991; Rogers, 2003; Sait et al., 2004; Venkatesh et al., 2003).

As mentioned before, policy and legal environment (PLE) includes all the relevant governmental regulations that have impacts on mCommerce adoption and use in organizations. The above analysis suggested that three items (PLE1, PLE2, and PLE3) are related to the factor PLE. The above findings showed that PLE can have a positive effect on the intention to adopt mCommerce in Saudi banks and telecoms. This finding supports previous mCommerce studies such as O'Donnell et al. (2007), OECD (2007), Sharma, Murthy, and Sundar (2006), Tiwari et al. (2006), and Yang (2005).

Based on the above findings, social influence (SI) as a component describes how other organizations affect the organizational decision to adopt mCommerce services. The above analysis suggested that three items associated with two factors (social factor (SF) and subjective norms (SN)) loaded to the SI component. The current study found that SI can have a positive effect on the intention to adopt mCommerce in Saudi banks and telecoms. Venkatesh et al. (2003) indicate that SI is one of the significant determinants for the adoption of information technology in organizations. Yaseen and Zayed (2010) revealed that social and cultural values significantly affect the adoption of mCommerce by individuals. The literature also suggested that the diffusion of new technologies in organizations can be influenced by SF (Al-Somali, Gholami, & Clegg, 2009; Dutta & Roy, 2003; Thompson et al., 1991; Venkatesh et al., 2003). Additionally, Bhatti (2007) stated that SN can be a major determinant in the adoption of mCommerce. The literature also revealed that SN can predict the users' intention to use and adopt new technologies (Davis et al., 1989; Mathieson, 1991; Taylor & Todd, 1995; Venkatesh & Davis, 2000; Venkatesh et al., 2003).

As mentioned before, top management support (TMS) refers to "the senior executives' favorable attitude toward, and explicit support for information systems" (Sabherwal, Jeyaraj, & Chowa, 2006). Based on the above findings, only two items loaded to the TMS component. The previous analysis suggested that TMS can affect the intention to adopt mCommerce in Saudi banks and telecoms positively. Researchers also found that TMS affects the adoption and implementation of mCommerce (AlHaj Ali, 2005; Chang, Peng, Hung, Chang, & Hung, 2009) and of new technologies in organizations (Elahi & Hassanzadeh, 2009; Premkumar & Ramamurthy, 1995; Teo, Chan, & Parker, 2004).

Based on the findings, three components can have a significant effect on the adoption of mCommerce in Saudi banks and telecoms. These components are performance expectancy, organizational readiness, and mCommerce features and opportunities. Performance expectancy is the most important component as it explains almost 34.48 per cent of the total variance. The second significant component is the organizational readiness, which explains 13.34 per cent of the total variance. The third important component is the features and opportunities associated with the introduction of mCommerce services in organizations; it explains approximately 6.38 per cent of the total variance. These three components in total explain 54.2 per cent of the total variance.

There are some limitations to the current study. The first limitation of the research is that it is concentrated on the Saudi market. This can be a limitation since it is focused on one country only and the results may not apply in another context unless confirmed by other research. The second limitation of this research is that the sample size of the research was relatively small with 102 complete cases. The third limitation is that the number of female participants can be considered as quite low.

REFERENCES

Al-Somali, S. A., Gholami, R., & Clegg, B. (2009). An investigation into the acceptance of online banking in Saudi Arabia. *Technovation*, *29*(2), 130–141. doi:10.1016/j.technovation.2008.07.004

Alfahl, H., Sanzogni, L., & Houghton, L. (2012). Mobile commerce adoption in organizations: A literature review and future research directions. *Journal of Electronic Commerce in Organizations*, *10*(2), 61–78. doi:10.4018/jeco.2012040104

AlHaj Ali, E. I. (2005). *Mobile commerce adoption across the supply chain in businesses in New Zealand* (Master Thesis), Auckland University of Technology (AUT), Auckland, New Zealand.

Armeanu, D., & Lache, L. (2008). Application of the model of principal components analysis on Romanian insurance market. *Journal Theoretical and Applied Economics*, *6*(6), 11–20.

Balasubramanian, S., Peterson, R. A., & Jarvenpaa, S. L. (2002). Exploring the implications of m-commerce for markets and marketing. *Journal of the Academy of Marketing Science*, *30*(4), 348–361. doi:10.1177/009207002236910

Benou, P., & Vassilakis, C. (2010). The conceptual model of context for mobile commerce applications. *Electronic Commerce Research*, *10*(2), 139–165. doi:10.100710660-010-9050-4

Bhatti, T. (2007). Exploring factors influencing the adoption of mobile commerce. *Journal of Internet Banking and Commerce*, *12*(3).

Chang, S.-I., Peng, T.-C., Hung, Y.-C., Chang, I.-C., & Hung, W.-H. (2009). *Critical success factors of mobile commerce adoption: A study based on the system life cycle and diamond model.* Paper presented at the 8th International Conference on Mobile Business (ICMB 2009), Dalian University of Technology (DUT), Dalian, China. 10.1109/ICMB.2009.29

Chapman, D. W., & Carter, J. F. (1979). Translation procedures for the cross cultural use of measurement instruments. *Educational Evaluation and Policy Analysis*, *1*(3), 71–76. doi:10.3102/01623737001003071

CITC. (2014). *CITC electronic newsletter*. Communications and Information Technology Commission in Saudi Arabia.

Davis, F. D. (1986). *A Technology acceptance model for empirically testing new end-user information systems: Theory and results* (Doctoral Dissertation). Massachusetts Institute of Technology, Cambridge, MA.

Davis, F. D. (1989). Perceived usefulness, perceived ease of use and user acceptance of information technology. *Management Information Systems Quarterly, 13*(3), 319–340. doi:10.2307/249008

Davis, F. D., Bagozzi, R. P., & Warshaw, P. R. (1989). User acceptance of computer technology: A comparison of two theoretical models. *Management Science, 35*(8), 982–1003. doi:10.1287/mnsc.35.8.982

Dutta, A., & Roy, R. (2003). Anticipating internet diffusion. *Communications of the ACM, 46*(2), 66–71. doi:10.1145/606272.606275

Elahi, S., & Hassanzadeh, A. (2009). A framework for evaluating electronic commerce adoption in Iranian companies. *International Journal of Information Management, 29*(1), 27–36. doi:10.1016/j.ijinfomgt.2008.04.009

Field, A. (2013). *Discovering statistics using IBM SPSS statistics* (4th ed.). London, UK: SAGE.

Fishbein, M., & Ajzen, I. (1975). *Belief, attitude, intention, and behavior: An introduction to theory and research*. Reading, MA: Addison-Wesley.

Grandon, E., & Pearson, J. M. (2004). Electronic commerce adoption: An empirical study of small and medium US businesses. *Information & Management, 42*(1), 197–216. doi:10.1016/j.im.2003.12.010

Gulfnews. (2013). *Digital awakening spurs m-commerce*. Retrieved 13 July, 2013, from http://gulfnews.com/business/retail/digital-awakening-spurs-m-commerce-1.1022923

Hassinen, M., Hyppönen, K., & Trichina, E. (2008). Utilizing national public-key infrastructure in mobile payment systems. *Electronic Commerce Research and Applications, 7*(2), 214–231. doi:10.1016/j.elerap.2007.03.006

Henten, A., Olesen, H., Saugstrup, D., & Tan, S. (2004). Mobile communications: Europe, Japan and South Korea in a comparative perspective. *Info, 6*(3), 197-207.

Hutcheson, G. D., & Sofroniou, N. (1999). *The multivariate social scientist: Introductory statistics using generalized linear models*. London, UK: SAGE Publications, Ltd. doi:10.4135/9780857028075

Kaiser, H. (1970). A second generation little jiffy. *Psychometrika, 35*(4), 401–415. doi:10.1007/BF02291817

Kaiser, H. (1974). An index of factorial simplicity. *Psychometrika, 39*(1), 31–36. doi:10.1007/BF02291575

Léger, P.-M., Cassivi, L., & Fosso Wamba, S. (2004). *Determinants of the adoption of customer-oriented mobile commerce initiatives*. Paper presented at the Twelfth International Association of Management of Technology (IAMOT'04), Washington, DC.

López Catalán, B., & Díaz Luque, P. (2008). *M-commerce adoption: TAM vs technology provider perspective through cognitive maps*. Paper presented at the Building Bridges in a Global Economy, Salmanca, Spain.

Mallat, N., & Tuunainen, V. K. (2008). Exploring merchant adoption of mobile payment systems: An empirical study. *e-Service Journal, 6*(2), 24–57. doi:10.2979/esj.2008.6.2.24

Mathieson, K. (1991). Predicting user intentions: Comparing the technology acceptance model with the theory of planned behavior. *Information Systems Research, 2*(3), 173–191. doi:10.1287/isre.2.3.173

Molla, A., & Licker, P. S. (2005). Perceived e-readiness factors in e-commerce adoption: An empirical investigation in a developing country. *International Journal of Electronic Commerce*, *10*(1), 83–110. doi:10.1080/10864415.2005.11043963

Moore, G. C., & Benbasat, I. (1991). Development of an instrument to measure the perceptions of adopting an information technology innovation. *Information Systems Research*, *2*(3), 192–222. doi:10.1287/isre.2.3.192

Narduzzi, E. (2001). *Is m-business the same game as the e-business?* Paper presented at the M-conference: Seizing the Mobile Advantage, Rotterdam, The Netherlands.

O'Donnell, J., Jackson, M., Shelly, M., & Ligertwood, J. (2007). Australian case studies in mobile commerce. *Journal of Theoretical and Applied Electronic Commerce Research*, *2*(2), 1–18.

OECD. (2007). *Mobile commerce*. Organisation for Economic Co-operation and Development.

Okazaki, S. (2005). New perspectives on m-commerce Research. *Journal of Electronic Commerce Research*, *6*(3), 160–164.

Pallant, J. (2011). *SPSS survival manual: A step by step guide to data analysis using the SPSS program* (4th ed.). Crows Nest, NSW, Australia: Allen & Unwin.

Premkumar, G., & Ramamurthy, K. (1995). The role of interorganizational and organizational factors on the decision mode for adoption of interorganizational systems. *Decision Sciences*, *26*(3), 303–336. doi:10.1111/j.1540-5915.1995.tb01431.x

Rogers, E. M. (2003). *Diffusion of innovations* (5th ed.). New York: Free Press.

Sabherwal, R., Jeyaraj, A., & Chowa, C. (2006). Information system success: Individual and organizational determinants. *Management Science*, *52*(12), 1849–1864. doi:10.1287/mnsc.1060.0583

Saidi, E. (2009). Mobile opportunities, mobile problems: Assessing mobile commerce implementation issues in Malawi. *Journal of Internet Banking and Commerce*, *14*(1).

Sait, S. M., Al-Tawil, K. M., & Hussain, S. A. (2004). E-commerce in Saudi Arabia: Adoption and perspectives. *AJIS. Australian Journal of Information Systems*, *12*(1), 54–74.

SAMA. (2012). *Saudi Arabian Monetary Agency - Forty eighth annual report*. Saudi Arabian Monetary Agency (SAMA). Retrieved from http://www.sama.gov.sa/sites/samaen/ReportsStatistics/ReportsStatisticsLib/5600_R_Annual_En_48_2013_02_19.pdf

SAMA. (2013). *Saudi banks*. Retrieved 19 May, 2013, from http://www.sama.gov.sa/sites/samaen/Links/Pages/SaudiBanks.aspx

Saporta, G., & Niang, N. (2009). Principal component analysis: Application to statistical process control. In G. Govaert (Ed.), *Data Analysis*. Hoboken, NJ: John Wiley & Sons, Inc. doi:10.1002/9780470611777.ch1

Sgriccia, M., Nguyen, H., Edra, R., Alworth, A., & Brandeis, O., Escandon, R., . . . Seal, K. (2007). Drivers of mobile business models: Lessons from four asian countries. *International Journal of Mobile Marketing*, *2*(2), 58–67.

Sharma, D., Murthy, R., & Sundar, K. (2006). *Government policies and regulations: Impact on mobile commerce in Indian context.* Paper presented at the Second European Conference on Mobile Goverment (EURO mGOV).

Siau, K., Lim, E.-P., & Shen, Z. (2001). Mobile commerce: Promises, challenges, and research agenda. *Journal of Database Management, 12*(3), 4–13. doi:10.4018/jdm.2001070101

Snowden, S., Spafford, J., Michaelides, R., & Hopkins, J. (2006). Technology acceptance and m-commerce in an operational environment. *Journal of Enterprise Information Management, 19*(6), 525–539. doi:10.1108/17410390610703657

Starkweather, J., & Herrington, R. (2014). Principal components analysis in SPSS. *SPSS Short Course in the Research and Statistical Support.* Retrieved 31 January, 2014, from http://www.unt.edu/rss/class/Jon/SPSS_SC/Module9/M9_PCA/SPSS_M9_PCA1.htm

Stoica, M., Miller, D. W., & Stotlar, D. (2005). New technology adoption, business strategy and government involvement: The case of mobile commerce. *Journal of Nonprofit & Public Sector Marketing, 13*(1&2), 213–232. doi:10.1300/J054v13n01_12

Stoica, M., & Roach, B. (2006). Sustainable development in the rural US midwest: The m-commerce solution. The wireless critical infrastructure. *International Journal of Critical Infrastructures, 2*(4), 331–346. doi:10.1504/IJCIS.2006.011343

Subramanian, G. H. (1998). A replication of perceived usefulness and perceived ease of use measurement. *Decision Sciences, 25*(5-6), 863–874. doi:10.1111/j.1540-5915.1994.tb01873.x

Taylor, S., & Todd, P. A. (1995). Understanding information technology usage: A test of competing models. *Information Systems Research, 6*(2), 144–176. doi:10.1287/isre.6.2.144

Teo, T., Chan, C., & Parker, C. (2004). *Factors affecting e-commerce adoption by SMEs: A meta-analysis.* Paper presented at the 15th Annual Australasian conference on information systems, Hobart, Australia.

Thompson, R. L., Higgins, C. A., & Howell, J. M. (1991). Personal computing: Toward a conceptual model of utilization. *Management Information Systems Quarterly, 15*(1), 124–143. doi:10.2307/249443

Tiwari, R., Buse, S., & Herstatt, C. (2006). From electronic to mobile commerce: Opportunities through technology convergence for business services. *Asia-Pacific Tech Monitor*, 38-45.

Varshney, U., Mallow, A., Ahluwalia, P., & Jain, R. (2004). Wireless in the enterprise: Requirements, solutions and research directions. *International Journal of Mobile Communications, 2*(4), 354. doi:10.1504/IJMC.2004.005856

Varshney, U., & Vetter, R. (2000). Emerging wireless and mobile networks. *Communications of the ACM, 43*(7), 73–81. doi:10.1145/336460.336478

Venkatesh, V., & Davis, F. D. (2000). A theoretical extension of the technology acceptance model: Four longitudinal Field Study. *Management Science, 46*(2), 186–204. doi:10.1287/mnsc.46.2.186.11926

Venkatesh, V., Morris, M. G., Davis, G. B., & Davis, F. D. (2003). User acceptance of information technology: Toward a unified view. *Management Information Systems Quarterly, 27*(2).

Vrechopoulos, A., Constantiou, I., Sideris, I., Doukidis, G., & Mylonopoulos, N. (2003). The critical role of consumer behavior research in mobile commerce. *International Journal of Mobile Communications*, *1*(2), 329–340.

Yang, K. C. C. (2005). Exploring factors affecting the adoption of mobile commerce in Singapore. *Telematics and Informatics*, *22*(3), 257–277. doi:10.1016/j.tele.2004.11.003

Yaseen, S. G., & Zayed, S. (2010). Exploring critical determinants in deploying mobile commerce technology. *American Journal of Applied Sciences*, *7*(1), 120–126. doi:10.3844/ajassp.2010.120.126

Yuan, Y., & Zhang, J. J. (2003). Towards an appropriate business model for m-commerce. *International Journal of Mobile Communications*, *1*(1-2), 35–56. doi:10.1504/IJMC.2003.002459

Zeeshan, S. A., Cheung, Y., & Scheepers, H. (2007). *Developing a collaborative orgnizational mobile commerce model*. Paper presented at the International Conference on Business and Information, Tokyo, Japan.

Zheng, P., & Ni, L. (2006). *Mobile application challenges. In Smart Phone and Next Generation Mobile Computing* (pp. 407–512). Burlington: Morgan Kaufmann. doi:10.1016/B978-012088560-2/50009-5

Chapter 11
Using Integrated Performance Indicator Systems in the Digital Economy:
A Critical Review

Ana Maria Ifrim
Titu Maiorescu University, Romania

Alina Stanciu
1 Decembrie 1918 University, Romania

Rodica Gherghina
The Bucharest University of Economic Studies, Romania

Ioana Duca
Titu Maiorescu University, Romania

ABSTRACT

The digital era has brought along the exponential growth of the economic and technological opportunities that entities can access and implement in the development of their own activities, along with a series of threats with strategic impact. Being a global, multinational, sustainable, profitable, and credible concept, it also involves a leadership connected to market threats for the entity. Moreover, this leadership must be adaptable, identifying with the vision of the entity and conveying it to its members through the organizational culture it cultivates, but above all a leader who understands and is aware of the functioning of the entity, both managerially and economically. And in order to achieve this, a permanent assessment and re-evaluation of the entity's performance is imperative. This chapter seeks to understand the economic and managerial mechanisms of operation to base the making of pertinent, real, and especially timely decisions in counteracting the threats of a turbulent environment while increasing the potential of the entity.

DOI: 10.4018/978-1-5225-8455-1.ch011

INTRODUCTION

Every entrepreneur is even now facing the influences of the megatrend and scenario; thus, it is vital for the future of the business to take prudent decision in order to assure its stability and growth (Leyer, Stumpf-Wollersheim & Kronsbein, 2017). The first step in using planning and using megatrend and scenario analysis for the longer-term business strategy development is to determine its relevance to the business. Comparing megatrends with the current business to create a collision with it and therefore revealing the point where the megatrend would intersect the business (Paton & McCalman, 2008). At that point, the megatrend forces the business to change its development course and the entrepreneurs are also forced to consider three possibilities: intersection with their business which implies "leaving the business in the dust", providing acceleration for the business, and a parallel position of the megatrends in the business with no direct impact on it. All these future challenges can be avoided when entrepreneurs/decision-makers assess the projected value of innovation against a range of scenarios using a full set of strategic key performance indicators (KPIs).

KPIs are the vital navigation instruments used by entrepreneurs to understand whether their business is having an increasing trend or whether it needs a change of direction. The right set of the indicators will shine light on performance and highlight areas that need attention. Without the right KPIs the entrepreneurs/decisions-makers are just sailing blindly. They understand the performance of all the key dimensions of their business by distilling them down in to critical KPIs who will equip them with the skills to understand, measure and interpret the most important aspects of the business.

However, the question that is on the wall of each entrepreneur is how are they going to build a strong KPIs system? Defining the strategy and the objectives that the business is aiming to achieve represents the first step in building the KPIs strength (Olson, Slater, Tomas & Hult, 2005). The key indicator must be related to the most critical aspects of the business. If the KPI is linked to the strategy and strategic priorities, then it must be meaningful and relevant. They become meaningful if they help decisions-makers answer to a key business question (KPQs). For this reason, it is recommended to develop between one and three key performance questions for each of the strategic objectives. Those questions help the entrepreneurs identify the real information needed and guide it to the right indicators. Because every company has a different strategy and strategic priorities, every company requires a unique set of KPIs (Lin, Peng & Kao, 2008).

KPIs have to be owned and understood by everyone in the organization (Guo, Chen, Long, Lu & Long, 2017). People must understand the rationality of measuring the performance and have some level of ownership of the metric. In that way, the KPI become the critical decision support tools. For entrepreneurs, it is important to explain to the company the way in which the KPI is linked to the strategic objectives and how KPI respond at strategic questions.

Same authors consider the KPIs be the "measures that help decision makers define and measure progress toward business goals. KPI metrics translate complex measures into a simple indicator that allows decision makers to assess the current situation and act quickly" (Meuer, 2017; Hurley, 2002).

The KPIs are the result of Druker development idea "A strategy without metrics is just a wish. And metrics that are not aligned with strategic objectives are a waste of time" (Guo, Chen, Long, Lu & Long, 2017). Despite the availability of enabling technologies, dashboard use didn't become popular until the late 1990s, with the rise of key performance indicators (KPIs), and the introduction of Kaplan and Norton's Balanced Scorecard (Hartnell, Ou & Kinicki, 2011). Today, the use of dashboards forms an important part of Management by Objectives (MBO), a management model that aims to improve performance by clearly defining objectives that are agreed to by both management and employees and align to overall organizational objectives (Hurley, 2002). A principle of Management by Objectives is the establishment of a management information system to measure actual performance and achievements against the defined objectives. MBO benefits include improving employee motivation and engagement, and better communication between management and employees. A KPI Framework groups related KPIs together to provide greater structure and context, and optimize efforts and understand how performance of certain KPIs impact other KPIs (Pieper, Trevor, Weller & Duchon, 2017). Examining individual and cross-organizational metrics and making use of the information is much easier with a well-designed KPI dashboard. You can make comparisons, see trends over time, see distribution, and see relationships between different areas of the organization. Sharing information across multiple parts of the organization supports more streamlined problem-solving, collaboration, and forecasting (Paton & McCalman, 2008).

To develop a powerful KPIs dashboard the entrepreneurs must choose three priority goals and have no more than three KPIs per goal. Focus on linking KPIs or measures to the goals that are most direct and supply the most evidence (Homburg & Pflesser, 2000). KPIs may need to be adjusted, but when they are, is important to keep them relevant, and keep the overall number of KPIs lean using SMART criteria. Properly designed, KPI dashboards let know if the business needs maintenance or if it is running at peak performance. They are easy to read and understand, easy to update, aligned to best practices around visual presentation of information and constructed to enable decisions to be made at a glance. The KPIs dashboards are a storehouse for current status snapshots and historical trends that will help the decision makers answer to critical questions: "Does my company is strong enough to face all that changes? / Does my decisions are based on real predictions that are aimed to provide me a sustainable business? / What are the key elements that make a successful company? / I can measure this key element?"

Based on past data, a key performance indicator is necessarily reactive. In other words, it shows you that a problem has occurred. The decision-makers can examine contributing factors to find any culprits for poor overall performance, and take the right remedial action (Pieper, Trevor, Weller & Duchon, 2017). However, damage may already have been done. Dissatisfied customers may voice their complaints to others. In general they are more likely to criticize an enterprise than satisfied customers are to praise it. By the time your KPI has shown you there is something wrong, you may have lost valuable customer goodwill together with future revenues and profits. It would clearly be preferable to have indicators that give you information about what is likely to happen in the future, and not only what has happened in the past. Depending on who is talking about them, you may hear such indicators being called KPPs (key performance predictors).

Demand forecasting and planning are examples of predictions that use indicators in order to reach a conclusion. Those indicators may include sales information about with deals to be closed this month, deals in progress and the number of new leads generated per month. They may also include information about the economy and about exchange rate trends, if goods and services are being supplied in different countries (Hartnell, Ou & Kinicki, 2011).

The future usually contains more unknowns than the past. Whereas many standard industry models exist for the "rear-view" or diagnostic KPIs we were discussing before, the prognostic KPI (or KPP) that looks ahead will often need to be customized. Predictive indicators can be used to take preparatory actions to ensure that indicators stay at 100%. It is also worth mentioning that KPIs based on historical data (the rear-view, diagnostic KPIs) may also have predictive capabilities. Trend analysis from historical data may also give a glimpse of the future. Looking at past results for KPIs can reveal deeper underlying changes or seasonal effects, both of which can be used to enhance the predictive power of the KPI concerned.

On the other hand, Benchmarking in today's volatile, uncertain, complex, and ambiguous economic environment is the key to controlling entities that have understood and accepted that in order to remain on the market, it is necessary, regardless of the field of activity, to consider Vision Pillar - Innovation as essential (Henczel, 2002). Against the backdrop of rising generations, scarcity of resources, the rate of change is known to continue to accelerate. New social, technological, environmental, political trends converge to create disruptive and disturbing forces, remodeling consumers' behaviors and preferences, going in-depth and responding to how / when / where?

On the other hand, the managers are an element that profoundly marks organizational culture (Amagoh, 2008). The special qualities of the managers, their professional and managerial training, and the specific capacities directly influence the organizational culture. Of course, the highest influence is given by top level managers, then middle managers (Ashkanasy, 2011). They can adopt a simple strategy that moves in the middle of employees to communicate with them and to sensitize them to the values they would like them to adhere to.

Many managers develop and report on their subordinates to communicate their organization's values and objectives. Other times, video cassettes are distributed to employees to highlight the role of each in achieving the company's goals. Each manager is concerned with communicating the values of the organization and integrating these values into their own actions (Rowland & Hall, 2014).

Foreign managers present in Romania appreciate the good professional training of Romanians, innovation, creativity, sociability, ability to engage in solving situations, the ability to learn quickly and to adopt everything that is Western, but disapprove of the inappropriate use of time, the tendency to solve the tasks at the last moment, the work in jumps, the impression that they can do anything and they are good at everything. It has been found that Romanians are particularly motivated by rewards, and especially by the material ones. Also, Romania's economic situation, the level of inflation, the devaluation of the national currency, the standard of living directly and indirectly affects the components of organizational culture: the aspirations of employees, their expectations, beliefs, behaviors.

In Romanian companies it is necessary to create a model of values compatible with the basic rules of the market economy, to form and consolidate a strong managerial organizational culture. In an organization characterized by such an organizational culture, the values must not only be declared but supported by concrete actions.

The experience of competitive Western firms shows that sometimes the values of organizational culture conflict with the system of objectives. Surviving through a strong organizational culture requires attachment to values, even with the sacrifice of short-term financial interests.

Most initiatives of benchmarking across an entity have pursued competitive advantage through time, quality, cost, effectiveness, and customer satisfaction. The motivation to apply benchmarking by the leader of an entity suggests that it wants one of the processes within the entity to be consolidated.

This chapter intends to identify and analyze the perspective of benchmarking and key performance indicators in Romanian SMEs from the perspective of quality, cost, effectiveness, and customer satisfaction.

BACKGROUND

Today, organizational culture is one of the concepts of widespread use in practice and in management theory, benefiting from continuous development (Cameron & Quinn, 2011). Specialists are currently trying to explain and demonstrate the role of organizational culture in increasing the efficiency, performance and competitiveness of the firm (Barney, 1986; Lim, 1995; Denison, 1990; Hartnell, Ou & Kinicki, 2011; Schneider & Somers, 2006; Tong & Arvey, 2015).

In Romania we identify mainly two types of organizational cultures: bureaucratic culture and entrepreneurial culture.

Bureaucratic culture is the one that characterizes state-owned enterprises, educational and health institutions belonging to the state, military institutions. This culture is arrogant, focused on the inside of the system and highly politicized. An adaptation of this culture to the environment is difficult because there is no strategic thinking and knowledge of performance management issues. Within these organizations, hostile relationships between employees, between employees and managers are distinguished, and work results are not considered important.

Entrepreneurial culture can be distinguished mostly within private organizations, characterized by greater power of adaptation to the environment and by greater openness to new values and strategies that lead to positive results. Employees are given a set of values, rules that lead to the creation of a relaxed and professional environment: respect and respect for the client, employees and community, creativity, involvement, courage and attachment to the organization.

Successful companies increasingly manifest themselves as true open systems, whose position in the market depends not only on their internal resources, but also their relations with configuration and external entities with complementary skills. External network of the company is basically an extension of the internal borders between the two types of networks becoming increasingly difficult to identify.

External networks of companies, based mainly on cooperation, may develop spontaneously with operators working in the same territory, usually in close proximity and belonging or industry, or suppliers, specialized service providers, distributors etc. to rationalize the various phases of production and distribution of goods (Allan, 1993; Henczel, 2002; Deutsch & Silcox, 2003). Integration into external networks such synergistic effects materialized in generating competitive advantages for its members.

The managerial vision implies both a good knowledge of the past and the present, as well as ability to make attractive and practical reflections for the future that resonate with the soul and mind of the members of the organization (Tajeddini, 2015). Realistically, the second level prepares the guidelines that the organization must follow to succeed.

Benchmarking as the management tool and the leader's vision is outlined. Some entities, by applying this method, have even changed and improved the field in which they operate, raising it to a different level, shaping new horizons, and even becoming themselves Benchmark / standards of excellence, used in the process of measuring practices, performances an entity, markets, industries. Regardless of the motivation, cultivating an external view of industry and competitors must be a priority to manage the business carried out in this economic vortex (Fisher, 2010).

In addition, specialist literature brings attention to several variants whereby an entity may decide to apply the Benchmarking method to improve its performance (Arsenault & Faerman, 2014; Ahearne et al., 2010; Delaney & Huselid, 1996). It may mean applying:

- **Strategic Benchmarking:** Used when the organization wishes to improve its overall performance by examining strategies and approaches that have made it possible to achieve high performance "by certain entities;
- **Process Benchmarking:** Used when trying to improve processes and critical operations in generating organizational performance;

- **Competitive Benchmarking:** Enhanced performance of the entity by benchmarking of key product and service characteristics obtained by competitors;
- **Functional Benchmarking:** The entity's performance is analyzed in comparison with other selected entities in different sectors of activity. The purpose of this type of analysis is to improve the performance of similar functions to other entities;
- **Internal Benchmarking:** Improves the performance of a department of an entity (eg "business unit") as compared to another department within the same entity;
- **External Benchmarking:** The entity's performances are analyzed against the "best in class" of the market;
- **International Benchmarking:** An entity's performance analysis is performed by comparison with the performance of other entities on a particular international market.

Leaders' decision to apply Benchmarking to their entity can be taken as a result of the desire to continuously improve performance as a result of preventing threats that may arise or as a result of capitalizing on the external or internal environment (Hurley, 2002; Becker & Huselid, 1998).

Applying the Benchmarking method involves passing it through a complex process of performance comparison, a process that will take place within a predetermined time, and on which it is imperative to establish stages to justify its deployment at the end and to ensure the efficiency reflected in the synchronization of the vision leader with increasing entity performance (Alstete & Beutell, 2018; Kaplan & Norton, 2006; Galbraith & Lawler, 1993).

The classic Benchmarking method requires that complex performance benchmarking and process compiling go through several stages (Lin, Peng & Kao, 2008):

- **Planning Phase, Which Involves:** Identifying the area of the subject being treated by benchmarking / Defining the objectives and criteria that will be used to assess the performance of the entity / Selecting the benchmarking type / Identifying the competitors / Producing an action plan / Developing a communication strategy / Allocation of resources and selecting the project team / Obtaining the leader's agreement;
- **Data and Information Gathering, Seeks:** Gathering performance information / Selecting and contacting competitors / Developing together with competitors a mutual understanding of the procedures to be followed / Preparing the questions, agreeing on the terminology and performance indicators that will be Use / Gather information using the chosen method, questionnaires, interviews, visits, telephone, fax, email / Examining and comparing the results for analysis;
- **Analyzing the Results:** Identifying performance differences between the entity being analyzed and competitors / Explaining these performance differences / Ensuring that these comparisons are relevant and credible / identifying opportunities to improve performance;
- **Recommendations:** Examine the feasibility of measures to improve performance according to the entity's own conditions / agree on performance improvement measures / Produce a report on the benchmarking project, report containing proposed recommendations / obtaining stakeholder support for action corresponding to the recommendations;
- **Implementation of Recommendations:** Implementation of action plans / Performance monitoring / informing stakeholder;

- **Monitoring and Review:** Evaluation of the benchmarking process and results related to performance objectives and criteria as well as overall efficiency / Periodic reassessment of performance benchmarks.

Among the advantages that turn benchmarking into a strategic tool include: helps identify opportunities for improvement, is the source of creativity and change; generates potential improvements in efficiency and effectiveness, both in current operations and strategy; helps establish internal priorities, align with strategy and customer expectations; supports improving productivity strategies (Behery, Jabeen & Parakandi, 2014); provide qualitative and quantitative information; helps to know your own activity and to appreciate all dimensions of performance; is a tool that links the organization (Akgün, Keskin & Byrne, 2009); people need to cooperate and learn how they work and how others think; this generates interdepartmental knowledge; is an effective tool for planning and implementing the change process that leads to improvement when knowledge is converted into action plans that lead to competitive advantages; increases the company's understanding of its forces and weaknesses towards competitors and signals the existence of competitive disadvantages; sets pragmatic goals based on an external vision (Chan, Shaffer & Snape, 2004).

A too high rate of personnel change within the organization may have many negative aspects. Among these, the most important is the cost of staff change. Business organizations will scale up their initial staff costs as well as the costs associated with their change so that the profitability targets are not compromised.

The change of staff, however necessary, will cause changes in the organizational structure. Employees have to work in addition to being a substitute for the vacancy. Many plans can be or need to be reconsidered, and teamwork may no longer be possible when one of the participants is no longer present. If the employee in the organization was popular and loved by others, this change may be due to a general morale, which negatively affects motivation.

The employee's decision to stay or to be the organization is one that can be analyzed with the tools specific to the theory of economics, as we would expect the organization to do when calculating it. Profitability of the workforce flow. In the case of the employee, the cost-benefit analysis can be applied to explain his decision to the organization; the determining factor is mainly the incentive system that characterizes the organizational environment.

Although all these advantages recommend it as a strategic tool that leads to improved performance, there are also critics, circumspect in terms of its usefulness. In this respect, through a review of literature, Longbottom identifies three trends in the literature (Agha, Alrubaiee & Jamhour, 2012):

- **Traditionalists:** Who explain how Benchmarking works and insist on its major long-term advantage;
- **Criticism:** Shows that rapid changes in the environment alter the importance of change through Benchmarking, so it generates slow and significant improvements. They are the followers of radical improvement through business process reengineering;
- **Modernists:** Argue for the use of global (integrated) models. They accept that Benchmarking is often perceived as an act of imitation or copying, but it shows that it actually supports more innovation than imitation.

In this context, what the leader can do is build, orientate managerial culture, and provide a logical and credible view of where the business should go and what performance is required of its members (Cocca & Alberti, 2010). Leaders must therefore ensure that they have created the right organizational framework for company employees to showcase their skills and initiative, to capitalize on their knowledge at the highest levels without the need to build sophisticated or inflexible control systems.

USING INTEGRATED PERFORMANCE INDICATOR SYSTEMS IN THE DIGITAL ECONOMY: A CRITICAL REVIEW

Various methods and tools have been designed and used over time to assess organizational phenomena, culture and organizational performance respectively (de Waal & Kourtit, 2013; Taticchi, Tonelli & Cagnazzo, 2010). One of the questions frequently raised by management specialists relates to what is important for the organization to be assessed: the organizational climate or organizational performance of the firm?

In-depth analysis of organizational performance research requires the consideration of both quantitative and qualitative research (Yadav & Sagar, 2013). Qualitative research involves an interpretative approach to the subject under study by using and collecting empirical materials (case studies, observation, visual materials, interviews, human stories) describing common and special moments in the lives of individuals and organizations. Among the methods used by a series of sciences, applicable to organizational culture research, the most important are: observation method, experiment method, method of conversation, psychological investigation method, biographical method, modeling and simulation method, psychometric test method, monograph method.

The method of observation lies in the intentional pursuit and accurate recording of the various behavioral manifestations of the members of the organization (Anand & Kodali, 2010). In essence, the method involves observing conduct, verbal expressions, physical products (uniforms, offices and outward appearance), interpersonal relationships, cultural norms and values, attitudes and beliefs, habits and work processes. The observation allows the direct knowledge of reality, identifying both the material elements of the organizational performance and some behavioral manifestations of the organization's members, negative or positive.

Applying this research method also involves a number of disadvantages, such as the fact that it is not economic, having to passively anticipate the behavior; unintentional changes can be made to the facts studied; the factors involved cannot be tracked simultaneously; the information is often very rich, but not all of the same importance.

The psychological investigation method allows us to obtain information about the psychic life of a group of individuals by using oral or written questions (Alhyari et al., 2013). Researchers use two forms of this survey: based on an interview when questions are asked orally and based on a questionnaire when questions are written.

The information resulting from organizational performance research must be processed and presented in an accessible, synthetic and relevant form. Thus, statistical and mathematical methods and graphical methods are used in practice, such as: prediction tests, group conversations, in-depth conversations, motivational study, factorial, multidimensional analysis, etc.

In many cases, the employee's lack of satisfaction (material and professional) contributes decisively to the decision to resign. It may simply fail to find interest in the job, when the task becomes overly monotonous or boring, or it is possible that it does not use its knowledge or skill in its execution. Not knowing about wages and other material benefits, working hours or job security are also a powerful incentive to change the job. The organization, however, has much more control over the elements that affect the resignation of employees, these being related to the personnel policy adopted in the field of work or the decisions taken by the governing body.

Sometimes employees are very happy with the work they do, but they have problems with the company itself. The work environment is a tool and they cannot do anything about creating better working conditions. Employees who are not happy with the working conditions will give their superiors or colleagues negative feelings about the organization and its rules, the opportunities it offers, and the chances of the organization and organization become bigger.

This method is used both to create a clearer picture of the company's cultural profile and to provide a database for further interventions. Based on other methods of identifying organizational culture, S.W.O.T. aims to rearrange the elements of the cultural profile corresponding to the following categories: Strengths, Weaknesses, Opportunities and Threats. Based on the Benchmarking, the strengths and weaknesses, the causes that generated them and their implications for the performance of the organization will be analyzed and presented.

Morphological analysis is a way to analyze and predict the components of organizational performance. This allows the decomposition of performance into component elements and their analysis in the context of profound changes in organizational culture in response to changes in the company's external environment.

Value analysis is another technique of organizing and processing the values of individuals and organizational performance (Andriole, 2010). This method provides information about what people value more or less, about what they value as desirable in correspondence with certain intentions, expectations and ideals. In organizations where employees are more concerned with meeting the basic, elementary needs, their behavioral choices are restricted, which leads to a decrease in their contribution to increasing the efficiency of their work. In strong economic firms, employees have higher aspirations, both spiritually and materially, which leads to their participation in organizational performance.

Impact analysis helps to get insight into the interaction between organizational performance and the external environment (Becker & Huselid, 2006). This type of method provides the possibility to anticipate the possible consequences of managerial decisions as a result of the impact of different environmental changes on the organizational performance in order to guide and control the development of the firm.

As a major difference, this method analyzes managerial performance by trying to assess its context, connect it to the performance of the organization, and discover ways to change it.

Critical Incident Technique Classification as a qualitative method is due to the possibility of a profound approach to the subject, of obtaining a rich material of high authenticity and allowing individuals to clarify the meanings they associate with certain organizational components (Olson et al., 2005).

As one of the most studied subjects in the management, the integrated systems of performance indicators and their influence in the ascension of an organization are today the ground for the assertion of many ideas, much of them controversial, a state determined by the various ways of approaching its problem, which led to the shaping of major research directions. The use of the method aims at identifying common themes and perceptions and on this basis identifies predominant behavioral patterns of the members of the community in certain circumstances.

Acceptance and assumption by top managers not only of their formal role within an entity but also of the informal one contributes to building a strong managerial performance. Involving managers in setting the mission and objectives of the entity in defining policies and action strategies that only make operational the stakeholder's vision make the managerial culture of an entity the link between all the elements that can ensure organizational performance.

SOLUTIONS AND RECOMMENDATIONS

Regardless of the method used, of a qualitative or quantitative nature, it is important for the initiators of the audit of organizational performance and / or management performance to consider establishing conclusions that provide generally valid information in the context of the diversity of values, beliefs, opinions and attitudes of individuals of an organization.

Studies based on ethnographic analysis require a great involvement of researchers in the life of the organization so that they perceive the whole social construction of the organization, but within it, and even experimenting with these elements themselves (Chen & Fu, 2008; Rowland & Hall, 2014; Homburg & Pflesser, 2000). Therefore researchers must observe the daily activities of the organization, study ceremonies and rituals, to understand the significance given various artefacts, study verbal and nonverbal languages used to capture existing stories and myths etc.

The analysis of organizational evolution can be an information base for the analysis of organizational performance. It is advisable, however, to treat information sources carefully since much of the documents in which these reports are presented are likely to appeal to the general public and are therefore often changing financial information's. For this reason, the analysis of organizational evolution is usually associated with other methods of investigation and analysis of organizational performance.

FUTURE RESEARCH DIRECTIONS

Today's world differs, through a series of essential aspects, from what we have been used to for a long time. The value and performance are the successful formula for effective and modern management of companies. "Measuring performance means appreciating value, and knowing value, means" to translate 'performance'.

Traditional entity operations are now disruptive by new technologies that remove barriers to entry for agile players. Challenged by the evolution of a fragmented market, the pragmatic adoption of new technologies represents new opportunities for new market players to innovate and develop business models that generate profit. Even powerful leadership entities have difficulty finding and finding anchorages in this new economic environment that will keep their competitive advantage and face the new threats to remain performing. The impact of Internet of Things (IoT), Cloud Computing, Distributed Intelligence, and Robotics on entities in 2020-2030 will be very strong. Only a thorough knowledge of the entity and the operations, transparency of management processes and financial knowledge of the external environment especially threats innovation in order to increase product and service quality, diversification and creation of internal mechanisms to respond to forces disruptive together with a managerial culture in which the leader has the force to influence from almost to the world, ensures that he remains in the market.

CONCLUSION

Considering the megatrends of economic environment and the concept of "vision" developed at level of strategic union (European Union), country/state (Kenya, Saudi Arabia) or economic sector (construction, oil and gas industry) and to gain some understanding of the future, four possible scenarios of how the economic environment could look in twenty years, have been developed to help the companies to create sustainable business plans, flexible and adaptable. Two variables: conflict versus harmony and evolution versus revolution and the interaction of these two variables has resulted in four scenarios of the state of the business world in 2030.

Megatrends signify major changes to the economy, society, and our personal lives – therefore they may represent material opportunities or challenges for businesses. External to companies, megatrends can give rise to new competitors, business models, customer segments or needs, and business contexts altogether. And internal to companies, megatrends can result in a need for new capabilities, offering, marketing mix, go-to-market models, and production processes. For these reasons, companies that consider megatrends and their impact on their business should be better positioned for long-term sustained growth. Key performance indicators is already used by numerous supply chains to improve management and performance. New horizons of the entities in improving their performance bring in action predictive KPIs or KPPs into the mix. These predictive KPIs are likely to be more specific to the enterprise concerned than the historical KPIs used so far. On the other hand, looking at how other sectors are using predictive business intelligence is likely to yield additional inspiration for improving supply chain

For many Romanian organizations, Benchmarking is still a little overlooked, on the one hand because of the lack of necessary financial resources, on the other hand, of a poor awareness of the importance of these investments in the medium and long term.

From the point of view of the improvement of the organizational performance, the following proposals can be recommended:

- In a world where competition is fierce, a leader can no longer meet his responsibilities without having managerial skills and knowledge. It is proposed that the managers go through specialization courses to help them successfully solve the problems, which are becoming more and more complex;
- The impact of Benchmarking on company performance is obvious and does not require much demonstration. The increase in performance gives the firm greater opportunities to adapt to the market, greater flexibility and chances of success compared with competition, and seek to improve financial results;
- The development of Benchmarking can offer the creation and observance of ethical codes that guide their activity and eliminate as far as possible the adoption of unethical behaviors with negative impact on the image of the company on the market;
- The initiation of partnerships, mergers, takeovers that will lead to the reinvigoration of the firm's activity becomes possible by taking into account the organizational element that influences the result of the company.

For the time being, the only alternatives for developing small and medium-sized businesses in Romania are: the ability to create new products and services, the ability to improve internal and external relationships so as to favor the creation of competitive advantages that will ensure success in the market.

REFERENCES

Agha, S., Alrubaiee, L., & Jamhour, M. (2012). Effect of core competence on competitive advantage and organizational performance. *International Journal of Business and Management*, *7*(1), 192–204.

Ahearne, M., Lam, S. K., Mathieu, J. E., & Bolander, W. (2010). Why are some sales people better at adapting to organizational change? *Journal of Marketing*, *74*(3), 65–79. doi:10.1509/jmkg.74.3.65

Akgün, A. E., Keskin, H., & Byrne, J. (2009). Organizational emotional capability, product and process innovation, and firm performance: An empirical analysis. *Journal of Engineering and Technology Management*, *26*(3), 103–130. doi:10.1016/j.jengtecman.2009.06.008

Alhyari, S., Alazab, M., Venkatraman, S., Alazab, M., & Alazab, A. (2013). Performance evaluation of e-government services using balanced scorecard. *Benchmarking: An International Journal*, *20*(4), 512–536. doi:10.1108/BIJ-08-2011-0063

Allan, F. (1993). Benchmarking: Practical aspects for information professionals. *Special Libraries*, *84*(3), 123–130.

Alstete, J. W., & Beutell, N. J. (2018). Designing learning spaces for management education: A mixed methods research approach. *Journal of Management Development*, *37*(2), 201–211. doi:10.1108/JMD-08-2017-0247

Amagoh, F. (2008). Perspectives on organizational change: Systems and complexity theories. *The Innovation Journal*, *13*(3), 1–14.

Anand, G., & Kodali, R. (2010). A mathematical model for the evaluation of roles and responsibilities of human resources in a lean manufacturing environment. *International Journal of Human Resources Development and Management*, *10*(1), 63–100. doi:10.1504/IJHRDM.2010.029447

Andriole, S. J. (2010). Business impact of Web 2.0 Technologies. *Communications of the ACM*, *53*(12), 67–79. doi:10.1145/1859204.1859225

Arsenault, P., & Faerman, S. R. (2014). Embracing paradox in management: The value of the competing values framework. *Organizational Management Journal*, *11*(3), 147–158. doi:10.1080/15416518.2014.949614

Ashkanasy, N. (2011, February). International happiness; a multilevel perspective. *The Academy of Management Perspectives*, 23–29.

Barney, J. B. (1986). Organizational culture: Can it be a source of sustained competitive advantage. *Academy of Management Review*, *11*(3), 656–665. doi:10.5465/amr.1986.4306261

Becker, B. E., & Huselid, M. A. (1998). High performance work systems and firm performance: A synthesis of research and managerial implications. *Research in Personnel and Human Resources Management*, *16*, 53–101.

Becker, B. E., & Huselid, M. A. (2006). Strategic human resources management: Where do we go from here? *Journal of Management*, *32*(6), 898–925. doi:10.1177/0149206306293668

Behery, M., Jabeen, F., & Parakandi, M. (2014). Adopting a contemporary performance management system. *International Journal of Productivity and Performance Management, 63*(1), 22–43. doi:10.1108/IJPPM-07-2012-0076

Cameron, K. S., & Quinn, R. E. (2011). *Diagnosing and Changing Organizational Culture: Based on the Competing Values Framework*. San Francisco, CA: Jossey-Bass.

Chan, L. L., Shaffer, M. A., & Snape, E. (2004). In search of sustained competitive advantage: The impact of organizational culture, competitive strategy and human resource management practices on firm performance. *International Journal of Human Resource Management, 15*(1), 17–35. doi:10.1080/0958519032000157320

Chen, H. M., & Fu, P. C. (2008). A systematic framework for performance appraisal and compensation strategy. *Human Systems Management, 27*, 161–175.

Cocca, P., & Alberti, M. (2010). A framework to assess performance measurement in SMEs. *International Journal of Productivity and Performance Management, 59*(2), 186–200. doi:10.1108/17410401011014258

Davila, A. (2012). New trends in performance measurement and management control. *In Performance Measurement and Management Control. Global Issues (Washington, D.C.), 25*, 65–87.

de Waal, A. A., & Kourtit, K. (2013). Performance measurement and management in practice. *International Journal of Productivity and Performance Management, 62*(5), 446–473. doi:10.1108/IJPPM-10-2012-0118

Delaney, J. T., & Huselid, M. A. (1996). The impact of human resource management practices on perceptions of organizational performance. *Academy of Management Journal, 39*, 949–969.

Denison, D. R. (1990). *Corporate Culture and Organizational Effectiveness*. New York, NY: Wiley.

Deutsch, P., & Silcox, B. (2003). Learning from other libraries: Benchmarking to assess library performance. *Information Outlook, 7*(7), 18–25.

Fisher, C. D. (2010). Happiness at Work. *International Journal of Management Reviews, 12*(4), 384–412. doi:10.1111/j.1468-2370.2009.00270.x

Galbraith, J. R., & Lawler, E. E. (1993). *Organizing for the Future: The New Logic for Managing Complex Organizations*. San Francisco, CA: Jossey-Bass.

Guo, D., Chen, H., Long, R., Lu, H., & Long, Q. (2017). A Co-Word Analysis of Organizational Constraints for Maintaining Sustainability. *Sustainability, 9*(11), 1928. doi:10.3390u9101928

Hartnell, C. A., Ou, A. Y., & Kinicki, A. (2011). Organizational culture and organizational effectiveness: A meta-analytic investigation of the competing values framework's theoretical suppositions. *The Journal of Applied Psychology, 96*(4), 677–694. doi:10.1037/a0021987 PMID:21244127

Henczel, S. (2002). Benchmarking – measuring and comparing for continuous improvement. *Information Outlook, 6*(7), 12–20.

Homburg, C., & Pflesser, C. (2000). A Multiple Layer Model of Market-Oriented Organizational Culture: Measurement Issues and Performance Outcomes. *JMR, Journal of Marketing Research, 37*(4), 449–462. doi:10.1509/jmkr.37.4.449.18786

Hurley, R. F. (2002). Putting people back into organizational learning. *Journal of Business and Industrial Marketing*, *17*(4), 270–281. doi:10.1108/08858620210431679

Kaplan, R. S., & Norton, D. P. (2006). How to implement a new strategy without disrupting your organization. *Harvard Business Review*, *84*(3), 100. PMID:16515159

Leyer, M., Stumpf-Wollersheim, J., & Kronsbein, D. (2017). Stains on the bright side of process-oriented organizational design: An empirical investigation of advantages and disadvantages. *Schmalenbach Business Review*, *17*(1), 29–47. doi:10.100741464-016-0020-9

Lim, B. (1995). Examining the organizational culture and organizational performance link. *Leadership and Organization Development Journal*, *16*(5), 16–21. doi:10.1108/01437739510088491

Lin, C. H., Peng, C. H., & Kao, D. T. (2008). The innovativeness effect of market orientation and learning orientation on business performance. *International Journal of Manpower*, *29*(8), 752–772. doi:10.1108/01437720810919332

Meuer, J. (2017). Exploring the Complementarities within High-Performance Work Systems: A Set-Theoretic Analysis of UK Firms. *Human Resource Management*, *56*(4), 651–672. doi:10.1002/hrm.21793

Olson, E. M., Slater, S. F., Tomas, G., & Hult, M. (2005). The performance implications of fit among business strategy, marketing organization structure, and strategic behavior. *Journal of Marketing*, *69*(3), 49–65. doi:10.1509/jmkg.69.3.49.66362

Paton, R. A., & McCalman, J. (2008). *Change Management: A Guide to Effective Implementation*. London: SAGE Publications.

Pieper, J. R., Trevor, C. O., Weller, I., & Duchon, D. (2017). Referral Hire Presence Implications for Referrer Turnover and Job Performance. *Journal of Management*, *19*, 14–20.

Rowland, C., & Hall, R. (2014). Management learning, performance and reward: Theory and practice revisited. *Journal of Management Development*, *33*(4), 342–356. doi:10.1108/JMD-08-2012-0110

Schneider, M., & Somers, M. (2006). Organizations as complex adaptive systems: Implications of complexity theory for leadership research. *The Leadership Quarterly*, *17*(4), 351–365. doi:10.1016/j.leaqua.2006.04.006

Tajeddini, K. (2015). Exploring the antecedents of effectiveness and efficiency. *International Journal of Hospitality Management*, *49*(7), 125–135. doi:10.1016/j.ijhm.2015.06.007

Taticchi, P., Tonelli, F., & Cagnazzo, L. (2010). Performance measurement and management: A literature review and a research agenda. *Measuring Business Excellence*, *14*(1), 4–18. doi:10.1108/13683041011027418

Tong, Y. K., & Arvey, R. D. (2015). Managing complexity via the Competing Values Framework. *Journal of Management Development*, *34*(6), 653–673. doi:10.1108/JMD-04-2014-0029

Yadav, N., & Sagar, M. (2013). Performance measurement and management frameworks. *Business Process Management Journal*, *19*(6), 947–971. doi:10.1108/BPMJ-01-2013-0003

ADDITIONAL READING

Chen, D., Li, O. Z., & Xin, F. (2017). Five-year plans, China finance and their consequences. *China Journal of Accounting Research*, *10*(3), 189–230. doi:10.1016/j.cjar.2017.06.001

Koksal, B., & Orman, C. (2015). Determinants of capital structure: Evidence from a major developing economy. *Small Business Economics*, *44*(2), 255–282. doi:10.100711187-014-9597-x

Weining, N., & Qingduo, Z. (2018). Corporate financing with loss aversion and disagreement. *Finance Research Letters*, *21*, 1–24.

Zenner, M., McInnes, P., Chivukula, R., & Le, P. (2017). A Primer on the Financial Policies of Chinese Firms: A Multi-country Comparison. *Journal of Applied Corporate Finance*, *28*(4), 86–94.

Chapter 12
A Noble Algorithm to Secure Online Data Transmission One Hundred Percent at Zero Cost

Alok Sharma
Baba Mast Nath University, India

Nidhi Sharma
Baba Mast Nath University, India

ABSTRACT

This noble algorithm to provide security to online data transfer is an excellent means by which security can be received in transferring data over the network, and it cannot be detected by any technique or tools available in the market with attacker, unwanted parties, and intruder. In this chapter, a noble algorithm to secure data in online transmission is proposed that provides one hundred percent security to online data. This process makes the communication one hundred percent secure.

INTRODUCTION

Transfer of information and sharing of information to distant locations has increased to large extent in today's digital world. So it has become compulsory to secure this information transferred over internet. There are lots of techniques available to secure information transferred over internet example public key cryptography, private key cryptography, hashing algorithms and steganographic techniques. This algorithm will cover main advantage of steganographic techniques to keep the existence of secret message unrevealed along with the benefit of making it impossible for intruder, attacker and third party to retrieve even a single bit of secret message. This algorithm is NP-Hard algorithm on network for intruder, attacker and third party but polynomial at receiver end. This is a basic algorithm and many applications based on different type of communication like Alpha-Numeric communication and other communication may be communicated by this ago. Case 2 of this algorithm gives one example of alpha-numeric communication which may be used by different security agencies with hundred percent security to data, lifelong two way communication with zero cost on security software and hardware (Pratheek, 2017).

DOI: 10.4018/978-1-5225-8455-1.ch012

BACKGROUND

Type of Encryption Algorithms Detectable by Bit Comparison Tools

1. LSB in GIF.
2. Steganographic Technique based on Difference Expansion method.
3. Hiding behind Corners.
4. Hiding Secret Message in Edges of the Image (RELSB).
5. Steganographic Technique based on Modulus Function and Pixel Value Differencing.
6. Data hiding method based on interpolation technique.
7. LSB principle of image steganography.

LSB in GIF

Palette based images, such as GIF images, are popular image file format commonly used on the Internet. GIF images are indexed images where the colors used in the image are stored in a palette or a color lookup table. GIF images can also be used for LSB steganography, although extra care should be taken. The main issue with the palette based approach is that if one changes the least significant bit of a pixel, it could result in an entirely different color since the index to the color palette gets modified. One possible solution to this problem is to sort the palette so that the color differences between consecutive colors are minimized. The main drawback of using GIF images in LSB steganography is that GIF images use to have a bit depth of 8 which means that information to be embedded is vey less as compared to other image formats. Second problem with GIF images is that these images are not secure to statistical as well as visual attacks, as the processing of palette processing to be done on the GIF images use to leave a clear signature on the image. This approach was dependent on the file format as well as the image itself, since a wrong choice of image could results in the message being visible (LSB in GIF, 2017).

Steganographic Technique Based on Difference Expansion Method

Difference Expansion (DE) is a more efficient and simple technique of data embedding used in digital images and is reversible in nature. In DE technique, one bit can be embedded into two pixels which are consecutive to each other. So it gives the maximum embedding capacity of 0.5 bpp. The main advantage of this technique was that it discovers extra storage space by exploring the redundancy in the image content. Both the payload capacity limit as well as the visual quality of embedded images of the DE method are the best along with a low computational complexity. The main problem with the difference expansion (DE) based reversible data hiding methods is that this technique is use to double differences between pixels in successive iteration. So this technique could not gain popularity. The DE is keen to statistical attacks as the level of distortions is high. DE based techniques use to have low payload capacity and could not be used for applications due to demand of high visual quality (Fridrich, Goljan & Du, 2001).

Hiding Behind Corners

There are techniques which do not take into account the cover image original information these cases use to drop certain marks on the cover image/stego image. In the technique of Hiding behind Corners

(HBC), cover image original information is not taken into account. Two algorithms were used in HBC based on using image filters to determine the effective hiding places in an image. They were Filter First and Battle Steg. The strength of Filter First was that it eliminates the need to provide any additional information such as original image. It was also very effective in hiding information (Wu & Tsai, 2003). Whereas the weakness of Filter First was that it was not secure, as an attacker can repeat the filtering process. It could be also much easier to retrieve the hidden information once the stego image is identified. The strength of Battle Steg was that it requires a password to retrieve the message. Its weakness includes the absence of a random seed so it was impossible to know where to place the shots and also it was possible for Battle Steg to never have a hit. Hiding behind Corners approach effectively utilizes edge areas but embedding capacity is less (Ni, Shi, Ansari & Su,2006).

Hiding Secret Message in Edges of the Image (RELSB)

Hiding Secret Message in Edges of the image introduced a new least significant bit embedding algorithm for hiding secret messages in non-adjacent pixel locations at the edges of images. Here the messages were hidden in regions which were least like their neighboring pixels i.e. regions that contain edges, corners, thin lines etc so that an attacker will have less suspicion of the presence of message bits in edges, because pixels in edges of an image appears to be much brighter or dimmer than their neighbors. Edges can be detected by edge detection filters such as a 3x3 window Laplacian edge detector. One common disadvantage of LSB embedding was that it created an imbalance between the neighboring pixels. Here this imbalance was avoided by flipping the gray-scale values among 2i-1, 2i and 2i+1. The various strengths of this scheme were that an attacker will have less suspicion to the presence of message bits in edges because pixels in edges appear to be either much brighter or dimmer than their neighbors and it was also secure against blind steganalysis. It also limits the length of the secret message to be embedded. The main disadvantage with this scheme was that the embedding capacity was relatively low. It could not make full use of edges during embedding (Li, Zeng & Yang, 2008).

Adaptive Data Hiding in Edge Areas of Images With Spatial LSB Domain Systems (AE-LSB)

Here a new adaptive least-significant bit (LSB) steganographic method based on pixel-value differencing (PVD) was proposed. The difference value of two consecutive pixels estimates how many secret bits to be embedded into the two pixels. Pixels located in the edge areas were embedded with more secret bits than that located in smooth areas. The range of difference values were adaptively divided into lower level, middle level, and higher level. It is ensured in the phase of readjustment that the level of consecutive pixels remains same both before and after embedding. The division of range [0, 255] values is done between different levels. It is required for extraction that the value of difference should belong to same level before and after embedding. This scheme provides more capacity and better quality than the PVD and was an improved version of PVD. The main disadvantage with this scheme was that it was less tolerant to steganalysis (Wu & Tsai, 2003).

Steganographic Method Based on Pixel Value Differencing and Modulus Function

High Quality Steganographic method with PVD and Modulus function was an extension of PVD based approach. This technique first calculates the difference value between two consecutive pixels and then modulus operation was used to calculate their remainder. To embed the secret data between two pixels their remainder is modified. The difference value taken use to decide the hiding capacity of the two consecutive. It is assumed that as much Lesser is the difference value that much smoother is the area, this means that only less secret data will be embedded and vice versa. The strength of the scheme was that it could greatly reduce the visibility of the hidden data than the PVD method. Since the scheme used the remainder of the two consecutive pixels it was more flexible. However, a loophole exists in the PVD method. Presence of secret data is revealed with the help of unusual steps in the histogram of pixel differences in this technique pixels which are modified are to be dispersed all around the whole cover medium or stego image and this contaminates many smooth regions (Marvel, Boncelet & Retter, 2007).

Data Hiding Method Based on Interpolation Technique

Reversible data hiding method based on Interpolation Technique (IT) concealed data into interpolation errors. Instead of using the nearest neighbor interpolation technique, an image interpolation algorithm was used to obtain the interpolation errors. The reference pixels are adaptively selected in the cover image and pixels other than the reference pixels are interpolated. Interpolation errors are obtained by subtracting the interpolated pixels from the original image. Data bits were concealed by modifying the interpolation errors. Because reference pixel values were not changed in the embedding process, the same set of interpolated pixels could be obtained in the decoding process and thus, the embedded data bits could be extracted and the original image was restored. In this technique, they reduced the number of reference pixels in smooth regions and increased the number of reference pixels in complex regions. But the distortions in the output image were\ much higher in histogram shifting method. However, in most cases, the number of reference pixels affects the payload and the stego image quality (Mao, Chen & Lian, 2004).

Edge Adaptive Image Steganography Based on LSB Matching (EA-LSBMR)

The least significant bit (LSB) based steganography is the most common type of steganographic approach. In most existing approaches, the choice of data hiding positions within the input cover image mainly depends on a pseudo random number generator (PRNG). Here the relationship between the image content and the size of the secret message to be embedded is not considered.

Even very low embedding rate will modify the smoother regions in the stego / cover image which will make the poor quality of image. It is easy for the stegano analyst to identify this type of images. In the techniques like LSB Matching Revisited (LSBMR) user has the option to select the region based on threshold value to embed the data. The threshold value will be calculated based on the size of secret message and the difference between two adjacent pixels in the cover image (S-Tools for Windows).

Synthesis of Literature Review

It is concluded that no available technique claim hundred percent security in communication. If we make search on google about hundred percent secure communication then scientificamerican.com and many other website say that nothing is hundred percent secure in communication. Along with this available techniques are very costly and not in reach of ordinary man, requiring millions of dollar cost on hardware and software.

MAIN FOCUS OF THE CHAPTER

This is an algorithm to create session for secure communication which is two way and lifelong. In this algorithm to create session between two parties both receiver and sender first mutually agrees on one BIT Table with values 0 and 1 in table and retains one (Same) copy of BIT Table with each and maintains it secret as the case of physically key exchange method in key based algorithm where both parties take their key physically (By transportation). As it is known that all communication on computer is in binary form that is 0 and 1. So message to be sent is converted into binary and it is spread in bit table such that 0 of message match with 0 of bit table and 1 with 1 as explained in example given below. After spreading binary bits of message in bit table locations of bit table are stored where bits of message are spread and location array with these locations is transferred over network as explained in example given below. On the receiver end values in location array location are retrieved from bit table available at receiver end received initially physically. These values are converted into character form which gives original message. Important point in this algorithm is that it is two way algorithm as sender can become receiver any time and receiver can become sender any time as both parties have same bit table mutually agreed and received physically (by transportation) as keys are exchanged in key based algorithms in the starting session.

NOBEL ALGORITHM TO PROVIDE A HUNDRED PERCENT SECURITY IN ONLINE TRANSMISSION AT ZERO COST

Encryption Algorithm (Explained in Figure 1)

1. Take BIT Table mutually agreed upon by receiver and sender in starting of session;
2. Take secret message;
3. Convert secret message into binary;
4. Spread the binary message such that 0 and 1 of message match with 0 and 1 of BIT Table;
5. Store the location of BIT Table where digits of secret message are stored in their sequence;
6. Make an location array of BIT Table locations;
7. Transfer the location array over internet to receiver.

Figure 1. Flow diagram of proposed algorithm

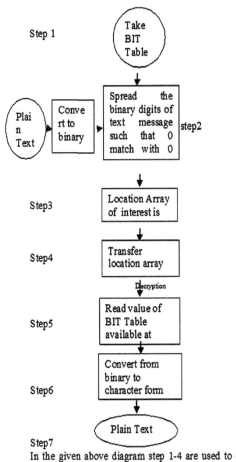

Step1

Step2

Step3

Step4

Step5

Step6

Step7

In the given above diagram step 1-4 are used to encrypt the message which cover Encryption Algorithm.
And step 5-7 are used to decrypt the message which cover Decryption algorithm.

Decryption Algorithm (Explained in Figure 1)

1. Receiver side those values in location of BIT Table are read as given in location array;
2. Store those values in sequence;
3. Convert from binary to text form;
4. Original message is retrieved;
5. Decryption is complete.

Example

Suppose the message to be sent is digit 32 online using this noble algorithm. First convert 32 into binary which is:

1 0 0 0 0 0

Suppose the given below BIT Table is mutually agreed upon by sender and receiver, copy given to both in start of session physically as key exchange mechanism in key based algorithm:

Receiver end	Sender end
0 1 0	0 1 0
0 0 0	0 0 0
1 0 0	1 0 0
1 1 1	1 1 1

Sender spread the message in underlined locations that is:

0 <u>1</u> 0
<u>0</u> <u>0</u> <u>0</u>
1 <u>0</u> 0
1 1 1

So location array of BIT Table is:

1,2	first row second column
1,3	first row third column
2,1	second row first column
2,2	second row second column
2,3	second row third column
3,2	third row second column

Send this location array online over network and at receiver end read the values of BIT Table at locations given in Location array which is:

1,2	first row second column value retrieved is 1
1,3	first row third column value retrieved is 0
2,1	second row first column value retrieved is 0
2,2	second row second column value retrieved is 0
2,3	second row third column value retrieved is 0
3,2	third row second column value retrieved is 0

When these values are changed to character gives 32 which is original message.

CASE 2 (ALPHA-NUMERIC COMMUNICATION)

To make a session for alpha-numeric communication both receiver and sender has to mutually agree on Alpha-numeric table and distribute it by physical transportation means in starting once as bit table is exchanged in case 1.

Suppose both receiver and sender agree on given below Alpha-numeric table and retains it confidentially:

S	Z	A	1	T
1	2	3	4	5
V	Y	3	B	2
6	7	8	9	10
5	D	E	C	4
11	12	13	14	15
7	8	6	F	P
16	17	18	19	20
0	9	G	J	M
21	22	23	24	25
H	Q	X	P	N
26	27	28	29	30
M	R	I	L	A
31	32	33	34	35
L	K	J	O	V
36	37	38	39	40
R	W	N	X	U
41	42	43	44	45
A	S	T	R	W
46	47	48	49	50

Alpha numeric table with plain text above and cipher below.

Example

Suppose the message to be send is:

UNIQUE ALGORITHM NO 1

Then the cipher to be sent by any media orally, telephonically or by internet etc. is:

45,43,33,27,45,13,3,34,23,39,49,33,48,26,31,43,39,4

and on the receiver side above cipher text is received and their respective plain text values are found from Alpha-numeric table available with receiver.

ISSUES, CONTROVERSIES, PROBLEMS

Expected Outcomes

1. To design an algorithm which makes steganography undetectable by bit comparison tools or any other technique available over the internet;

2. New algorithm to secure image steganoghraphic file will be designed to provide hundred percent security and confidentiality in online transmission of data over internet with zero cost which is urgent need of today's digital world as internet / world- wide web has become part of everyone's life;

3. Lifelong two way communication session will be created;

4. Using this research cost of security software and hardware will be reduced to zero;

5. Easy to use session with basic knowledge of computer will be created.

Problems

Steganography is the latest field of encryption and decryption where existence of hidden data cannot be detected. Secondly techniques available in market are detectable by bit comparison tools and other techniques which do not confirm hundred percent security, confidentiality of data transmitted over network. Most widely acceptable technique available is LSB (least significant bit) but this technique also do not ensure hundred percent security to data transferred using this technique.

Computer Code

Implementation

This implementation (shown in Figure 2–Figure 13) is done in MATLAB and works according to algorithm of Encryption and Decryption explained above.

Figure 2.

Figure 3.

Figure 4.

Comparison to Available Technique

According to Scientific American and other data available online on search to google.com for 'Hundred percent secure online communication' no available technique has claimed hundred percent security in online communication. According to ScientificAmerican.com nothing is hundred percent secure but our algorithm gives hundred percent security in communication.

Figure 5.

Figure 6.

SOLUTIONS AND RECOMMENDATIONS

Quality Analysis and Hardness of Nobel Algorithm

In this algorithm BIT Table is transferred manually as key are exchanged manually in key based algorithms. This makes this communication two way which means that receiver and sender can mutually exchange each other and receiver can become sender, sender can become receiver as BIT Table is same with both receiver and sender.

Figure 7.

Figure 8.

Secondly only location array is transferred over network which do not carry data values but carry the locations of BIT Table whose data values are to be picked to retrieve the original message. In this way it is like sending the memory address without allowing access to data values in those memory addresses which makes impossible for intruder, attacker and third parties to access the data which makes this algorithm as NP-Hard. NP-Hard is justified as data cannot be recovered by any means by intruder/attacker/third party and makes this unbreakable by third parties. On the other hand at the receiver end it

Figure 9.

Figure 10.

is polynomial as both BIT Table and location array are available. This is NP-Hard on network as BIT-Table is not available over network which is transferred manually as key exchange mechanism in key based algorithms.

This analysis confirms that it is hundred percent secure algorithm to transfer data over internet with zero cost of algorithm and within approach of every civilian. What is required to use this algorithm is internet connection with basic knowledge of computer fundamental.

Figure 11.

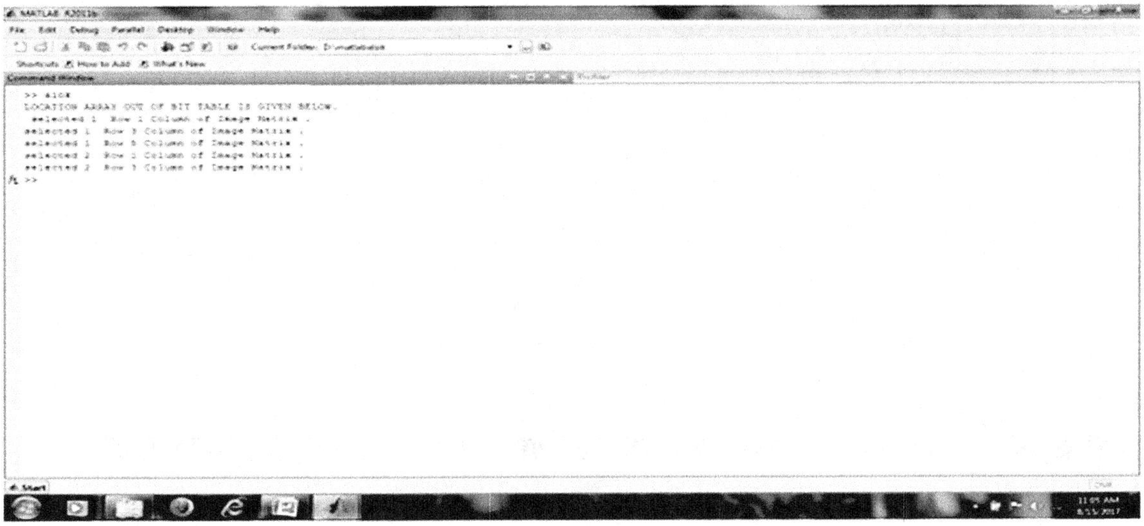

Figure 12.

FUTURE RESEARCH DIRECTIONS

This algorithm is a example of Basic research so gives a basic concept should be used for all type of communication and may be extended for image, video and for file with other extensions in communication. In future it is expected from our side that all communication of govt. organizations across the world, all private organizations across the world and every individual over net should use this algorithm.

This algorithm do not impose any type of limitation for binary and alpha-numeric communication but security of BIT Table/ Alpha-numeric table is must to get all advantage of this communication.

Figure 13.

CONCLUSION

This algorithm confirms hundred percent security and integrity of data transferred using this algorithm. This algorithm is free of cost as any internet user with basic knowledge of computer fundamental can use it without any external requirement. Along with the above mentioned benefits the session made using this algorithm can be used for life long and for other communications like Alpha-numeric communication along with binary communication with zero cost on security software and hardware without any type of network complexity. The session made through this algorithm are two way as sender and receiver can mutually exchange each other and easy to use. If all network communication is shifted to principle of this algorithm security problems will be reduced to zero. When use of this algorithm is made for communication, quality of network becomes immaterial for data security point of view as this algo is NP-Hard over network and even unsafe network can not compromise the security of data transferred over net using this algorithm. The behind this is that location of data in BIT table/ Alpha-numeric table is transferred over net not the real data which is equivalent to sending memory address without allowing access to them. By making use of this algorithm cost on network security is reduced to zero as there is no importance of security quality of network as it is taken care by algorithm itself. If all communication is done using this algorithm it will reduce the billions of cost spent on network security software, hardware and anti-virus etc. to zero benefitting the society completely. The significance of this technique is for all defense purpose across the world, for govt. organizations across the world, all private organizations across the world and every individual over net as this technique is in reach of every organization or individual over net requiring basic knowledge of computer and internet connection.

ACKNOWLEDGMENT

Many people have contributed to this work, either directly or indirectly. To start with, I must thank all the researcher who have contributed in the field of Steganography because their work enabled me to do further enhancement in this area.

I would like to thank Dr. S.C. Batra, Dean, Faculty of Management & Commerce, Dr. Satpal, Professor & Head, Dept of Computer Science, Prof. (Dr.) Ramphool Sharma, Prof. (Dr.) Ajay Bamba and other faculty members who had helped a lot during my research work. I would like to thank Dr. Vinod Srivastava, Professor, my Ph.D. research supervisor, who provided me with the great opportunity to do research in the area of steganography. Without his valuable guidance and priceless suggestions, this work would not have been possible. He helped me a lot in broadening my knowledge in this area. His understanding, encouragement and personal guidance have provided a good foundation for the research. His tolerance of having deep discussion, sacrificing his personal time, is extremely insightful and hereby greatly appreciated.

I am also thankful to the faculty members and staff members of Baba Mast Nath University, who had conducted course work in Ph.D.

Finally I would like to thank my family members, friends and relatives for their valuable support and understanding.

REFERENCES

Fridrich, J., Goljan, M., & Du, R. (2001). Detecting LSB steganography in color, and gray-scale images. *IEEE MultiMedia*, 8(4), 22–28. doi:10.1109/93.959097

Li, X., Zeng, T., & Yang, B. (2008). Detecting LSB matching by applying calibration technique for difference image. *Proc. 10th ACM Workshop on Multimedia and Security*, 133–138. 10.1145/1411328.1411353

LSB in GIF. (2017). Retrieved from http://www.ijsce.org/attachments/File/v3i5/E190011351 .pdf

Mao, Y. B., Chen, G., & Lian, S. G. (2004). A novel fast image Encryption scheme based on the 3D chaotic baker map. *International Journal of Bifurcation and Chaos in Applied Sciences and Engineering*, 14(10), 3613–3624. doi:10.1142/S021812740401151X

Marvel, L. M., Boncelet, C. G., & Retter, C. (2007). Spread Spectrum Steganography. *IEEE Transactions on Image Processing*, 8(8), 160–178. PMID:18267522

Ni, Z., Shi, Y. Q., Ansari, N., & Su, W. (2006). Reversible data hiding. *IEEE Transactions on Circuits and Systems for Video Technology*, 16(3), 354–362. doi:10.1109/TCSVT.2006.869964

Pratheek, P. K. (2017). *Steganography Using Visual Cryptography*. Retrieved from https://books.google.com/books?id=Z8WiAwAAQBAJ

S-Tools for Windows. (n.d.). Retrieved from http://www.modemac.com/s-tools.html

Wu, D., & Tsai, W. (2003). A steganographic method for images by pixel value differencing. *Pattern Recognition Letters*, 24(9-10), 1613–1626. doi:10.1016/S0167-8655(02)00402-6

Chapter 13
Stimulating Local and Regional Economic Projects and Technological Innovation

Louis Delcart
European Academy of the Regions, Belgium

ABSTRACT

The literature on the development of SMEs is clear: one of the most important obstacles to developing a private sector that also creates jobs is access to financial resources. This chapter presents the various economic players and their accessibility to finance: the public authorities, national, regional and local, the enterprises, and then in particular the SMEs and the traditional civil society. It also shows the conditions that succeed with the most effective results, incentives for start-ups and further developing companies, and the way targets are to be measured.

INTRODUCTION

In his introduction to the book "Internationalisation of SMEs. How to succeed abroad?" present chairman of the EU Parliament and former vice-president of the EU Commission, Antonio Tajani wrote: "The shortage of appropriate funding is one of the crucial factors preventing SMEs from exploring the potential of global markets. I would thus welcome and encourage every initiative that can improve access to finance at the European, national or regional levels. At a time when European enterprises, in particular start-ups and enterprises in an early growth phase, face unfavourable lending conditions, we need a concerted effort to establish financial instruments and a legal framework that would enable SMEs to expand beyond Europe's Single Market" (Lernoux, Boschmans, Bouyon, Martin & Van Caillie, 2013). Access to finance varies greatly between countries and ranges from about 5 percent of the adult population in Papua New Guinea and Tanzania to 100 percent in the Netherlands (Demirgüç-Kunt, Beck & Honohan, 2008).

DOI: 10.4018/978-1-5225-8455-1.ch013

One of the incentives for regional involvement is to stimulate them in taking responsibility on the management of the European Regional Development Funds based upon a regionally developed strategy (EU, 2016). The difference in approach is striking: the UK manages the ERDF per member state of the Union: England, Scotland, Wales (2 programs!), Northern-Ireland and Gibraltar. Countries organizing the ERDF funds in a centralized way are Romania, Slovakia, Slovenia, Croatia, Malta, Luxembourg, Lithuania, Latvia, Hungary, Finland, Estonia, Denmark, Cyprus, Czech Republic, Bulgaria and Austria. Countries having developed various strategic plans for their regions –and enabling them most likely to manage the funds themselves- are Belgium, France, Germany, Greece, Ireland, Italy, Netherlands, Poland, Portugal, Spain and Sweden. And then there is an overwhelming offer of some 330 cross border collaboration plans. Hereby the regional approach is aiming transnational regions, such as countries alongside the coast of the Adriatic and Ionian Sea, the Low Countries and the North of France, the Danube countries or the countries alongside the Baltic Sea.

There will always be inequalities in economic development within a country. The composition of the population, the presence of large economic players, the presence of good schools and universities make the ascendance of a population towards economic improvement easier in one region compared with other ones. But to arrive to these results, the effort should not come from the sole national government. Local and regional authorities can have an immense impact on the development of their region and city. Even if they only have authority and a lack of budget, their creativity and local cohesion and dynamics can achieve important improvements for their local population. One should read the testimonials within the list of mayors selected for the "Mayor of the World competition", to be convinced that mayors and governors can make a difference. The mayor of the Greek island of Lesbos, Galinos (2016), for example, is among the top-10 mayors of 2016. "Although he didn't have any responsibility with the immigration issue because he is a mayor and not a Minister of immigration policy, he bears the whole weight on his back, he helped the refugees as much as he could, and he created a very good camp, the best in Greece probably. He did the best for his island, and for the residents even many of them don't understand it. If the mayor Galinos was not there at this time, the chaos would have arisen."

This chapter intends hereby to develop the various aspects of the various economic players and their accessibility to finance: the public authorities, national, regional and local, the enterprises and then in particular the SMEs and the traditional civil society.

BACKGROUND

National, Regional, and Local Authorities

Authorities have the potential to create jobs. Their financial means are in many cases substantial and come from direct taxes and indirect taxes. Direct Taxes are taxes that are directly paid to the government by the taxpayer. It is a tax applied on individuals and organizations directly by the government e.g. income tax, corporation tax, wealth tax etc. Indirect Taxes are applied on the manufacture or sale of goods and services. Direct taxes can be determined and collected as well by national, regional as local authorities. Indirect taxes are mostly collected on a higher level than the local one. Both together create a budget on an authority's level. Expenses should be done based upon the level of the budget. When the budget is exceeding the foreseen income, authorities start to have debts. Nowadays, authorities try to reach their goals by combining their means with the means of the private sector, under public-private-partnership (PPP) constructions. In such cases the authorities provide with basic means, such as land, on which the private partner builds a motorway or an office building. The motorway or the office building is then managed by the private company during a long-term contract period against a rent for the use. This rent can be collected through payment booths on the motorway, or through an annual rent received from the authority that occupies the building with its staff. The purpose of the PPP-tool is that payment of the rent is integrated in the authority's expense budget and is taken out of the authority's investment budget and gives it space to perform other urgent investments which they are bound to do alone. One of the many examples of this methodology is the construction of the motorway Recife-João Pessoa in North-East Brazil, where the use of the motorway paid back the investment in ½ years' time. Sometimes local authorities appeal to good citizenship of the entrepreneurs of the region in order to sponsor events or sports teams, or in order to give a grant for the restauration of a city centre, like it was the case in the Turkish city of Gaziantep.

To this enumeration is added in recent years the technique of crowd funding. Crowd funding is a method of raising capital through the collective effort of friends, family, customers, and individual investors. This approach taps into the collective efforts of a large pool of individuals - primarily online via social media and crowd funding platforms - and leverages their networks for greater reach and exposure (The startups.co platform, 2018). Although crowd funding has been created in the first place to serve start-ups or starting initiatives who are unable to receive funds from the banks or from venture capitalists, because of the lack of return on investment, crowd funding is nowadays also used by local public authorities to set up programs with a large public benefit, such as erecting or repairing monuments, purchasing new attractive pieces for the local museum etc. The return is in this case not expressed in financial benefits, but in social benefits, such as being mentioned as crowd funder on the website, having free access to the museum etc. Last but not least, authorities can fund through grant and lending international programs. Grants are - generally partial - investments of an international body into a project defined and proposed by a regional or local authority, who also funds the non-covered part of the program. European Fund for Regional Development (EFRD funds) are one of these examples. In many countries, these means are used in order to reshape city centers and make them more attractive for inhabitants, visitors and investors. The reshape of Constanta city center in South-East Romania is a nice large scale example of this, whereas the construction of a multifunctional day center for socio-medical assistance in the neighboring municipality of Cumpana is a nice small scale example. Loans are also provided to governments or regional authorities who guarantee the reimbursement of these. The APEX-loans granted by the European Investment Bank to governments of the Eastern Partnership enabled the latter to work out large scale turnaround programs for the agricultural sector in order to make them more competitive to the European market. In this way the government of Moldova was not only able to modernise its wine production sector, but also to set up a program for replacing traditional low performing crops in the agricultural sector into perennial crops such as nuts, apricots, apples and berries such as mulberries, blueberries, raspberries. A similar scenario took place in the Western Balkans. Since 2009, the EIB, the European Commission, the Council of Europe Development Bank and the European Bank for Reconstruction and Development have been cooperating under the Western Balkans Investment Framework (WBIF). This provides a joint grant facility and a joint lending facility for priority investments in the region. The objective is to simplify access to credit by pooling and coordinating different sources of finance and technical assistance, with a focus on infrastructure sectors, including social infrastructure.

Small and Medium Sized Enterprises

Small and medium-sized enterprises (SMEs) are often referred to as the backbone of the European economy, providing a potential source for jobs and economic growth. SMEs are defined by the European Commission as having less than 250 persons employed. They should also have an annual turnover of up to EUR 50 million, or a balance sheet total of no more than EUR 43 million (Commission Recommendation of 6 May 2003). The EU administration makes a distinction between micro-enterprises, with less than 10 persons employed, small sized enterprise with 10-49 persons employed and medium-sized enterprises: with 50-249 persons employed. Most SMEs are micro-enterprises (MSMEs) created by private individuals to create employment for themselves and their family. Their first ambition is to survive and only few of them have also the ambition to expand. In many cases the first mentioned have trouble in finding the appropriate funding, especially when they are in the start-up phase. They can usually only borrow from private investors or relatives, who would typically ask between 100% and 120% interest rate. In case microfinance organisations exist in their country they also can appeal to this type of non-banking financial institution. The required interest rates of these organisations are also quite high (30%) because of the labour intensive type of service provided to MSMEs, where bank agents have to visit the farms, help them in setting up project and a reimbursement scheme, following up the project on a regular basis. They also pointed out that MSMEs have generally no access to regular banks due to a lack of collateral. Thanks to their specific structure, collateral is sometimes not required by this type of financial institution.

The banking sector plays its role for SMEs with a proven track record and a solid business plan. There are as well venture capital companies that take financial participations in companies as banks that give credits and credit lines according to the demand for working capital or for investments. But even in countries where access to finance is very much available, start-ups have still trouble in finding the necessary financial means. Support to SMEs is prevailing, even in well-established Western European countries.

The support to SMEs is a typical matter for decentralisation. The difference in approach is striking: the UK manages the ERDF funds per member state of the Union: England, Scotland, Wales (2 programs!), Northern-Ireland and Gibraltar. Countries still organizing the ERDF funds in a centralized way are Romania, Slovakia, Slovenia, Croatia, Malta, Luxembourg, Lithuania, Latvia, Hungary, Finland, Estonia, Denmark, Cyprus, Czech Republic, Bulgaria and Austria. Countries having developed various strategic plans for their regions –and enabling them most likely to manage the funds themselves- are Belgium, France, Germany, Greece, Ireland, Italy, Netherlands, Poland, Portugal, Spain and Sweden (Delcart, 2017). The aim for a decentralized approach is also promoted in non-EU European countries. For the last 3 years Ukrainian law authorises local governments to retain taxes and to use them for the development of their regions. Several regions and cities such as Kiev and Lviv have a fund to stimulate the development of SMEs. Kyiv has also a budget for stimulating IT-companies to increase added value. IT sector companies are numerous in Kyiv, but most of them just execute orders from international companies. In Albania all municipalities were merged into 61 new entities, which were regrouped into 12 counties. The municipalities focus nowadays on practical development of their areas, on urban development and leave strategic development and the acquisition of funds for those purposes to the regional council.

The main obstacle in access to finance for SMEs is the following: how to cover risks in areas where there are insufficient assets to use as pledge? Even when assets are available as collateral, it is real value is difficult to calculate, since in many transitional economies the real estate market is inactive. One of the newly developed support tools to SMEs is the risk sharing tool. In this case an international development bank guarantees a part of a credit bank's portfolio in case some of the attributed credit become defective. Thanks to this tool, selected banks are able to give credit to customer companies who were hindered in their access to finance, and thus their development, because of a lack of collateral: start-ups, service companies without assets, companies investing in assets that become an investment product when they are operational (e.g. power plants to be built up). Customers appreciate the guarantee facility because it enables them to borrow the required sum, based on their real needs. The guarantee enables the bank also to extend the tenor of the loan.

Another type of guarantee is the counter guarantee. In this case a back-to-back guarantee from an international development bank is involved to a national financial guarantee institution that in turn provides guarantees to SMEs. This type of guarantee is only successful in Turkey. Other countries hesitate in setting it up.

In democracies, governments cannot influence the interest rates charged or offered by the Central Bank to the banking sector. And the interest rate of the Central Bank is influenced by the international appreciation or rating of a country's economy. Therefore, in some cases, ministries also subsidize interest payments of loans to individual companies, when the charged interest rates are considered a main obstacle for development. Enterprise Georgia e.g. manages the state programs for economic development. They have a budget of some 5 m GEL for interest rate subsidies to manufacturing companies and the hospitality sector (during 42 months), and can also provide with an interest subsidy for 2 years for the leasing component. In Moldova e.g. agricultural producers groups receive 75% of the investment's interest payments from the state agency AIPA. Young farmers and women farmers receive 15% on top of the regular subsidies.

Another tool for development is the creation of producers groups or co-operatives. A co-operative is a form of self-organisation of producers and consumers, aimed at increasing economic power and achieving economies of scale (Delcart, 2015). Although promoted by the EU, and although in effective in many countries, former communist countries talk about producers groups, and not about the very socialist oriented co-operatives. Co-operatives are again appreciated as a development tool of a region, but have to be run efficiently and require solidarity among the shareholder. In Cape Verde for example coffee planters as well as vineyards are organised in co-operations that buy the products at a fixed price and proceed to the fabrication of the end product and the commercialisation. But the coffee plants and vines are not planted and maintained structurally in order to forecast a certain production quantity (Delcart, (2016). In that case it is preferable to have solid contracts with post-harvest producers, who guarantee the buy up of the harvest.

Innovation as Key Lever for Regional Economic Development

One of the two winners of the 2018 Nobel Prize for Economy, Paul Romer, demonstrates how knowledge can function as a driver of long-term economic growth. When annual economic growth of a few per cent accumulates over decades, it transforms people's lives. Previous macroeconomic research had emphasised technological innovation as the primary driver of economic growth, but had not modelled how economic decisions and market conditions determine the creation of new technologies. Paul Romer solved this problem by demonstrating how economic forces govern the willingness of firms to produce new ideas and innovations. In that spirit, a joint initiative was taken in December 2012, between the EIB, the EIF, the European Commission, the Council of Europe Development Bank and the European Bank for Reconstruction and Development to launch the Western Balkans Enterprise Development and

Innovation Facility (WB EDIF). It contains a guarantee fund in which local banks are encouraged to build up new portfolios of SME transactions and thereby improving access to finance to SMEs in the Western Balkans countries. Enterprise Innovation Fund (ENIF) supports innovative SMEs in the Western Balkans in their early and expansion stage by providing equity finance through local funds management companies.

Civil Society Organisations

By civil society, we understand in Western Europe in the first place: chambers of commerce, labour organisations, employers organisations, cultural organisations, health care organisations, universities and technical university colleges and the press (Delcart, 2017). Civil society organisations in Eastern Europe are based upon the legal statute of the organisation, which has to be a non-profit organisation. All above mentioned organisations, who constitute the pillar of Western Europe's "Fourth power", are in many countries public organisations and therefore not included in the list. The American consultants, who set up the system in the last decade of the previous century, have been counting heads, and did not base their appreciation on the content of the organisation's activity, when they have determined the power and impact of civil society in post-communist European countries. Which makes that nowadays most "not-for-profit" organisations in post-communist societies have been set up by political parties in order to influence the public opinion. And are therefore also not intending to collaborate, on the contrary (Nikolov, 2017). But according to international habits, non-profit organisations are financed with a mixture of means: private donations or charity, national, regional and local governmental subsidies paid with tax payers' money, grants coming from European or international projects, and nowadays crowd-funding. On the other hand, non-profit organisations can also create an income through their activities. A recent visit to the Chamber of Commerce of Moldova showed that this private non-profit organization has to develop its own income, through membership fees as well as through courses and seminars and through the organization of trade fairs.

PREFERENTIAL ACCESS TO FINANCE

In a democracy, one cannot avoid that projects with no benefit for society or without employment opportunities but with only the benefit for a limited number of investors are launched and financed. But when efforts are made with tax money, such as local, regional or national grants, one could expect that each project considered should meet a certain number of requirements:

1. A project should in the first place create employment. In countries with low labour cost, often there is a form of solidarity among the population, in which people are put more easily at work. Western economists consider this pattern with disdain and are reluctant in front of this lack of productivity. Due to high unemployment and low labour costs in Eastern European countries, lots of SMEs are overstaffed. While they have a turnover well below the €50m threshold of SMEs, they often employ more than 250 staff and therefore are officially not considered as SMEs anymore by European bureaucrats;
2. A project should be sustainable on the long run. Many subsidised projects in the past focused on the payment of salaries, but offering services for free to the public. Many cultural projects saw the

light in this way but disappeared as quickly once the pot of subventions was emptied. A project should focus on offering a service that is sufficiently attractive that other companies or private individuals should be willing to pay for it. This requires as well investment in machinery as in expertise. But also in market knowledge. This means that projects need stakeholders: government, the personnel, the business community, customers, the neighbourhood, the press etc. Even cultural or sportive initiatives should create direct or indirect sustainable income. It is therefore important that projects are thought over thoroughly, according to a structured implementation scheme. Result based management, considering the input and the resources to be introduced, the activity/ies to be developed, the various outputs to be delivered, but also considering the outcome on the long run and even a certain impact on society should be described in the business plan. This methodology enables the initiator to consider also the investments to be made and the turnover to be examined;

3. The results of a project should also be measurable. This implies that measurement criteria should be fixed in advance. Measurement indicators should be agreed upon, also with the financial partners. But this is only part of the game. Enablers (Assumptions and Risks) & Constraints (assumptions and Risks) should be defined in advance and should be monitored on a regular basis and reported annually. Planning and monitoring should also be linked to accountability and success. Because in the end, the business person who introduces the project is to be held accountable, not only for success bit also for failure.

START-UPS, SCALE-UPS, AND ACCESS TO FINANCE

Start-ups are the group that incurs the most difficulties in its search for finance. Especially when their projects are based upon innovation and develop a new market. Often they have to rely on family or relatives who believe in them. Interesting initiatives have been taken in several Western European countries (The Netherlands, Belgium) where national or regional authorities create a guarantee fund protecting partially the seed capital they collect from relatives and family. In countries with microcredit institutions, these organisations give loans up to 10.000 € also to start-ups. In urban centres their customers often start grocery stores, bakeries, small retail businesses or renovate rooms in their houses for AirBNB or Booking.com application. At the outskirts of the city the loans tend to be for green houses, cattle and poultry raising for the supply of the city. Credit officers do a monthly follow up by personal visit or phone, asking for additional needs.

A scale up (company) is a company who has an average annualised return of at least 20% in the past 3 years with at least 10 employees in the beginning of the period (OECD Eurostat, 2018). The need of a scale cannot be met by traditional fund suppliers coming from the family. So-called "business angles", venture capital suppliers but also regional and local authorities provide with capital or guarantee bank loans enabling the company to increase its capacity and enter into new markets.

When it comes to venture capital, the European Investment Fund created since 2015 a South Central Ventures fund focused on the Balkans. These investments are intended to fuel the international business expansion and growth of the most promising tech startups that can show traction and prove their potential to "make it big". Shares from already 17 companies started in Croatia, Serbia, Macedonia, Greece have been taken into the portfolio of the Fund together with the necessary technical support. These companies deal with various technological aspects such as booking for tourism and solutions for recreational boats, optimisation of advertising on social media platforms, fintech, connecting parents and medical specialist in child treatment, telecom services, sales technology, business information and credit risk mitigation, generation of productivity reports in companies, helping farmers to reach sustainable, resource-efficient and profitable production, etc. The same European Investment Fund is also managing a fund-of-funds for seed and venture investments in Croatia. EIF is currently in the process of selecting a fund management team that will set up an accelerator and a Venture Capital fund, with a focus on investments in start-ups, mentoring, incubation and follow-on VC investments in the successful portfolio companies (Delcart, 2017).

SOLUTIONS AND RECOMMENDATIONS

Digital economy plays the key role in regional development. In the first place there is IT and the Internet that are to be considered as the single most important sources of growth for national economies around the world. It is clear that European SMEs grow two to three times faster when they embrace digital technologies. And many of the applications that are developed in that way, are effective on a regional level.

The most important characteristics of virtual enterprises are: virtual enterprise value is created not added. The purpose of virtual enterprise is to create value by changing opportunities in its environment; Virtual enterprise is a temporary cooperation objectives. To capture a new opportunity quickly, cooperation between distributed sites is required.

The Internet of Things is a new approach that steps outside the classical ICT environment creates a vast opportunity to young engineers and ICT experts to find new markets. They have to consider various service sectors, such as buildings, energy, consumer and home, healthcare, traditional industries, transportation, retail and public safety, find various application groups such as commercial and industrial applications, but also infrastructure, elderly care, entertainment, safety, resource automation, surveillance equipment and tracking, store hospitality and many more. Developments of remote health control and intervention assurance are thought over and installed. The skill needed is ICT, but the environment can almost be every human activity there is.

The economy of the future will be made to scale ever higher, will be electronic and will be based on the forms developed by the Internet. The Internet is proving to be successful by creating and improving the shopping and ways of doing business. Soon, and this will go faster than we can imagine new or other specialist Internet economy will be the largest part of the infrastructure of the global economy.

The share economy took a new breath once apps on the smart phone were available: the principle of rental received a whole new content. The Green Economy collaborates together with the Share Economy, where bikes and electric cars are shared and used to bridge the last mile. And this phenomenon is not limited to Europe and the US, on the contrary: more than 2 million inhabitants of Bogota take the bike, scooter, roller skates or go on foot every week on the weekly cycloid. In addition, more than 120 km of public road is then closed for motorized traffic between 7 and 2 pm. The driverless car makes companies dream of car fleets that are shared among users that only order a car when they need to use one. The same can be done by companies who need personnel on a temporary basis, and that are unwilling to fill in the necessary paperwork. Online staffing applications offer companies the possibility to share staff. The same principle is offered to restaurants that make lunches that are not consumed in their restaurant, but in the customer's home. The bikers are able to pass through heavy traffic and deliver hot meals within minutes. The same bikers deliver also parcels in the framework of e-commerce. Together with the classic examples such as AirBnB and Uber, this new type of industry offers powerful perspectives on a regional and local level.

FUTURE RESEARCH DIRECTIONS

Economic regionalization is one of the key features of the world economy in the post-war period. It has led to the formation of new power centres, which exert an increasing influence on the ratio of forces in the contemporary economy. As with globalization, regionalization has emerged as an effect of increasing interdependencies due to the development of the world labour division and the diversification of international specializations. Regionalization requires complementarity based on a similar level of development in order to be a coherent whole.

Regions and cities take more responsibility than ever. Not because national governments fail, but because they face problems that are specific to their environment. Really democratic countries consider this trend as an opportunity and share power with lower levels not reluctantly but with conviction. And even the classic lack of funds through taxes to realize something is tackled by the many alternatives that are at our disposal nowadays: crowd funding, charities, co-operatives, cross-border co-operation, European cohesion funds etc. But empowering cities and regions means also disposing of charismatic politicians with a vision and with a heart from their population and not for their pockets. Local and regional politicians are much more in the picture and more vulnerable to criticism. But their capacity to change things quickly is much higher.

CONCLUSION

There are advantages and disadvantages in the globalized world. Young people study longer and acquire more know-how. Thanks to technology, they also have a much larger window on the world. But they are often confronted with a hopeless situation created by politicians who act only out of their own interests and who neglect the interests of the country. But there, too, there are breakthroughs. We visited countries where the rule of law is applied much more strictly than in the past. We visited European countries with a young population who dare to take risks and who want to live in a stable country and have the necessary attention to that aspect. A stable political environment: that is the basic requirement for economic growth. But that stability must also be sustainable. Growth is reversed when government leaders lose against sight of the general interest and are only committed to securing their own re-election.

We strongly believe in the role of regional players in the development of an economy. This approach can arrive at a very effective stage thanks to the triple-helix approach. The Triple Helix concept comprises three basic elements: (1) a more prominent role for the university in innovation, on a par with industry and government in a knowledge–based society; (2) a movement toward collaborative relationships among the three major institutional spheres, in which innovation policy is increasingly an outcome of interaction rather than a prescription from government; (3) in addition to fulfilling their traditional functions, each institutional sphere also "takes the role of the other" performing new roles as well as their traditional function (Etzkowitz, 2003). Institutions taking non-traditional roles are viewed as a major potential source of innovation in innovation.

The entrepreneurial university takes a pro-active stance in putting knowledge to use and in broadening the input into the creation of academic knowledge. Thus it operates according to an interactive rather than a linear model of innovation. As firms raise their technological level, they engage in higher levels of training and in sharing of knowledge. Government acts as a public entrepreneur and venture capitalist, in addition to its traditional regulatory role in setting the rules of the game. Globalization becomes decentralized and takes place through regional networks among universities as well as through multinational corporations and international organizations. As universities develop links, they can combine discrete pieces of intellectual property and jointly exploit them. In current international competitive circumstances, innovation is too important to be left to the individual firm, or even a group of firms, the individual researcher or even a cross-national collaboration of researchers. Innovation has expanded from an internal process within and even among firms to an activity that involves institutions not traditionally thought of as having a direct role in innovation such as universities (Etzkowitz, 2003).

The basic requirement for economic growth is access to finance. That has also been understood by the international community. She will respond to this. No longer by giving loans to nations that are then filled in incorrectly. But by going to the end consumer: the SMEs. Because past crises have shown it: fraudulent management is not spent on SMEs. It is the exclusive area of large companies, which are regarded as dairy cows by shareholders or by overpowered managers. There is a lot of know-how available in emerging economies: both technological and with market knowledge. Only the elaboration of projects to make them sustainable and thus proposing them to financial partners requires foreign know-how. But it also requires a smoother collateral policy from the local government or central bank. And that is only possible when fraud with collateral is severely punished by the rule of law. In the meantime, much can be solved by offering guarantees from international development banks, through the organization of serious follow-up at the banks, by requiring an accounting at the companies, by introducing project-based thinking among the managers of SMEs.

REFERENCES

Commission Recommendation of 6 May 2003. (2003). Retrieved October 27, 2018, from http://ec.europa.eu/eurostat/web/structural-business-statistics/structural-business-statistics/sme?p_p_id=NavTreeportletprod_WAR_NavTreeportletprod_INSTANCE_vxlB58HY09rg&p_p_lifecycle=0&p_p_state=normal&p_p_mode=view&p_p_col_id=column-2&p_p_col_pos=1&p_p_col_count=4

Delcart, L. (2015). Can traditional and new civil society organizations play a role in regional development? *LinkedIn Pulse*. Retrieved October 22, 2018, from https://www.linkedin.com/pulse/can-traditional-new-civil-society-organisations-play-role-delcart/

Delcart, L. (2016). Economic development and internationalization in Cape Verde. *LinkedIn Pulse*. Retrieved October 24, 2018, from https://www.linkedin.com/pulse/economic-development-internationalisation-cape-verde-louis-delcart/

Delcart, L. (2017). *The regional call for autonomy: a curse for Europe?* Retrieved October 22, 2018, from https://lodelcar.tumblr.com/post/169307969510/the-regional-call-for-autonomy-a-curse-for

Delcart, L. (2017). *The role of civil society as engine for regional development.* Retrieved October 24, 2018, from https://lodelcar.tumblr.com/post/150068173340/the-role-of-civil-society-as-engine-for-regional

Demirgüç-Kunt, A., Beck, T., & Honohan, P. (2008). *Finance for All? Policies and Pitfalls in Expanding Access.* Washington, DC: The World Bank. Retrieved March 21, 2008, from http://siteresources.worldbank.org/INTFINFORALL/Resources/4099583-1194373512632/FFA_book.pdf

Etzkowitz, H. (2003). Innovation in Innovation: The Triple Helix of University-Industry-Government Relations. Social Science Information. doi:10.1177/05390184030423002

European Investment Fund. (2018). Retrieved October 28, 2018, from http://www.eif.org/what_we_do/resources/CVCiFoF/index.htm

European Regional Policy. (2016). Retrieved October 22, 2018, from http://ec.europa.eu/regional_policy/en/atlas/programmes/

OECD Eurostat. (2018). *ECD Manual on Business Demography Statistics.* Eurostat-OECD.

Galinos, S. (2016). *Mayor of Lesbos (Greece). Nomination of Andel P. Berlin.* Retrieved October 22, 2017, from http://www.worldmayor.com/contest_2016/lesbos-mayor-galinos.html https://www.linkedin.com/pulse/can-traditional-new-civil-society-organisations-play-role-delcart/

Lernoux, F., Boschmans, K., Bouyon, S., Martin, I., & Van Caillie, D. (2013). *Internationalisation of SMEs. How to succeed abroad?* Brussels: De Boeck & Larcier.

Nikolov, M. (2017). President of the Centre for economic analyses quoted in Louis Delcart, which future for the western Balkans? *LinkedIn Pulse.* Retrieved October 28, 2018, from https://www.linkedin.com/pulse/which-future-western-balkans-louis-delcart/

The Startups.co Platform. (2018). Retrieved October 22, 2018, from https://www.fundable.com/learn/resources/guides/crowdfunding-guide/what-is-crowdfunding

Compilation of References

Abdulghader, A. A., Dalbir, S., & Ibrahim, M. (2012). Potential E-Commerce Adoption Strategies for Libyan Organization. *IJICT, 1*(7), 321–328.

Adler, R., Everett, A. M., & Waldron, M. (2000). Advanced Management Accounting Techniques in Manufacturing: Utilization, Benefits, and Barriers to Implementation. *Accounting Forum, 24*(2), 131–150. doi:10.1111/1467-6303.00032

Agha, S., Alrubaiee, L., & Jamhour, M. (2012). Effect of core competence on competitive advantage and organizational performance. *International Journal of Business and Management, 7*(1), 192–204.

Agrawal, N., & Tapaswi, S. (2017). Defense schemes for variants of distributed denial-of-service (DDoS) attacks in cloud computing: A survey. *Information Security Journal: A Global Perspective, 26*(1), 1-13.

Ahearne, M., Lam, S. K., Mathieu, J. E., & Bolander, W. (2010). Why are some sales people better at adapting to organizational change? *Journal of Marketing, 74*(3), 65–79. doi:10.1509/jmkg.74.3.65

Akgün, A. E., Keskin, H., & Byrne, J. (2009). Organizational emotional capability, product and process innovation, and firm performance: An empirical analysis. *Journal of Engineering and Technology Management, 26*(3), 103–130. doi:10.1016/j.jengtecman.2009.06.008

Akyuz, K. C., Yıldırım, I., & Balaban, Y. (2015). Measuring efficiencies of the firms in paper sector by using data envelopment analysis. *International Journal of Economic and Administrative Studies, 14*, 23–38.

Alamin, T. H. M., & Yassin, A. A. (2015). Measuring hospitals efficiency using data envelopment analysis tool: Study on governmental hospitals services at Ministry of Health–Khartoum State. *International Journal of Science and Research, 4*(2), 1586–1592.

Alfahl, H., Sanzogni, L., & Houghton, L. (2012). Mobile commerce adoption in organizations: A literature review and future research directions. *Journal of Electronic Commerce in Organizations, 10*(2), 61–78. doi:10.4018/jeco.2012040104

AlHaj Ali, E. I. (2005). *Mobile commerce adoption across the supply chain in businesses in New Zealand* (Master Thesis), Auckland University of Technology (AUT), Auckland, New Zealand.

Alhyari, S., Alazab, M., Venkatraman, S., Alazab, M., & Alazab, A. (2013). Performance evaluation of e-government services using balanced scorecard. *Benchmarking: An International Journal, 20*(4), 512–536. doi:10.1108/BIJ-08-2011-0063

Allan, F. (1993). Benchmarking: Practical aspects for information professionals. *Special Libraries, 84*(3), 123–130.

Alsmadi, I., Burdwell, R., Aleroud, A., Wahbeh, A., Al-Qudah, M. A., & Al-Omari, A. (2018). *Network Security. In International Conference on Practical Information Security* (pp. 121-138). Springer.

Al-Somali, S. A., Gholami, R., & Clegg, B. (2009). An investigation into the acceptance of online banking in Saudi Arabia. *Technovation, 29*(2), 130–141. doi:10.1016/j.technovation.2008.07.004

Alstete, J. W., & Beutell, N. J. (2018). Designing learning spaces for management education: A mixed methods research approach. *Journal of Management Development, 37*(2), 201–211. doi:10.1108/JMD-08-2017-0247

Al-Tuwaijri, S. A., Christensen, T. E., & Hughes, K. II. (2004). The Relations among Environmental Disclosure, Environmental Performance and Economic Performance: A Simultaneous Equations. *Approach. Accounting, Organizations and Society, 29*(5-6), 447–471. doi:10.1016/S0361-3682(03)00032-1

Amagoh, F. (2008). Perspectives on organizational change: Systems and complexity theories. *The Innovation Journal, 13*(3), 1–14.

Ambec, S., & Lanoie, P. (2008). Does it pay to be green? A systematic overview. *The Academy of Management Perspectives, 22*(4), 45–62. doi:10.5465/amp.2008.35590353

Anand, G., & Kodali, R. (2010). A mathematical model for the evaluation of roles and responsibilities of human resources in a lean manufacturing environment. *International Journal of Human Resources Development and Management, 10*(1), 63–100. doi:10.1504/IJHRDM.2010.029447

Andreassen, H. K., Bujnowska-Fedak, M. M., Chronaki, C. E., Duritru, R. C., Pudele, I., Santana, S., ... Wynn, R. (2007). European citizens' use of E-health services: A study of seven countries. *BMC Public Health, 7*(53), 1–14. PMID:17425798

Andress, A. (2003). *Surviving Security: How to Integrate People, Process, and Technology*. Boca Raton, FL: Auerbach Publications. doi:10.1201/9780203501405

Andriole, S. J. (2010). Business impact of Web 2.0 Technologies. *Communications of the ACM, 53*(12), 67–79. doi:10.1145/1859204.1859225

Ansari, L. S., Bell, J. E., Cypher, J. H., Dears, P. H., Dutton, J. J., Ferguson, M. D., ... Zampino, P. A. (1997b). *Target Costing: The Next Frontier in Strategic Cost Management*. Chicago: Irwin Professional Publishing.

Anton, W. R. Q., Deltas, G., & Khanna, M. (2004). Incentives for Environmental Self-regulation and Implications for Environmental Performance. *Journal of Environmental Economics and Management, 48*(1), 632–654. doi:10.1016/j.jeem.2003.06.003

Aras, G., & Crowther, D. (2009). The durable organization in a time of financial and economic crisis. *Economics and Management, 14*, 210–216.

Arens, A. A., Elder, R. J., & Beasley, M. S. (2008). *Auditing and Assurance Services. An Integrated Approach* (12th ed.). Pearson Prentice Hall.

Armeanu, D., & Lache, L. (2008). Application of the model of principal components analysis on Romanian insurance market. *Journal Theoretical and Applied Economics, 6*(6), 11–20.

Arsenault, P., & Faerman, S. R. (2014). Embracing paradox in management: The value of the competing values framework. *Organizational Management Journal, 11*(3), 147–158. doi:10.1080/15416518.2014.949614

Arukonda, S., & Sinha, S. (2015). The innocent perpetrators: Reflectors and reflection attacks. *Advanced Computer Science, 4*, 94–98.

Asaduzzaman, A., Mazumder, S., & Salinas, S. (2018). A promising security protocol for protecting near field communication devices from networking attacks. *International Journal of Security and Networks, 13*(2), 98–107. doi:10.1504/IJSN.2018.092448

Ashkanasy, N. (2011, February). International happiness; a multilevel perspective. *The Academy of Management Perspectives*, 23–29.

Association of Certified Fraud Examiners (ACFE). (2014). *Fraud Examiners Manual* (International Edition).

Association of Certified Fraud Examiners (ACFE). (2018). *Report to the Nations. Global Study on Occupational Fraud and Abuse*. Retrieved from https://www.acfe.com/fraud-resources.aspx

Atkinson, J. H., Hohner, G., Mundt, B., Troxel, R. B., & Winchell, W. (1991). *Current Trends in Cost of Quality - Linking the Cost of Quality and Continuous Improvement*. Montvale, NJ: NAA.

Aytekin, S. (2011). The performance measurement of the health hospitals with low bed occupancy rates: An application of data envelopment analysis. *Uludag Journal of Economy and Society, 30*(1), 113–138.

Azhari, F. (2014). Quick detection of NFC vulnerability: Implementation weakness exploitation. *Information Management & Computer Security, 22*(2), 134–140. doi:10.1108/IMCS-09-2013-0067

Balasubramanian, S., Peterson, R. A., & Jarvenpaa, S. L. (2002). Exploring the implications of m-commerce for markets and marketing. *Journal of the Academy of Marketing Science, 30*(4), 348–361. doi:10.1177/009207002236910

Bal, V. (2013). Data envelopment analysis and medical image archiving and communication systems to investigate the effects of the performance of public hospitals. *Journal of Suleyman Demirel University Institute of Social Sciences, 17*, 31–50.

Bal, V., & Bilge, H. (2013). Efficiency measurement with data envelopment analysis in education and research hospitals. *Manas Journal of Social Studies, 2*(2), 1–14.

Barney, J. B. (1986). Organizational culture: Can it be a source of sustained competitive advantage. *Academy of Management Review, 11*(3), 656–665. doi:10.5465/amr.1986.4306261

Bartsiotas, G. A., & Achamkulangare, G. (2016). *Fraud Prevention, Detection and Response in United Nations System Organizations*. Geneva: United Nations. Retrieved from https://www.acfe.com/fraud-resources.aspx

Bayraktutan, Y., Arslan, I., & Bal, V. (2010). The evaluation of the effects of health information systems to the performance of hospitals by data enveloping analysis: An application in the thoracic medicine hospitals. *Gaziantep Medical Journal, 16*(3), 13–18.

Beasley, M. S., Buckless, F. A., Glover, S. M., & Prawitt, D. F. (2009). *Auditing Cases. An Interactive Learning Approach* (4th ed.). Prentice Hall.

Beaudin, K. (2015). College and university data breaches: Regulating higher educaiton cybersecurity under state and federal law. *The Journal of College and University Law, 41*(3), 657–694.

Becker, B. E., & Huselid, M. A. (1998). High performance work systems and firm performance: A synthesis of research and managerial implications. *Research in Personnel and Human Resources Management, 16*, 53–101.

Becker, B. E., & Huselid, M. A. (2006). Strategic human resources management: Where do we go from here? *Journal of Management, 32*(6), 898–925. doi:10.1177/0149206306293668

Behery, M., Jabeen, F., & Parakandi, M. (2014). Adopting a contemporary performance management system. *International Journal of Productivity and Performance Management, 63*(1), 22–43. doi:10.1108/IJPPM-07-2012-0076

Bell, C. L. (1997). The ISO 14001 Environmental Management Systems Standard: One American's View. In C. Sheldon (Ed.), *ISO 14000 and Beyond: Environmental Management Systems in the Real World* (pp. 61–92). Sheffield, UK: Greenleaf Publishing. doi:10.9774/GLEAF.978-1-909493-05-6_5

Benjamin, V., & Chen, H. (2012). *Securing cyberspace: Identifying key actors in hacker communities. IEEE International Conference on Intelligence and Security Informatics (ISI)*, Arlington, VA. 10.1109/ISI.2012.6283296

Benou, P., & Vassilakis, C. (2010). The conceptual model of context for mobile commerce applications. *Electronic Commerce Research, 10*(2), 139–165. doi:10.100710660-010-9050-4

Beylik, U., Kayral, İ. H., & Naldöken, Ü. (2015). Public hospital unions' performance analysis in terms of health care services efficiency. *Cumhuriyet University the Journal of Social Sciences, 39*(2), 203–224.

Bhatti, T. (2007). Exploring factors influencing the adoption of mobile commerce. *Journal of Internet Banking and Commerce, 12*(3).

Bircan, H. (2011). Measurement of the efficiency of village clinics in the Sivas by data envelopment Analysis. *Cumhuriyet University Journal of Economics and Administrative Sciences, 12*(1), 331–347.

Bishop, T. J. F., & Hydoski, F. E. (2009). *Corporate Resiliency. Managing the Growing Risk of Fraud and Corruption*. John Wiley & Sons, Inc.

Blengini, G. A., & Shields, D. J. (2010). Green labels and sustainability reporting: Overview of the building supply chain in Italy. *Management of Environmental Quality*, *21*(4), 477–493. doi:10.1108/14777831011049115

Boiral, O. (2013). Sustainability reports as simulacra? A counter-account of A and A+ GRI reports. *Accounting, Auditing & Accountability Journal*, *26*(7), 1036–1071. doi:10.1108/AAAJ-04-2012-00998

Bolman, L. G., & Deal, T. E. (1999). 4 Steps to keeping change efforts heading in the right direction. *Journal for Quality and Participation*, *22*(3), 6–11.

Bonn, S. (2008). Transitioning from Traditional to Hybrid and Online Teaching. In Information and Communication Technology in Education. ICFAI University Press.

Bostan, I. (2016). Investigating the Effectiveness of Programs on Health Financing Based on Audit Procedures. *Iranian Journal of Public Health*, *45*(8), 1074–1079. PMID:27928534

Boyton, W. C., & Johnson, R. N. (2006). *Modern Auditing. Assurance Services and the Integrity of Financial Reporting* (8th ed.). John Wiley & Sons.

Briggs, D., Cruickshank, M., & Paliadelis, P. (2012). Health managers and health reform. *Journal of Management & Organization*, *18*(5), 641–658. doi:10.1017/S1833367200000584

Broadbent, A., & Schaffner, C. (2016). Quantum cryptography beyond quantum key distribution. *Designs, Codes and Cryptography*, *78*(1), 351–382. doi:10.100710623-015-0157-4

Bruntland, G. H., Julio, F., & Cristopher, J. L. M. (2003). Who Assessment of Health Systems Performance. *Lancet*, *361*(9375), 2155. doi:10.1016/S0140-6736(03)13702-6 PMID:12826452

Bukachi, F., & Pakenham-Walsh, N. (2007). Information technology for health in developing countries. *Chest Journal*, *132*(5), 1624–1630. doi:10.1378/chest.07-1760 PMID:17998362

Burrows, G., & Chenhall, R. H. (2012). Target costing: First and second comings. *Accounting History Review*, *22*(2), 127–142. doi:10.1080/21552851.2012.681124

Cameron, K. S., & Quinn, R. E. (2011). *Diagnosing and Changing Organizational Culture: Based on the Competing Values Framework*. San Francisco, CA: Jossey-Bass.

CAM-I (Consortium for Advanced Management–International) et SMAC (Society of Management Accounting of Canada). (1994). *Implementing Target Costing, Management Accounting Guideline, April*. Author.

Campbell, B., Kay, R., & Avison, D. (2005). Strategic Alignment: A Practitioner's Perspective. *Journal of Enterprise Information Management*, *18*(6), 653–664. doi:10.1108/17410390510628364

Căpuşneanu, S., & Briciu, S. (2011). Analysis of the Possibility to Organize the Management Accounting through the Target Costing (TC) Method in the Romanian Entities. *Theoretical and Applied Economics*, *9*(562), 71–88.

Celik, T., & Esmeray, A. (2014). Measurement of cost efficiency in private hospitals in Kayseri using by data envelopment analysis. *International Journal of Alanya Faculty of Business, 6*(2), 45–54.

Chalikias, M., Kyriakopoulos, G., Skordoulis, M., & Koniordos, M. (2014). *Core ICT indicators: Partnership on ICT measurement for development.* Retrieved from http://www.itu.int/ITU-D/ict/partnership

Chandramouli, R. (2011). *Emerging social media threats: Technology and Policy Perspectives. Second Worldwide Cybersecurity Summit.* London, UK: WCS.

Chang, S.-I., Peng, T.-C., Hung, Y.-C., Chang, I.-C., & Hung, W.-H. (2009). *Critical success factors of mobile commerce adoption: A study based on the system life cycle and diamond model.* Paper presented at the 8th International Conference on Mobile Business (ICMB 2009), Dalian University of Technology (DUT), Dalian, China. 10.1109/ICMB.2009.29

Chan, L. L., Shaffer, M. A., & Snape, E. (2004). In search of sustained competitive advantage: The impact of organizational culture, competitive strategy and human resource management practices on firm performance. *International Journal of Human Resource Management, 15*(1), 17–35. doi:10.1080/0958519032000157320

Chapman, D. W., & Carter, J. F. (1979). Translation procedures for the cross cultural use of measurement instruments. *Educational Evaluation and Policy Analysis, 1*(3), 71–76. doi:10.3102/01623737001003071

Chen, H. M., & Fu, P. C. (2008). A systematic framework for performance appraisal and compensation strategy. *Human Systems Management, 27,* 161–175.

Chen, H., Ge, L., & Xie, L. A. (2015). User Authentication Scheme Based on Elliptic Curves Cryptography for Wireless Ad Hoc Networks. *Sensors (Basel), 15*(7), 17057–17075. doi:10.3390150717057 PMID:26184224

Chen, L. D. (2008). A model of consumer acceptance of mobile payment. *International Journal of Mobile Communications, 6*(1), 32–52. doi:10.1504/IJMC.2008.015997

Choi, Y., Lee, D., Kim, J., Jung, J., Nam, J., & Won, D. (2014). Security Enhanced User Authentication Protocol for Wireless Sensor Networks Using Elliptic Curves Cryptography. *Sensors (Basel), 14*(6), 10081–10106. doi:10.3390140610081 PMID:24919012

Choras, M. (2013). Comprehensive approach to information sharing for increased network security and survivability. *Cybernetics and Systems: An International Journal, 44*(6-7), 550–568. doi:10.1080/01969722.2013.818433

CITC. (2014). *CITC electronic newsletter.* Communications and Information Technology Commission in Saudi Arabia.

Cocca, P., & Alberti, M. (2010). A framework to assess performance measurement in SMEs. *International Journal of Productivity and Performance Management, 59*(2), 186–200. doi:10.1108/17410401011014258

Cohen, E. (2004). Compromise or Customize: XBRL's Paradoxical Power. CAP Forum on E-Business: Compromise or Customize: XBRL's Paradoxical Power. *Canadian Accounting Perspectives, 2*(3), 187–206. doi:10.1506/YAHN-CAE8-5CWQ-H4TE

Cohen, E. (2015). XBRL: The standardised business language for 21st century reporting and governance. *International Journal of Disclosure and Governance, 4*(2), 368–394.

Cokins, G. (2002). Integrations of Target Costing and ABC. *Journal of Cost Management, 6*(4), 13–22.

Coleman, L., & Purcell, B. M. (2015). Data breaches in higher education. *Journal of Business Cases and Applications, 15,* 1–7.

Collins, C., Steg, L., & Koning, M. (2007). Customers' values, beliefs on sustainable corporate performance, and buying behavior. *Psychology and Marketing, 24*(6), 555–577. doi:10.1002/mar.20173

Collins, S., & McCombie, S. (2012). Stuxnet: The emergence of a new cyber weapon and its implications. *Journal of Policing. Intelligence and Counter Terrorism, 7*(1), 80–91. doi:10.1080/18335330.20 12.653198

Coltman, T., Tallon, P., Sharma, R., & Queiroz, M. (2015). Strategic IT alignment: Twenty-five years on. *Journal of Information Technology, 30*(2), 91–100. doi:10.1057/jit.2014.35

Commission Recommendation of 6 May 2003. (2003). Retrieved October 27, 2018, from http://ec.europa.eu/eurostat/web/structural-business-statistics/structural-business-statistics/ sme?p_p_id=NavTreeportletprod_WAR_NavTreeportletprod_INSTANCE_vxlB58HY09rg&p_p_ lifecycle=0&p_p_state=normal&p_p_mode=view&p_p_col_id=column-2&p_p_col_pos=1&p_p_ col_count=4

Constantin, D.M., Topor, D.I., & Căpuşneanu, S., Barbu & C.M., Bogan, E. (2016). The monitoring of carbon monoxide air pollutant, as part of the air quality management. Case study: Olt County, Romania. *Annales Universitatis Apulensis Series Oeconomica, 2*(18), 27–34.

Conti, M., Dragoni, N., & Lesyk, V. (2016). A survey of man in the middle attacks. *IEEE Communications Surveys and Tutorials, 18*(3), 2027–2051. doi:10.1109/COMST.2016.2548426

Cooper, R., & Slagmulder, R. (1997). *Target Costing and Value Engineering*. Portland, OR: Productivity Press.

Cormier, D., Gordon, I., & Magnan, M. (2004). Corporate environmental disclosure: Contrasting management's perceptions with reality. *Journal of Business Ethics, 49*(2), 143–165. doi:10.1023/ B:BUSI.0000015844.86206.b9

Cox, P., Brammer, S., & Millington, A. (2004). An Empirical Examination of Institutional Investor Preferences for Corporate Social Performance. *Journal of Business Ethics, 52*(1), 27–43. doi:10.1023/ B:BUSI.0000033105.77051.9d

Creswell, J. W. (2013). *Research Design: Qualitative, Quantitative, and Mixed Methods Approaches* (4th ed.). London: SAGE Publications, Inc.

Croteau, A., & Li, P. (2003). Critical success factors of CRM technological initiatives. *Canadian Journal of Administrative Sciences, 20*(1), 21–34. doi:10.1111/j.1936-4490.2003.tb00303.x

Custer, W. L. (2010). Information Security Issues in Higher Education and Institutional Research. *New Directions for Institutional Research, 1,* 46. doi:10.1002/ir.341

Davila, A. (2012). New trends in performance measurement and management control. *In Performance Measurement and Management Control. Global Issues (Washington, D.C.), 25,* 65–87.

Davis, F. D. (1986). *A Technology acceptance model for empirically testing new end-user information systems: Theory and results* (Doctoral Dissertation). Massachusetts Institute of Technology, Cambridge, MA.

Davis, F. D. (1989). Perceived usefulness, perceived ease of use and user acceptance of information technology. *Management Information Systems Quarterly, 13*(3), 319–340. doi:10.2307/249008

Davis, F. D., Bagozzi, R. P., & Warshaw, P. R. (1989). User acceptance of computer technology: A comparison of two theoretical models. *Management Science, 35*(8), 982–1003. doi:10.1287/mnsc.35.8.982

de Waal, A. A., & Kourtit, K. (2013). Performance measurement and management in practice. *International Journal of Productivity and Performance Management, 62*(5), 446–473. doi:10.1108/IJPPM-10-2012-0118

Dekker, H., & Smidt, P. (2003). A survey of the adoption and use of target costing in Dutch firms. *International Journal of Production Economics, 84*(3), 293–305. doi:10.1016/S0925-5273(02)00450-4

Delaney, J. T., & Huselid, M. A. (1996). The impact of human resource management practices on perceptions of organizational performance. *Academy of Management Journal, 39,* 949–969.

Delcart, L. (2015). Can traditional and new civil society organizations play a role in regional development? *LinkedIn Pulse.* Retrieved October 22, 2018, from https://www.linkedin.com/pulse/can-traditional-new-civil-society-organisations-play-role-delcart/

Delcart, L. (2016). Economic development and internationalization in Cape Verde. *LinkedIn Pulse.* Retrieved October 24, 2018, from https://www.linkedin.com/pulse/economic-development-internationalisation-cape-verde-louis-delcart/

Delcart, L. (2017). *The regional call for autonomy: a curse for Europe?* Retrieved October 22, 2018, from https://lodelcar.tumblr.com/post/169307969510/the-regional-call-for-autonomy-a-curse-for

Delcart, L. (2017). *The role of civil society as engine for regional development.* Retrieved October 24, 2018, from https://lodelcar.tumblr.com/post/150068173340/the-role-of-civil-society-as-engine-for-regional

Deloitte. (2018). *Effective dates of IFRSs and amendments.* Retrieved from https://www.iasplus.com

Demirgüç-Kunt, A., Beck, T., & Honohan, P. (2008). *Finance for All? Policies and Pitfalls in Expanding Access.* Washington, DC: The World Bank. Retrieved March 21, 2008, from http://siteresources.worldbank.org/INTFINFORALL/Resources/4099583-1194373512632/FFA_book.pdf

Denison, D. R. (1990). *Corporate Culture and Organizational Effectiveness.* New York, NY: Wiley.

Derman, D. T. (2005). Avoiding Accounting Fixation: Determinants of Cognitive Adaptation to Differences in Accounting Method. *Contemporary Accounting Research, 22*(2), 351–384. doi:10.1506/RQ40-UR50-5CRL-YU8A

Deutsch, P., & Silcox, B. (2003). Learning from other libraries: Benchmarking to assess library performance. *Information Outlook, 7*(7), 18–25.

Dewangga, A., Goldsmith, S., & Pegram, N. (2008). *Social responsibility guideline and sustainable development: Integrating a common goal of a sustainable society* (Master's thesis). Retrieved from WorldCat Dissertations. (OCLC: 747412684)

Dias, J., Matos, J. N., & Oliveira, A. S. (2014). The charge collector system: A new NFC and smartphone-based toll collection system. *Procedia Technology, 17*, 130–137. doi:10.1016/j.protcy.2014.10.220

Dobrescu, P. (2010). *Viclenia globalizării. Asaltul asupra puterii americane*. Bucureşti, România: Institul European.

Dogan, N. O., & Gencan, S. (2014). Performance assessment using DEA/AHP integrated method: An application on public hospitals in Ankara. *Gazi Universitesi Iktisadi ve Idari Bilimler Fakultesi Dergisi, 16*(2), 88–112.

Downing, M. (2013). *The Importance of Network Monitoring*. Retrieved from http://www.animate.com/the-importance-of-network-monitoring/

Du, J., Wang, J., Chen, Y., Chou, S. Y., & Zhu, J. (2014). Incorporating health outcomes in Pennsylvania Hospital efficiency: An additive super efficiency DEA approach. *Annals of Operations Research, 221*(1), 161–172. doi:10.100710479-011-0838-y

Dumitriu, C. (2003). *Management şi marketing ecologic. O abordare strategică*. Iaşi, România: Editura Tehnopress.

Dutta, A., & Roy, R. (2003). Anticipating internet diffusion. *Communications of the ACM, 46*(2), 66–71. doi:10.1145/606272.606275

Duţu, M. (2010). *Dreptul mediului*. Bucureşti, România: Editura C.H. Beck.

Dyllick, T., & Hockerts, K. (2002). Beyond the business case for corporate sustainability. *Business Strategy and the Environment, 11*(2), 130–141. doi:10.1002/bse.323

Edge, I. E. (2010). Employ five fundamental principles to produce a SOLID, secure network. *Information Security Journal: A Global Perspective, 19*(3), 153-159. doi:10.1080/19393551003649008

El Zarki, M., Mehrotra, S., Tsudik, G., & Venkatasubramanian, N. (2002, February). Security issues in a future vehicular network. *International Conference on European Wireless*, 2.

Elahi, S., & Hassanzadeh, A. (2009). A framework for evaluating electronic commerce adoption in Iranian companies. *International Journal of Information Management, 29*(1), 27–36. doi:10.1016/j.ijinfomgt.2008.04.009

Elkington, J. (1997). *Cannibals with forks – Triple bottom line of 21st century business*. Stoney Creek, CT: New Society Publishers.

Enachi, M., & Andone, I. (2015). The Progress of XBRL in Europe – Projects, Users and Prospects. *Procedia Economics and Finance*, *20*, 185–192. doi:10.1016/S2212-5671(15)00064-7

Enagi, M. A., & Ochoche, A. (2013). The Role of Enterprise Architecture in Aligning Business and Information Technology in Organisations: Nigerian Government Investment on Information Technology. *IACSIT International Journal of Engineering and Technology*, *3*(1), 59–65.

Epstein, M. (2008). *Making sustainability work: Best practices in managing and measuring corporate social, environmental, and economic impacts*. San Francisco: Greenleaf.

Ericksen, J., & Dyer, L. (2005). Toward a strategic human resource management model of high reliability organization performance. *International Journal of Human Resource Management*, *16*(6), 907–925. doi:10.1080/09585190500120731

Eriksson, P., & Kovalainen, A. (2015). Qualitative Methods in Business Research: A Practical Guide to Social Research. *Sage (Atlanta, Ga.)*.

Esty, D. C., & Winston, A. S. (2006). *Green to Gold*. Yale University Press.

Etzkowitz, H. (2003). Innovation in Innovation: The Triple Helix of University-Industry-Government Relations. Social Science Information. doi:10.1177/05390184030423002

European Investment Fund. (2018). Retrieved October 28, 2018, from http://www.eif.org/what_we_do/resources/CVCiFoF/index.htm

European Regional Policy. (2016). Retrieved October 22, 2018, from http://ec.europa.eu/regional_policy/en/atlas/programmes/

European Security and Markets Authority. (2017). *ESEF Reporting Manual*. https://www.esma.europa.eu

European Security and Markets Authority. (2017). *European single electronic format*. Retrieved from https://www.esma.europa.eu

Falaki, H., Mahajan, R., Kandula, S., Lymberopoulos, D., Govindan, R., & Estrin, D. (2010, June). Diversity in smartphone usage. In *Proceedings of the 8th international conference on Mobile systems, applications, and services* (pp. 179-194). ACM.

Farahani, A. J. (2008). E-learning: A New Paradigm in Education. In Tehnologia informaţiei şi comunicării în educaţie. ICFAI University Press.

Feil, P., Yook, K.-H., & Kim, I.-W. (2004, Spring). Japanese Target Costing: A Historical Perspective. *International Journal of Strategic Cost Management*, 10-19.

Fennelly, L. (2016). *Effective physical security*. Butterworth-Heinemann.

Field, A. (2013). *Discovering statistics using IBM SPSS statistics* (4th ed.). London, UK: SAGE.

Finkenzeller, K. (2010). *RFID handbook: fundamentals and applications in contactless smart cards, radio frequency identification and near-field communication*. John Wiley & Sons. doi:10.1002/9780470665121

Fischbacher-Smith, D. (2016). Breaking bad? In search of a (softer) systems view of security ergonomics. *Security Journal, 29*(1), 5–22. doi:10.1057j.2015.41

Fishbein, M., & Ajzen, I. (1975). *Belief, attitude, intention, and behavior: An introduction to theory and research*. Reading, MA: Addison-Wesley.

Fisher, C. D. (2010). Happiness at Work. *International Journal of Management Reviews, 12*(4), 384–412. doi:10.1111/j.1468-2370.2009.00270.x

Fontinelle, A. (2018). *Introduction to Accounting Information Systems*. Investopedia. Retrieved from https://www.investopedia.com/

Frame, B., & Newton, B. (2007). Promoting sustainability through social marketing: Examples from New Zealand. *International Journal of Consumer Studies, 31*(6), 571–581. doi:10.1111/j.1470-6431.2007.00600.x

Frese, M., & Fay, D. (2001). Personal initiative: An active performance concept for work in the 21st century. *Research in Organizational Behavior, 23*, 133–187. doi:10.1016/S0191-3085(01)23005-6

Fridrich, J., Goljan, M., & Du, R. (2001). Detecting LSB steganography in color, and gray-scale images. *IEEE MultiMedia, 8*(4), 22–28. doi:10.1109/93.959097

Friedberg, I., McLaughlin, K., Smith, P., Laverty, D., & Sezer, S. (2016). STPA-SafeSec: Safety and security analysis for cyber-physical systems. *Journal of Information Security and Applications, 29*, 1–12.

Fryxell, G. E., & Vryza, M. (1999). Managing environmental issues across multiple functions: An empirical study of corporate environmental departments and functional co-ordination. *Journal of Environmental Management, 55*(1), 39–56. doi:10.1006/jema.1998.0241

Gaidelys, V., & Valodkiene, G. (2011). The Methods of Selecting and Assessing Potential Consumers Used of by Competitive Intelligence. *Inzinerine Ekonomika-Engineering Economics, 22*(2), 196–202.

Galbraith, J. R., & Lawler, E. E. (1993). *Organizing for the Future: The New Logic for Managing Complex Organizations*. San Francisco, CA: Jossey-Bass.

Galbreath, J. (2006). Corporate social responsibility strategy: Strategic options, global considerations. *Corporate Governance, 6*(2), 175–187. doi:10.1108/14720700610655178

Galbreath, J. (2009). Building corporate social responsibility into strategy. *European Business Review, 21*(2), 109–127. doi:10.1108/09555340910940123

Galinos, S. (2016). *Mayor of Lesbos (Greece). Nomination of Andel P. Berlin*. Retrieved October 22, 2017, from http://www.worldmayor.com/contest_2016/lesbos-mayor-galinos.html https://www.linkedin.com/pulse/can-traditional-new-civil-society-organisations-play-role-delcart/

Gandino, F., Celozzi, C., & Rebaudengo, M. (2017). A Key Management Scheme for Mobile Wireless Sensor Networks. *Applied Sciences, 7*(5), 490. doi:10.3390/app7050490

Gemmel, P., Vandaele, D., & Tambeur, W. (2001). Hospital Process Orientation (HPO): The development of a measurement tool. *Total Quality Management & Business Excellence*, *19*(12), 1207–1217. doi:10.1080/14783360802351488

Gopalakrishnan, B., Kokatnur, A., & Gupta, D. P. (2007). Design and development of a target-costing system for turning operation. *Journal of Manufacturing Technology Management*, *18*(2), 217–238. doi:10.1108/17410380710722917

Grama, J. (2014). *Just in time research:Data breaches in higher education.* Retrieved from https://net.educause.edu/ir/library/pdf/ECP1402.pdf

Grandon, E., & Pearson, J. M. (2004). Electronic commerce adoption: An empirical study of small and medium US businesses. *Information & Management*, *42*(1), 197–216. doi:10.1016/j.im.2003.12.010

Gregory, W. H., & Grama, J. (2013). *Information Security (Research Bulletin).* Louisville, CO: EDU-CAUSE Center for Applied Research. Retrieved from http://www.educause.edu/ecar

GRI. (2011). *Sustainability Reporting Guidelines.* Amsterdam: Global Reporting Initiativ.

Grimson, J., Grimson, W., & Hasselbring, W. (2000). The system integration challenge in health care. *Communications of the ACM*, *43*(6), 49–55. doi:10.1145/336460.336474

Grinnel, D. J., & Hunt, H. G. (2000). Development of an integrated course in accounting: Focus on environmental issues. *Issues in Accounting Education*, *15*(1), 19–42. doi:10.2308/iace.2000.15.1.19

Gulfnews. (2013). *Digital awakening spurs m-commerce.* Retrieved 13 July, 2013, from http://gulfnews.com/business/retail/digital-awakening-spurs-m-commerce-1.1022923

Gülsevin, G., & Türkan, A. H. (2012). Evaluation of efficiencies of hospitals in Afyonkarahisar using data envelopment analysis. *Afyon Kocatepe University Journal of Sciences*, *20*, 1–8.

Gunn, J. (2007). XBRL: Opportunities and Challenges in Enhancing Financial Reporting and Assurance Processes. *American Accounting Association.*, *1*, A36–A43.

Guo, D., Chen, H., Long, R., Lu, H., & Long, Q. (2017). A Co-Word Analysis of Organizational Constraints for Maintaining Sustainability. *Sustainability*, *9*(11), 1928. doi:10.3390u9101928

Gupta, N. (2013). *Customer perception towards online shopping.* Retrieved from retailing.jrps.in/uploads/july 2013/customer _perfection_by_nidhi_gupta.pdf

Hadad, S., Hadad, Y., & Simon-Tuval, T. (2013). Determinants of healthcare system's efficiency in OECD countries. *The European Journal of Health Economics*, *14*(2), 253–265. doi:10.100710198-011-0366-3 PMID:22146798

Hadžiosmanović, D., Bolzoni, D., & Hartel, P. H. (2012). A log mining approach for process monitoring in SCADA. *International Journal of Information Security*, *11*(4), 231–251. doi:10.100710207-012-0163-8

Hair, J. F. J., Hult, G. T. M., Ringle, C., & Sarstedt, M. (2014). A primer on partial least squares structural equation modeling (PLS-SEM). *Long Range Planning*, *46*, 328. doi:10.1016/j.lrp.2013.01.002

Hajji, T., Ouerdi, N., Azizi, A., & Azizi, M. (2018). EMV Cards Vulnerabilities Detection Using Deterministic Finite Automaton. *Procedia Computer Science, 127*, 531–538. doi:10.1016/j.procs.2018.01.152

Hamood, H. H., Omar, N., & Sulaiman, S. (2011). Target Costing Practices: A Review of Literature. *Asia-Pacific Management Accounting Journal, 6*(1), 1–24.

Harris, S. (2013). *All-In-One CISSP Exam Guide* (6th ed.). McGraw Hill.

Harshita, S. T., & Tanwar, S. (2018). Security Issues and Countermeasures of Online Transaction in E-Commerce. In Mobile Commerce: Concepts, Methodologies, Tools, and Applications (pp. 982-1013). IGI Global.

Hartnell, C. A., Ou, A. Y., & Kinicki, A. (2011). Organizational culture and organizational effectiveness: A meta-analytic investigation of the competing values framework's theoretical suppositions. *The Journal of Applied Psychology, 96*(4), 677–694. doi:10.1037/a0021987 PMID:21244127

Haselsteiner, E., & Breitfuß, K. (2006, July). Security in near field communication (NFC). In *Workshop on RFID security* (pp. 12-14). Academic Press.

Hasselbring, W. (2000). Information system integration. *Communications of the ACM, 43*(6), 33–38. doi:10.1145/336460.336472

Hassinen, M., Hyppönen, K., & Trichina, E. (2008). Utilizing national public-key infrastructure in mobile payment systems. *Electronic Commerce Research and Applications, 7*(2), 214–231. doi:10.1016/j.elerap.2007.03.006

He, D., Chen, C., Chan, S., & Bu, J. (2012). Secure and efficient handover authentication based on bilinear pairing functions. *IEEE Transactions on Wireless Communications, 11*(1), 48–53. doi:10.1109/TWC.2011.110811.111240

Hedrick, G. W., & Grama, J. (2013). *Information Security*. Retrieved from https://library.educause.edu/resources/2013/6/information-security

HEISC. (2014). *Information Security Guide - Communications Security*. Retrieved from https://spaces.internet2.edu/display/2014infosecurityguide/Communications+Security

Henczel, S. (2002). Benchmarking – measuring and comparing for continuous improvement. *Information Outlook, 6*(7), 12–20.

Henten, A., Olesen, H., Saugstrup, D., & Tan, S. (2004). Mobile communications: Europe, Japan and South Korea in a comparative perspective. *Info, 6*(3), 197-207.

Hermanson, R. H., Loeb, S. E., Saada, J. M., & Strawser, R. H. (1976). *Auditing Theory and Practice*. Homewood, IL: Richard D. Irwin, Inc.

Higher Education Information Security Council (HEISC). (2013). *Information Security Program Assessment Tool*. Retrieved from http://www.educause.edu

Hiller, J., & Russel, R. (2013). The challenge and imperative of private sector cybersecurity: An international comparison. *Computer Law & Security Review*, 29(3), 236–245. doi:10.1016/j.clsr.2013.03.003

Hjortdal, M. (2011). China's use of cyber warfare: Espionage meets strategic deterrence. *The Journal of Strategic Studies*, 4(2), 1–24.

Hodge, F. D., Kennedy, J. J., & Maines, L. A. (2004). Does search-facilitating technology improve the transparency of financial reporting? *The Accounting Review*, 79(3), 687–703. doi:10.2308/accr.2004.79.3.687

Hoffman, C. (2006). *Financial Reporting Using XBRL*. UBmatrix Inc.

Hoffman, C., & Raynier F. (2017). *Intelligent Digital Financial Reporting*. CC0 1.0 Universal Public Domain Dedication.

Hoffman, C. (2017). *Digital Financial Reporting Manifesto*. Universal Public Domain Dedication.

Holger, D., Luzi, H., Christian, L., & Rodrigo, V. (2008). *Mandatory IFRS Reporting Around the World: Early Evidence on the Economic Consequences. Initiative on Global Markets*. University of Chicago, Graduate School of Business.

Homburg, C., & Pflesser, C. (2000). A Multiple Layer Model of Market-Oriented Organizational Culture: Measurement Issues and Performance Outcomes. *JMR, Journal of Marketing Research*, 37(4), 449–462. doi:10.1509/jmkr.37.4.449.18786

Hong, J., Kim, J., & Cho, J. (2010). The trend of the security research for the insider cyber threat. *International Journal of Future Generation Communication and Networking*, 3(2), 31–40.

Horváth, P., Niemand, S., & Wolbold, M. (1993), Target Costing: State of the Art Report. Arlington, TX: Computer Aided Manufacturing-International (CAM-I).

Huang, N., & Jiao, Z. (2014). On campus network security system of college and university. *Journal of Emerging Technologies in Web Intelligence*, 6(4).

Huitsing, P., Chandia, R., Papa, M., & Shenoi, S. (2008). Attack taxonomies for the Modbus protocols. *International Journal of Critical Infrastructure Protection*, 1, 37–44. doi:10.1016/j.ijcip.2008.08.003

Huo, W., Dong, Q., & Chen, Y. (2015). *ECC-based RFID/NFC Mutual Authentication Protocol*. Academic Press.

Hurley, R. F. (2002). Putting people back into organizational learning. *Journal of Business and Industrial Marketing*, 17(4), 270–281. doi:10.1108/08858620210431679

Husseini, A. (2001). *Industrial Environmental Standards and Their Implementation in the World*. National Environmental Management Seminar (EM 2001), Kuala Lumpur, Malaysia.

Hutcheson, G. D., & Sofroniou, N. (1999). *The multivariate social scientist: Introductory statistics using generalized linear models*. London, UK: SAGE Publications, Ltd. doi:10.4135/9780857028075

IAASB. (2015). *Handbook of International Quality Control, Auditing, Review, Other Assurance, and Related Services Pronouncements* (Vol. 1). New York: International Federation of Accountants.

Ibbs, C. W., & Kwak, Y. H. (2000). Assessing project management maturity. *Project Management Journal, 31*(1), 32–43. doi:10.1177/875697280003100106

Iles, A. (2008). Shifting to green chemistry: The need for innovations in sustainability marketing. *Business Strategy and the Environment, 17*(8), 524–535. doi:10.1002/bse.547

Ilias, A., Razak, M. Z. A., & Rahman, R. A. (2015). The expectation of perceived benefit of extensible business reporting language (XBRL): A case in Malaysia. *Journal of Developing Areas, 49*(5), 263–271. doi:10.1353/jda.2015.0060

Ionac, N., & Ciulache, S. (2005). *Ghid de cercetare environmentală*. Bucureşti, România: Editura Ars Docendi.

ISO/IEC 21827. (2008). *Information technology - Security techniques - Systems security engineering - Capability maturity model (SSE-CMM)*. Retrieved from http://www.iso.org/iso/catalogue_detail.htm?csnumber=44716

ISO/IEC 27002. (2013). *Information technology Security techniques - Code of practice for information security controls*. Retrieved from http://www.iso.org/iso/catalogue_detail?csnumber=54533

Ivan, O. R., Căpuşneanu, S., Topor, D. I., & Oprea, D. M. (2017). Environmental changes and their influences on performance of a company by using eco-dashboard. *Journal of Environmental Protection and Ecology, 18*(1), 399–409.

Jayapandian, N., Rahman, A. M. Z., Koushikaa, M., & Radhikadevi, S. (2016, February). A novel approach to enhance multi level security system using encryption with fingerprint in cloud. In *Futuristic Trends in Research and Innovation for Social Welfare (Startup Conclave), World Conference on* (pp. 1-5). IEEE. 10.1109/STARTUP.2016.7583903

Jayapandian, N., Rahman, A. M. Z., Radhikadevi, S., & Koushikaa, M. (2016, February). Enhanced cloud security framework to confirm data security on asymmetric and symmetric key encryption. In *Futuristic Trends in Research and Innovation for Social Welfare (Startup Conclave), World Conference on* (pp. 1-4). IEEE. 10.1109/STARTUP.2016.7583904

Jayapandian, N., & Rahman, A. M. Z. (2017). Secure and efficient online data storage and sharing over cloud environment using probabilistic with homomorphic encryption. *Cluster Computing, 20*(2), 1561–1573. doi:10.100710586-017-0809-4

Johnson, D., Menezes, A., & Vanstone, S. (2001). The elliptic curve digital signature algorithm (ECDSA). *International Journal of Information Security, 1*(1), 36–63. doi:10.1007102070100002

Jones, D. (2011). *New ideas and tips for PDF financial reports*. Retrieved from http://irwebreport.com

Juhmani, O. I. H. (2010). Adoption and Benefits of Target Costing in Bahraini Manufacturing Companies. *Journal of Academy of Business and Economics*, *10*(1), 113–122.

Kaiser, H. (1970). A second generation little jiffy. *Psychometrika*, *35*(4), 401–415. doi:10.1007/BF02291817

Kaiser, H. (1974). An index of factorial simplicity. *Psychometrika*, *39*(1), 31–36. doi:10.1007/BF02291575

Kaplan, R. S., & Norton, D. P. (2006). How to implement a new strategy without disrupting your organization. *Harvard Business Review*, *84*(3), 100. PMID:16515159

Karim, H. V. (2007). *Strategic security management: a risk assessment guide for decision makers.* Elsevier Inc.

Kaspersky, E., & Furnell, S. (2014). A security education Q&A. *Information Management & Computer Security*, *22*(2), 130–133. doi:10.1108/IMCS-01-2014-0006

Kato, Y. (1993). Target costing support systems: Lessons from leading Japanese companies. *Management Accounting Research*, *4*(1), 33–47. doi:10.1006/mare.1993.1002

Kesan, P. J., & Hayes, M. C. (2012). Mitigative counterstriking: Self-defense and deterrence in cyberspace. *Harvard Journal of Law & Technology*, *25*(2), 474–529.

Khan, A. A. (2016). *Spoofing protection for secure-element identifiers.* U.S. Patent Application No. 14/474,737.

Khan, S., Gani, A., Wahab, A. W. A., Shiraz, M., & Ahmad, I. (2016). Network forensics: Review, taxonomy, and open challenges. *Journal of Network and Computer Applications*, *66*, 214–235. doi:10.1016/j.jnca.2016.03.005

Kirchgeorg, M., & Winn, M. (2006). Sustainability marketing for the poorest of the poor. *Business Strategy and the Environment*, *15*(3), 171–184. doi:10.1002/bse.523

Kizil, C., & Burhan, K. (2018). Accounting Scandals and Eye-Catching Frauds: USA-Japan Comparison by Considering the Role of Auditing. *Journal of Asian Research*, *2*(3), 1–14. doi:10.22158/jar.v2n3p123

Knapp, M. C. (2006). *Contemporary Auditing* (6th ed.). Thomson South-Western.

Koch, R., Stelte, B., & Golling, M. (2012). *Attack Trends in Present Computer Networks. 4th International Conference on Cyber Conflict (CYCON)*, Tallinn, Estonia.

Kocsoy, M., Gurdal, K., & Karabayir, M. E. (2008). Target Costing in Turkish Manufacturing Enterprises. *European Journal of Soil Science*, *7*(2), 92–105.

Kortvedt, H., & Mjolsnes, S. (2009, November). Eavesdropping near field communication. In *The Norwegian Information Security Conference (NISK)* (*Vol. 27*, p. 5768). Academic Press.

Kothari, S.P., Shu, S. & Wysocki, P.D. (2009). Do Managers Withhold Bad News? *Journal of Accounting Research*, *47*(1).

Kotulic, A. G., & Clark, J. G. (2004). Why there aren't more information security research studies. *Information & Management, 41*(5), 597–607. doi:10.1016/j.im.2003.08.001

KPMG. (2018). *Asia Pacific Tax Profiles.* Retrieved from https://home.kpmg.com

Krombholz, K., Hobel, H., Huber, M., & Weippl, E. (2015). Advanced social engineering attacks. *Journal of Information Security and Applications, 22,* 113–122. doi:10.1016/j.jisa.2014.09.005

Kumar, G., & Kumar, K. (2014). Network security – an updated perspective. *Systems Science & Control Engineering, 2*(1), 325–334. doi:10.1080/21642583.2014.895969

Kumar, U., & Gambhir, S. (2014). A literature review of security threats to wireless networks. *International Journal of Future Generation Communication and Networking, 7*(4), 25–34. doi:10.14257/ijfgcn.2014.7.4.03

Kurasaka, H. (1997). *Status and Progress of Environmental Assessment in Japan.* Paper presented at the Recent Developments with National and International Environmental Impact Assessment Processes, New Orleans, LA.

Kurosawa, K., Ohta, H., & Kakuta, K. (2017). How to make a linear network code (strongly) secure. *Designs, Codes and Cryptography, 82*(3), 559–582. doi:10.100710623-016-0180-0

Landoll, D. J. (2010). The security risk assessment handbook: a complete guide for performing security risk assessment (2nd ed.). CRC Press, Taylor & Francis Group.

Laur, S., & Nyberg, K. (2006, December). Efficient mutual data authentication using manually authenticated strings. In *International Conference on Cryptology and Network Security* (pp. 90-107). Springer. 10.1007/11935070_6

Lee, J. I., Kim, K. Y., Park, H. W., Park, S. J., & Kim, J. H. (2016). *Image forming apparatus supporting function of near field communication and method of setting NFC operation mode thereof.* U.S. Patent No. 9,256,386. Washington, DC: U.S. Patent and Trademark Office.

Lee, Y. H., Yang, C. C., & Chen, T. T. (2016). Barriers to incident-reporting behavior among nursing staff: A study based on the theory of planned behavior. *Journal of Management & Organization, 22*(1), 1–18. doi:10.1017/jmo.2015.8

Léger, P.-M., Cassivi, L., & Fosso Wamba, S. (2004). *Determinants of the adoption of customer-oriented mobile commerce initiatives.* Paper presented at the Twelfth International Association of Management of Technology (IAMOT'04), Washington, DC.

Lehmann, J. (1999). *Befunde empirischer Forschung zu Umweltbildung und Umweltbewusstsein (Findigs from empirical research on environmental education and environmental awareness).* OpladenŞ Leske and Budrich.

Lernoux, F., Boschmans, K., Bouyon, S., Martin, I., & Van Caillie, D. (2013). *Internationalisation of SMEs. How to succeed abroad?* Brussels: De Boeck & Larcier.

Leyer, M., Stumpf-Wollersheim, J., & Kronsbein, D. (2017). Stains on the bright side of process-oriented organizational design: An empirical investigation of advantages and disadvantages. *Schmalenbach Business Review*, *17*(1), 29–47. doi:10.100741464-016-0020-9

Liaudanskienel, R., Ustinovicius, L., & Bogdanovicius, A. (2009). Evaluation of Construction Process Safety Solutions Using the TOPSIS Method. *Inzinerine Ekonomika-Engineering Economics*, *64*(4), 32–40.

Lim, B. (1995). Examining the organizational culture and organizational performance link. *Leadership and Organization Development Journal*, *16*(5), 16–21. doi:10.1108/01437739510088491

Lin, C. H., Peng, C. H., & Kao, D. T. (2008). The innovativeness effect of market orientation and learning orientation on business performance. *International Journal of Manpower*, *29*(8), 752–772. doi:10.1108/01437720810919332

Lin, Z., Lin, D., & Pei, D. (2017). Practical construction of ring LFSRs and ring FCSRs with low diffusion delay for hardware cryptographic applications. *Cryptography and Communications*, *9*(4), 431–440. doi:10.100712095-016-0183-8

Lippman, E. (2010). *Case study on sustainability: Accountants' role in developing a new business model*. Retrieved from http://papers.ssrn.com/sol3/papers.cfm?abstract_id=1662648

Liu, S., Zhang, J., Keil, M., & Chen, T. (2010). Comparing senior executive and project manager perceptions of IT project risk: A Chinese Delphi study. *Information Systems Journal*, *20*(4), 319–355. doi:10.1111/j.1365-2575.2009.00333.x

Li, X., Zeng, T., & Yang, B. (2008). Detecting LSB matching by applying calibration technique for difference image. *Proc. 10th ACM Workshop on Multimedia and Security*, 133–138. 10.1145/1411328.1411353

López Catalán, B., & Díaz Luque, P. (2008). *M-commerce adoption: TAM vs technology provider perspective through cognitive maps*. Paper presented at the Building Bridges in a Global Economy, Salmanca, Spain.

Lord & Benoit Report. (2006). *Do the Benefits of Section 404 Exceed the Cost?* Retrieved from https://www.businesswire.com

Louwers, T. J., Ramsay, R. J., Sinason, D. H., & Strawser, J. R. (2007). *Auditing and Assurance Services* (2nd ed.). New York: McGraw-Hill Irwin.

Low, C., & Chen, Y. H. (2012). Criteria for the evaluation of a cloud-based hospital information system outsourcing provider. *Journal of Medical Systems*, *36*(6), 3543–3553. doi:10.100710916-012-9829-z PMID:22366976

LSB in GIF. (2017). Retrieved from http://www.ijsce.org/attachments/File/v3i5/E190011351 .pdf

Madlmayr, G., Langer, J., Kantner, C., & Scharinger, J. (2008, March). NFC devices: Security and privacy. In *Availability, Reliability and Security, 2008. ARES 08. Third International Conference on* (pp. 642-647). IEEE.

Malatras, A., Geneiatakis, D., & Vakalis, I. (2016). On the efficiency of user identification: A system-based approach. *International Journal of Information Security, 15*(1), 1–19.

Mallat, N., & Tuunainen, V. K. (2008). Exploring merchant adoption of mobile payment systems: An empirical study. *e-Service Journal, 6*(2), 24–57. doi:10.2979/esj.2008.6.2.24

Mao, Y. B., Chen, G., & Lian, S. G. (2004). A novel fast image Encryption scheme based on the 3D chaotic baker map. *International Journal of Bifurcation and Chaos in Applied Sciences and Engineering, 14*(10), 3613–3624. doi:10.1142/S021812740401151X

Martínez-Argüelles, M. J., Castán, J. M., & Juan, A. A. (2010). Using the critical incident technique to identify factors of service quality in online higher education. *International Journal of Information Systems in the Service Sector, 2*(4), 57–72. doi:10.4018/jisss.2010100104

Marvel, L. M., Boncelet, C. G., & Retter, C. (2007). Spread Spectrum Steganography. *IEEE Transactions on Image Processing, 8*(8), 160–178. PMID:18267522

Mathieson, K. (1991). Predicting user intentions: Comparing the technology acceptance model with the theory of planned behavior. *Information Systems Research, 2*(3), 173–191. doi:10.1287/isre.2.3.173

McDonald, S., & Oates, C. J. (2006). Sustainability: Consumer Perceptions and Marketing Strategies. *Special Issue: Sustainability Marketing, 15*(3), 157–170.

Mei-Yu, W., & Ming-Hsien, Y. (2013). Enterprise information security management based on context-aware RBAC and communication monitoring technology. *Mathematical Problems in Engineering*, 1–11. doi:10.1155/2013/569562

Messier, W. F., Glover, S. M., & Prawitt, D. F. (2008). *Auditing and Assurance Services. A Systematic Approach* (5th ed.). New York: McGraw-Hill Irwin.

Meuer, J. (2017). Exploring the Complementarities within High-Performance Work Systems: A Set-Theoretic Analysis of UK Firms. *Human Resource Management, 56*(4), 651–672. doi:10.1002/hrm.21793

Molla, A., & Licker, P. S. (2005). Perceived e-readiness factors in e-commerce adoption: An empirical investigation in a developing country. *International Journal of Electronic Commerce, 10*(1), 83–110. doi:10.1080/10864415.2005.11043963

Monden, Y., & Lee, J. (1993). How a Japanese auto maker reduces costs. *Management Accounting, 72*(2), 22.

Montabon, F., Melnyk, S. A., Sroufe, R., & Calantone, R. J. (2000). ISO 14000: Assessing its perceived impact on corporate performance. *The Journal of Supply Chain Management, 36*(2), 4–16. doi:10.1111/j.1745-493X.2000.tb00073.x

Moore, G. C., & Benbasat, I. (1991). Development of an instrument to measure the perceptions of adopting an information technology innovation. *Information Systems Research, 2*(3), 192–222. doi:10.1287/isre.2.3.192

Morak, J., Kumpusch, H., Hayn, D., Modre-Osprian, R., & Schreier, G. (2012). Design and evaluation of a telemonitoring concept based on NFC-enabled mobile phones and sensor devices. *IEEE Transactions on Information Technology in Biomedicine, 16*(1), 17–23. doi:10.1109/TITB.2011.2176498 PMID:22113811

Narduzzi, E. (2001). *Is m-business the same game as the e-business?* Paper presented at the M-conference: Seizing the Mobile Advantage, Rotterdam, The Netherlands.

National Accreditation Board of Ghana (NAB). (2016). *Number of accredited tertiary institutions in Ghana per category as at September 2016.* Retrieved from www.nab.gov.gh

Nelson, M., Elliot, J., & Tarpley, R. (2002). How Are Earnings Managed? Examples from Auditors. *The Accounting Review, 77,* 175–202. doi:10.2308/accr.2002.77.s-1.175

Nikolov, M. (2017). President of the Centre for economic analyses quoted in Louis Delcart, which future for the western Balkans? *LinkedIn Pulse.* Retrieved October 28, 2018, from https://www.linkedin.com/pulse/which-future-western-balkans-louis-delcart/

Nishimura, A. (2002). Asia Economic Growth and Management Accounting. *Malaysian Accounting Review, 1*(1), 87–101.

Ni, Z., Shi, Y. Q., Ansari, N., & Su, W. (2006). Reversible data hiding. *IEEE Transactions on Circuits and Systems for Video Technology, 16*(3), 354–362. doi:10.1109/TCSVT.2006.869964

Norris, P. (2001). *Digital Divide: Civic Engagement, Information Poverty and the Internet Worldwide.* New York: Cambridge University Press. doi:10.1017/CBO9781139164887

O'Donnell, J., Jackson, M., Shelly, M., & Ligertwood, J. (2007). Australian case studies in mobile commerce. *Journal of Theoretical and Applied Electronic Commerce Research, 2*(2), 1–18.

Oblinger, D. G. (2015). *Ten reasons to tackle the top 10 IT issues.* Retrieved from http://er.educause.edu/articles/2015/1/ten-reasons-to-tackle-the-top-10-it-issues

OECD Eurostat. (2018). *ECD Manual on Business Demography Statistics.* Eurostat-OECD.

OECD. (2007). *Mobile commerce.* Organisation for Economic Co-operation and Development.

Okazaki, S. (2005). New perspectives on m-commerce Research. *Journal of Electronic Commerce Research, 6*(3), 160–164.

Olson, E. M., Slater, S. F., Tomas, G., & Hult, M. (2005). The performance implications of fit among business strategy, marketing organization structure, and strategic behavior. *Journal of Marketing, 69*(3), 49–65. doi:10.1509/jmkg.69.3.49.66362

Oracle's Financial Management Solutions: Transition to IFRS with Oracle E-Business Suite. (n.d.). Retrieved from www.oracle.com

Ortiz, S. (2006). Is near-field communication close to success? *Computer, 39*(3), 18-20.

Ozcan, Y. A. (2008). *Healthcare benchmarking and performance evaluation an assessment using data envelopment analysis (DEA).* Springer.

Pakizeh, F., Vali, S., Hanzaei, T., & Moradi, M. (2013). Feasibility Assessment of Target Costing in Yasuj Cement Factory. *International Journal of Advanced Studies in Humanities and Social Science*, *1*(4), 290–297.

Pallant, J. (2011). *SPSS survival manual: A step by step guide to data analysis using the SPSS program* (4th ed.). Crows Nest, NSW, Australia: Allen & Unwin.

Pan, E., Johnston, D., Walker, J., Adler-Milstein, J., Bates, D. W., & Middleton, B. (2005). *The Value of Healthcare Information Exchange and Interoperability*. Chicago: Health Information Management and Systems Society.

Paton, R. A., & McCalman, J. (2008). *Change Management: A Guide to Effective Implementation*. London: SAGE Publications.

Patton, M. (2015). Battling data breaches: For higher education institutions, Data Breach Prevention is More Complex than for Industry and Business. *Community College Journal*, *86*(1), 20–24.

Paunica, M., Matac, M. L., Motofei, C., & Manole, A. (2009). Some aspects regarding the use of business intelligence in the financial management. *Metalurgia International*, *1*(14), 180–181.

Pelletier, M. P., Trépanier, M., & Morency, C. (2011). Smart card data use in public transit: A literature review. *Transportation Research Part C, Emerging Technologies*, *19*(4), 557–568. doi:10.1016/j.trc.2010.12.003

Pelone, F., Kringos, D. S., Romaniello, A., Archibugi, M., Salsiri, C., & Ricciardi, W. (2015). Primary care efficiency measurement using data envelopment analysis: A systematic review. *Journal of Medical Systems*, *39*(1), 1–14. doi:10.100710916-014-0156-4 PMID:25486892

Peltier, T. R. (2010). Information security risk analysis (3rd ed.). CRC Press, Taylor & Francis Group, Auerbach Publications.

Pettigrew, A. M., Woodman, R. W., & Cameron, K. S. (2001). Studying organizational change and development: Challenges for future research. *Academy of Management Journal*, *44*(4), 697–713.

Pfleeger, S. L., & Caputo, D. D. (2012). *Leveraging behavioral science to mitigate cyber-security risk*. MITRE Technical Report 12-0499. Bedford, MA: MITRE Corporation.

Pieper, J. R., Trevor, C. O., Weller, I., & Duchon, D. (2017). Referral Hire Presence Implications for Referrer Turnover and Job Performance. *Journal of Management*, *19*, 14–20.

Poll, H. (2015). *Pearson student mobile device survey 2015*. Retrieved from http://www.pearsoned.com/wp-content/uploads/2015-Pearson-Student-Mobile-Device-Survey-College.pdf

Pratheek, P. K. (2017). *Steganography Using Visual Cryptography*. Retrieved from https://books.google.com/books?id=Z8WiAwAAQBAJ

Premkumar, G., & Ramamurthy, K. (1995). The role of interorganizational and organizational factors on the decision mode for adoption of interorganizational systems. *Decision Sciences*, *26*(3), 303–336. doi:10.1111/j.1540-5915.1995.tb01431.x

PWC Report. (2015). *The Global State of Information Security Survey 2015*. Retrieved from http://www.pwc.com/gx/en/issues/cyber-security/ information-security-survey/download.html

Ragatz, J.A. (2015). *The Fraud Triangle can be an Ethics Crystal Ball*. The American College of Financial Services, TAC Digital Commons, Faculty Publications, Paper 261.

Rattray, C. J., Lord, B. R., & Shanahan, Y. P. (2007). Target costing in New Zealand manufacturing firms. *Pacific Accounting Review*, *19*(1), 68–83. doi:10.1108/01140580710754656

Reichenberg, N. (2014). Improving Security via Proper Network Segmentation. *Security Week*. Retrieved from http://www.securityweek.com/improving-security-proper-network-segmentation

Reichenberg, N., & Wolfgang, M. (2014). Segmenting for security: Five steps to protect your network. *Network World*. Retrieved from http://www.networkworld.com

Reisinger, B. (2017). XBRL in Progress – Financial Reporting Policy Frameworks and their Effects on the Adoption of XBRL. *Financial Communications*, *8*, 1–20.

Ricchiute, D. N. (2006). Auditing (8th ed.). Thomson South-Western.

Richards, D. A., Melancon, B. C., & Ratley, J. D. (2008). *Managing the Business Risk of Fraud: A Practical Guide*. Retrieved from https://www.acfe.com/fraud-resources.aspx

Richardson, A. J., & Welker, M. (2001). Social disclosure, financial disclosure and the cost capital of equity capital. *Accounting, Organizations and Society*, *26*(7), 597–616. doi:10.1016/S0361-3682(01)00025-3

Rittenberg, L. E., & Schwieger, B. J. (2005). *Auditing. Concepts for a Changing Environment* (5th ed.). Thomson South-Western.

Rogers, E. M. (2003). *Diffusion of innovations* (5th ed.). New York: Free Press.

Rojanschi, V., Grigore, F., & Ciomoș, V. (2008). *Ghidul evaluatorului și auditoriului de mediu*. București, România: Editura Economică.

Roșca, I. (Ed.). (1993). Designing financial and accounting information systems. Didactic and Pedagogical Publishing House.

Rowbottom, N., Allam, A., & Lymer, A. (2005). An exploration of the potential for studying the usage of investor relations information through the analysis of web server logs. *International Journal of Accounting Information Systems*, *6*(1), 31–53. doi:10.1016/j.accinf.2004.08.002

Rowland, C., & Hall, R. (2014). Management learning, performance and reward: Theory and practice revisited. *Journal of Management Development*, *33*(4), 342–356. doi:10.1108/JMD-08-2012-0110

Rubenstein, D.B. (1994). *Environmental Accounting for the sustainable corporation – Strategies and Techniques*. Quorum Books.

Sabherwal, R., Jeyaraj, A., & Chowa, C. (2006). Information system success: Individual and organizational determinants. *Management Science*, *52*(12), 1849–1864. doi:10.1287/mnsc.1060.0583

Saidi, E. (2009). Mobile opportunities, mobile problems: Assessing mobile commerce implementation issues in Malawi. *Journal of Internet Banking and Commerce*, *14*(1).

SAINT. (2016). *Vulnerability management, penetration testing, configuration assessment and compliance.* Retrieved from http://www.saintcorporation.com

Sait, S. M., Al-Tawil, K. M., & Hussain, S. A. (2004). E-commerce in Saudi Arabia: Adoption and perspectives. *AJIS. Australian Journal of Information Systems*, *12*(1), 54–74.

SAMA. (2012). *Saudi Arabian Monetary Agency - Forty eighth annual report.* Saudi Arabian Monetary Agency (SAMA). Retrieved from http://www.sama.gov.sa/sites/samaen/ReportsStatistics/ ReportsStatisticsLib/5600_R_Annual_En_48_2013_02_19.pdf

SAMA. (2013). *Saudi banks.* Retrieved 19 May, 2013, from http://www.sama.gov.sa/sites/samaen/Links/ Pages/SaudiBanks.aspx

SANS Institute. (2006). *Penetration testing: Assessing your overall security before attackers do.* Retrieved from https://www.sans.org/reading-room/whitepapers/ analyst/penetration-testing-assessing-security-attackers-34635

SANS Institute. (2013). *Network security resources.* Retrieved from https://www.sans.org/network-security/

Santos, M., & Filho, W. (2005). An analysis of the relationship between sustainable development and the anthropsystem construct. *International Journal of Environment and Sustainable Development*, *4*(1), 78–87. doi:10.1504/IJESD.2005.006775

Saporta, G., & Niang, N. (2009). Principal component analysis: Application to statistical process control. In G. Govaert (Ed.), *Data Analysis*. Hoboken, NJ: John Wiley & Sons, Inc. doi:10.1002/9780470611777.ch1

Schamberger, R., Madlmayr, G., & Grechenig, T. (2013, February). Components for an interoperable NFC mobile payment ecosystem. In *Near Field Communication (NFC), 2013 5th International Workshop on* (pp. 1-5). IEEE. 10.1109/NFC.2013.6482440

Schneider, D. (2012). The state of network security. *Network Security*, *2*(2), 14–20. doi:10.1016/S1353-4858(12)70016-8

Schneider, M., & Somers, M. (2006). Organizations as complex adaptive systems: Implications of complexity theory for leadership research. *The Leadership Quarterly*, *17*(4), 351–365. doi:10.1016/j.leaqua.2006.04.006

Sebetci, Ö., & Uysal, İ. (2017). The Efficiency of Clinical Departments in Medical Faculty Hospitals: A Case Study Based on Data Envelopment Analysis. *International Journal on Computer Science and Engineering*, *5*(7), 1–8.

Sgriccia, M., Nguyen, H., Edra, R., Alworth, A., & Brandeis, O., Escandon, R., . . . Seal, K. (2007). Drivers of mobile business models: Lessons from four asian countries. *International Journal of Mobile Marketing*, *2*(2), 58–67.

Sharma, D., Murthy, R., & Sundar, K. (2006). *Government policies and regulations: Impact on mobile commerce in Indian context.* Paper presented at the Second European Conference on Mobile Goverment (EURO mGOV).

Sherman, H. D., Young, D. S., & Collingwood, H. (2003). *Profits you can Trust. Spotting & Surviving Accounting Landmines.* Financial Times Prentice Hall.

Shkurti, R., & Muça, E. (2014). An Analysis of Cloud Computing and Its Role in Accounting Industry in Albania. *Global Perspectives on Accounting Education, 8*(2), 219–229.

Shrivastava, P., & Hart, S. (1992). Greening organizations. *Academy of Management Best Paper Proceedings, 52*(1), 185–189. doi:10.5465/ambpp.1992.17515480

Siau, K., Lim, E.-P., & Shen, Z. (2001). Mobile commerce: Promises, challenges, and research agenda. *Journal of Database Management, 12*(3), 4–13. doi:10.4018/jdm.2001070101

Singer, W. P., & Friedman, A. (2014). *Cyber Security and Cyber War: What Everyone Needs to Know.* New York: Oxford University Press.

Singh, A., & Fhom, H. C. S. (2017). Restricted usage of anonymous credentials in vehicular ad hoc networks for misbehavior detection. *International Journal of Information Security, 16*(2), 195–201. doi:10.100710207-016-0328-y

Škrinjar, R., Bosilj-Vukšić, V., & Indihar-Štemberger, M. (2008). The impact of business process orientation on financial and non-financial performance. *Business Process Management Journal, 14*(5), 738–754. doi:10.1108/14637150810903084

Smart, N. P. (2001, December). The exact security of ECIES in the generic group model. In *IMA International Conference on Cryptography and Coding* (pp. 73-84). Springer. 10.1007/3-540-45325-3_8

Smith, D. (2005). Dancing with the mysterious forces of chaos: Issues around complexity, knowledge and the management of uncertainty. *Clinician in Management, (3/4),* 115–123.

Smith, M. (1999). *Management Accounting for Competitive Advantage* (1st ed.). Sydney: LBC Information Services.

Smyth, G. (2008). Wireless Technologies: Bridging the Digital Divide in Education. In A. Varma (Ed.), Information and Communication Technology in Education. ICFAI University Press.

Snowden, S., Spafford, J., Michaelides, R., & Hopkins, J. (2006). Technology acceptance and m-commerce in an operational environment. *Journal of Enterprise Information Management, 19*(6), 525–539. doi:10.1108/17410390610703657

Soltani, B. (2007). *Auditing. An International Approach.* Harlow, UK: Pearson Education.

Souissi, M., & Ito, K. (2004). Integrating target costing and the balanced scorecard. *Journal of Corporate Accounting & Finance, 15*(6), 57–62. doi:10.1002/jcaf.20057

Starkweather, J., & Herrington, R. (2014). Principal components analysis in SPSS. *SPSS Short Course in the Research and Statistical Support*. Retrieved 31 January, 2014, from http://www.unt.edu/rss/class/Jon/SPSS_SC/Module9/M9_PCA/SPSS_M9_PCA1.htm

Stepchenko, D., & Voronova, I. (2015). Assessment of Risk Function Using Analytical Network Process. *Inzinerine Ekonomika-Engineering Economics*, *26*(3), 264–271.

Stoica, M., Miller, D. W., & Stotlar, D. (2005). New technology adoption, business strategy and government involvement: The case of mobile commerce. *Journal of Nonprofit & Public Sector Marketing*, *13*(1&2), 213–232. doi:10.1300/J054v13n01_12

Stoica, M., & Roach, B. (2006). Sustainable development in the rural US midwest: The m-commerce solution. The wireless critical infrastructure. *International Journal of Critical Infrastructures*, *2*(4), 331–346. doi:10.1504/IJCIS.2006.011343

S-Tools for Windows. (n.d.). Retrieved from http://www.modemac.com/s-tools.html

Subramanian, G. H. (1998). A replication of perceived usefulness and perceived ease of use measurement. *Decision Sciences*, *25*(5-6), 863–874. doi:10.1111/j.1540-5915.1994.tb01873.x

Symantec. (2014). *Internet Security Threat Report 2014*. Retrieved from http://www.symantec.com

Tajeddini, K. (2015). Exploring the antecedents of effectiveness and efficiency. *International Journal of Hospitality Management*, *49*(7), 125–135. doi:10.1016/j.ijhm.2015.06.007

Tani, T. (1995). Interactive control in target cost management. *Management Accounting Research*, *6*(4), 399–414. doi:10.1006/mare.1995.1028

Tani, T., Okano, H., Shimizu, N., Iwabuchi, Y., Fukuda, J., & Cooray, S. (1994). Target cost management in Japanese companies: Current state of the art. *Management Accounting Research*, *5*(1), 67–81. doi:10.1006/mare.1994.1005

Taticchi, P., Tonelli, F., & Cagnazzo, L. (2010). Performance measurement and management: A literature review and a research agenda. *Measuring Business Excellence*, *14*(1), 4–18. doi:10.1108/13683041011027418

Taylor, J. (2011). *Forensic Accounting*. Edinburgh Gate, UK: Pearson Education Ltd.

Taylor, S., & Todd, P. A. (1995). Understanding information technology usage: A test of competing models. *Information Systems Research*, *6*(2), 144–176. doi:10.1287/isre.6.2.144

Teo, T., Chan, C., & Parker, C. (2004). *Factors affecting e-commerce adoption by SMEs: A meta-analysis*. Paper presented at the 15th Annual Australasian conference on information systems, Hobart, Australia.

The Startups.co Platform. (2018). Retrieved October 22, 2018, from https://www.fundable.com/learn/resources/guides/crowdfunding-guide/what-is-crowdfunding

Thibodeau, J. C., & Freie, D. (2007). *Auditing after Sarbanes-Oxley. Illustrative Cases*. New York: McGraw-Hill Irwin.

Thompson, R. L., Higgins, C. A., & Howell, J. M. (1991). Personal computing: Toward a conceptual model of utilization. *Management Information Systems Quarterly, 15*(1), 124–143. doi:10.2307/249443

Tiago, O., Manoj, T., & Espadanal, M. (2014). Assessing the determinants of cloud computing adoption: An analysis of the manufacturing and services sectors. *Information & Management, 51*(5), 497–510. doi:10.1016/j.im.2014.03.006

Tickner, P. (2010). *How to be a successful auditor. A practical guide to investigating fraud in the workplace for internal auditors and managers.* West Sussex, UK: John Wiley and Sons Ltd Publication.

Tiwari, R., Buse, S., & Herstatt, C. (2006). From electronic to mobile commerce: Opportunities through technology convergence for business services. *Asia-Pacific Tech Monitor*, 38-45.

Tong, Y. K., & Arvey, R. D. (2015). Managing complexity via the Competing Values Framework. *Journal of Management Development, 34*(6), 653–673. doi:10.1108/JMD-04-2014-0029

Tropina, T., & Callanan, C. (2015). *Self- and Co-regulation in Cybercrime, Cybersecurity and National Security.* New York: Springer International Publishing. doi:10.1007/978-3-319-16447-2

Turner, E. C., & Dasgupta, S. (2003). *Privacy And Security In E-Business.* Academic Press.

Țuțuianu, O. (2006). *Evaluarea și raportarea performanței de mediu. Indicatori de mediu.* București, România: Editura AGIR.

Uçkun, N., Girginer, N., Köse, T., & Şahin, Ü. (2016). Analysis efficiency of public hospitals of metropolitan municipalities in Turkey. *International Journal of Innovative Research in Education, 3*(2), 102–108.

United States Computer Emergency Readiness Team (US-CERT). (2013). *Security tip. Understanding Encryption.* Retrieved from https://www.us-cert.gov/ncas/tips/ST04-019

US GAO. (2012). *Information security: Better implementation of controls for mobile devices should be encouraged.* Retrieved from http://www.gao.gov/products/GAO-12-757

Valentine, S. V., & Savage, V. R. (2010) A Strategic Environmental Management Framework: Evaluating The Profitability of Being Green. In *Sustainability matters- Environmental Management in Asia.* Academic Press. Retrieved from http://www.worldscientific.com/worldscibooks/10.1142/7901#t=doi

Valentine, S. V. (2009). The Green Onion: A Corporate Environmental Strategy Framework. *Corporate Social Responsibility and Environmental Management.* doi:10.1002/csr.217

van der Wende, M. C. (2001a). The International Dimension in National Higher Education Policies: What Has Changed in Europe over the Last Five Years? *European Journal of Education, 36*(4), 431–441. doi:10.1111/1467-3435.00080

Varabyova, Y., & Müller, J. M. (2016). The efficiency of health care production in OECD countries: A systematic review and meta-analysis of cross-country comparisons. *Health Policy (Amsterdam), 120*(3), 252–263. doi:10.1016/j.healthpol.2015.12.005 PMID:26819140

Varma, A. (2008). ICT in the Field of Education. In A. Varma (Ed.), Information and Communication Technology in Education. ICFAI University Press.

Varshney, U., Mallow, A., Ahluwalia, P., & Jain, R. (2004). Wireless in the enterprise: Requirements, solutions and research directions. *International Journal of Mobile Communications*, 2(4), 354. doi:10.1504/IJMC.2004.005856

Varshney, U., & Vetter, R. (2000). Emerging wireless and mobile networks. *Communications of the ACM*, 43(7), 73–81. doi:10.1145/336460.336478

Venkatesh, V., & Davis, F. D. (2000). A theoretical extension of the technology acceptance model: Four longitudinal Field Study. *Management Science*, 46(2), 186–204. doi:10.1287/mnsc.46.2.186.11926

Venkatesh, V., Morris, M. G., Davis, G. B., & Davis, F. D. (2003). User acceptance of information technology: Toward a unified view. *Management Information Systems Quarterly*, 27(2).

Verdult, R., & Kooman, F. (2011, February). Practical attacks on NFC enabled cell phones. In *Near Field Communication (NFC), 2011 3rd International Workshop on* (pp. 77-82). IEEE. 10.1109/NFC.2011.16

Verizon. (2013). *The 2013 data breach investigations report*. Retrieved from www.verizonenterprise.com

Vrechopoulos, A., Constantiou, I., Sideris, I., Doukidis, G., & Mylonopoulos, N. (2003). The critical role of consumer behavior research in mobile commerce. *International Journal of Mobile Communications*, 1(2), 329–340.

Wadhwa, L., & Virender, P. (2012). Forensic Accounting and Fraud Examination in India. *International Journal of Applied Engineering Research*, 7(11), 1–29.

Wang, W., & Hu, L. (2014). A secure and efficient handover authentication protocol for wireless networks. *Journal of Sensors*, 14(7), 11379–11394. doi:10.3390140711379 PMID:24971471

Want, R. (2011). Near field communication. *IEEE Pervasive Computing*, 10(3), 4–7. doi:10.1109/MPRV.2011.55

Whittington, O. R., & Pany, K. (2008). *Principles of Auditing & Other Assurance Services* (16th ed.). New York: McGraw-Hill Irwin.

Winkler, I. (2010). *Justifying IT Security – Managing Risk & Keeping your network Secure*. Qualys Inc.

Wu, D., & Tsai, W. (2003). A steganographic method for images by pixel value differencing. *Pattern Recognition Letters*, 24(9-10), 1613–1626. doi:10.1016/S0167-8655(02)00402-6

Xiao, L., & Wang, Z. (2011). Internet of things: A new application for intelligent traffic monitoring system. *Journal of Networks*, 6(6), 887.

Yadav, N., & Sagar, M. (2013). Performance measurement and management frameworks. *Business Process Management Journal*, 19(6), 947–971. doi:10.1108/BPMJ-01-2013-0003

Yakhou, M., & Dorweiler, V. P. (2004). Environmental accounting: An essential component of business strategy. *Business Strategy and the Environment*, *13*(2), 65–77. doi:10.1002/bse.395

Yami, S., Castaldo, S., Dagnino, B., & Le Roy, F. (Eds.). (2010). *Coopetition: winning strategies for the 21st century*. Edward Elgar Publishing. doi:10.4337/9781849807241

Yang, C. N., Wu, C. C., & Wang, D. S. (2014). A discussion on the relationship between probabilistic visual cryptography and random grid. *Information Sciences*, *278*, 141–173. doi:10.1016/j.ins.2014.03.033

Yang, J., & Papazoglou, M. P. (2000). Interoperation support for electronic business. *Communications of the ACM*, *43*(6), 39–47. doi:10.1145/336460.336473

Yang, K. C. C. (2005). Exploring factors affecting the adoption of mobile commerce in Singapore. *Telematics and Informatics*, *22*(3), 257–277. doi:10.1016/j.tele.2004.11.003

Yan, W., Chen, C., & Chang, W. (2009). An investigation into sustainable product constructualization using a design knowledge hierarchy and Hopfield network. *Computers & Industrial Engineering*, *56*(4), 617–626. doi:10.1016/j.cie.2008.10.015

Yaokumah, W., Brown, S., & Adjei, P. O. (2015). Information technology governance barriers, drivers, IT/Business alignment, and maturity in Ghanaian universities. *International Journal of Information Systems in the Service Sector*, *7*(4), 66–83. doi:10.4018/IJISSS.2015100104

Yaseen, S. G., & Zayed, S. (2010). Exploring critical determinants in deploying mobile commerce technology. *American Journal of Applied Sciences*, *7*(1), 120–126. doi:10.3844/ajassp.2010.120.126

Yiğit, V. (2017). Technical Efficiency of Physicians In Performance Based Supplementary Payment System: Application In A University Hospital. *Electronic Journal of Social Sciences*, *16*(62), 854–866.

Yilmaz, R., & Baral, G. (2010). Target costing as a strategic cost management tool for success of balanced scorecard system. *China-USA Business Review*, *9*(3), 39–53.

Yuan, Y., & Zhang, J. J. (2003). Towards an appropriate business model for m-commerce. *International Journal of Mobile Communications*, *1*(1-2), 35–56. doi:10.1504/IJMC.2003.002459

Yusuf, M. O., & Onasanya, S. A. (2004). Information and communication technology (ICT) and technology in tertiary institution. In E.A. Ogunsakin (Ed.), Teaching in Tertiary Institutions (pp. 67-76). Ilorin: Faculty of Education.

Zeeshan, S. A., Cheung, Y., & Scheepers, H. (2007). *Developing a collaborative orgnizational mobile commerce model*. Paper presented at the International Conference on Business and Information, Tokyo, Japan.

Zentner, A. (2008). Online sales, Internet use, file sharing, and the decline of retail music specialty stores. *Information Economics and Policy*, *20*(3), 288–300. doi:10.1016/j.infoecopol.2008.06.006

Zhang, D., & Adipat, B. (2005). Challenges, methodologies, and issues in the usability testing of mobile applications. *International Journal of Human-Computer Interaction, 18*(3), 293–308. doi:10.120715327590ijhc1803_3

Zheng, P., & Ni, L. (2006). *Mobile application challenges. In Smart Phone and Next Generation Mobile Computing* (pp. 407–512). Burlington: Morgan Kaufmann. doi:10.1016/B978-012088560-2/50009-5

Related References

To continue our tradition of advancing information science and technology research, we have compiled a list of recommended IGI Global readings. These references will provide additional information and guidance to further enrich your knowledge and assist you with your own research and future publications.

Abtahi, M. S., Behboudi, L., & Hasanabad, H. M. (2017). Factors Affecting Internet Advertising Adoption in Ad Agencies. *International Journal of Innovation in the Digital Economy*, 8(4), 18–29. doi:10.4018/IJIDE.2017100102

Agrawal, S. (2017). The Impact of Emerging Technologies and Social Media on Different Business(es): Marketing and Management. In O. Rishi & A. Sharma (Eds.), *Maximizing Business Performance and Efficiency Through Intelligent Systems* (pp. 37–49). Hershey, PA: IGI Global. doi:10.4018/978-1-5225-2234-8.ch002

Alnoukari, M., Razouk, R., & Hanano, A. (2016). BSC-SI: A Framework for Integrating Strategic Intelligence in Corporate Strategic Management. *International Journal of Social and Organizational Dynamics in IT*, 5(2), 1–14. doi:10.4018/IJSODIT.2016070101

Alnoukari, M., Razouk, R., & Hanano, A. (2016). BSC-SI, A Framework for Integrating Strategic Intelligence in Corporate Strategic Management. *International Journal of Strategic Information Technology and Applications*, 7(1), 32–44. doi:10.4018/IJSITA.2016010103

Altındağ, E. (2016). Current Approaches in Change Management. In A. Goksoy (Ed.), *Organizational Change Management Strategies in Modern Business* (pp. 24–51). Hershey, PA: IGI Global. doi:10.4018/978-1-4666-9533-7.ch002

Alvarez-Dionisi, L. E., Turner, R., & Mittra, M. (2016). Global Project Management Trends. *International Journal of Information Technology Project Management*, 7(3), 54–73. doi:10.4018/IJITPM.2016070104

Anantharaman, R. N., Rajeswari, K. S., Angusamy, A., & Kuppusamy, J. (2017). Role of Self-Efficacy and Collective Efficacy as Moderators of Occupational Stress Among Software Development Professionals. *International Journal of Human Capital and Information Technology Professionals*, 8(2), 45–58. doi:10.4018/IJHCITP.2017040103

Aninze, F., El-Gohary, H., & Hussain, J. (2018). The Role of Microfinance to Empower Women: The Case of Developing Countries. *International Journal of Customer Relationship Marketing and Management*, *9*(1), 54–78. doi:10.4018/IJCRMM.2018010104

Arsenijević, O. M., Orčić, D., & Kastratović, E. (2017). Development of an Optimization Tool for Intangibles in SMEs: A Case Study from Serbia with a Pilot Research in the Prestige by Milka Company. In M. Vemić (Ed.), *Optimal Management Strategies in Small and Medium Enterprises* (pp. 320–347). Hershey, PA: IGI Global. doi:10.4018/978-1-5225-1949-2.ch015

Aryanto, V. D., Wismantoro, Y., & Widyatmoko, K. (2018). Implementing Eco-Innovation by Utilizing the Internet to Enhance Firm's Marketing Performance: Study of Green Batik Small and Medium Enterprises in Indonesia. *International Journal of E-Business Research*, *14*(1), 21–36. doi:10.4018/IJEBR.2018010102

Atiku, S. O., & Fields, Z. (2017). Multicultural Orientations for 21st Century Global Leadership. In N. Baporikar (Ed.), *Management Education for Global Leadership* (pp. 28–51). Hershey, PA: IGI Global. doi:10.4018/978-1-5225-1013-0.ch002

Atiku, S. O., & Fields, Z. (2018). Organisational Learning Dimensions and Talent Retention Strategies for the Service Industries. In N. Baporikar (Ed.), *Global Practices in Knowledge Management for Societal and Organizational Development* (pp. 358–381). Hershey, PA: IGI Global. doi:10.4018/978-1-5225-3009-1.ch017

Ávila, L., & Teixeira, L. (2018). The Main Concepts Behind the Dematerialization of Business Processes. In M. Khosrow-Pour, D.B.A. (Ed.), Encyclopedia of Information Science and Technology, Fourth Edition (pp. 888-898). Hershey, PA: IGI Global. doi:10.4018/978-1-5225-2255-3.ch076

Bartens, Y., Chunpir, H. I., Schulte, F., & Voß, S. (2017). Business/IT Alignment in Two-Sided Markets: A COBIT 5 Analysis for Media Streaming Business Models. In S. De Haes & W. Van Grembergen (Eds.), *Strategic IT Governance and Alignment in Business Settings* (pp. 82–111). Hershey, PA: IGI Global. doi:10.4018/978-1-5225-0861-8.ch004

Bashayreh, A. M. (2018). Organizational Culture and Organizational Performance. In W. Lee & F. Sabetzadeh (Eds.), *Contemporary Knowledge and Systems Science* (pp. 50–69). Hershey, PA: IGI Global. doi:10.4018/978-1-5225-5655-8.ch003

Bedford, D. A. (2018). Sustainable Knowledge Management Strategies: Aligning Business Capabilities and Knowledge Management Goals. In N. Baporikar (Ed.), *Global Practices in Knowledge Management for Societal and Organizational Development* (pp. 46–73). Hershey, PA: IGI Global. doi:10.4018/978-1-5225-3009-1.ch003

Benmoussa, F., Nakara, W. A., & Jaouen, A. (2016). The Use of Social Media by SMEs in the Tourism Industry. In I. Lee (Ed.), *Encyclopedia of E-Commerce Development, Implementation, and Management* (pp. 2159–2170). Hershey, PA: IGI Global. doi:10.4018/978-1-4666-9787-4.ch155

Berger, R. (2016). Indigenous Management and Bottom of Pyramid Countries: The Role of National Institutions. In U. Aung & P. Ordoñez de Pablos (Eds.), *Managerial Strategies and Practice in the Asian Business Sector* (pp. 107–123). Hershey, PA: IGI Global. doi:10.4018/978-1-4666-9758-4.ch007

Bharwani, S., & Musunuri, D. (2018). Reflection as a Process From Theory to Practice. In M. Khosrow-Pour, D.B.A. (Ed.), Encyclopedia of Information Science and Technology, Fourth Edition (pp. 1529-1539). Hershey, PA: IGI Global. doi:10.4018/978-1-5225-2255-3.ch132

Bhatt, G. D., Wang, Z., & Rodger, J. A. (2017). Information Systems Capabilities and Their Effects on Competitive Advantages: A Study of Chinese Companies. *Information Resources Management Journal, 30*(3), 41–57. doi:10.4018/IRMJ.2017070103

Bhushan, M., & Yadav, A. (2017). Concept of Cloud Computing in ESB. In R. Bhadoria, N. Chaudhari, G. Tomar, & S. Singh (Eds.), *Exploring Enterprise Service Bus in the Service-Oriented Architecture Paradigm* (pp. 116–127). Hershey, PA: IGI Global. doi:10.4018/978-1-5225-2157-0.ch008

Bhushan, S. (2017). System Dynamics Base-Model of Humanitarian Supply Chain (HSCM) in Disaster Prone Eco-Communities of India: A Discussion on Simulation and Scenario Results. *International Journal of System Dynamics Applications, 6*(3), 20–37. doi:10.4018/IJSDA.2017070102

Biswas, A., & De, A. K. (2017). On Development of a Fuzzy Stochastic Programming Model with Its Application to Business Management. In S. Trivedi, S. Dey, A. Kumar, & T. Panda (Eds.), *Handbook of Research on Advanced Data Mining Techniques and Applications for Business Intelligence* (pp. 353–378). Hershey, PA: IGI Global. doi:10.4018/978-1-5225-2031-3.ch021

Bücker, J., & Ernste, K. (2018). Use of Brand Heroes in Strategic Reputation Management: The Case of Bacardi, Adidas, and Daimler. In A. Erdemir (Ed.), *Reputation Management Techniques in Public Relations* (pp. 126–150). Hershey, PA: IGI Global. doi:10.4018/978-1-5225-3619-2.ch007

Bureš, V. (2018). Industry 4.0 From the Systems Engineering Perspective: Alternative Holistic Framework Development. In R. Brunet-Thornton & F. Martinez (Eds.), *Analyzing the Impacts of Industry 4.0 in Modern Business Environments* (pp. 199–223). Hershey, PA: IGI Global. doi:10.4018/978-1-5225-3468-6.ch011

Buzady, Z. (2017). Resolving the Magic Cube of Effective Case Teaching: Benchmarking Case Teaching Practices in Emerging Markets – Insights from the Central European University Business School, Hungary. In D. Latusek (Ed.), *Case Studies as a Teaching Tool in Management Education* (pp. 79–103). Hershey, PA: IGI Global. doi:10.4018/978-1-5225-0770-3.ch005

Campatelli, G., Richter, A., & Stocker, A. (2016). Participative Knowledge Management to Empower Manufacturing Workers. *International Journal of Knowledge Management, 12*(4), 37–50. doi:10.4018/IJKM.2016100103

Căpusneanu, S., & Topor, D. I. (2018). Business Ethics and Cost Management in SMEs: Theories of Business Ethics and Cost Management Ethos. In I. Oncioiu (Ed.), *Ethics and Decision-Making for Sustainable Business Practices* (pp. 109–127). Hershey, PA: IGI Global. doi:10.4018/978-1-5225-3773-1.ch007

Carneiro, A. (2016). Maturity in Health Organization Information Systems: Metrics and Privacy Perspectives. *International Journal of Privacy and Health Information Management*, 4(2), 1–18. doi:10.4018/IJPHIM.2016070101

Chan, R. L., Mo, P. L., & Moon, K. K. (2018). Strategic and Tactical Measures in Managing Enterprise Risks: A Study of the Textile and Apparel Industry. In K. Strang, M. Korstanje, & N. Vajjhala (Eds.), *Research, Practices, and Innovations in Global Risk and Contingency Management* (pp. 1–19). Hershey, PA: IGI Global. doi:10.4018/978-1-5225-4754-9.ch001

Chandan, H. C. (2016). Motivations and Challenges of Female Entrepreneurship in Developed and Developing Economies. In N. Baporikar (Ed.), *Handbook of Research on Entrepreneurship in the Contemporary Knowledge-Based Global Economy* (pp. 260–286). Hershey, PA: IGI Global. doi:10.4018/978-1-4666-8798-1.ch012

Charlier, S. D., Burke-Smalley, L. A., & Fisher, S. L. (2018). Undergraduate Programs in the U.S: A Contextual and Content-Based Analysis. In J. Mendy (Ed.), *Teaching Human Resources and Organizational Behavior at the College Level* (pp. 26–57). Hershey, PA: IGI Global. doi:10.4018/978-1-5225-2820-3.ch002

Chaudhuri, S. (2016). Application of Web-Based Geographical Information System (GIS) in E-Business. In U. Panwar, R. Kumar, & N. Ray (Eds.), *Handbook of Research on Promotional Strategies and Consumer Influence in the Service Sector* (pp. 389–405). Hershey, PA: IGI Global. doi:10.4018/978-1-5225-0143-5.ch023

Choudhuri, P. S. (2016). An Empirical Study on the Quality of Services Offered by the Private Life Insurers in Burdwan. In U. Panwar, R. Kumar, & N. Ray (Eds.), *Handbook of Research on Promotional Strategies and Consumer Influence in the Service Sector* (pp. 31–55). Hershey, PA: IGI Global. doi:10.4018/978-1-5225-0143-5.ch002

Dahlberg, T., Kivijärvi, H., & Saarinen, T. (2017). IT Investment Consistency and Other Factors Influencing the Success of IT Performance. In S. De Haes & W. Van Grembergen (Eds.), *Strategic IT Governance and Alignment in Business Settings* (pp. 176–208). Hershey, PA: IGI Global. doi:10.4018/978-1-5225-0861-8.ch007

Damnjanović, A. M. (2017). Knowledge Management Optimization through IT and E-Business Utilization: A Qualitative Study on Serbian SMEs. In M. Vemić (Ed.), *Optimal Management Strategies in Small and Medium Enterprises* (pp. 249–267). Hershey, PA: IGI Global. doi:10.4018/978-1-5225-1949-2.ch012

Daneshpour, H. (2017). Integrating Sustainable Development into Project Portfolio Management through Application of Open Innovation. In M. Vemić (Ed.), *Optimal Management Strategies in Small and Medium Enterprises* (pp. 370–387). Hershey, PA: IGI Global. doi:10.4018/978-1-5225-1949-2.ch017

Daniel, A. D., & Reis de Castro, V. (2018). Entrepreneurship Education: How to Measure the Impact on Nascent Entrepreneurs. In A. Carrizo Moreira, J. Guilherme Leitão Dantas, & F. Manuel Valente (Eds.), *Nascent Entrepreneurship and Successful New Venture Creation* (pp. 85–110). Hershey, PA: IGI Global. doi:10.4018/978-1-5225-2936-1.ch004

David, F., van der Sijde, P., & van den Besselaar, P. (2016). Enterpreneurial Incentives, Obstacles, and Management in University-Business Co-Operation: The Case of Indonesia. In J. Saiz-Álvarez (Ed.), *Handbook of Research on Social Entrepreneurship and Solidarity Economics* (pp. 499–518). Hershey, PA: IGI Global. doi:10.4018/978-1-5225-0097-1.ch024

David, R., Swami, B. N., & Tangirala, S. (2018). Ethics Impact on Knowledge Management in Organizational Development: A Case Study. In N. Baporikar (Ed.), *Global Practices in Knowledge Management for Societal and Organizational Development* (pp. 19–45). Hershey, PA: IGI Global. doi:10.4018/978-1-5225-3009-1.ch002

Delias, P., & Lakiotaki, K. (2018). Discovering Process Horizontal Boundaries to Facilitate Process Comprehension. *International Journal of Operations Research and Information Systems*, 9(2), 1–31. doi:10.4018/IJORIS.2018040101

Denholm, J., & Lee-Davies, L. (2018). Success Factors for Games in Business and Project Management. In *Enhancing Education and Training Initiatives Through Serious Games* (pp. 34–68). Hershey, PA: IGI Global. doi:10.4018/978-1-5225-3689-5.ch002

Deshpande, M. (2017). Best Practices in Management Institutions for Global Leadership: Policy Aspects. In N. Baporikar (Ed.), *Management Education for Global Leadership* (pp. 1–27). Hershey, PA: IGI Global. doi:10.4018/978-1-5225-1013-0.ch001

Deshpande, M. (2018). Policy Perspectives for SMEs Knowledge Management. In N. Baporikar (Ed.), *Knowledge Integration Strategies for Entrepreneurship and Sustainability* (pp. 23–46). Hershey, PA: IGI Global. doi:10.4018/978-1-5225-5115-7.ch002

Dezdar, S. (2017). ERP Implementation Projects in Asian Countries: A Comparative Study on Iran and China. *International Journal of Information Technology Project Management*, 8(3), 52–68. doi:10.4018/IJITPM.2017070104

Domingos, D., Martinho, R., & Varajão, J. (2016). Controlled Flexibility in Healthcare Processes: A BPMN-Extension Approach. In M. Cruz-Cunha, I. Miranda, R. Martinho, & R. Rijo (Eds.), *Encyclopedia of E-Health and Telemedicine* (pp. 521–535). Hershey, PA: IGI Global. doi:10.4018/978-1-4666-9978-6.ch040

Domingos, D., Respício, A., & Martinho, R. (2017). Reliability of IoT-Aware BPMN Healthcare Processes. In C. Reis & M. Maximiano (Eds.), *Internet of Things and Advanced Application in Healthcare* (pp. 214–248). Hershey, PA: IGI Global. doi:10.4018/978-1-5225-1820-4.ch008

Dosumu, O., Hussain, J., & El-Gohary, H. (2017). An Exploratory Study of the Impact of Government Policies on the Development of Small and Medium Enterprises in Developing Countries: The Case of Nigeria. *International Journal of Customer Relationship Marketing and Management*, 8(4), 51–62. doi:10.4018/IJCRMM.2017100104

Durst, S., Bruns, G., & Edvardsson, I. R. (2017). Retaining Knowledge in Smaller Building and Construction Firms. *International Journal of Knowledge and Systems Science*, 8(3), 1–12. doi:10.4018/IJKSS.2017070101

Edvardsson, I. R., & Durst, S. (2017). Outsourcing, Knowledge, and Learning: A Critical Review. *International Journal of Knowledge-Based Organizations*, 7(2), 13–26. doi:10.4018/IJKBO.2017040102

Edwards, J. S. (2018). Integrating Knowledge Management and Business Processes. In M. Khosrow-Pour, D.B.A. (Ed.), Encyclopedia of Information Science and Technology, Fourth Edition (pp. 5046-5055). Hershey, PA: IGI Global. doi:10.4018/978-1-5225-2255-3.ch437

Ejiogu, A. O. (2018). Economics of Farm Management. In *Agricultural Finance and Opportunities for Investment and Expansion* (pp. 56–72). Hershey, PA: IGI Global. doi:10.4018/978-1-5225-3059-6.ch003

Ekanem, I., & Abiade, G. E. (2018). Factors Influencing the Use of E-Commerce by Small Enterprises in Nigeria. *International Journal of ICT Research in Africa and the Middle East*, 7(1), 37–53. doi:10.4018/IJICTRAME.2018010103

Ekanem, I., & Alrossais, L. A. (2017). Succession Challenges Facing Family Businesses in Saudi Arabia. In P. Zgheib (Ed.), *Entrepreneurship and Business Innovation in the Middle East* (pp. 122–146). Hershey, PA: IGI Global. doi:10.4018/978-1-5225-2066-5.ch007

El Faquih, L., & Fredj, M. (2017). Ontology-Based Framework for Quality in Configurable Process Models. *Journal of Electronic Commerce in Organizations*, 15(2), 48–60. doi:10.4018/JECO.2017040104

El-Gohary, H., & El-Gohary, Z. (2016). An Attempt to Explore Electronic Marketing Adoption and Implementation Aspects in Developing Countries: The Case of Egypt. *International Journal of Customer Relationship Marketing and Management*, 7(4), 1–26. doi:10.4018/IJCRMM.2016100101

Entico, G. J. (2016). Knowledge Management and the Medical Health Librarians: A Perception Study. In J. Yap, M. Perez, M. Ayson, & G. Entico (Eds.), *Special Library Administration, Standardization and Technological Integration* (pp. 52–77). Hershey, PA: IGI Global. doi:10.4018/978-1-4666-9542-9.ch003

Faisal, M. N., & Talib, F. (2017). Building Ambidextrous Supply Chains in SMEs: How to Tackle the Barriers? *International Journal of Information Systems and Supply Chain Management*, 10(4), 80–100. doi:10.4018/IJISSCM.2017100105

Fernandes, T. M., Gomes, J., & Romão, M. (2017). Investments in E-Government: A Benefit Management Case Study. *International Journal of Electronic Government Research*, 13(3), 1–17. doi:10.4018/IJEGR.2017070101

Fouda, F. A. (2016). A Suggested Curriculum in Career Education to Develop Business Secondary Schools Students' Career Knowledge Management Domains and Professional Thinking. *International Journal of Technology Diffusion*, 7(2), 42–62. doi:10.4018/IJTD.2016040103

Gallardo-Vázquez, D., & Pajuelo-Moreno, M. L. (2016). How Spanish Universities are Promoting Entrepreneurship through Your Own Lines of Teaching and Research? In L. Carvalho (Ed.), *Handbook of Research on Entrepreneurial Success and its Impact on Regional Development* (pp. 431–454). Hershey, PA: IGI Global. doi:10.4018/978-1-4666-9567-2.ch019

Gao, S. S., Oreal, S., & Zhang, J. (2018). Contemporary Financial Risk Management Perceptions and Practices of Small-Sized Chinese Businesses. In I. Management Association (Ed.), Global Business Expansion: Concepts, Methodologies, Tools, and Applications (pp. 917-931). Hershey, PA: IGI Global. doi:10.4018/978-1-5225-5481-3.ch041

Garg, R., & Berning, S. C. (2017). Indigenous Chinese Management Philosophies: Key Concepts and Relevance for Modern Chinese Firms. In B. Christiansen & G. Koc (Eds.), *Transcontinental Strategies for Industrial Development and Economic Growth* (pp. 43–57). Hershey, PA: IGI Global. doi:10.4018/978-1-5225-2160-0.ch003

Gencer, Y. G. (2017). Supply Chain Management in Retailing Business. In U. Akkucuk (Ed.), *Ethics and Sustainability in Global Supply Chain Management* (pp. 197–210). Hershey, PA: IGI Global. doi:10.4018/978-1-5225-2036-8.ch011

Giacosa, E. (2016). Innovation in Luxury Fashion Businesses as a Means for the Regional Development. In L. Carvalho (Ed.), *Handbook of Research on Entrepreneurial Success and its Impact on Regional Development* (pp. 206–222). Hershey, PA: IGI Global. doi:10.4018/978-1-4666-9567-2.ch010

Giacosa, E. (2018). The Increasing of the Regional Development Thanks to the Luxury Business Innovation. In L. Carvalho (Ed.), *Handbook of Research on Entrepreneurial Ecosystems and Social Dynamics in a Globalized World* (pp. 260–273). Hershey, PA: IGI Global. doi:10.4018/978-1-5225-3525-6.ch011

Gianni, M., & Gotzamani, K. (2016). Integrated Management Systems and Information Management Systems: Common Threads. In P. Papajorgji, F. Pinet, A. Guimarães, & J. Papathanasiou (Eds.), *Automated Enterprise Systems for Maximizing Business Performance* (pp. 195–214). Hershey, PA: IGI Global. doi:10.4018/978-1-4666-8841-4.ch011

Gianni, M., Gotzamani, K., & Linden, I. (2016). How a BI-wise Responsible Integrated Management System May Support Food Traceability. *International Journal of Decision Support System Technology*, 8(2), 1–17. doi:10.4018/IJDSST.2016040101

Glykas, M., & George, J. (2017). Quality and Process Management Systems in the UAE Maritime Industry. *International Journal of Productivity Management and Assessment Technologies*, 5(1), 20–39. doi:10.4018/IJPMAT.2017010102

Glykas, M., Valiris, G., Kokkinaki, A., & Koutsoukou, Z. (2018). Banking Business Process Management Implementation. *International Journal of Productivity Management and Assessment Technologies*, 6(1), 50–69. doi:10.4018/IJPMAT.2018010104

Gomes, J., & Romão, M. (2017). The Balanced Scorecard: Keeping Updated and Aligned with Today's Business Trends. *International Journal of Productivity Management and Assessment Technologies*, 5(2), 1–15. doi:10.4018/IJPMAT.2017070101

Gomes, J., & Romão, M. (2017). Aligning Information Systems and Technology with Benefit Management and Balanced Scorecard. In S. De Haes & W. Van Grembergen (Eds.), *Strategic IT Governance and Alignment in Business Settings* (pp. 112–131). Hershey, PA: IGI Global. doi:10.4018/978-1-5225-0861-8.ch005

Grefen, P., & Turetken, O. (2017). Advanced Business Process Management in Networked E-Business Scenarios. *International Journal of E-Business Research*, *13*(4), 70–104. doi:10.4018/IJEBR.2017100105

Haider, A., & Saetang, S. (2017). Strategic IT Alignment in Service Sector. In S. Rozenes & Y. Cohen (Eds.), *Handbook of Research on Strategic Alliances and Value Co-Creation in the Service Industry* (pp. 231–258). Hershey, PA: IGI Global. doi:10.4018/978-1-5225-2084-9.ch012

Haider, A., & Tang, S. S. (2016). Maximising Value Through IT and Business Alignment: A Case of IT Governance Institutionalisation at a Thai Bank. *International Journal of Technology Diffusion*, *7*(3), 33–58. doi:10.4018/IJTD.2016070104

Hajilari, A. B., Ghadaksaz, M., & Fasghandis, G. S. (2017). Assessing Organizational Readiness for Implementing ERP System Using Fuzzy Expert System Approach. *International Journal of Enterprise Information Systems*, *13*(1), 67–85. doi:10.4018/IJEIS.2017010105

Haldorai, A., Ramu, A., & Murugan, S. (2018). Social Aware Cognitive Radio Networks: Effectiveness of Social Networks as a Strategic Tool for Organizational Business Management. In H. Bansal, G. Shrivastava, G. Nguyen, & L. Stanciu (Eds.), *Social Network Analytics for Contemporary Business Organizations* (pp. 188–202). Hershey, PA: IGI Global. doi:10.4018/978-1-5225-5097-6.ch010

Hall, O. P. Jr. (2017). Social Media Driven Management Education. *International Journal of Knowledge-Based Organizations*, *7*(2), 43–59. doi:10.4018/IJKBO.2017040104

Hanifah, H., Halim, H. A., Ahmad, N. H., & Vafaei-Zadeh, A. (2017). Innovation Culture as a Mediator Between Specific Human Capital and Innovation Performance Among Bumiputera SMEs in Malaysia. In N. Ahmad, T. Ramayah, H. Halim, & S. Rahman (Eds.), *Handbook of Research on Small and Medium Enterprises in Developing Countries* (pp. 261–279). Hershey, PA: IGI Global. doi:10.4018/978-1-5225-2165-5.ch012

Hartlieb, S., & Silvius, G. (2017). Handling Uncertainty in Project Management and Business Development: Similarities and Differences. In Y. Raydugin (Ed.), *Handbook of Research on Leveraging Risk and Uncertainties for Effective Project Management* (pp. 337–362). Hershey, PA: IGI Global. doi:10.4018/978-1-5225-1790-0.ch016

Hass, K. B. (2017). Living on the Edge: Managing Project Complexity. In Y. Raydugin (Ed.), *Handbook of Research on Leveraging Risk and Uncertainties for Effective Project Management* (pp. 177–201). Hershey, PA: IGI Global. doi:10.4018/978-1-5225-1790-0.ch009

Hassan, A., & Privitera, D. S. (2016). Google AdSense as a Mobile Technology in Education. In J. Holland (Ed.), *Wearable Technology and Mobile Innovations for Next-Generation Education* (pp. 200–223). Hershey, PA: IGI Global. doi:10.4018/978-1-5225-0069-8.ch011

Hassan, A., & Rahimi, R. (2016). Consuming "Innovation" in Tourism: Augmented Reality as an Innovation Tool in Digital Tourism Marketing. In N. Pappas & I. Bregoli (Eds.), *Global Dynamics in Travel, Tourism, and Hospitality* (pp. 130–147). Hershey, PA: IGI Global. doi:10.4018/978-1-5225-0201-2.ch008

Hawking, P., & Carmine Sellitto, C. (2017). Developing an Effective Strategy for Organizational Business Intelligence. In M. Tavana (Ed.), *Enterprise Information Systems and the Digitalization of Business Functions* (pp. 222–237). Hershey, PA: IGI Global. doi:10.4018/978-1-5225-2382-6.ch010

Hawking, P., & Sellitto, C. (2017). A Fast-Moving Consumer Goods Company and Business Intelligence Strategy Development. *International Journal of Enterprise Information Systems*, *13*(2), 22–33. doi:10.4018/IJEIS.2017040102

Hawking, P., & Sellitto, C. (2017). Business Intelligence Strategy: Two Case Studies. *International Journal of Business Intelligence Research*, *8*(2), 17–30. doi:10.4018/IJBIR.2017070102

Haynes, J. D., Arockiasamy, S., Al Rashdi, M., & Al Rashdi, S. (2016). Business and E Business Strategies for Coopetition and Thematic Management as a Sustained Basis for Ethics and Social Responsibility in Emerging Markets. In M. Al-Shammari & H. Masri (Eds.), *Ethical and Social Perspectives on Global Business Interaction in Emerging Markets* (pp. 25–39). Hershey, PA: IGI Global. doi:10.4018/978-1-4666-9864-2.ch002

Hee, W. J., Jalleh, G., Lai, H., & Lin, C. (2017). E-Commerce and IT Projects: Evaluation and Management Issues in Australian and Taiwanese Hospitals. *International Journal of Public Health Management and Ethics*, *2*(1), 69–90. doi:10.4018/IJPHME.2017010104

Hernandez, A. A. (2018). Exploring the Factors to Green IT Adoption of SMEs in the Philippines. *Journal of Cases on Information Technology*, *20*(2), 49–66. doi:10.4018/JCIT.2018040104

Hernandez, A. A., & Ona, S. E. (2016). Green IT Adoption: Lessons from the Philippines Business Process Outsourcing Industry. *International Journal of Social Ecology and Sustainable Development*, *7*(1), 1–34. doi:10.4018/IJSESD.2016010101

Hollman, A., Bickford, S., & Hollman, T. (2017). Cyber InSecurity: A Post-Mortem Attempt to Assess Cyber Problems from IT and Business Management Perspectives. *Journal of Cases on Information Technology*, *19*(3), 42–70. doi:10.4018/JCIT.2017070104

Igbinakhase, I. (2017). Responsible and Sustainable Management Practices in Developing and Developed Business Environments. In Z. Fields (Ed.), *Collective Creativity for Responsible and Sustainable Business Practice* (pp. 180–207). Hershey, PA: IGI Global. doi:10.4018/978-1-5225-1823-5.ch010

Ilahi, L., Ghannouchi, S. A., & Martinho, R. (2016). A Business Process Management Approach to Home Healthcare Processes: On the Gap between Intention and Reality. In M. Cruz-Cunha, I. Miranda, R. Martinho, & R. Rijo (Eds.), *Encyclopedia of E-Health and Telemedicine* (pp. 439–457). Hershey, PA: IGI Global. doi:10.4018/978-1-4666-9978-6.ch035

Iwata, J. J., & Hoskins, R. G. (2017). Managing Indigenous Knowledge in Tanzania: A Business Perspective. In P. Jain & N. Mnjama (Eds.), *Managing Knowledge Resources and Records in Modern Organizations* (pp. 198–214). Hershey, PA: IGI Global. doi:10.4018/978-1-5225-1965-2.ch012

Jabeen, F., Ahmad, S. Z., & Alkaabi, S. (2016). The Internationalization Decision-Making of United Arab Emirates Family Businesses. In N. Zakaria, A. Abdul-Talib, & N. Osman (Eds.), *Handbook of Research on Impacts of International Business and Political Affairs on the Global Economy* (pp. 1–22). Hershey, PA: IGI Global. doi:10.4018/978-1-4666-9806-2.ch001

Jain, P. (2017). Ethical and Legal Issues in Knowledge Management Life-Cycle in Business. In P. Jain & N. Mnjama (Eds.), *Managing Knowledge Resources and Records in Modern Organizations* (pp. 82–101). Hershey, PA: IGI Global. doi:10.4018/978-1-5225-1965-2.ch006

Jamali, D., Abdallah, H., & Matar, F. (2016). Opportunities and Challenges for CSR Mainstreaming in Business Schools. *International Journal of Technology and Educational Marketing*, 6(2), 1–29. doi:10.4018/IJTEM.2016070101

James, S., & Hauli, E. (2017). Holistic Management Education at Tanzanian Rural Development Planning Institute. In N. Baporikar (Ed.), *Management Education for Global Leadership* (pp. 112–136). Hershey, PA: IGI Global. doi:10.4018/978-1-5225-1013-0.ch006

Janošková, M., Csikósová, A., & Čulková, K. (2018). Measurement of Company Performance as Part of Its Strategic Management. In R. Leon (Ed.), *Managerial Strategies for Business Sustainability During Turbulent Times* (pp. 309–335). Hershey, PA: IGI Global. doi:10.4018/978-1-5225-2716-9.ch017

Jean-Vasile, A., & Alecu, A. (2017). Theoretical and Practical Approaches in Understanding the Influences of Cost-Productivity-Profit Trinomial in Contemporary Enterprises. In A. Jean Vasile & D. Nicolò (Eds.), *Sustainable Entrepreneurship and Investments in the Green Economy* (pp. 28–62). Hershey, PA: IGI Global. doi:10.4018/978-1-5225-2075-7.ch002

Jha, D. G. (2016). Preparing for Information Technology Driven Changes. In S. Tiwari & L. Nafees (Eds.), *Innovative Management Education Pedagogies for Preparing Next-Generation Leaders* (pp. 258–274). Hershey, PA: IGI Global. doi:10.4018/978-1-4666-9691-4.ch015

Joia, L. A., & Correia, J. C. (2018). CIO Competencies From the IT Professional Perspective: Insights From Brazil. *Journal of Global Information Management*, 26(2), 74–103. doi:10.4018/JGIM.2018040104

Juma, A., & Mzera, N. (2017). Knowledge Management and Records Management and Competitive Advantage in Business. In P. Jain & N. Mnjama (Eds.), *Managing Knowledge Resources and Records in Modern Organizations* (pp. 15–28). Hershey, PA: IGI Global. doi:10.4018/978-1-5225-1965-2.ch002

K., I., & A, V. (2018). Monitoring and Auditing in the Cloud. In K. Munir (Ed.), *Cloud Computing Technologies for Green Enterprises* (pp. 318-350). Hershey, PA: IGI Global. doi:10.4018/978-1-5225-3038-1.ch013

Kabra, G., Ghosh, V., & Ramesh, A. (2018). Enterprise Integrated Business Process Management and Business Intelligence Framework for Business Process Sustainability. In A. Paul, D. Bhattacharyya, & S. Anand (Eds.), *Green Initiatives for Business Sustainability and Value Creation* (pp. 228–238). Hershey, PA: IGI Global. doi:10.4018/978-1-5225-2662-9.ch010

Kaoud, M. (2017). Investigation of Customer Knowledge Management: A Case Study Research. *International Journal of Service Science, Management, Engineering, and Technology*, 8(2), 12–22. doi:10.4018/IJSSMET.2017040102

Kara, M. E., & Fırat, S. Ü. (2016). Sustainability, Risk, and Business Intelligence in Supply Chains. In M. Erdoğdu, T. Arun, & I. Ahmad (Eds.), *Handbook of Research on Green Economic Development Initiatives and Strategies* (pp. 501–538). Hershey, PA: IGI Global. doi:10.4018/978-1-5225-0440-5.ch022

Katuu, S. (2018). A Comparative Assessment of Enterprise Content Management Maturity Models. In N. Gwangwava & M. Mutingi (Eds.), *E-Manufacturing and E-Service Strategies in Contemporary Organizations* (pp. 93–118). Hershey, PA: IGI Global. doi:10.4018/978-1-5225-3628-4.ch005

Khan, M. A. (2016). MNEs Management Strategies in Developing Countries: Establishing the Context. In M. Khan (Ed.), *Multinational Enterprise Management Strategies in Developing Countries* (pp. 1–33). Hershey, PA: IGI Global. doi:10.4018/978-1-5225-0276-0.ch001

Khan, M. A. (2016). Operational Approaches in Organizational Structure: A Case for MNEs in Developing Countries. In M. Khan (Ed.), *Multinational Enterprise Management Strategies in Developing Countries* (pp. 129–151). Hershey, PA: IGI Global. doi:10.4018/978-1-5225-0276-0.ch007

Kinnunen, S., Ylä-Kujala, A., Marttonen-Arola, S., Kärri, T., & Baglee, D. (2018). Internet of Things in Asset Management: Insights from Industrial Professionals and Academia. *International Journal of Service Science, Management, Engineering, and Technology*, 9(2), 104–119. doi:10.4018/IJSSMET.2018040105

Klein, A. Z., Sabino de Freitas, A., Machado, L., Freitas, J. C. Jr, Graziola, P. G. Jr, & Schlemmer, E. (2017). Virtual Worlds Applications for Management Education. In L. Tomei (Ed.), *Exploring the New Era of Technology-Infused Education* (pp. 279–299). Hershey, PA: IGI Global. doi:10.4018/978-1-5225-1709-2.ch017

Kożuch, B., & Jabłoński, A. (2017). Adopting the Concept of Business Models in Public Management. In M. Lewandowski & B. Kożuch (Eds.), *Public Sector Entrepreneurship and the Integration of Innovative Business Models* (pp. 10–46). Hershey, PA: IGI Global. doi:10.4018/978-1-5225-2215-7.ch002

Kumar, J., Adhikary, A., & Jha, A. (2017). Small Active Investors' Perceptions and Preferences Towards Tax Saving Mutual Fund Schemes in Eastern India: An Empirical Note. *International Journal of Asian Business and Information Management*, 8(2), 35–45. doi:10.4018/IJABIM.2017040103

Lassoued, Y., Bouzguenda, L., & Mahmoud, T. (2016). Context-Aware Business Process Versions Management. *International Journal of e-Collaboration*, 12(3), 7–33. doi:10.4018/IJeC.2016070102

Lavassani, K. M., & Movahedi, B. (2017). Applications Driven Information Systems: Beyond Networks toward Business Ecosystems. *International Journal of Innovation in the Digital Economy*, 8(1), 61–75. doi:10.4018/IJIDE.2017010104

Lazzareschi, V. H., & Brito, M. S. (2017). Strategic Information Management: Proposal of Business Project Model. In G. Jamil, A. Soares, & C. Pessoa (Eds.), *Handbook of Research on Information Management for Effective Logistics and Supply Chains* (pp. 59–88). Hershey, PA: IGI Global. doi:10.4018/978-1-5225-0973-8.ch004

Lederer, M., Kurz, M., & Lazarov, P. (2017). Usage and Suitability of Methods for Strategic Business Process Initiatives: A Multi Case Study Research. *International Journal of Productivity Management and Assessment Technologies*, 5(1), 40–51. doi:10.4018/IJPMAT.2017010103

Lee, I. (2017). A Social Enterprise Business Model and a Case Study of Pacific Community Ventures (PCV). In V. Potocan, M. Üngan, & Z. Nedelko (Eds.), *Handbook of Research on Managerial Solutions in Non-Profit Organizations* (pp. 182–204). Hershey, PA: IGI Global. doi:10.4018/978-1-5225-0731-4. ch009

Lee, L. J., & Leu, J. (2016). Exploring the Effectiveness of IT Application and Value Method in the Innovation Performance of Enterprise. *International Journal of Enterprise Information Systems*, 12(2), 47–65. doi:10.4018/IJEIS.2016040104

Lee, Y. (2016). Alignment Effect of Entrepreneurial Orientation and Marketing Orientation on Firm Performance. *International Journal of Customer Relationship Marketing and Management*, 7(4), 58–69. doi:10.4018/IJCRMM.2016100104

Leon, L. A., Seal, K. C., Przasnyski, Z. H., & Wiedenman, I. (2017). Skills and Competencies Required for Jobs in Business Analytics: A Content Analysis of Job Advertisements Using Text Mining. *International Journal of Business Intelligence Research*, 8(1), 1–25. doi:10.4018/IJBIR.2017010101

Leu, J., Lee, L. J., & Krischke, A. (2016). Value Engineering-Based Method for Implementing the ISO14001 System in the Green Supply Chains. *International Journal of Strategic Decision Sciences*, 7(4), 1–20. doi:10.4018/IJSDS.2016100101

Levy, C. L., & Elias, N. I. (2017). SOHO Users' Perceptions of Reliability and Continuity of Cloud-Based Services. In M. Moore (Ed.), *Cybersecurity Breaches and Issues Surrounding Online Threat Protection* (pp. 248–287). Hershey, PA: IGI Global. doi:10.4018/978-1-5225-1941-6.ch011

Levy, M. (2018). Change Management Serving Knowledge Management and Organizational Development: Reflections and Review. In N. Baporikar (Ed.), *Global Practices in Knowledge Management for Societal and Organizational Development* (pp. 256–270). Hershey, PA: IGI Global. doi:10.4018/978-1-5225-3009-1.ch012

Lewandowski, M. (2017). Public Organizations and Business Model Innovation: The Role of Public Service Design. In M. Lewandowski & B. Kożuch (Eds.), *Public Sector Entrepreneurship and the Integration of Innovative Business Models* (pp. 47–72). Hershey, PA: IGI Global. doi:10.4018/978-1-5225-2215-7.ch003

Lhannaoui, H., Kabbaj, M. I., & Bakkoury, Z. (2017). A Survey of Risk-Aware Business Process Modelling. *International Journal of Risk and Contingency Management*, 6(3), 14–26. doi:10.4018/IJRCM.2017070102

Li, J., Sun, W., Jiang, W., Yang, H., & Zhang, L. (2017). How the Nature of Exogenous Shocks and Crises Impact Company Performance?: The Effects of Industry Characteristics. *International Journal of Risk and Contingency Management*, 6(4), 40–55. doi:10.4018/IJRCM.2017100103

Lu, C., & Liu, S. (2016). Cultural Tourism O2O Business Model Innovation-A Case Study of CTrip. *Journal of Electronic Commerce in Organizations, 14*(2), 16–31. doi:10.4018/JECO.2016040102

Machen, B., Hosseini, M. R., Wood, A., & Bakhshi, J. (2016). An Investigation into using SAP-PS as a Multidimensional Project Control System (MPCS). *International Journal of Enterprise Information Systems, 12*(2), 66–81. doi:10.4018/IJEIS.2016040105

Malega, P. (2017). Small and Medium Enterprises in the Slovak Republic: Status and Competitiveness of SMEs in the Global Markets and Possibilities of Optimization. In M. Vemić (Ed.), *Optimal Management Strategies in Small and Medium Enterprises* (pp. 102–124). Hershey, PA: IGI Global. doi:10.4018/978-1-5225-1949-2.ch006

Malewska, K. M. (2017). Intuition in Decision-Making on the Example of a Non-Profit Organization. In V. Potocan, M. Üngan, & Z. Nedelko (Eds.), *Handbook of Research on Managerial Solutions in Non-Profit Organizations* (pp. 378–399). Hershey, PA: IGI Global. doi:10.4018/978-1-5225-0731-4.ch018

Maroofi, F. (2017). Entrepreneurial Orientation and Organizational Learning Ability Analysis for Innovation and Firm Performance. In N. Baporikar (Ed.), *Innovation and Shifting Perspectives in Management Education* (pp. 144–165). Hershey, PA: IGI Global. doi:10.4018/978-1-5225-1019-2.ch007

Martins, P. V., & Zacarias, M. (2017). A Web-based Tool for Business Process Improvement. *International Journal of Web Portals, 9*(2), 68–84. doi:10.4018/IJWP.2017070104

Matthies, B., & Coners, A. (2017). Exploring the Conceptual Nature of e-Business Projects. *Journal of Electronic Commerce in Organizations, 15*(3), 33–63. doi:10.4018/JECO.2017070103

McKee, J. (2018). Architecture as a Tool to Solve Business Planning Problems. In M. Khosrow-Pour, D.B.A. (Ed.), Encyclopedia of Information Science and Technology, Fourth Edition (pp. 573-586). Hershey, PA: IGI Global. doi:10.4018/978-1-5225-2255-3.ch050

McMurray, A. J., Cross, J., & Caponecchia, C. (2018). The Risk Management Profession in Australia: Business Continuity Plan Practices. In N. Bajgoric (Ed.), *Always-On Enterprise Information Systems for Modern Organizations* (pp. 112–129). Hershey, PA: IGI Global. doi:10.4018/978-1-5225-3704-5.ch006

Meddah, I. H., & Belkadi, K. (2018). Mining Patterns Using Business Process Management. In R. Hamou (Ed.), *Handbook of Research on Biomimicry in Information Retrieval and Knowledge Management* (pp. 78–89). Hershey, PA: IGI Global. doi:10.4018/978-1-5225-3004-6.ch005

Mendes, L. (2017). TQM and Knowledge Management: An Integrated Approach Towards Tacit Knowledge Management. In D. Jaziri-Bouagina & G. Jamil (Eds.), *Handbook of Research on Tacit Knowledge Management for Organizational Success* (pp. 236–263). Hershey, PA: IGI Global. doi:10.4018/978-1-5225-2394-9.ch009

Mnjama, N. M. (2017). Preservation of Recorded Information in Public and Private Sector Organizations. In P. Jain & N. Mnjama (Eds.), *Managing Knowledge Resources and Records in Modern Organizations* (pp. 149–167). Hershey, PA: IGI Global. doi:10.4018/978-1-5225-1965-2.ch009

Mokoqama, M., & Fields, Z. (2017). Principles of Responsible Management Education (PRME): Call for Responsible Management Education. In Z. Fields (Ed.), *Collective Creativity for Responsible and Sustainable Business Practice* (pp. 229–241). Hershey, PA: IGI Global. doi:10.4018/978-1-5225-1823-5.ch012

Muniapan, B. (2017). Philosophy and Management: The Relevance of Vedanta in Management. In P. Ordóñez de Pablos (Ed.), *Managerial Strategies and Solutions for Business Success in Asia* (pp. 124–139). Hershey, PA: IGI Global. doi:10.4018/978-1-5225-1886-0.ch007

Muniapan, B., Gregory, M. L., & Ling, L. A. (2016). Marketing Education in Sarawak: Looking at It from the Employers' Viewpoint. In B. Smith & A. Porath (Eds.), *Global Perspectives on Contemporary Marketing Education* (pp. 112–130). Hershey, PA: IGI Global. doi:10.4018/978-1-4666-9784-3.ch008

Murad, S. E., & Dowaji, S. (2017). Using Value-Based Approach for Managing Cloud-Based Services. In A. Turuk, B. Sahoo, & S. Addya (Eds.), *Resource Management and Efficiency in Cloud Computing Environments* (pp. 33–60). Hershey, PA: IGI Global. doi:10.4018/978-1-5225-1721-4.ch002

Mutahar, A. M., Daud, N. M., Thurasamy, R., Isaac, O., & Abdulsalam, R. (2018). The Mediating of Perceived Usefulness and Perceived Ease of Use: The Case of Mobile Banking in Yemen. *International Journal of Technology Diffusion*, 9(2), 21–40. doi:10.4018/IJTD.2018040102

Naidoo, V. (2017). E-Learning and Management Education at African Universities. In N. Baporikar (Ed.), *Management Education for Global Leadership* (pp. 181–201). Hershey, PA: IGI Global. doi:10.4018/978-1-5225-1013-0.ch009

Naidoo, V., & Igbinakhase, I. (2018). Opportunities and Challenges of Knowledge Retention in SMEs. In N. Baporikar (Ed.), *Knowledge Integration Strategies for Entrepreneurship and Sustainability* (pp. 70–94). Hershey, PA: IGI Global. doi:10.4018/978-1-5225-5115-7.ch004

Nayak, S., & Prabhu, N. (2017). Paradigm Shift in Management Education: Need for a Cross Functional Perspective. In N. Baporikar (Ed.), *Management Education for Global Leadership* (pp. 241–255). Hershey, PA: IGI Global. doi:10.4018/978-1-5225-1013-0.ch012

Ndede-Amadi, A. A. (2016). Student Interest in the IS Specialization as Predictor of the Success Potential of New Information Systems Programmes within the Schools of Business in Kenyan Public Universities. *International Journal of Information Systems and Social Change*, 7(2), 63–79. doi:10.4018/IJISSC.2016040104

Nedelko, Z., & Potocan, V. (2016). Management Practices for Processes Optimization: Case of Slovenia. In G. Alor-Hernández, C. Sánchez-Ramírez, & J. García-Alcaraz (Eds.), *Handbook of Research on Managerial Strategies for Achieving Optimal Performance in Industrial Processes* (pp. 545–561). Hershey, PA: IGI Global. doi:10.4018/978-1-5225-0130-5.ch025

Nedelko, Z., & Potocan, V. (2017). Management Solutions in Non-Profit Organizations: Case of Slovenia. In V. Potocan, M. Üngan, & Z. Nedelko (Eds.), *Handbook of Research on Managerial Solutions in Non-Profit Organizations* (pp. 1–22). Hershey, PA: IGI Global. doi:10.4018/978-1-5225-0731-4.ch001

Nedelko, Z., & Potocan, V. (2017). Priority of Management Tools Utilization among Managers: International Comparison. In V. Wang (Ed.), *Encyclopedia of Strategic Leadership and Management* (pp. 1083–1094). Hershey, PA: IGI Global. doi:10.4018/978-1-5225-1049-9.ch075

Nedelko, Z., Raudeliūnienė, J., & Črešnar, R. (2018). Knowledge Dynamics in Supply Chain Management. In N. Baporikar (Ed.), *Knowledge Integration Strategies for Entrepreneurship and Sustainability* (pp. 150–166). Hershey, PA: IGI Global. doi:10.4018/978-1-5225-5115-7.ch008

Nguyen, H. T., & Hipsher, S. A. (2018). Innovation and Creativity Used by Private Sector Firms in a Resources-Constrained Environment. In S. Hipsher (Ed.), *Examining the Private Sector's Role in Wealth Creation and Poverty Reduction* (pp. 219–238). Hershey, PA: IGI Global. doi:10.4018/978-1-5225-3117-3.ch010

Nycz, M., & Pólkowski, Z. (2016). Business Intelligence as a Modern IT Supporting Management of Local Government Units in Poland. *International Journal of Knowledge and Systems Science*, *7*(4), 1–18. doi:10.4018/IJKSS.2016100101

Obaji, N. O., Senin, A. A., & Olugu, M. U. (2016). Supportive Government Policy as a Mechanism for Business Incubation Performance in Nigeria. *International Journal of Information Systems and Social Change*, *7*(4), 52–66. doi:10.4018/IJISSC.2016100103

Obicci, P. A. (2017). Risk Sharing in a Partnership. In *Risk Management Strategies in Public-Private Partnerships* (pp. 115–152). Hershey, PA: IGI Global. doi:10.4018/978-1-5225-2503-5.ch004

Obidallah, W. J., & Raahemi, B. (2017). Managing Changes in Service Oriented Virtual Organizations: A Structural and Procedural Framework to Facilitate the Process of Change. *Journal of Electronic Commerce in Organizations*, *15*(1), 59–83. doi:10.4018/JECO.2017010104

Ojasalo, J., & Ojasalo, K. (2016). Service Logic Business Model Canvas for Lean Development of SMEs and Start-Ups. In N. Baporikar (Ed.), *Handbook of Research on Entrepreneurship in the Contemporary Knowledge-Based Global Economy* (pp. 217–243). Hershey, PA: IGI Global. doi:10.4018/978-1-4666-8798-1.ch010

Ojo, O. (2017). Impact of Innovation on the Entrepreneurial Success in Selected Business Enterprises in South-West Nigeria. *International Journal of Innovation in the Digital Economy*, *8*(2), 29–38. doi:10.4018/IJIDE.2017040103

Okdinawati, L., Simatupang, T. M., & Sunitiyoso, Y. (2017). Multi-Agent Reinforcement Learning for Value Co-Creation of Collaborative Transportation Management (CTM). *International Journal of Information Systems and Supply Chain Management*, *10*(3), 84–95. doi:10.4018/IJISSCM.2017070105

Ortner, E., Mevius, M., Wiedmann, P., & Kurz, F. (2016). Design of Interactional Decision Support Applications for E-Participation in Smart Cities. *International Journal of Electronic Government Research*, *12*(2), 18–38. doi:10.4018/IJEGR.2016040102

Pal, K. (2018). Building High Quality Big Data-Based Applications in Supply Chains. In A. Kumar & S. Saurav (Eds.), *Supply Chain Management Strategies and Risk Assessment in Retail Environments* (pp. 1–24). Hershey, PA: IGI Global. doi:10.4018/978-1-5225-3056-5.ch001

Palos-Sanchez, P. R., & Correia, M. B. (2018). Perspectives of the Adoption of Cloud Computing in the Tourism Sector. In J. Rodrigues, C. Ramos, P. Cardoso, & C. Henriques (Eds.), *Handbook of Research on Technological Developments for Cultural Heritage and eTourism Applications* (pp. 377–400). Hershey, PA: IGI Global. doi:10.4018/978-1-5225-2927-9.ch018

Parry, V. K., & Lind, M. L. (2016). Alignment of Business Strategy and Information Technology Considering Information Technology Governance, Project Portfolio Control, and Risk Management. *International Journal of Information Technology Project Management*, 7(4), 21–37. doi:10.4018/IJITPM.2016100102

Pashkova, N., Trujillo-Barrera, A., Apostolakis, G., Van Dijk, G., Drakos, P. D., & Baourakis, G. (2016). Business Management Models of Microfinance Institutions (MFIs) in Africa: A Study into Their Enabling Environments. *International Journal of Food and Beverage Manufacturing and Business Models*, 1(2), 63–82. doi:10.4018/IJFBMBM.2016070105

Patiño, B. E. (2017). New Generation Management by Convergence and Individual Identity: A Systemic and Human-Oriented Approach. In N. Baporikar (Ed.), *Innovation and Shifting Perspectives in Management Education* (pp. 119–143). Hershey, PA: IGI Global. doi:10.4018/978-1-5225-1019-2.ch006

Pawliczek, A., & Rössler, M. (2017). Knowledge of Management Tools and Systems in SMEs: Knowledge Transfer in Management. In A. Bencsik (Ed.), *Knowledge Management Initiatives and Strategies in Small and Medium Enterprises* (pp. 180–203). Hershey, PA: IGI Global. doi:10.4018/978-1-5225-1642-2.ch009

Pejic-Bach, M., Omazic, M. A., Aleksic, A., & Zoroja, J. (2018). Knowledge-Based Decision Making: A Multi-Case Analysis. In R. Leon (Ed.), *Managerial Strategies for Business Sustainability During Turbulent Times* (pp. 160–184). Hershey, PA: IGI Global. doi:10.4018/978-1-5225-2716-9.ch009

Perano, M., Hysa, X., & Calabrese, M. (2018). Strategic Planning, Cultural Context, and Business Continuity Management: Business Cases in the City of Shkoder. In A. Presenza & L. Sheehan (Eds.), *Geopolitics and Strategic Management in the Global Economy* (pp. 57–77). Hershey, PA: IGI Global. doi:10.4018/978-1-5225-2673-5.ch004

Pereira, R., Mira da Silva, M., & Lapão, L. V. (2017). IT Governance Maturity Patterns in Portuguese Healthcare. In S. De Haes & W. Van Grembergen (Eds.), *Strategic IT Governance and Alignment in Business Settings* (pp. 24–52). Hershey, PA: IGI Global. doi:10.4018/978-1-5225-0861-8.ch002

Perez-Uribe, R., & Ocampo-Guzman, D. (2016). Conflict within Colombian Family Owned SMEs: An Explosive Blend between Feelings and Business. In J. Saiz-Álvarez (Ed.), *Handbook of Research on Social Entrepreneurship and Solidarity Economics* (pp. 329–354). Hershey, PA: IGI Global. doi:10.4018/978-1-5225-0097-1.ch017

Pérez-Uribe, R. I., Torres, D. A., Jurado, S. P., & Prada, D. M. (2018). Cloud Tools for the Development of Project Management in SMEs. In R. Perez-Uribe, C. Salcedo-Perez, & D. Ocampo-Guzman (Eds.), *Handbook of Research on Intrapreneurship and Organizational Sustainability in SMEs* (pp. 95–120). Hershey, PA: IGI Global. doi:10.4018/978-1-5225-3543-0.ch005

Petrisor, I., & Cozmiuc, D. (2017). Global Supply Chain Management Organization at Siemens in the Advent of Industry 4.0. In L. Saglietto & C. Cezanne (Eds.), *Global Intermediation and Logistics Service Providers* (pp. 123–142). Hershey, PA: IGI Global. doi:10.4018/978-1-5225-2133-4.ch007

Pierce, J. M., Velliaris, D. M., & Edwards, J. (2017). A Living Case Study: A Journey Not a Destination. In N. Silton (Ed.), *Exploring the Benefits of Creativity in Education, Media, and the Arts* (pp. 158–178). Hershey, PA: IGI Global. doi:10.4018/978-1-5225-0504-4.ch008

Radosavljevic, M., & Andjelkovic, A. (2017). Multi-Criteria Decision Making Approach for Choosing Business Process for the Improvement: Upgrading of the Six Sigma Methodology. In J. Stanković, P. Delias, S. Marinković, & S. Rochhia (Eds.), *Tools and Techniques for Economic Decision Analysis* (pp. 225–247). Hershey, PA: IGI Global. doi:10.4018/978-1-5225-0959-2.ch011

Radovic, V. M. (2017). Corporate Sustainability and Responsibility and Disaster Risk Reduction: A Serbian Overview. In M. Camilleri (Ed.), *CSR 2.0 and the New Era of Corporate Citizenship* (pp. 147–164). Hershey, PA: IGI Global. doi:10.4018/978-1-5225-1842-6.ch008

Raghunath, K. M., Devi, S. L., & Patro, C. S. (2018). Impact of Risk Assessment Models on Risk Factors: A Holistic Outlook. In K. Strang, M. Korstanje, & N. Vajjhala (Eds.), *Research, Practices, and Innovations in Global Risk and Contingency Management* (pp. 134–153). Hershey, PA: IGI Global. doi:10.4018/978-1-5225-4754-9.ch008

Raman, A., & Goyal, D. P. (2017). Extending IMPLEMENT Framework for Enterprise Information Systems Implementation to Information System Innovation. In M. Tavana (Ed.), *Enterprise Information Systems and the Digitalization of Business Functions* (pp. 137–177). Hershey, PA: IGI Global. doi:10.4018/978-1-5225-2382-6.ch007

Rao, Y., & Zhang, Y. (2017). The Construction and Development of Academic Library Digital Special Subject Databases. In L. Ruan, Q. Zhu, & Y. Ye (Eds.), *Academic Library Development and Administration in China* (pp. 163–183). Hershey, PA: IGI Global. doi:10.4018/978-1-5225-0550-1.ch010

Ravasan, A. Z., Mohammadi, M. M., & Hamidi, H. (2018). An Investigation Into the Critical Success Factors of Implementing Information Technology Service Management Frameworks. In K. Jakobs (Ed.), *Corporate and Global Standardization Initiatives in Contemporary Society* (pp. 200–218). Hershey, PA: IGI Global. doi:10.4018/978-1-5225-5320-5.ch009

Renna, P., Izzo, C., & Romaniello, T. (2016). The Business Process Management Systems to Support Continuous Improvements. In W. Nuninger & J. Châtelet (Eds.), *Handbook of Research on Quality Assurance and Value Management in Higher Education* (pp. 237–256). Hershey, PA: IGI Global. doi:10.4018/978-1-5225-0024-7.ch009

Rezaie, S., Mirabedini, S. J., & Abtahi, A. (2018). Designing a Model for Implementation of Business Intelligence in the Banking Industry. *International Journal of Enterprise Information Systems*, *14*(1), 77–103. doi:10.4018/IJEIS.2018010105

Riccò, R. (2016). Diversity Management: Bringing Equality, Equity, and Inclusion in the Workplace. In J. Prescott (Ed.), *Handbook of Research on Race, Gender, and the Fight for Equality* (pp. 335–359). Hershey, PA: IGI Global. doi:10.4018/978-1-5225-0047-6.ch015

Romano, L., Grimaldi, R., & Colasuonno, F. S. (2017). Demand Management as a Success Factor in Project Portfolio Management. In L. Romano (Ed.), *Project Portfolio Management Strategies for Effective Organizational Operations* (pp. 202–219). Hershey, PA: IGI Global. doi:10.4018/978-1-5225-2151-8.ch008

Rostek, K. B. (2016). Risk Management: Role and Importance in Business Organization. In D. Jakóbczak (Ed.), *Analyzing Risk through Probabilistic Modeling in Operations Research* (pp. 149–178). Hershey, PA: IGI Global. doi:10.4018/978-1-4666-9458-3.ch007

Rouhani, S., & Savoji, S. R. (2016). A Success Assessment Model for BI Tools Implementation: An Empirical Study of Banking Industry. *International Journal of Business Intelligence Research*, *7*(1), 25–44. doi:10.4018/IJBIR.2016010103

Ruan, Z. (2016). A Corpus-Based Functional Analysis of Complex Nominal Groups in Written Business Discourse: The Case of "Business". *International Journal of Computer-Assisted Language Learning and Teaching*, *6*(2), 74–90. doi:10.4018/IJCALLT.2016040105

Ruhi, U. (2018). Towards an Interdisciplinary Socio-Technical Definition of Virtual Communities. In M. Khosrow-Pour, D.B.A. (Ed.), Encyclopedia of Information Science and Technology, Fourth Edition (pp. 4278-4295). Hershey, PA: IGI Global. doi:10.4018/978-1-5225-2255-3.ch371

Ryan, J., Doster, B., Daily, S., & Lewis, C. (2016). A Case Study Perspective for Balanced Perioperative Workflow Achievement through Data-Driven Process Improvement. *International Journal of Healthcare Information Systems and Informatics*, *11*(3), 19–41. doi:10.4018/IJHISI.2016070102

Safari, M. R., & Jiang, Q. (2018). The Theory and Practice of IT Governance Maturity and Strategies Alignment: Evidence From Banking Industry. *Journal of Global Information Management*, *26*(2), 127–146. doi:10.4018/JGIM.2018040106

Sahoo, J., Pati, B., & Mohanty, B. (2017). Knowledge Management as an Academic Discipline: An Assessment. In B. Gunjal (Ed.), *Managing Knowledge and Scholarly Assets in Academic Libraries* (pp. 99–126). Hershey, PA: IGI Global. doi:10.4018/978-1-5225-1741-2.ch005

Saini, D. (2017). Relevance of Teaching Values and Ethics in Management Education. In N. Baporikar (Ed.), *Management Education for Global Leadership* (pp. 90–111). Hershey, PA: IGI Global. doi:10.4018/978-1-5225-1013-0.ch005

Sambhanthan, A. (2017). Assessing and Benchmarking Sustainability in Organisations: An Integrated Conceptual Model. *International Journal of Systems and Service-Oriented Engineering*, 7(4), 22–43. doi:10.4018/IJSSOE.2017100102

Sambhanthan, A., & Potdar, V. (2017). A Study of the Parameters Impacting Sustainability in Information Technology Organizations. *International Journal of Knowledge-Based Organizations*, 7(3), 27–39. doi:10.4018/IJKBO.2017070103

Sánchez-Fernández, M. D., & Manríquez, M. R. (2018). The Entrepreneurial Spirit Based on Social Values: The Digital Generation. In P. Isaias & L. Carvalho (Eds.), *User Innovation and the Entrepreneurship Phenomenon in the Digital Economy* (pp. 173–193). Hershey, PA: IGI Global. doi:10.4018/978-1-5225-2826-5.ch009

Sanchez-Ruiz, L., & Blanco, B. (2017). Process Management for SMEs: Barriers, Enablers, and Benefits. In M. Vemić (Ed.), *Optimal Management Strategies in Small and Medium Enterprises* (pp. 293–319). Hershey, PA: IGI Global. doi:10.4018/978-1-5225-1949-2.ch014

Sanz, L. F., Gómez-Pérez, J., & Castillo-Martinez, A. (2018). Analysis of the European ICT Competence Frameworks. In V. Ahuja & S. Rathore (Eds.), *Multidisciplinary Perspectives on Human Capital and Information Technology Professionals* (pp. 225–245). Hershey, PA: IGI Global. doi:10.4018/978-1-5225-5297-0.ch012

Sarvepalli, A., & Godin, J. (2017). Business Process Management in the Classroom. *Journal of Cases on Information Technology*, 19(2), 17–28. doi:10.4018/JCIT.2017040102

Satpathy, B., & Muniapan, B. (2016). Ancient Wisdom for Transformational Leadership and Its Insights from the Bhagavad-Gita. In U. Aung & P. Ordoñez de Pablos (Eds.), *Managerial Strategies and Practice in the Asian Business Sector* (pp. 1–10). Hershey, PA: IGI Global. doi:10.4018/978-1-4666-9758-4.ch001

Saygili, E. E., Ozturkoglu, Y., & Kocakulah, M. C. (2017). End Users' Perceptions of Critical Success Factors in ERP Applications. *International Journal of Enterprise Information Systems*, 13(4), 58–75. doi:10.4018/IJEIS.2017100104

Saygili, E. E., & Saygili, A. T. (2017). Contemporary Issues in Enterprise Information Systems: A Critical Review of CSFs in ERP Implementations. In M. Tavana (Ed.), *Enterprise Information Systems and the Digitalization of Business Functions* (pp. 120–136). Hershey, PA: IGI Global. doi:10.4018/978-1-5225-2382-6.ch006

Seidenstricker, S., & Antonino, A. (2018). Business Model Innovation-Oriented Technology Management for Emergent Technologies. In M. Khosrow-Pour, D.B.A. (Ed.), Encyclopedia of Information Science and Technology, Fourth Edition (pp. 4560-4569). Hershey, PA: IGI Global. doi:10.4018/978-1-5225-2255-3.ch396

Senaratne, S., & Gunarathne, A. D. (2017). Excellence Perspective for Management Education from a Global Accountants' Hub in Asia. In N. Baporikar (Ed.), *Management Education for Global Leadership* (pp. 158–180). Hershey, PA: IGI Global. doi:10.4018/978-1-5225-1013-0.ch008

Sensuse, D. I., & Cahyaningsih, E. (2018). Knowledge Management Models: A Summative Review. *International Journal of Information Systems in the Service Sector*, *10*(1), 71–100. doi:10.4018/IJISSS.2018010105

Sensuse, D. I., Wibowo, W. C., & Cahyaningsih, E. (2016). Indonesian Government Knowledge Management Model: A Theoretical Model. *Information Resources Management Journal*, *29*(1), 91–108. doi:10.4018/irmj.2016010106

Seth, M., Goyal, D., & Kiran, R. (2017). Diminution of Impediments in Implementation of Supply Chain Management Information System for Enhancing its Effectiveness in Indian Automobile Industry. *Journal of Global Information Management*, *25*(3), 1–20. doi:10.4018/JGIM.2017070101

Seyal, A. H., & Rahman, M. N. (2017). Investigating Impact of Inter-Organizational Factors in Measuring ERP Systems Success: Bruneian Perspectives. In M. Tavana (Ed.), *Enterprise Information Systems and the Digitalization of Business Functions* (pp. 178–204). Hershey, PA: IGI Global. doi:10.4018/978-1-5225-2382-6.ch008

Shaikh, A. A., & Karjaluoto, H. (2016). On Some Misconceptions Concerning Digital Banking and Alternative Delivery Channels. *International Journal of E-Business Research*, *12*(3), 1–16. doi:10.4018/IJEBR.2016070101

Shams, S. M. (2016). Stakeholder Relationship Management in Online Business and Competitive Value Propositions: Evidence from the Sports Industry. *International Journal of Online Marketing*, *6*(2), 1–17. doi:10.4018/IJOM.2016040101

Shamsuzzoha, A. (2016). Management of Risk and Resilience within Collaborative Business Network. In R. Addo-Tenkorang, J. Kantola, P. Helo, & A. Shamsuzzoha (Eds.), *Supply Chain Strategies and the Engineer-to-Order Approach* (pp. 143–159). Hershey, PA: IGI Global. doi:10.4018/978-1-5225-0021-6.ch008

Shaqrah, A. A. (2018). Analyzing Business Intelligence Systems Based on 7s Model of McKinsey. *International Journal of Business Intelligence Research*, *9*(1), 53–63. doi:10.4018/IJBIR.2018010104

Sharma, A. J. (2017). Enhancing Sustainability through Experiential Learning in Management Education. In N. Baporikar (Ed.), *Management Education for Global Leadership* (pp. 256–274). Hershey, PA: IGI Global. doi:10.4018/978-1-5225-1013-0.ch013

Shetty, K. P. (2017). Responsible Global Leadership: Ethical Challenges in Management Education. In N. Baporikar (Ed.), *Innovation and Shifting Perspectives in Management Education* (pp. 194–223). Hershey, PA: IGI Global. doi:10.4018/978-1-5225-1019-2.ch009

Sinthupundaja, J., & Kohda, Y. (2017). Effects of Corporate Social Responsibility and Creating Shared Value on Sustainability. *International Journal of Sustainable Entrepreneurship and Corporate Social Responsibility*, 2(1), 27–38. doi:10.4018/IJSECSR.2017010103

Škarica, I., & Hrgović, A. V. (2018). Implementation of Total Quality Management Principles in Public Health Institutes in the Republic of Croatia. *International Journal of Productivity Management and Assessment Technologies*, 6(1), 1–16. doi:10.4018/IJPMAT.2018010101

Smuts, H., Kotzé, P., Van der Merwe, A., & Loock, M. (2017). Framework for Managing Shared Knowledge in an Information Systems Outsourcing Context. *International Journal of Knowledge Management*, 13(4), 1–30. doi:10.4018/IJKM.2017100101

Soares, E. R., & Zaidan, F. H. (2016). Information Architecture and Business Modeling in Modern Organizations of Information Technology: Professional Career Plan in Organizations IT. In G. Jamil, J. Poças Rascão, F. Ribeiro, & A. Malheiro da Silva (Eds.), *Handbook of Research on Information Architecture and Management in Modern Organizations* (pp. 439–457). Hershey, PA: IGI Global. doi:10.4018/978-1-4666-8637-3.ch020

Sousa, M. J., Cruz, R., Dias, I., & Caracol, C. (2017). Information Management Systems in the Supply Chain. In G. Jamil, A. Soares, & C. Pessoa (Eds.), *Handbook of Research on Information Management for Effective Logistics and Supply Chains* (pp. 469–485). Hershey, PA: IGI Global. doi:10.4018/978-1-5225-0973-8.ch025

Spremic, M., Turulja, L., & Bajgoric, N. (2018). Two Approaches in Assessing Business Continuity Management Attitudes in the Organizational Context. In N. Bajgoric (Ed.), *Always-On Enterprise Information Systems for Modern Organizations* (pp. 159–183). Hershey, PA: IGI Global. doi:10.4018/978-1-5225-3704-5.ch008

Steenkamp, A. L. (2018). Some Insights in Computer Science and Information Technology. In *Examining the Changing Role of Supervision in Doctoral Research Projects: Emerging Research and Opportunities* (pp. 113–133). Hershey, PA: IGI Global. doi:10.4018/978-1-5225-2610-0.ch005

Studdard, N., Dawson, M., Burton, S. L., Jackson, N., Leonard, B., Quisenberry, W., & Rahim, E. (2016). Nurturing Social Entrepreneurship and Building Social Entrepreneurial Self-Efficacy: Focusing on Primary and Secondary Schooling to Develop Future Social Entrepreneurs. In Z. Fields (Ed.), *Incorporating Business Models and Strategies into Social Entrepreneurship* (pp. 154–175). Hershey, PA: IGI Global. doi:10.4018/978-1-4666-8748-6.ch010

Sun, Z. (2016). A Framework for Developing Management Intelligent Systems. *International Journal of Systems and Service-Oriented Engineering, 6*(1), 37–53. doi:10.4018/IJSSOE.2016010103

Swami, B., & Mphele, G. T. (2016). Problems Preventing Growth of Small Entrepreneurs: A Case Study of a Few Small Entrepreneurs in Botswana Sub-Urban Areas. In N. Baporikar (Ed.), *Handbook of Research on Entrepreneurship in the Contemporary Knowledge-Based Global Economy* (pp. 479–508). Hershey, PA: IGI Global. doi:10.4018/978-1-4666-8798-1.ch020

Tabach, A., & Croteau, A. (2017). Configurations of Information Technology Governance Practices and Business Unit Performance. *International Journal of IT/Business Alignment and Governance, 8*(2), 1–27. doi:10.4018/IJITBAG.2017070101

Talaue, G. M., & Iqbal, T. (2017). Assessment of e-Business Mode of Selected Private Universities in the Philippines and Pakistan. *International Journal of Online Marketing, 7*(4), 63–77. doi:10.4018/IJOM.2017100105

Tam, G. C. (2017). Project Manager Sustainability Competence. In *Managerial Strategies and Green Solutions for Project Sustainability* (pp. 178–207). Hershey, PA: IGI Global. doi:10.4018/978-1-5225-2371-0.ch008

Tambo, T. (2018). Fashion Retail Innovation: About Context, Antecedents, and Outcome in Technological Change Projects. In I. Management Association (Ed.), Fashion and Textiles: Breakthroughs in Research and Practice (pp. 233-260). Hershey, PA: IGI Global. doi:10.4018/978-1-5225-3432-7.ch010

Tambo, T., & Mikkelsen, O. E. (2016). Fashion Supply Chain Optimization: Linking Make-to-Order Purchasing and B2B E-Commerce. In S. Joshi & R. Joshi (Eds.), *Designing and Implementing Global Supply Chain Management* (pp. 1–21). Hershey, PA: IGI Global. doi:10.4018/978-1-4666-9720-1.ch001

Tandon, K. (2016). Innovative Andragogy: The Paradigm Shift to Heutagogy. In S. Tiwari & L. Nafees (Eds.), *Innovative Management Education Pedagogies for Preparing Next-Generation Leaders* (pp. 238–257). Hershey, PA: IGI Global. doi:10.4018/978-1-4666-9691-4.ch014

Tantau, A. D., & Frăţilă, L. C. (2018). Information and Management System for Renewable Energy Business. In *Entrepreneurship and Business Development in the Renewable Energy Sector* (pp. 200–244). Hershey, PA: IGI Global. doi:10.4018/978-1-5225-3625-3.ch006

Teixeira, N., Pardal, P. N., & Rafael, B. G. (2018). Internationalization, Financial Performance, and Organizational Challenges: A Success Case in Portugal. In L. Carvalho (Ed.), *Handbook of Research on Entrepreneurial Ecosystems and Social Dynamics in a Globalized World* (pp. 379–423). Hershey, PA: IGI Global. doi:10.4018/978-1-5225-3525-6.ch017

Trad, A., & Kalpić, D. (2016). The E-Business Transformation Framework for E-Commerce Architecture-Modeling Projects. In I. Lee (Ed.), *Encyclopedia of E-Commerce Development, Implementation, and Management* (pp. 733–753). Hershey, PA: IGI Global. doi:10.4018/978-1-4666-9787-4.ch052

Trad, A., & Kalpić, D. (2016). The E-Business Transformation Framework for E-Commerce Control and Monitoring Pattern. In I. Lee (Ed.), *Encyclopedia of E-Commerce Development, Implementation, and Management* (pp. 754–777). Hershey, PA: IGI Global. doi:10.4018/978-1-4666-9787-4.ch053

Trad, A., & Kalpić, D. (2018). The Business Transformation Framework, Agile Project and Change Management. In M. Khosrow-Pour, D.B.A. (Ed.), Encyclopedia of Information Science and Technology, Fourth Edition (pp. 620-635). Hershey, PA: IGI Global. doi:10.4018/978-1-5225-2255-3.ch054

Trad, A., & Kalpić, D. (2018). The Business Transformation and Enterprise Architecture Framework: The Financial Engineering E-Risk Management and E-Law Integration. In B. Sergi, F. Fidanoski, M. Ziolo, & V. Naumovski (Eds.), *Regaining Global Stability After the Financial Crisis* (pp. 46–65). Hershey, PA: IGI Global. doi:10.4018/978-1-5225-4026-7.ch003

Turulja, L., & Bajgoric, N. (2018). Business Continuity and Information Systems: A Systematic Literature Review. In N. Bajgoric (Ed.), *Always-On Enterprise Information Systems for Modern Organizations* (pp. 60–87). Hershey, PA: IGI Global. doi:10.4018/978-1-5225-3704-5.ch004

van Wessel, R. M., de Vries, H. J., & Ribbers, P. M. (2016). Business Benefits through Company IT Standardization. In K. Jakobs (Ed.), *Effective Standardization Management in Corporate Settings* (pp. 34–53). Hershey, PA: IGI Global. doi:10.4018/978-1-4666-9737-9.ch003

Vargas-Hernández, J. G. (2017). Professional Integrity in Business Management Education. In N. Baporikar (Ed.), *Management Education for Global Leadership* (pp. 70–89). Hershey, PA: IGI Global. doi:10.4018/978-1-5225-1013-0.ch004

Vasista, T. G., & AlAbdullatif, A. M. (2017). Role of Electronic Customer Relationship Management in Demand Chain Management: A Predictive Analytic Approach. *International Journal of Information Systems and Supply Chain Management, 10*(1), 53–67. doi:10.4018/IJISSCM.2017010104

Vergidis, K. (2016). Rediscovering Business Processes: Definitions, Patterns, and Modelling Approaches. In P. Papajorgji, F. Pinet, A. Guimarães, & J. Papathanasiou (Eds.), *Automated Enterprise Systems for Maximizing Business Performance* (pp. 97–122). Hershey, PA: IGI Global. doi:10.4018/978-1-4666-8841-4.ch007

Vieru, D., & Bourdeau, S. (2017). Survival in the Digital Era: A Digital Competence-Based Multi-Case Study in the Canadian SME Clothing Industry. *International Journal of Social and Organizational Dynamics in IT, 6*(1), 17–34. doi:10.4018/IJSODIT.2017010102

Vijayan, G., & Kamarulzaman, N. H. (2017). An Introduction to Sustainable Supply Chain Management and Business Implications. In M. Khan, M. Hussain, & M. Ajmal (Eds.), *Green Supply Chain Management for Sustainable Business Practice* (pp. 27–50). Hershey, PA: IGI Global. doi:10.4018/978-1-5225-0635-5.ch002

Vlachvei, A., & Notta, O. (2017). Firm Competitiveness: Theories, Evidence, and Measurement. In A. Vlachvei, O. Notta, K. Karantininis, & N. Tsounis (Eds.), *Factors Affecting Firm Competitiveness and Performance in the Modern Business World* (pp. 1–42). Hershey, PA: IGI Global. doi:10.4018/978-1-5225-0843-4.ch001 von Rosing, M., Fullington, N., & Walker, J. (2016). Using the Business Ontology and Enterprise Standards to Transform Three Leading Organizations. *International Journal of Conceptual Structures and Smart Applications*, 4(1), 71–99. doi:10.4018/IJCSSA.2016010104

von Rosing, M., & von Scheel, H. (2016). Using the Business Ontology to Develop Enterprise Standards. *International Journal of Conceptual Structures and Smart Applications*, 4(1), 48–70. doi:10.4018/IJCSSA.2016010103

Walczak, S. (2016). Artificial Neural Networks and other AI Applications for Business Management Decision Support. *International Journal of Sociotechnology and Knowledge Development*, 8(4), 1–20. doi:10.4018/IJSKD.2016100101

Wamba, S. F., Akter, S., Kang, H., Bhattacharya, M., & Upal, M. (2016). The Primer of Social Media Analytics. *Journal of Organizational and End User Computing*, 28(2), 1–12. doi:10.4018/JOEUC.2016040101

Wang, C., Schofield, M., Li, X., & Ou, X. (2017). Do Chinese Students in Public and Private Higher Education Institutes Perform at Different Level in One of the Leadership Skills: Critical Thinking?: An Exploratory Comparison. In V. Wang (Ed.), *Encyclopedia of Strategic Leadership and Management* (pp. 160–181). Hershey, PA: IGI Global. doi:10.4018/978-1-5225-1049-9.ch013

Wang, F., Raisinghani, M. S., Mora, M., & Wang, X. (2016). Strategic E-Business Management through a Balanced Scored Card Approach. In I. Lee (Ed.), *Encyclopedia of E-Commerce Development, Implementation, and Management* (pp. 361–386). Hershey, PA: IGI Global. doi:10.4018/978-1-4666-9787-4.ch027

Wang, J. (2017). Multi-Agent based Production Management Decision System Modelling for the Textile Enterprise. *Journal of Global Information Management*, 25(4), 1–15. doi:10.4018/JGIM.2017100101

Wiedemann, A., & Gewald, H. (2017). Examining Cross-Domain Alignment: The Correlation of Business Strategy, IT Management, and IT Business Value. *International Journal of IT/Business Alignment and Governance*, 8(1), 17–31. doi:10.4018/IJITBAG.2017010102

Wolf, R., & Thiel, M. (2018). Advancing Global Business Ethics in China: Reducing Poverty Through Human and Social Welfare. In S. Hipsher (Ed.), *Examining the Private Sector's Role in Wealth Creation and Poverty Reduction* (pp. 67–84). Hershey, PA: IGI Global. doi:10.4018/978-1-5225-3117-3.ch004

Wu, J., Ding, F., Xu, M., Mo, Z., & Jin, A. (2016). Investigating the Determinants of Decision-Making on Adoption of Public Cloud Computing in E-government. *Journal of Global Information Management*, 24(3), 71–89. doi:10.4018/JGIM.2016070104

Xu, L., & de Vrieze, P. (2016). Building Situational Applications for Virtual Enterprises. In I. Lee (Ed.), *Encyclopedia of E-Commerce Development, Implementation, and Management* (pp. 715–724). Hershey, PA: IGI Global. doi:10.4018/978-1-4666-9787-4.ch050

Yablonsky, S. (2018). Innovation Platforms: Data and Analytics Platforms. In *Multi-Sided Platforms (MSPs) and Sharing Strategies in the Digital Economy: Emerging Research and Opportunities* (pp. 72–95). Hershey, PA: IGI Global. doi:10.4018/978-1-5225-5457-8.ch003

Yusoff, A., Ahmad, N. H., & Halim, H. A. (2017). Agropreneurship among Gen Y in Malaysia: The Role of Academic Institutions. In N. Ahmad, T. Ramayah, H. Halim, & S. Rahman (Eds.), *Handbook of Research on Small and Medium Enterprises in Developing Countries* (pp. 23–47). Hershey, PA: IGI Global. doi:10.4018/978-1-5225-2165-5.ch002

Zanin, F., Comuzzi, E., & Costantini, A. (2018). The Effect of Business Strategy and Stock Market Listing on the Use of Risk Assessment Tools. In *Management Control Systems in Complex Settings: Emerging Research and Opportunities* (pp. 145–168). Hershey, PA: IGI Global. doi:10.4018/978-1-5225-3987-2.ch007

Zgheib, P. W. (2017). Corporate Innovation and Intrapreneurship in the Middle East. In P. Zgheib (Ed.), *Entrepreneurship and Business Innovation in the Middle East* (pp. 37–56). Hershey, PA: IGI Global. doi:10.4018/978-1-5225-2066-5.ch003

About the Contributors

Ionica Oncioiu holds a Ph.D. in economy and accounting. Her research interests include the development of SMEs innovation, Project Management, Accounting Information Systems, Asset Management and E-Commerce Marketing. She had more than 10 years of experience in this area and has published 10 text books and more than 70 papers in scholarly peer reviewed international journals.

* * *

Husam AlFahl holds a PhD in Management Information Systems from Griffith Business School, Griffith University and his specialization is Electronic Commerce. His research interest includes information technology adoption, electronic commerce, management information systems, ERP and mobile commerce. Dr. Husam holds a Bachelor of Science degree in Management Information Systems from KFUPM, and Master of Business Administration and Master of Information Technology (MBA/ MIT) from Newcastle University.

Mădălina-Gabriela Anghel graduated the Faculty of Finance and Accounting, the 2003 promotion, the Management-Marketing Faculty, the 2007 promotion, the Master of Financial and Banking and Insurance Management (2007), the Management of Small and Medium Enterprises in the Field of Social Economy (2008), she obtained the title of Ph.D. in Economics Sciences, Finance domain, awarded by the Academy of Economic Studies in Bucharest in 2013, with the thesis „The Management of the Portfolio of Financial Instruments". In 2005, she became a university lecturer at the "Artifex" University of Bucharest, Department of Finance and Accounting, progressing in his academic career, currently having the academic degree of associate professor. The main areas of didactic and interest competence are: statistics, financial-banking-money modeling, capital market, credit institutions, currency. She has published as an author or co-author of over 23 books of didactic and scientific content and over 280 articles in specialized journals from the country or abroad ISI (web of knowledge) or indexed in international databases in volumes of international conferences or other scientific events, as well as in other journals recognized in the field. For teaching and research, she received 25 distinctions, awards and diplomas from associations, institutions and professional organizations. She is a vice-president, member of the Board of Directors and the executive committee of the Romanian Statistical Society, also a member of the General Association of Economists in Romania.

Constantin Anghelache is graduate of the Bucharest University of Economic Studies, Faculty of Economic Calculation and Economic Cybernetics and of the Bucharest University, Faculty of Law. He is a Phd of Economics, and a university professor at the Bucharest University of Economic Studies/ „Artifex" University of Bucharest specialized in quantitative economics (statistics, econometrics, economic modeling, financial-banking and monetary modeling, economic proportions and correlations, economic forecasting and quantitative methods of economic analysis). He is a member of the Doctoral School of the Bucharest University of Economic Studies, being a PhD supervisor. Prepares students for bachelor and master study programs. He has published over 118 papers (books) with scientific and didactic content. At the same time, he published 20 books of economic analysis regarding the "Romania's economic condition". He has also published over 950 specialized articles in ISI (web of knowledge) and BDI review and has participated with communications at over 200 scientific national and international meetings. He is the head of the National Scientific Statistical Seminar "Octav Onicescu". He is the first vice-president of the General Association of Economists of Romania, the first vice-president of the Romanian Statistical Society, founding member of the Romanian Society of Statistics (1999); Member of the Board of Directors of the Association "Reseau des Pays du Groupe de Vysegrad", the chairman of the Methodological Advisory Council, a member of the scientific colleges of some specialised reviews. For teaching and research, he was rewarded with prizes, medals and diplomas of excellence, The "Petre S. Aurelian" Prize, awarded by the Romanian Academy, Opera Omnia.

Alex Ansah Dawson is a research assistant and an MSc student at Kwame Nkrumah University of Science and Technology, Kumasi, Ghana. He is a CEO of IT Marketing Company, with a vast experience in Web marketing. His research interest includes Information Security, Data Management, and IT Governance.

Cristian-Marian Barbu, PhD, is a graduate of the Academy of Economic Studies in Bucharest, Romania, and after passing the Bachelor exam in 1997, he received the degree of Economist. He received his PhD degree in Economics from the Academy of Economic Studies in Bucharest in 2005 with the dissertation entitled „Agricultural sustainable economic development in the mountain areas in Romania". After graduation, he took the academic career and started working in higher education in 1998, in „ARTIFEX" University of Bucharest. He held the positions of instructor, starting with 1998, teaching assistant starting with 2000, lecturer starting with 2003, associate professor starting with 2008, and University professor starting with 2017. His expertise in teaching and research, as tenured teaching staff in higher education, since 2003, in Political Economics, Microeconomics, Macroeconomics, Prices and Competition, Economic Policies, made him allocate time to research and the dissemination of the findings, which resulted into books, monographs, studies, and articles published, as well as participation in national and international conferences, and research grants. In his capacity of tenured teaching staff in higher education, he wrote specialized handbooks, as author and co-author, which have been aids for students and enriched the data in the field. The recognition and the appreciation of his prestige in research and scientific activity are translated in the membership in editorial/scientific boards of IDB indexed journals and conferences editorial boards.

Alexandra Botoş graduated in Accounting and Management Information Systems and have a master's degree in Accounting and Audit at Petru Maior University. In 2012 she started working as a Chef Accountant in an accounting services providing firm. In 2014 she became probationer at CECCAR and started postgraduate studies in psycho-pedagogics, being then accepted at The 1st of December 1918 University in Alba Iulia, for PhD studies in Accounting. In 2016 she have obtained the certification of

Expert Accountant and she became a member and a project coordinator at Junior Chamber International. In 2017 she became vice president of the local chapter JCI Tîrgu Mures and in 2018 national board officer for JCI Romania as Vice President for Economic Policies.

Sorinel Căpușneanu is a PhD. associate professor at the Dimitrie Cantemir Christian University of Bucharest, Department of Finance, Banking and Accountancy and Regional Public Relations Manager for Human Resource Management Academic Research Society. Also, he is the Editor in Chief of International Journal of Academic Research in Accounting, Finance and Management Sciences and Academic Journal of Economic Studies. His research focus is the area of Management Accounting, Management Performance, Management Information Systems, Audit and Controlling, and Business Ethics. He is the author of the following books: Elements of Cost Management, Economica Publishing House (2008) and Management Accounting. Performance Assessment Tool, University Publishing House (2013) and co-author of Ethics and Decision-Making for Sustainable Business Practices (Chapter 7 Business Ethics and Cost Management in SME's. Theories of Business Ethics and Cost Management Ethos) published by IGI-Global (USA, 2017). He has participated in numerous national and international conferences and has made a remarkable contribution to managerial accounting by publishing several articles.

Marilena Ciobanasu holds a Ph.D. in management. Her research interests include the financial analysis, human resources, strategic management.

Dana Maria Constantin is a PhD. lecturer at the University of Bucharest, Department of Meteorology and Hydrology. Her research focus is the area of biometeorology, bioclimatology, meteorology, climatology. She is the author of the book: The relation between the climate and the environment pollution in the area of Slatina (2013). She has published numerous articles on meteorology and climatology and she has participated in numerous national and international conferences.

Tatiana Dănescu is a Ph.D. Professor at University of Medicine, Pharmacy, Sciences and Technology of Targu-Mures, Ph.D supervisor in accounting at "1 Decembrie 1918" University in Alba Iulia, actively participates in the accreditation process for universities in Romania (Member of the Economic Sciences Committee – ARACIS, with over 70 graduated university programs and studies). University didactic expertise and professional development of practitioners: title holder for the following courses: Epistemological approaches to accounting and auditing, Financial audit, Internal audit, Financial accounting, held at Universities in Romania (UPM, UAB, Sapientia University in Cluj – Napoca); Financial audit trainer for the Romanian Chamber of Financial Auditors and trainer in tax matters regarding the conditions of application for IFRS in Romania (For the Ministry of Finance, in collaboration with the Department For International Development of the UK Government).

Louis Delcart is the former president of the «European Marketing Confederation» and vice-president of the Belgian-Ukrainian Chamber of Commerce. After a carreer of 18 years at the BACOB Bank in Brussels, he started his own consulting firm, Cardone Consulting. In March 2004 he was appointed general manager of Haviland, the inter-municipal development agency of the Halle-Vilvoorde, the district around Brussels. In March 2010 he became director Internationalisation and Innovation at VOKA – Chamber of Commerce Halle-Vilvoorde, a function of which he retired in June 2014. Since then he is again active as consultant in internationalisation of SMEs, in training and consultancy of banks as service provider to SMEs and in consultancy for local authorities in their role of stimulating the development of new business in their action area.

Ana Maria Ifrim is teaching at the Titu Maiorescu University. She is the author of two books, over 15 articles to various national and international conferences.

Jayapandian N is a PhD. assistant professor at the Christ University, Department of Computer Science and Engineering, Bangalore, India. His research interest includes information security, cloud computing, and grid computing. Dr. Jayapandian holds a Bachelor of Technology degree in Information Technology from IRTT, Anna University and Master of Engineering in Computer Science and Engineering from KEC, Anna University. He is published various research article in reputed international journals. He is an active reviewer of reputed international journals. He has participated in numerous national and international conferences and has made a remarkable contribution to cloud data security field and publishing several articles.

Alexandru Manole is a graduate of the Bucharest University of Economic Studies, The Faculty of Accounting and Management Information Systems (1999). He is teaching various IT in economics disciplines at the "ARTIFEX" University of Bucharest, The Faculty of Finances and Accounting, The Department of Financial and Accounting. He holds a PhD in Accounting, granted in 2007. As a Professor, he teaches subjects such as database management systems, decision support systems, programming etc. He published articles in scientific journals, two books on databases and decision support systems, co-authored several books and his main interests are the applications of information technology in accounting and finance.

Andreea Marin-Pantelescu is a graduate of the Bucharest University of Economic Studies, The Faculty of Commerce, the specialization Tourism-Services (2002) and of the postgraduate program in International Tourism (2003). In February 2007, she becomes a teacher in the Bucharest University of Economic Studies, The Faculty of Commerce, The Department of Tourism-Services. She obtains her PhD in Economics in the year 2008 with a thesis in services, and in 2010 a Master's Degree in the domain Economics and International Business. As a Lecturer in the Department of Tourism and Geography, the Faculty of Business and Tourism, the Bucharest University of Economic Studies, she teaches subjects like the technique of tourism operations, the technique of hotels operations, development strategies for the tertiary sector, services economy, business ethics, etc. She writes articles published in scientific journals and her research interests are in the field of services, tourism and booking systems (Amadeus and Travelport). Currently, she is focused on the services economy course and conducts research in the domain of creative services. She is a founding member of the Academic Association for Research in Tourism and Services (CACTUS).

Catalina Motofei is a graduate of the Bucharest University of Economic Studies, The Faculty of Accounting and Management Information Systems (1995). She has 20 years of experience in business accounting and controlling working in different industries: manufacturing, trade, retail and consultancy. In October 2016, she starts teaching in the Bucharest University of Economic Studies, The Faculty of Accounting and Management Information Systems, The Department of Financial and Economic Analysis and Valuation. She obtains her PhD in Economics in the year 2012 with a thesis in accounting field.

As an Assistant Professor in the Department of Financial and Economic Analysis and Valuation, the Faculty of Accounting and Management Information Systems, she teaches subjects like introduction and fundamentals of economic and financial analysis, business performance measurement. She writes articles published in scientific journals and her research interests are in the field of financial analysis. Currently, she is focused on the business performance course.

Anca Gabriela Petrescu is teaching at the University Valahia. The whole period was marked of academic activities, coordination of scientific publications, courses, textbooks and scientific research. She is the author of 5 books, over 50 articles to various national and international conferences.

Ileana-Sorina Rakos is a PhD. lecturer at the University of Petrosani, Department of Economic Sciences. Her research focus is the area of Finance and Accounting. She is the author of the book: Management of public institutions. Theoretical and Applied Fundamentals (2018). She has published numerous articles on Finance and Accounting and she has participated in numerous national and international conferences.

Ioan Ovidiu Spătăcean is a PhD lecturer Spătăcean Ioan Ovidiu has accumulated a valuable educational, professional and research experience during his 15 years of activity performed in the university environment. Research concerns are anchored in areas such as financial audit, corporate governance, or financial markets and have resulted in over 40 papers published as author or co-author in journals with international visibility. The professional expertise was largely acquired as a result of more than 13 years of collaboration with the Goldring Investment Firm from Târgu Mureş, where specific experiences and skills for risk management, financial reporting and compliance were accumulated. Also, the professional activity performed as a financial auditor and chartered accountant, member of the Romanian Chamber of Financial Auditors (since 2011) and the Body of Experts' and Licensed Accountants of Romania (2013), contributed in a significant manner to strengthening teaching and research skills.

Alina Stanciu is a highly skilled professional with extended expertise in Management and Public Relation gained in multinational environment in the past 10 years. Experienced in Business2Business Strategy and New Business with a strong understanding of management concepts, leadership, business policies and talent acquisition, having solid track record in building and motivating strong teams. Involved in external relations with business organizations, persuasive and empathic character with strong communication skills.

Dan Ioan Topor is a PhD. lecturer at the 1 Decembrie 1918 University of Alba-Iulia, Faculty of Economic Sciences. His research focus is the area of Management Accounting, Management Performance and Management Information Systems, Audit and Controlling, and Business Ethics. He is the author of the following books: New dimensions of cost-related cost information for winemaking (2014), Basics of Accounting (2016) and co-author of Ethics and Decision-Making for Sustainable Business Practices (Chapter 7 Business Ethics and Cost Management in SME's. Theories of Business Ethics and Cost Management Ethos) published by IGI-Global (USA, 2017). He has published numerous articles on Managerial Accounting and Management Control and has participated in numerous national and international conferences.

Mirela Catalina Turkes is a PhD lecturer at the Dimitrie Cantemir Christian University of Bucharest, Department of Finance, Banking and Accountancy. Her research focus is the area of Marketing and Communications. She is the author of the following books: The Basics of Marketing (2014), The Marketing of Financial-Banking Services (2013), Another Way to Learn Marketing (2016) and The Basics of Marketing Revised Edition (2017). She has published numerous articles on Marketing and has participated in numerous national and international conferences.

Winfred Yaokumah is the Dean of the Faculty of Engineering, Science and Computing at the Pentecost University College, Accra, Ghana. He holds PhD in Information Technology with specialization in Information Assurance and Security. He has published extensively in several international journals, including the Journal of Information Management and Computer Security, Information Resources Management Journal, International Journal of Enterprise Information Systems, International Journal of E-Business Research, Journal of Information Technology Research, International Journal of Technology and Human Interaction, and the International Journal of Information Systems in the Service Sector. His research interest includes information security, e-services, IT governance, cloud computing, technology diffusion, information security governance, and IT leadership.

Index

A

Accountability 137, 140
Accounting Estimates 154, 156
Activity-Based Costing (ABC) 43
Administration 3, 5, 20, 25-26, 29, 62-63, 111, 132, 135, 139, 219

B

Benchmarking 14, 188-191, 193, 195
Big Data 60
business strategy 20, 91-92, 94-95, 171, 186

C

Communications Security 1-3, 6-7, 12-14
Corporate Governance 137, 139, 144-145
Creative Accounting 156
Credibility 46, 105, 154, 168

D

Data Base Management System (DBMS) 43
Data Definition 135
Data Security 14, 72, 80, 87, 90, 135, 214
Data Transfer Security 1-3, 5-7, 10-14, 18-19
Database 29-31, 33, 35, 43, 64, 75, 84, 99-100, 114, 118, 120, 126, 133-136, 193
decisional processes 134
Defense-in-depth 1, 4-5, 9, 13
Developing Companies 216
Digitization 45-46, 80

E

E-Business 54, 75-76
Encryption 1, 3, 5-6, 10, 12-14, 72, 74, 84-87, 90, 201, 204, 208
Entity 5, 20, 24-27, 39, 43, 46, 53-54, 56, 58-59, 91, 137, 139-140, 145, 147, 153, 156, 164, 185, 188-190, 193-194
Entrepreneur 186, 225
Environment 1, 3-4, 6, 14, 20-22, 40-41, 46, 56, 66, 68, 75, 80, 91-98, 102, 108-109, 133-134, 145, 151-153, 158, 171, 173, 179, 185, 188-191, 193-195, 223-224
Environmental Indicator 97, 108
Environmental Monitoring 108
Environmental Performance 92, 94-95, 99, 104, 109
E-Payment 72, 75, 90
E-Readiness 178

F

Fair Value 137, 156
Finance 9, 92, 216-222, 225
Financial Reporting 44-46, 52-56, 58, 137-141, 144-145, 147-154, 156
Financial Risks 168
Fraud Risk Assessment 147-148, 151-152
Fraud Triangle 151, 153

G

General Accounts Plan 24, 43
GIF 201

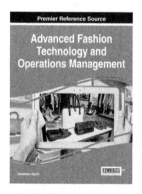

Ensure Quality Research is Introduced to the Academic Community

Become an IGI Global Reviewer for Authored Book Projects

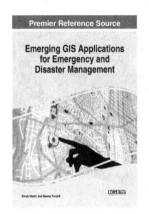

Premier Reference Source

Emerging GIS Applications for Emergency and Disaster Management

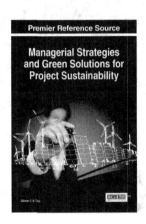

Premier Reference Source

Managerial Strategies and Green Solutions for Project Sustainability

Premier Reference Source

Comparative Approaches to Using R and Python for Statistical Data Analysis

Premier Reference Source

Solutions for High-Touch Communications in a High-Tech World

The overall success of an authored book project is dependent on quality and timely reviews.

In this competitive age of scholarly publishing, constructive and timely feedback significantly expedites the turnaround time of manuscripts from submission to acceptance, allowing the publication and discovery of forward-thinking research at a much more expeditious rate. Several IGI Global authored book projects are currently seeking highly qualified experts in the field to fill vacancies on their respective editorial review boards:

Applications may be sent to:
development@igi-global.com

Applicants must have a doctorate (or an equivalent degree) as well as publishing and reviewing experience. Reviewers are asked to write reviews in a timely, collegial, and constructive manner. All reviewers will begin their role on an ad-hoc basis for a period of one year, and upon successful completion of this term can be considered for full editorial review board status, with the potential for a subsequent promotion to Associate Editor.

If you have a colleague that may be interested in this opportunity, we encourage you to share this information with them.

Printed in the United States
By Bookmasters